'An entire room full of Hollywood screenwriters handcuffed to their laptops couldn't hope to dream up a crime story as gobsmacking as the true-life tale of Sister Ping.' *Boston Phoenix*

'Captivating. . . . A page-turner that reads like a crime novel. Peopled with dozens of colorful characters, it offers an authoritative history of the diaspora of the Chinese and their experience in the United States. . . . Keefe's account reminds us how much hope the American dream inspires and what a steep price some have paid to try to live it.' *San Jose Mercury News*

'Brilliant. . . . Keefe's account maintains the swift pace of a thriller. With the immigration debate still boiling, this exploration of how far people will go to achieve the American dream is a must-read.'
Publishers Weekly

'*The Snakehead* achieves what only the finest reporting can: it peels back an astonishing hidden world. Keefe takes the reader on a spellbinding journey . . . that will forever change your understanding of what it means to become an American.'
David Grann, author of *The Lost City of Z*

'Keefe has written a vivid non fiction thriller. *The Snakehead* reads like a Chinese-American version of *The Sopranos*, except that the mob boss is a grandmother who runs a human smuggling enterprise, and the story is true.' Jane Mayer, author of *The Dark Side*

'Bracing, vivid . . . Keefe writes gracefully, perceptively, insightfully about a vast array of characters. Without sacrificing one iota of narrative momentum, he untangles a dauntingly complicated [human smuggling] operation so a reader can effortlessly follow along. He makes Sister Ping . . . as memorable as any character in recent fiction . . . Riveting.' *The New York Times Book Review*

'Evocatively captures our yin and yang over immigration policy . . . This is one of the freshest accounts of modern-day migration I've read, one filled with moral ambiguity, one that doesn't pretend to have the answers, one that in these times feels like essential reading. A rich, beautifully told story, so suspenseful and with so many unexpected twists that in places it reads like a John le Carré novel.'

The Washington Post

'Timely and compelling . . . Keefe delineates a world of raids, bribes, global conspiracies and daily gun battles; he introduces us to gangsters, hit men, FBI agents, and the notorious, elusive Sister Ping. He places it all squarely in the context of the world's growing immigration crisis.' *The Wall Street Journal*

'A formidably well researched book that is as much a paean to its author's industriousness as it is a chronicle of crime.'

The New York Times

'A brilliant reporter's account of the Fujianese-American underworld.' *The New York Review of Books*

'Brilliant. . . . Keefe's mastery of this chapter of our ongoing immigration saga is impressive. He muses thoughtfully about its many conundrums and highlights how our ethos of welcoming the persecuted gets soured by bad policy and the pervasive exploitation of the helpless. There will be more chapters, no doubt, but this one was pretty riveting.' *Los Angeles Times*

'Reads like a mashup of *The Godfather* and *Chinatown*, complete with gun battles, a ruthless kingpin and a mountain of cash. Except that it's all true.' *Time*

'Painstakingly reported and vividly told. . . . As immigration reform languishes in Washington . . . everyone involved—from policymakers to activists to the undocumented—would be wise to read *The Snakehead*.' *Newsweek*

'Engrossing. . . . Keefe's narrative delves deeply into Chinatown and the labyrinthine smuggling routes between China and America, but it's also a glimpse into our conflicted feelings about illegals and the morass of America's immigration policy.' *New York Magazine*

'Epic. . . . Impressive. . . . A true-life thriller that examines just about every aspect of U.S. immigration policy.' *The Associated Press*

'Riveting. . . . Keefe deftly interweaves the political, legal and gun-slinging strands of Sister Ping's story, rendering scenes of White House policy deliberation and immigration court procedure as engagingly as scenes of Chinatown shootouts and high-seas rendezvous.' National Public Radio

'A masterwork. In this single tale about a global criminal, Keefe finds a story of quintessentially American hope.' *The Christian Science Monitor*

'An eye-opener. . . . Compelling and informative. . . . Keefe maintains a commendable fairness and objectivity reporting a fascinating story.' *USA Today*

'Exceptional . . . [Keefe] tells this story with a masterful fluidity, shifting among multiple characters—gangsters at shootouts, passengers fishing off the drifting freighter, maneuvering politicians—all backed up in pages of meticulous citations . . . An adventure story, crime drama, political thriller and a contemplative look into immigration policy all at once. Each element could be a compelling book in its own right, but [Keefe] combines them for an illuminating whole.' *Cleveland Plain Dealer*

The Snakehead

Patrick Radden Keefe is an award-winning staff writer at *The New Yorker* and the author of the international bestsellers *Empire of Pain: The Secret History of the Sackler Dynasty* (winner of the Baillie Gifford Prize for Non-Fiction), *Say Nothing: A True Story of Murder and Memory in Northern Ireland* (winner of the Orwell Prize), and *Rogues: True Stories of Grifters, Killers, Rebels, and Crooks*. He is also the writer and host of the eight-part podcast *Wind of Change*, about the strange convergence of Cold War espionage and heavy metal music, which *The Guardian* named the #1 podcast of 2020. He grew up in Boston and now lives in New York.

蛇頭

蕭洪題

The Snakehead

AN EPIC TALE
OF THE
CHINATOWN UNDERWORLD
AND THE
AMERICAN DREAM

PATRICK RADDEN KEEFE

PICADOR

First published 2009 by Doubleday
A division of Random House, Inc., New York

First published in the UK 2023 by Picador
an imprint of Pan Macmillan
The Smithson, 6 Briset Street, London EC1M 5NR
EU representative: Macmillan Publishers Ireland Ltd, 1st Floor,
The Liffey Trust Centre, 117–126 Sheriff Street Upper, Dublin 1, D01 YC43
Associated companies throughout the world
www.panmacmillan.com

ISBN 978-1-5290-9988-1

Snakehead calligraphy by Dr. Tang Xiao Xiong

The epigraph is from Roger Daniels, *Coming to America: A History of Immigration and Ethnicity in American Life* (New York: Harper Perennial, 1990; 2nd edn 2002).

5 7 9 8 6

A CIP catalogue record for this book is available from the British Library.

Printed and bound by CPI Group (UK) Ltd, Croydon, CR0 4YY

FSC www.fsc.org
MIX
Paper | Supporting responsible forestry
FSC® C116313

TO JUSTYNA

In at least some parts of nineteenth-century Norway, people called those who intended to emigrate "Americans" even before they left.

—ROGER DANIELS,
Coming to America:
A History of Immigration and
Ethnicity in American Life

Contents

Dramatis Personae xv

Map of Chinatown xix

Book I

1 Pilgrims 3

2 Leaving Fujian 22

3 Eighteen-Thousand-Dollar Woman 38

4 *Dai Lo* of the Fuk Ching 59

5 Swiftwater 83

6 Year of the Snake 99

Book II

7 Mombasa 121

8 The Phantom Ship 137

9 The Teaneck Massacre 150

10 Mutiny in the Atlantic 168

11 A Well-founded Fear 182

12 The Fat Man 207

13 Freedom Birds 227

Book III

14 The Goldfish and the Great Wall 251

15 Parole 263

16	Snakeheads International	280
17	Catching Lilly Zhang	293
18	The Mother of All Snakeheads	306
	Epilogue	329
	Acknowledgments	345
	A Note on Sources	350
	Notes	353
	Index	412

Dramatis Personae

GIVEN THE historical and geographical sweep of this story, there are, of necessity, many characters. Because *The Snakehead* is an account of people transplanted from one country to another, many of the individuals described go by more than one name. In order to minimize confusion for readers who may be unaccustomed to Chinese names, I have defaulted in many instances to the English names adopted by some of the Chinese characters. Thus Chung Sing Chau, who upon arriving in America took the name Sean Chen, will be Sean Chen for the purposes of this story. Because some of the characters in the book are involved in organized crime, and because Chinese mobsters share with their cousins in the Italian Mafia a wonderful facility for nicknames, I have opted to refer to some characters primarily by their nicknames—like Mr. Charlie, or the Fat Man—simply on the grounds that the nicknames will be easier for the reader to keep straight.

Chinese names are customarily rendered with the family name preceding the individual name, so Sister Ping's full name is Cheng Chui Ping, Cheng being her surname. I have followed the Chinese form, with a few exceptions, such as Kin Sin Lee and Pin Lin, where through some consensus prosecutors, immigration attorneys, *Golden Venture* passengers, and the friends and associates of the individual in question have all elected to reverse the order, putting the first name first and the surname last, and for me to do otherwise would be formalistic. In what follows, the boldface name is the one used in the body of the book, nicknames are placed in quotation marks, and inside the parentheses are aliases, birth names (if the person has adopted an English name or a nickname), and traditional Chinese renderings (in the few cases where I otherwise depart from them).

"Ah Kay" (Guo Liang Qi), *leader of the Fuk Ching gang*

"Ah Wong" (Guo Liang Wong), *younger brother of Ah Kay who assumed control of smuggling operations*

Gloria Canales, *major people smuggler, based in Costa Rica*

Ann Carr, *British immigration attorney who represented Sean Chen in York, Pennsylvania*

Ying Chan, Daily News *reporter who covered the snakehead trade*

"Mr. Charlie" ("Char Lee," "Ma Lee," Lee Peng Fei), *Bangkok-based boat smuggler*

Sean Chen (Chung Sing Chau), *Fujianese teenager aboard the* Golden Venture

Cheng Chai Leung, *father of Sister Ping, early Fujianese snakehead*

Cheng Chui Ping ("Sister Ping"), *New York–based snakehead and underground banker*

Cheng Mei Yeung, *brother of Sister Ping, smuggler based in Guatemala, California, and Bangkok*

Monica Cheng (Cheng Hui Mui), *daughter and oldest child of Sister Ping and Cheung Yick Tak*

Susan Cheng (Cheng Tsui Wah), *Sister Ping's sister, procured travel documents for smuggled migrants*

Cheung Yick Tak ("Billy"), *husband of Sister Ping*

Beverly Church, *nurse and paralegal in York, Pennsylvania, became involved with the* Golden Venture *detainees*

Patrick Devine, *Buffalo-based INS investigator*

James Dullan, *driver on the Niagara smuggling route*

"The Fat Man" ("Four Star," Dickson Yao), *Hong Kong–based drug smuggler and informant for the DEA and the INS*

Kenny Feng, *Taiwanese snakehead and associate of Sister Ping, based in Guatemala*

Foochow Paul (Kin Fei Wong), *original head of the Fuk Ching gang*

Ed Garde, *investigator with the Niagara County Sheriff's Department*

Richard Kephart, *driver on the Niagara smuggling route*

Ray Kerr, *head of the FBI's C-6 squad, handled Dan Xin Lin*

Kin Sin Lee (Lee Kin Sin), *Mr. Charlie's deputy, chief snakehead enforcer aboard the* Golden Venture

Dougie Lee, *detective with the NYPD's Jade Squad*

Peter Lee, *FBI special agent, handled Sister Ping*

Dan Xin Lin (Lin Dan Xin), *Fuk Ching gang member, defected to start his own smuggling operation*

Li Xing Hua ("Stupid"), *Fuk Ching gang member, bodyguard to Ah Kay*

Sam Lwin, *Burmese first officer of the* Golden Venture, *subsequently took control of the ship*

Joan Maruskin, *Methodist minister in York, Pennsylvania, became involved with the* Golden Venture *detainees*

Billy McMurry, *FBI special agent, responsible for the Sister Ping investigation after 1997*

Doris Meissner, *commissioner of the INS, appointed by President Clinton after the* Golden Venture *incident*

Don Monica, *Nairobi-based INS officer*

Konrad Motyka, *FBI special agent who worked on both the Fuk Ching and the Sister Ping case*

Joe Occhipinti, *head of the INS's Anti-Smuggling Unit and lead investigator on Operation Hester*

Benny Ong ("Uncle Seven," Ong Kai Sui), *adviser for life to the Hip Sing tong in Chinatown*

"Paul" (Min Hoang), *Vietnamese smuggler based in Canada, piloted boats across the Niagara River*

"Peter" (Cheng Wai Wei), *brother-in-law of Sister Ping, husband of Susan, ran the Niagara smuggling route*

Pin Lin (Lin Pin), Golden Venture *passenger represented by Craig Trebilcock*

Pao Pong, *Pattaya Tourist Police officer, interrupted loading of the* Golden Venture *in Thailand*

Grover Joseph Rees III, *general counsel of the INS*

Luke Rettler, *prosecutor in the Manhattan district attorney's office, specialized in Asian gangs*

Mark Riordan, *Bangkok-based INS officer*

Eric Schwartz, *National Security Council staffer, coordinated the Washington response to the* Golden Venture *incident*

Gerald Shargel, *prominent criminal defense attorney, represented Ah Kay*

Sterling Showers, *retired factory worker in York, Pennsylvania, befriended* Golden Venture *detainees*

Bill Slattery, *district director of the INS in New York City*

Song You Lin, *Fuk Ching gang assassin*

Jerry Stuchiner, *INS officer in charge in Hong Kong and then in Honduras*

Alan Tam ("Ha Gwei"), *half African American Fuk Ching gang member, driver and fixer for the gang*

Amir Tobing, *Indonesian captain of the* Golden Venture

Craig Trebilcock, *York, Pennsylvania, litigator, led pro bono legal effort on behalf of* Golden Venture *detainees*

Wang Kong Fu, *close smuggling associate of Sister Ping's, introduced Sister Ping to Ah Kay*

Herbie Weizenblut, *associate of Jerry Stuchiner's, installed as Honduran consul in Hong Kong*

Weng Yu Hui, *Fujianese man smuggled by Sister Ping, later became a key* Golden Venture *snakehead*

Yang You Yi, *Fujianese* Golden Venture *passenger and lead folding-paper artist in the prison in York, Pennsylvania*

Chinatown

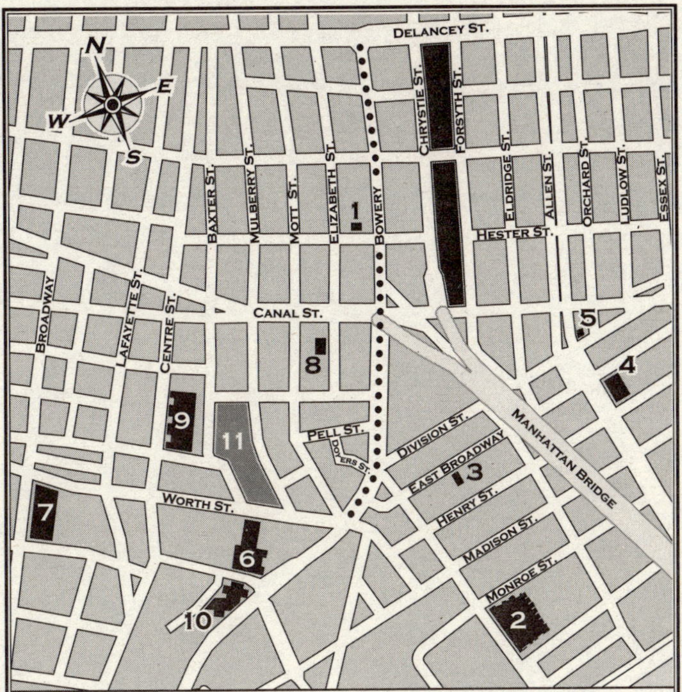

1. Tak Shun Variety Store
2. Sister Ping's Apartment
3. Yeung Sun Restaurant
4. Fukienese American Association
5. The Beeper Store
6. United States Courthouse
7. FBI Headquarters
8. NYPD 5th Precinct
9. Manhattan DA; Luke Rettler's Office
10. Metropolitian Correctional Center
11. Columbus Park

The Snakehead

Book I

Chapter One

Pilgrims

THE SHIP made land at last a hundred yards off the Rockaway Peninsula, a slender, skeletal finger of sand that forms a kind of barrier between the southern reaches of Brooklyn and Queens and the angry waters of the Atlantic. Dating back to the War of 1812, the people of New York erected battlements and positioned cannons along the beaches here, to defend against foreign invasion. Even before white settlers arrived, the local Canarsie Indians had identified in the eleven miles of dunes and grass something proprietary and exclusive. "Rockaway" derives from the Canarsie word *Reckouwacky,* which means "place of our own people."

A single road runs down the center of the peninsula, past the Marine Parkway Bridge, which connects to the mainland, through the sleepy winterized bungalows of the Breezy Point Cooperative, right out to the western tip of Rockaway, where weekend anglers reel in stripers and blues. Looking south, past the beach at the Atlantic, you wouldn't know you were on the southern fringe of one of the biggest cities in the world. But turn your head the other way, out across the bay side of the peninsula, and there's Coney Island in the distance, the grotty old Cyclone tracing a garish profile above the boardwalk.

At a quarter to two on a moonless Sunday morning, June 6, 1993, a single police cruiser drove east along that central road, its headlights illuminating the dark asphalt. A large stretch of the peninsula is national park land, and inside the car, a twenty-eight-year-old National Park Police officer named David Somma was doing a graveyard shift with his partner, Steve Divivier. At thirty, Divivier had been with the force for four years, but this was his first time on an overnight patrol.

It wasn't typically an eventful task. The Breezy Point neighborhood west of the bridge was close-knit. The families were mostly Irish Americans who had been in the area for generations, working-class city cops and firefighters whose fathers and grandfathers had bought modest summer homes along the beach in the fifties and sixties and at some point paved over the sandy lots and winterized their weekend shacks. At 98.5 percent white, Breezy Point had the peculiar distinction of being the least ethnically diverse neighborhood in New York City. A night patrol of the beach might turn up the occasional keg party or bonfire, but serious crime along that stretch was unheard of. The Breezy Point police force was a volunteer auxiliary. The officers had so little use for their handcuffs that they had taken to oiling them to stave off rust.

Somma was behind the wheel, and he saw it first. An earlier rain shower had left the ocean swollen with fog. But out to his right, beyond the beach, the darkness was pierced by a single pinprick of faint green illumination: a mast light.

The officers pulled over, got out of the car, and scrambled to the top of the dunes separating the road from the beach. In the distance they beheld the ghostly silhouette of a ship, a tramp steamer, perhaps 150 feet long. The vessel was listing ever so slightly to its side. Somma ran back to the car and got on the radio, alerting the dispatcher that a large ship was dangerously close to shore. He and Divivier climbed the dune for another look.

Then, from out across the water, they heard the first screams.

Half stifled by the wind, the cries were borne to them across the beach. To Somma they sounded desperate, the kind of sound people make when they know they are about to die. He had a flashlight with him, and pointed it in the direction of the ship. The sea was rough, the waves fierce and volatile. About 25 yards out, between the rolling swells, Somma saw four heads bobbing in the water. The officers turned and sprinted back to the car.

"We've got a large number of people in the water!" Somma shouted into the radio. Divivier had grabbed a life ring and was already running back to the beach. The officers charged into the water. It was cold—53 degrees—and the surf was violent, big swells breaking all around them and threatening to engulf the people in the distance. Guided by the wailing voices, Divivier and Somma strode out until they were waist-deep. As Divivier closed the distance to the four people, he hurled the life ring in their direction. But the wind and current carried it away. He reeled it in, walked deeper into the water, and cast the ring again. Again it failed to reach the people as they struggled in the swells.

Realizing that they couldn't do the rescue from solid ground, Divivier and Somma plunged into the water and began swimming, enormous waves twisting their bodies and crashing over their heads. The drowning people writhed in the cold ocean. Eventually Divivier and Somma reached them and shouted over the percussive surf, telling them to take hold of the life ring. Then the officers turned around and dragged the shipwrecked strangers back to shore. There the four collapsed, panting, on the sand. They were Asian men, the officers saw, diminutive and cadaverously thin. When Somma spoke to them, they didn't appear to understand. They just looked up, with terror in their eyes, and pointed in the direction of the ship.

From the ocean, the officers heard more screams.

Somma's first radio call to the Park Service Police dispatcher had gone out at 1:46 A.M. There was a Coast Guard station just across the peninsula from the beach, at the Rockaway end of the Marine Parkway Bridge. Charlie Wells, a tall, ruddy, nineteen-year-old seaman apprentice, was on radio duty from midnight to four in the morning. Wells, the son of an Emergency Medical Services captain, had grown up in Whitestone, Queens. He lived in the barracks; he'd been with the Coast Guard less than a year.

"A fishing boat sank off Reis Park," a dispatcher's voice said, crackling through the radio. "There's forty people in the water!"

Wells ran out of the barracks, started his truck, and drove a few hundred yards south down the access road in the direction of the ocean side beach. He pulled over in a clearing and ran up onto the beach, where he was startled by the sight of the ship in the distance. He mouthed a quiet *Wow.*

On the beach in front of him, it looked like some madcap game of capture the flag was under way. A dozen or so dark, wiry figures, some of them in ragged business suits, others in just their underwear, were running in every direction, and a number of burly police officers were giving chase. Three off-duty Park Service officers had joined Somma and Divivier and were scrambling after the Asian men who had managed to swim to shore.

"Help!" one of the officers shouted, spotting Wells.

Wells took off after one of the men, gained on him easily, and rugby-tackled him. He was much smaller than Wells, skinny, and soaked through. Wells held the man down and looked up to see more people emerging from the surf. It was a primordial scene—an outtake from a zombie movie—as hordes of men and women, gaunt and hollow-cheeked, walked out of the sea. Some collapsed, exhausted, on the sand. Others dashed immediately into the dunes, trying to evade the cops. Still more thrashed and bobbed and screamed in the crashing waves. Wells could just discern the outline of the ship in the darkness. There was movement on the deck, some sort of commotion. People were jumping overboard.

"We need a Coast Guard boat!" one of the officers shouted at Wells. "And a helicopter!"

Wells ran back to the van and radioed his station. "I need more help," he said. "There's a two-hundred-foot tanker that ran aground right off the beach, and these guys are jumping right into the water."

The tide was coming in, and a strong westerly crosscurrent was pulling the people in the water down along the shoreline. The officers ventured into the water again and again. They plucked people from the shallows and dragged them onto the shore. The survivors were terrified, eyes wild, teeth chattering, bellies grossly distended from gulping saltwater. They looked half dead. They were all Asian, and almost all men, but there were a few women among them, and a few children. They flung their arms around the officers in a tight clench, digging their fingers so deep that in the coming days the men would find discolored gouge marks on the skin of their shoulders and backs.

The night was still so dark that it was hard to locate the people in the water. The men relied on their flashlights, the narrow beams roving the waves in search of flailing arms or the whites of eyes. But the flashlights began to deteriorate from exposure to the saltwater, and when the lights failed, the rescuers had to wade out into the darkness and just listen for the screams. "We entered the water guided only by the sound of a human voice," one of the officers later wrote in an incident report. "When we were lucky, we could then use our flashlights to locate a person . . . When we weren't lucky, the voices just stopped." The rescue workers pulled dozens of people to shore. Every time they thought they had cleared the water, another pocket of screams would pick up, and they would head back in.

Those who were too tired to walk or move the officers carried, jackknifed over their shoulders, and deposited on higher ground. There they collapsed, vomiting saltwater, their bodies shaking, their faces slightly purple from exposure. The officers tried massaging their legs and arms to improve circulation. Some were hysterical, sobbing and pointing out at the ship. Others seemed delusional and rolled around covering themselves with fistfuls of sand, whether to insulate their frozen bodies or hide from the officers was unclear. Some were more collected—they were strong swimmers, or they had caught a generous current. They walked up out of the water, stripped off their wet clothes, produced a set of dry clothes from a plastic bag tied around an ankle, and changed right there on the beach. Some of them then sat among the growing number of survivors on the sand, waiting to see what would become of them. Others simply walked off over the dunes and disappeared into the dark suburban stillness of Breezy Point.

Across New York and New Jersey, telephones were beginning to ring. Cops and firefighters, rescue workers and EMTs, reached for pagers buzzing on darkened bedside tables and rolled out of bed. When a disaster occurs, most of us are hardwired to run in the opposite direction, to stop and gawk only when we've put some distance between ourselves and any immediate risk. But there's a particular breed of professional who always runs toward the danger, even as the rest of us run away. As word spread among the first responders in New York and New Jersey that a ship full of what appeared to be illegal immigrants who couldn't swim had run aground in the Atlantic, a massive rescue got under way. It would prove to be one of the biggest, and most unusual, rescue operations in New York history—"like a plane crash on the high seas," one of the rescue workers said.

A heavyset Coast Guard pilot named Bill Mundy got the call as he was finishing a maintenance run in his helicopter and had just touched down at the Coast Guard's hangar at Floyd Bennett Field in Brooklyn, across the bridge from Rockaway. The propeller was still spinning, and Mundy summoned his copilot and two rescue divers, climbed back aboard, and lifted off, ascending 50 feet into the air. The fog was clearing, and past the bridge, beyond the dark strip of roofs and trees on Rockaway, they could see the ship, just a few miles away as the crow flies, protruding from the slate-dark sea. The helicopter tore through the sky, and below they could see the bleeding strobe of emergency vehicles—ambulances, squad cars, a convoy of fire trucks hurtling over the bridge toward the beach.

The helicopter reached the scene in minutes, and Mundy saw people on the beach below and people in the ocean. The chopper's spotlight searched the scene, a pool of white light skimming across the black water and spilling onto the dark shapes aboard the vessel. The ship was called the *Golden Venture*, its name stenciled in block letters on the salt-streaked bow. Its green paint was scarred by rust along the waterline. Two rope ladders had been flung over the side, and people were climbing halfway down the ladders and jumping into the water.

Mundy couldn't believe it. He'd rescued a lot of people from the water, and what they always feared most was the unknown aspect of the sea—that voracious, limitless, consuming darkness of the ocean. But here these people were, in the middle of the night, in a strange place, 25 feet above the water, and they were just pouring over the side of the ship like lemmings. *This is very high on the "I'm gonna die" list,* Mundy thought. They were lining the decks, emerging through hatches from the bowels of the ship. They were moving as people in shock do, their bodies erratic, herky-jerky, as they dashed back and forth and cannonballed over the side.

Mundy hovered down, the chopper getting closer to the ship, training the bright searchlight, unsure what to focus on. The people on board looked up, alarmed, and dashed to and fro. "DO NOT JUMP," Mundy's copilot said over the loudspeaker. "STAY ON BOARD." But the whir of the propeller drowned him out. And even if they could hear, Mundy realized, these people weren't American; there was no telling what language they spoke. The helicopter descended closer still and Mundy and his colleagues tried signaling with their hands, using palm-extended gestures of restraint, hoping the people on deck would see them. But the rotor wash was strong enough to knock a man down, and as they came in close, the people just panicked, scattering to the other end of the deck.

From up here Mundy could see what had happened. A sandbar, a kind of shoal, had developed under the water a couple hundred yards from shore. The bow had plowed into that sandbar and ridden up onto it, so that the first 15 feet of the vessel cleared it altogether. The water around the ship must have looked shallow—they'd hit the sand, after all—but the water on the shore side fell off again, becoming deeper. And the waves were fierce. As Mundy circled the *Golden Venture*, he noticed that the propeller was still furiously churning water aft of the ship. The people in the water were getting pulled back toward the blades. Why hadn't the crew shut the engine down? "There's got to be a pilot on board," Mundy said. He set the radio to Channel 16, the international distress frequency, and addressed the ship. "Secure power!" Mundy commanded. "Shut the engine down!"

Before long three Coast Guard boats rounded the peninsula and tried to approach the *Golden Venture*. But the surf was so rough that they couldn't get close to the ship, lest a sudden swell should bash them against it. Eventually the smallest boat, a 22-foot Boston Whaler, managed to maneuver in close and come alongside the *Golden Venture*. Charlie Wells's roommate in the barracks, a junior seaman named Gilbert Burke, was on board, and along with two colleagues, Burke prepared to start persuading the passengers to jump into the Whaler instead of the water. But just as they approached the *Golden Venture*, an enormous wave came avalanching down on the bow of the Whaler, and the boat flipped clear out of the water, throwing all three crew members into the waves—then capsizing on top of them.

"The twenty-two just flipped over," a voice on Wells's radio announced.

Wells scanned the water around the *Golden Venture*. He could see the smaller vessel. "I'm looking right at it," he said. "It's not flipped over."

Then he realized: it was upside-down. Wells grabbed the radio.

"Coast Guard Station Rockaway Mobile One, our Boston Whaler just flipped over in the surf. Do you have a visual on our guys?"

Another Coast Guard helicopter had joined Mundy's now, along with several police choppers. They were stacked one on top of the other, all circling the stranded ship like buzzards. Mundy realized that they might be interfering with the flight path of heavy jets approaching Kennedy Airport, and he squawked his military code to the Federal Aviation Administration, asking the air traffic controllers to reroute any incoming flights around the rescue. His swimmers were wearing headsets, scanning the water below, and could not see Wells's roommate, Gilbert Burke, or either of the others from the overturned Whaler.

"We're looking for them," they radioed Wells. "We're looking."

The rescue swimmers descended into the roiling water to try to recover the crew, and finally they radioed again. "We've got one of your guys."

But it wasn't Burke; it was one of Burke's colleagues. When the Whaler flipped, the outboard engine had come crashing down and split the crewman's head open. The rescue swimmer loaded the bleeding man into a steel basket and signaled the crew to hoist him up.

As Wells stood on the beach, a figure walked out of the surf and approached him, drenched and shivering. It was the third man from the Whaler. "We all got separated," he said. There was still no sign of Burke.

After Mundy's team dropped off the injured Coast Guard man on the beach, they picked up two of the *Golden Venture* passengers who had reached the shore and gone into cardiac arrest. It was the first time Mundy had seen any of the passengers up close. They were dressed only in their underwear, and to Mundy they looked like "something from a concentration camp." They were all angles, bones and ribs, not a finger-and-thumb's worth of body fat between them. There was no insulation for their internal organs, and Mundy realized that when they hit the cold water, their blood vessels must have constricted, causing a heart attack. As he tried to revive the two men, he could feel the gristle of their bodies, the cartilage, their brittle ribs threatening to fracture under his powerful hands. The helicopter reached Floyd Bennett Field, where Emergency Medical Services had set up a triage station. But it was too late. Both men were DOA.

Even as he sat there with the corpses of these strangers, Mundy marveled at the resolve it must have required to expire on land and not at sea. The men had walked up out of the water, collapsed on the beach, and died.

When Gilbert Burke was thrown clear of the Boston Whaler, he got caught in a rip current and carried west, away from the *Golden Venture* and the rescue vehicles, out as far as the tip of the Rockaway Peninsula. Just before clearing the peninsula altogether, he managed to swim to a breakwater, and from there back to shore. If he hadn't, he would have been pulled farther out into the ocean.

Burke walked back east along the beach. By the time he arrived, the whole peninsula was a riot of rescue vehicles. A dozen boats surrounded the ship, four rescue helicopters swarmed overhead, and news helicopters had begun to arrive. Fifty-two ambulances lined the roads up and down the peninsula, ferrying the survivors from Breezy Point to Floyd Bennett Field and on to city hospitals.

Most of the survivors were corralled on the beach. They sat in clusters, looking dazed, hugging their knees and shivering. Their clothes were cheap and generic: acid-washed jeans and chunky Reebok knockoffs, vagabond suits, ill-fitting and frayed. Rescue workers unloaded truckloads of gray and blue blankets, and the survivors wrapped themselves in these, gazing out at the ocean from which they'd escaped. David Somma, the Park Police officer who had first spotted the ship, was walking among them on the beach, taking in the scene, when one of the men made eye contact with him. Somma approached the man and saw that he was clutching something in his hands. He held two hundred-dollar bills and a map of the New York City subway.

The sun was beginning to rise, casting a strange violet hue over the beach, and a makeshift command center had been established on shore, facing the ship. The brass from the fire department, police department, and mayor's office stood barking into radios at a folding table in the sand. Ray Kelly, the short, vulpine commissioner of police, arrived, wearing a crisp white shirt and tie under his blue NYPD windbreaker, despite the ungodly hour. Kelly was stunned by the vision—the ship, the people, the activity on the beach. Mayor David Dinkins showed up as well, and loped alongside Kelly, surveying the scene. The local and national media had descended, and correspondents were doing pieces to camera, the hulking ship framed over their shoulders in the background. "These are people who are apparently desperately trying to come to America," Dinkins told the cameras. "I would hope that those people who are already here would recognize how important the freedom is that they have here."

"Your heart goes out to them," Kelly added. "You don't know what the circumstances are that brought them here."

The people on the boat were Chinese. That much the officials had figured out. But the ship looked like a fishing boat or a short-haul freighter; it couldn't possibly have come all the way from China, much less transported so many people. Agents from the Immigration and Naturalization Service, or INS, had arrived, and were trying to segregate the passengers from the crew. But communication was a challenge. Many of the passengers were from China's Fujian Province, it emerged. They seemed to speak only limited Mandarin or Cantonese and conversed in a dialect of their own. Some of the men on the beach didn't look Chinese at all; their complexions were darker, their faces broader. They were Burmese and Indonesian, and as soon as the authorities surmised that these men were the crew members, they segregated them from the others in a crude cluster and circled them with yellow police tape.

In batches, the authorities began relocating the passengers to a building at Floyd Bennett Field. It was there that Sergeant Dougie Lee was sent when he reported to the scene. Dougie worked in the major case squad, the detective bureau of the NYPD. He was Cantonese American, tall and gangly, with a boyish face, prominent teeth, and a thick New York accent. He had been asleep in his apartment in Queens when the chief of detectives called and said, "You need to respond to Rockaway."

Dougie was thirty-eight and had lived in Hong Kong until he was twelve, when his family moved to New York. He spoke Cantonese and some Mandarin, and while he didn't speak Fujianese, he could understand some of it. As a member of the NYPD's Oriental Gang Unit—the Jade Squad, as it was known—he'd had a lot of exposure to Fujianese immigrants lately. "The Fooks," the cops called them. They had started showing up in the city, masses of them, new arrivals turning up at the sweatshops and employment agencies in Chinatown every week.

Dougie entered a large, brightly lit room filled with Chinese people. There were a few women, but it was mainly men, young to middle-aged, still wrapped in blankets, all of them wearing medical triage tags around their necks. The other officers standing watch were reluctant to get too close to the men. "Bad breath," they told Dougie. The men had been in the hold of a ship for some untold stretch of time, their clothes unwashed, their teeth unbrushed; their breath smelled of malnourishment and rot. Under fluorescent lights, they sat at long tables in a kind of rec room. Some sat alone, looking bedraggled and spent. Others were cheerful, grateful to be there, bereft of possessions in a foreign land, without so much as a dime for a phone call. They drank coffee from paper cups and ate cookies and potato chips, devouring whatever was put in front of them. They were desperate for cigarettes, bumming smokes off the cops, chanting "Marlboro! Marlboro! Marlboro!" Fearful of tuberculosis and that breath, rescue workers had given them all baby-blue antibacterial face masks.

Dougie Lee sat with the men. At first they didn't want to talk, eyeing him with nervous suspicion. But after a while they started warming up and coming over to him. Some spoke a little Mandarin or Cantonese. Soon they were queuing to tell him their stories. Dougie listened, and translated as best he could for the nurses who circulated through the room. The survivors all seemed to be from Fujian Province. A few had traveled with friends or cousins, but most had come alone. They had come for jobs, they said. Dougie needed to get people's names and find out whether they were hurt, but they flooded him with information—about brothers, sisters, parents, wives, the people they had left behind. They were afraid of the men who ran the ship, they said. On board, they had eaten only one meal a day.

One man said he had made a small scratch in the wall of the hold for every day they were at sea.

"How long was it?" Dougie asked.

"Months," the man replied.

Many of the survivors announced right there in the holding area at Floyd Bennett Field that they wanted political asylum in America. The officers interviewing them thought they sounded somewhat robotic, almost rehearsed, as if they had been coached on what to say when they arrived. The passengers expressed surprise at the kindness of Dougie and his colleagues. "American police are much nicer than police in China," they said.

As he listened to the passengers, Dougie found himself hoping that they would be able to obtain legal status in the United States. He himself had been lucky. His grandfather had come to America illegally, jumping ship and working in an old-school Chinese laundry in New York, where all the washing was done by hand. He had obtained his citizenship eventually; Dougie didn't know quite how, and even that—not knowing—was a kind of luxury. He had saved money and sent for the family, and that was how Dougie had come to America.

As he sat with the men from the ship, Dougie marveled at the way the Chinese treasured the United States—the way they borrowed money, left their loved ones, and risked their lives to get here. He had worked in Chinatown long enough to know that the nation the Chinese called the "Beautiful Country" was not always what it was cracked up to be. He had worked the kidnappings and the extortion rackets, busted sweatshops and massage parlors, been to basements where dozens of people shared a few hundred square feet, where people slept in rotation. Dougie looked at the men he was interviewing, saw the sacrifice they'd made, and came to a stark realization: *I couldn't do what they've done.*

By 8 A.M. the *Golden Venture* had slid off the sandbar with the rising tide and washed to shore. A team of officers boarded the boat and were greeted immediately by the odor of human feces. The deck was littered with shit, little piles of it everywhere. The *Golden Venture* was a small ship. It was hard to imagine that it had been occupied so recently by hundreds of people. The officers made their way down a single ladder into the hold, a dark space that was roughly the size of a three-car garage. In the dim light they encountered more stench—the sour reek of piss and perspiration—and squalor. "Slippers, purses, money, a remote control from a VCR, sweaters, pants—anything, everything that you could imagine," a Coast Guard officer recalled. "It was an overpowering aroma . . . The living space was being used as a bathroom."

Working with translators, authorities had plucked from the assembled survivors a sullen, heavyset, dark-skinned man in his forties. According to the Indonesian passport he was carrying, his name was Amir Humanthal Lumban Tobing, and according to the frightened passengers, he was the captain of the *Golden Venture*. Tobing was taken to an office at the Park Police headquarters and questioned by members of the INS and the Park Police. They gave him some hot food and read him his Miranda rights. He spoke some broken English; most captains do. One of the Park Police officers made a crude map of the world so the captain could trace the route the ship had taken.

Tobing said he had boarded the *Golden Venture* six months earlier, in January 1993, in Singapore. From Singapore he had sailed to Bangkok, where he took on ninety Chinese passengers and an onboard enforcer named Kin Sin Lee. From Bangkok the ship had sailed back to Singapore, where the generator was fixed for twelve days. As Tobing talked, a television in the office played the news, flashing images of the ship and the passengers on the beach. Suddenly Tobing sat up and pointed to one of the faces in the crowd on the television. "That's Kin Sin Lee," he said. He explained to the officers that Kin Sin Lee was the "owner of the boat."

From Singapore the ship sailed through the Strait of Malacca and across the Indian Ocean to Kenya, Tobing continued. In Mombasa it took on two hundred more passengers. With a finger, Captain Tobing indicated the route from Kenya: south along the east coast of Africa, down around the Cape of Good Hope, then up through the Atlantic, past Brazil and Central America to the East Coast of the United States. There was something peculiar about this route. It would have been vastly easier to cross the Pacific, in a straight line from China to California. The *Golden Venture* had traveled the wrong way around the planet, a journey of some 17,000 miles. In total, the trip had taken 120 days, twice as long as the storied voyage of the *Mayflower*, which brought the Pilgrims to Plymouth in 1620.

Even as the officers interrogated Tobing, the passengers were being led away. A convoy of blue-and-white Mass Transit Authority buses had been commandeered to transport the Chinese to an INS detention facility in a federal building at 201 Varick Street in downtown Manhattan. No one could pinpoint precisely when it had happened, but a subtle categorical shift had occurred; the passengers had been reclassified. They were no longer shipwrecked refugees, no longer the huddled masses, the wretched refuse of the teeming shore, no longer the homeless, tempest-tossed, that Emma Lazarus extolled in the 1883 poem inscribed in bronze on the Statue of Liberty a few short miles away. They were invaders. In the days and weeks to come, numerous people who were on the beach that morning would describe the arrival of hordes of Chinese as resembling the Normandy invasion—a storming of the beaches, a waterborne assault on the United States. Once the immediate logistical challenge of saving scores of people from drowning had subsided, the daunting gravity of the situation set in: some three hundred undocumented foreigners had just landed in the media capital of the United States. It was the single largest arrival of illegal immigrants in modern American history, and the whole thing was unfolding in real time on national television. Before the Chinese boarded the buses, someone determined that they should be handcuffed, and every major news channel captured footage of the men being frogmarched into the buses, decked out in surgical masks and triage tags and flexicuffed together in twos. As dozens of police officers stood guard, bus after bus filled up and slowly wheezed away.

All that remained on the beach were the strewn belongings that had washed ashore, cast-off possessions and crude souvenirs, the detritus of the crash and the rescue: discarded cardboard suitcases floating in the shallows; torn white plastic bags in which the jumpers had packed a dry change of clothes; empty gallon jugs of Taiwanese frying oil, which some had clung to for flotation; a few stray bottles of orange drink from Kenya. All this jetsam washed up through the morning, along with ragged bits of soggy blue paper: air-mail stationery, for letters home.

The only Chinese who remained on the beach were the dead. For a time it was unclear how many they were. The initial count was eight, but that was lowered after it was determined that some of the bodies had been counted twice. Along with the two cardiac arrest victims that Bill Mundy had dealt with, the bodies of three who had drowned washed up that morning, and another later in the day. In the coming weeks, clam dredgers and fishermen would stumble upon four more bodies, bringing the total who perished to ten.

Little was known about the dead. They were undocumented, in the most literal sense—they had no papers and offered no clues. A few had New York telephone numbers written in permanent marker on the waistbands of their underwear, which enabled authorities to track down family members in the city. Four of the bodies were identified and sent back to China for burial. But the others just lay there in refrigerated vaults in Manhattan, waiting to be claimed. Early on, two Chinatown residents who thought a relative might be among the dead ventured into the medical examiner's office, only to be accosted by immigration officials, handcuffed, and interrogated about their own immigration status. Word spread in the neighborhood, and no one took the risk of going to identify the bodies. Ten months later, six of the bodies were still there, unclaimed and unburied. Local residents pitched in $6,000 to pay for their cremation at a cemetery in New Jersey.

Of the survivors, thirty or so were taken to hospitals in Brooklyn and Queens and treated for hypothermia, exposure, exhaustion, and various injuries. The rest ended up in the INS holding center at 201 Varick. The facility had only 225 beds, not enough to accommodate the *Golden Venture* passengers. The immigration authorities were overwhelmed, ill-equipped to deal with this number of new arrivals.

President Bill Clinton had been in office for only six months. He had not yet appointed a director of the INS. As agency officials scrambled to house and process the passengers, they had to contend with the press as well. The arrival of the ship in New York was a sensational event. The *New York Times* alone assigned two dozen reporters to the story. The man who stepped into the leadership vacuum at the INS and presented himself to the cameras and microphones to address the situation was the agency's New York district director, Bill Slattery. Slattery had grown up in Newark, New Jersey, and done stints in the Marines and on the Texas Border Patrol before being assigned to the New York office of the INS, where he quickly rose through the ranks. He was extremely ambitious, and tough—tough on illegal immigrants and tough on his own subordinates. "A meat eater, not a grass eater," one colleague said.

"This is the twenty-fourth ship that the U.S. government has encountered since August of 1991," Slattery told reporters. "Almost all the aliens are Chinese nationals coming from Fukien province." (*Fujian* is sometimes pronounced "Fukien," and the Fujianese are also known as Fukienese.) In the past nine months alone, two thousand illegal Chinese had been captured trying to enter the country, he said. Two weeks earlier a freighter had slipped beneath the Golden Gate Bridge and deposited 240 Fujianese on a San Francisco pier. The following day, 57 more had been discovered locked in a warehouse in New Jersey.

The fee to reach America was $35,000, with a small down payment due before the trip began and the balance owed if the migrants survived the journey. Strictly speaking, this was "human smuggling" rather than "human trafficking." Though the terms are often used interchangeably, they describe two different crimes. Human trafficking generally involves some form of deception or exploitation, where an individual is misled about where she is going or what she will be doing when she gets there and is often pushed into sex work or forced labor. Human smuggling is a risky and often extremely dangerous undertaking, but migrants generally enter into it with their eyes open; no one is telling them they will be models or waitresses when they arrive, and incidents of smugglers forcing migrants into prostitution, while not unheard of, are exceedingly rare. Still, human smuggling is a rough and exploitative business. Slattery explained that the poor Chinese undertook enormous debts to make the journey and then spent years working as indentured servants, turning over their earnings to the shady underworld entrepreneurs who financed their passage.

"In effect, slavery here in the U.S.," one reporter prompted.

"That's right," Slattery replied.

Several miles away, inside a small shop at 47 East Broadway, in New York's Chinatown, a woman watched the news unfold on television. She was short and pudgy, with a broad face, small, wide-set eyes, and a hangdog expression. She spoke almost no English; her hair was cut in a sensible shoulder-length bob; and she favored the cheap, utilitarian apparel of her countrymen from Fujian Province. She worked long hours in the store, selling clothing and simple goods, and in a restaurant downstairs, which served Fujianese specialties like oyster cakes and fishball soup to the newly arrived Chinese peasants who had settled in the neighborhood. When a truckload of supplies came, neighbors saw her hauling the goods into the shop. She could have been mistaken for one of those destitute peasants herself.

But in fact she was a very wealthy woman, the owner of the shop and the restaurant and the five-story brick building that housed them. Her name was Cheng Chui Ping, but everyone in the neighborhood called her Ping Jie—Big Sister Ping, or simply Sister Ping, a casual honorific, a gesture of respect. At the age of forty-four, she wasn't just a shopkeeper and restaurateur but something like a village elder in the claustrophobically intimate corner of Chinatown where she resided. She was a banker of sorts, and something else as well. She was what the Chinese call a *shetou,* or snakehead, a kind of immigration broker who charges steep fees to smuggle people out of China and into other countries. She had pioneered the China-to-Chinatown route in the early 1980s, and from her humble shop on East Broadway she had developed a reputation as one of the most reliable—and successful—snakeheads on the planet. In Chinese communities from Europe to South America to the United States, Sister Ping had become a well-burnished brand name, one that connoted safe, illicit delivery from point A to point B; the Cadillac of global human smuggling.

But as she watched the news that morning, she brooded, and grumbled that she had come in for a run of bad luck lately. She had helped arrange the financing for the voyage of the *Golden Venture,* and she had personally received fees from two of the passengers on board. Sister Ping didn't know it yet, but one of those passengers was among the dead.

Chapter Two

Leaving Fujian

NO ONE knows precisely how many ethnic Chinese live outside of China, but estimates range from 40 to 50 million or more. After the descendants of African slaves, the overseas Chinese, as they are often called, represent the largest diaspora on the planet. America no doubt saw the occasional Chinese trader prior to the mid-nineteenth century, but the history of the Chinese in the United States did not really get under way until one January day in 1848, when a foreman at John Sutter's mill, on the south fork of the American River in northern California, fished several pieces of glittering metal from the water, metal that "could be beaten into a different shape, but not broken." It was gold that first drew the Chinese to America, and it was visions of a paradise where backbreaking labor was lavishly repaid that led the nineteenth-century Chinese fortune-seekers who first came to the country to call it Jinshan, or Golden Mountain. The colloquialism somehow managed to survive the actual privations that the pioneer experience held in store, the eventual disappearance of the gold itself, and the shifting fortunes of Chinese Americans over the ensuing decades. The name just stuck. So much so, in fact, that it still endures today.

China was in a state of upheaval during the mid-nineteenth century, demoralized by the Opium Wars with Great Britain. The first Chinese to arrive in California sent word back across the Pacific of a nation of unclaimed land, plentiful timber, and gold that you could pluck from the ground. At that time America was a sparsely populated country; only 23 million people lived in the United States, compared with 430 million in China. Young Chinese men began abandoning their villages and leaving for America in droves. Two thousand arrived in 1848; four years later, 20,000 entered through the port of San Francisco alone. But for all their numbers and the vastness of the nation in which they were born, the nineteenth-century Chinese who came to the Golden Mountain originated from a remarkably small corner of China—a handful of counties on the west side of the Pearl River Delta, around the southern city of Canton (or, as it's known today, Guangzhou). In fact, until the 1960s, most Chinese in America could trace their roots to an area roughly half the size of the state of Delaware.

By 1867, nearly 70 percent of all mineworkers west of the Rockies were Chinese. When the railroad barons elected to stitch together the fractious country with a single transcontinental rail network, constructing the Central Pacific Railroad to connect the Union Pacific with the existing eastern lines, Chinese workers dynamited the tunnels and laid the rails. Charlie Crocker, the chief contractor for the Central Pacific, was a big believer in Chinese labor and deployed recruiters to Canton, observing that a race of people who had managed to build the Great Wall could certainly build a railroad. It was thankless work. The Chinese were paid a pittance, less even than their Irish counterparts, and many died from accidental blasts, disease, abuse at the hands of their employers, or attacks from Native Americans, who may have recognized the railroad for what it was: an incursion upon their homeland that once established would be impossible to undo. More than one of the great fortunes of the Gilded Age was built on Chinese labor. But the endeavor took a devastating toll on the Chinese. Over a thousand Chinese workers perished while building the railroad. Twenty thousand pounds of bones were shipped back to China.

If analogies to slave labor spring to mind, they were hardly lost on Americans at the time. When the Civil War ended, some southern newspapers began explicitly editorializing that one way to compensate for the emancipation of black slaves was to shift agricultural work to imported "coolies" from China. "Emancipation has spoiled the Negro," the *Vicksburg Times* remarked. "We therefore say let the Coolies come." The demand for Chinese laborers was so intense that it gave rise to a highly efficient apparatus for importing them. Chinese "travel agencies," some of them affiliated with triads, the secret societies that dominated organized crime in China, sprang up in San Francisco and went into business securing transportation to America for migrant workers. Penniless gold rushers could book passage on American ships bound for California without putting any money down. In lieu of a fee they simply pledged a portion of their income once they arrived. The means of conveyance was so-called coolie clippers, which bore more than a passing resemblance to slave ships and confined their Chinese cargo to the hold, occasionally in chains or bamboo cages. Once they arrived, the workers paid their dues to the travel agencies, and when debtors failed to pay, the Chinese brokers sometimes arranged to hold their families hostage, as a form of human security.

One sorry irony of the early Chinese experience in America was the unintended consequences of the trans-American railroad the Cantonese laborers helped to construct. The euphoria of the gold rush began to dissipate almost as quickly as it had begun, when what surface gold could be easily snatched had already been snatched and what was left proved difficult to retrieve. Taxed as "foreign miners" and then driven out of the mining business altogether, and cut loose by the railroad once the golden spike joined the Central Pacific and Union Pacific lines in Promontory Summit, Utah, in 1863, the Chinese took up menial jobs in settlements throughout the West. But the very railroad tracks the Chinese had built enabled white homesteaders to traverse the continent in a mere eight days. As the post–Civil War recession set in, easterners began crossing the country in greater and greater numbers, arriving on the West Coast in search of work. Often willing to take any job and work for meager wages, largely unintegrated into frontier society, and present in daunting numbers, the Chinese were almost too easy a scapegoat for West Coast labor leaders and politicians and the embittered unemployed of the white working class. Before long, resentment blossomed into violence. "In San Francisco, some boys have stoned an inoffensive Chinaman to death," Mark Twain wrote in 1872. "Although a large crowd witnessed the shameful deed, no one interfered." Bloody anti-Chinese purges began occurring in settlements throughout the West.

On May 6, 1882, the anti-Chinese animus was codified in the Chinese Exclusion Act. The law, which strictly limited any further immigration from China and excluded Chinese already in the country from citizenship, was a landmark piece of legislation: the first broad restriction on immigration to the United States. Coming as it did at the end of a century of extraordinary growth and industrialization, and on the heels of a war that had questioned but ultimately solidified the concept of a coherent, unitary, sovereign America, the act created, in a very real sense, the concept of illegal immigration. In 1887, one Chinese laborer who had lived in San Francisco for the past twelve years sailed to China to visit his parents. When he returned the following year, he was denied reentry at the port of San Francisco. He challenged his exclusion, and the controversy made it as far as the Supreme Court. In the famous "Chinese Exclusion Case," the Court described the Chinese as "strangers in the land, residing apart by themselves, and adhering to the customs and usages of their own country." The ruling established Congress's plenary power over immigration and upheld its right to pass legislation that excludes noncitizens. In 1891 the United States appointed the first superintendent of immigration to process arriving immigrants. Ellis Island was established the following year.

The sudden reversal—from recruiting laborers in the 1850s to forcibly excluding them three decades later—was not the last instance when the Chinese in America would be the victims of larger circumstance, at the mercy of the capricious ebb and flow of the country's economic needs. The Chinese who remained were obliged, for their own survival, to withdraw from direct economic competition, retreating into two undertakings, the restaurant business and the laundry business, where they might be regarded as less of an economic threat. By 1920 fully half of the Chinese in America were engaged in one of these two occupations. The exclusion lasted six decades, halting further legal immigration and largely freezing the United States' Chinese population in place. But when Japan attacked Pearl Harbor, Franklin Delano Roosevelt sought Chinese support against the common enemy, and the ban on Chinese immigration suddenly seemed a bit awkward. Roosevelt wrote to Congress, asking lawmakers to "correct a historic mistake." They repealed the exclusion act in December 1943.

But the war had scarcely ended when the Communists took over in China and closed its borders, so the de facto consequences of the exclusion endured long after the law itself was repealed. In the 1950s, Beijing introduced a household registration system that tied the various entitlements of the welfare state to individually registered family residences. The policy was designed in part to prevent tens of millions of rural Chinese from flooding major cities in search of food and work. In practice it meant that if an individual wanted to relocate within China, he needed permission from Party officials both in the place he was leaving and in the place he was heading to. If you moved without permission, you lost your allotment of grain and the other benefits that the welfare state provided. The policy effectively rooted rural Chinese citizens to the land, preventing them from leaving the village of their birth. It became very difficult even to relocate to the neighboring province, much less to leave China altogether.

Sister Ping was born on January 9, 1949, ten months before Mao established the People's Republic of China. She grew up in a village in northern Fujian Province called Shengmei, or Prospering Beauty, a hardscrabble settlement of farmers and fishermen by the banks of the Min River, where chickens roamed a network of dirt lanes that turned muddy during the monsoon months of August and September, and rice farmers worked their modest paddies with water buffalo. She was one of five children born to a farmer from Shengmei, Cheng Chai Leung, and his wife, who had grown up in a neighboring village. As a girl, Sister Ping would leave the village elementary school when her classes were done for the day and return home to a long list of chores. She was responsible for chopping wood and for tending to a small plot of vegetables. She helped raise the family's pigs and rabbits. "I never went out to play. I always worked," she would later explain. "And I liked working."

During her formative years, Sister Ping bore witness to a procession of tragically misguided policy initiatives from Beijing. When she was barely ten, Mao's Great Leap Forward reassembled China's peasantry into communes in an effort to reinvent centuries-old agrarian communities as industrial proletariats. The result was severe food shortages, and ultimately the greatest famine in recorded history, which between 1958 and 1960 killed nearly 38 million people. All across China, peasant families like Sister Ping's suffered almost unimaginable hardship during these years, struggling to ward off starvation and eke out a living despite the frailty of their malnourished bodies and a government whose incompetence was matched only by its indifference in the face of civilian death. It was Mao's view that in a country as populous as China, individual human lives were anything but sacred. One incidental cost of the Great Leap Forward, he conceded, was that "half of China may well have to die." The millions of people who collapsed and died in the countryside were simply doing their part, he suggested: "They can fertilize the ground." In a country where filial piety and veneration of the dead had been cornerstones of the Confucian tradition for over two thousand years, the grieving families of the dead were instructed to plant crops atop their burial plots.

While she was still a pigtailed child, Sister Ping encountered a world in which human life could be casually extinguished at any moment, and in addition to fostering a slightly callous, unsentimental view of death, the experience seems to have forged in her a survivalist instinct—a fierce conviction that only through hard work could she and her loved ones prevail over adversity and escape the kind of fickle end that others had in store. One day when she was twelve years old, Sister Ping left the village to go cut wood for kindling. In order to reach a remote grove of trees on the far side of the Min River, she joined eight other people in a rowboat. There were only seven oars, and though she was still just a child, Sister Ping took one and did her part to row. But before they could reach the other side, the current picked up and the boat flipped over. Sister Ping was thrown into the water and managed to swim to shore. Afterward she learned that everyone who had been carrying an oar had survived the accident. The two who had not been rowing drowned. The incident made an indelible impression on the little girl, one that she would remember for the rest of her life. "The two people who were lazy and sat back while others worked ended up dead," she would later reflect. "This taught me to work hard."

If in her later life Sister Ping harbored a suspicion, bordering on contempt, of the authority of government and the laws and edicts of officials, her attitude here again may have been developed at an early age. When she was a teenager and attending the local high school, it was announced one day that the school was closing. Schools and universities across China were being shuttered and young people were being sent to work in the fields under the banner of the Cultural Revolution. Mao announced that "rebellion is justified" and encouraged the young to overturn the decadent "old culture" of China. Children turned on their elders, branding them reactionaries, class traitors, and capitalists. Students pilloried their teachers in the schoolyard, dousing them with black ink, jeering at them, and in some cases torturing them, forcing them to eat excrement or kneel in ground glass. Soon marauding bands of teenage Red Guards were burning books, destroying artworks, defacing monuments, and assaulting scholars and intellectuals. It was a bizarre, dystopian interlude in China's history, a bout of state-sanctioned madness in which the young indulged in a destructive kind of *Clockwork Orange* frenzy.

Sister Ping was not an especially political person. But she was a natural leader, and before long she had donned green, military-style work clothes and a red armband and become a leader of the Red Guard. No record exists of her activities during these cataclysmic, often violent years, and in later life she would be reticent about discussing it. "That was the trend. I had to go with the trend" was all she would say of her participation. "Gone with the old to welcome the new."

Mao had always been suspicious of Fujian, for reasons that perhaps were understandable. It is one of China's smaller provinces, a mountainous sliver of coast far from the official influence of Beijing and directly across the strait from Taiwan. It has always been one of China's most outward-looking regions, home to seafarers and traders, smugglers and explorers: a historic point of embarkation. Over a millennium of isolation from the rest of China and exposure to the outside world, the region and its people developed an adventurous, somewhat maverick sensibility. In the thirteenth century Marco Polo visited the port of Fuzhou and remarked on the great quantities of its chief exports, galangal and ginger. (He added that the people of Fuzhou were "addicted to eating human flesh, esteeming it more delicate than any other," but Marco Polo was not famed for his accurate reporting.) According to legend, a seven-foot-tall admiral named Zheng He set sail from Fuzhou a half-century before Columbus with an armada of 3,000 white-hulled junks and some 30,000 sailors, and ventured deep into the South Seas and as far away as Africa. By the 1570s, Fujianese merchants had established trading posts in Manila and Nagasaki. Seed communities of Fujianese traders were established throughout Southeast Asia, and today, centuries later, vast numbers of ethnic Fujianese are scattered throughout the region. Eighty percent of the Chinese in the Philippines can trace their roots to Fujian, as can 55 percent of the Chinese in Indonesia. Taiwan was a mere hundred miles across the strait, and the Fujianese settled there as well. So many made the crossing in the seventeenth and eighteenth centuries that modern Taiwanese speak a dialect similar to that spoken in the southern Fujianese port of Xiamen. Well over a million Chinese in Hong Kong, Macau, and Taiwan have roots in Tingjiang commune, which contains Shengmei village, where Sister Ping grew up.

It was from Fujian that the second great wave of Chinese came to America, in the 1980s and 1990s. In fact, even *Fujian* is too broad a description of the point of origin of this explosive population displacement. It was really just from northern Fujian that they came, where the regional capital of Fuzhou sits, 30 miles from the ocean, on the edge of the coastal plain, hemmed in on three sides by mountains and on the fourth side by the sea. When the Fujianese talk about Fuzhou, they tend to include not just the city but the main population centers of the surrounding countryside: the nearby city of Changle, the historic port of Mawei, and a string of townships along the northern banks of the Min River, where it flows into the ocean and meets the Taiwan Strait and the East China Sea. The mountains surrounding Fuzhou have preserved a subdialect, Minbei, or Northern Min, which differs from the language spoken in Xiamen and Taiwan; it's not so much Fujianese as Fuzhounese. Minbei was Sister Ping's mother tongue.

This peculiar type of population displacement, in which the people of a handful of villages seem to relocate en masse to another country within a short span of time, is actually not so unusual. In New York's Little Italy, the Calabrians who settled along Mulberry Street at the turn of the twentieth century self-segregated block by block, and even building by building, according to the particular village in southern Italy from which they came. Social scientists who study migration have observed the pattern in countries around the world: a few early pioneers venture out and lay roots in a faraway land; if they find it agreeable, they send first for their immediate family, then for their extended family, then for friends and fellow villagers. It is one of the peculiar ironies of global migration that an immigrant community in a given country is often highly atypical of the country from which the people came. If you put yourself in the shoes of the person contemplating where it is that he or she wants to resettle, it makes perfect sense: you go to the place where you have a sister or a cousin or an old friend from school. Of course, this model works only if you have a sending community that is close-knit to begin with, but that is where the traditional Fujianese devotion to family comes in. Those first explorers who left the village bore little resemblance to the impetuous young men of Western literature who turn their backs on family and society and leave to seek their fortunes. Migration, at least in Fujian Province, was anything but selfish or misanthropic. The family was regarded as an economic unit, and the first pioneers to leave the village generally did so with the aim of establishing a beachhead on a foreign shore and eventually sending for the family. Demographers call this process "chain migration" and use the concept to explain how it is that half the residents of crowded urban ghettos from Boston to Berlin often hail from the same few villages in whatever country they left behind. A more evocative Fujianese expression captures the same dynamic: "One brings ten. Ten bring a hundred."

Moreover, everywhere the Fujianese went, they seemed to succeed, often besting the local population and controlling a disproportionate amount of wealth. More than half of Asia's forty billionaires of Chinese ancestry in the year 2000 had roots in Fujian Province. What the Fujianese did best, it sometimes seems, was leave. They were fiercely independent by nature, wily, and doggedly entrepreneurial. When opportunity beckoned, from any remote corner of the earth, they followed, often against staggeringly difficult odds, and established enclaves in foreign lands.

Sister Ping might be described as one of the Fujianese pioneers who struck out for the unknown and settled in New York. But that would be an oversimplification. In fact she was not the first in her family to make the journey to America: her father was. Because Fujian is all mountains and coast, with little arable land, Fujianese men grew up knowing how to fish and sail, and opportunity could always be found at sea. For generations of Fujianese men, the sea offered a sometimes perilous but always reliable option: if you couldn't make ends meet on land, there was always work to be found on one of the merchant ships going in and out of the port at Mawei. During the 1960s, in the midst of the upheaval of the Great Leap Forward and the Cultural Revolution, Sister Ping's father, Cheng Chai Leung, left the family and joined the crew of a merchant ship bound for the United States. He faced a bitter reality: he could do more for his family by turning his back on them and finding work outside China than he could by staying put.

In those years, very few Chinese made it to America. Leaving China was forbidden, and in any event, Beijing and Washington had no diplomatic relations, so there was no legal process for applying to enter the United States. Those few who did manage to make it to America tended to arrive the way Cheng Chai Leung did: they either found jobs as sailors or simply stowed away, and when they arrived in the bustling port of Los Angeles, or Baltimore, or New York, they jumped ship, disappeared amid the dockhands and stevedores and all the chaos of unloading one cargo and loading another, and ventured into town. If they could find their way to a Chinatown, there would be people who spoke Cantonese or Mandarin, and they could find a place to stay and a job that paid cash, washing dishes in a restaurant or working in a Chinese laundry.

Cheng Chai Leung worked as a dishwasher for a decade. He wrote letters every few months—the family received three letters a year—and he sent money home. But he was largely absent during Sister Ping's youth. He left the family when she was fifteen and stayed in America for thirteen years. Eventually he slipped up somehow and alerted American authorities to his illegal status. They discovered that he was a deserted crewman, and he was deported back to China in 1977. According to authorities in Hong Kong and New York, it was upon his return to China that Sister Ping's father went into business smuggling people.

The origins of the term *snakehead* are shrouded in mystery. Some believe that the snake symbolizes a circuitous smuggling route, with the snake's head leading the way. Smuggled migrants are referred to as "snakes," or sometimes "snaketails." But they're just as often known as "ducks," or simply "customers." As smuggling operations grew more complex, a certain hierarchy evolved, with "little snakeheads" doing recruitment in Chinese villages and "big snakeheads" arranging financing and logistics, and pocketing the bulk of the profits, from the safety of New York or Hong Kong or Taipei. Historical records indicate that the indigenous Fujianese once venerated snakes as totems. The Fujianese were originally known as the Min, and the Mandarin character for the Min is composed of a symbol for a gate with a worm or a snake crawling underneath it. When emigrants slither through the wire fences strung along the border between one country and another, one of Sister Ping's snakehead associates once explained, "the shape of it looks like a snake."

One curiosity of the growth of the snakehead trade in Fujian Province during the 1980s and 1990s is that at the time Fujian had one of the fastest-growing economies in China. Mao died in 1976, and by the time Sister Ping's father returned from America the following year, Deng Xiaoping was already ushering in a period of critical reflection on the errors of the Mao era and moving toward a series of sweeping economic reforms designed to open up China somewhat to the outside world and experiment with a more market-based economy. In 1980 Beijing established a number of special economic zones, which were permitted to be more open to international trade and given certain tax incentives to lure foreign investment, and the southern Fujian city of Xiamen was selected. In 1984 fourteen other coastal cities were designated, and Fuzhou made the list.

Xiamen and, to a lesser extent, Fuzhou reinvented themselves as shipping and manufacturing centers in the 1980s, and the economy started to improve. It would seem that this development should have discouraged emigration from China. A rising tide lifts all boats, supposedly: why leave the province just as it is discovering prosperity? But as these changes swept through the region, many Fujianese who had for generations devoted themselves to subsistence fishing or tending a farm suddenly began to feel dislocated in the new economy—left behind. Demographers who have researched migration find that it is not actually absolute poverty that drives people to leave one country for another. The poorest provinces in western China have rarely been a source of outmigration. When everyone around you shares your own meager lifestyle, there is actually less of an inclination to leave. Instead, it is "relative deprivation" that tends to drive migration: income disparities, the experience of watching your neighbor do better than you. So, ironically, economic development sometimes causes people to leave rather than stay put.

Some did better than others when the economic reforms came to Fujian, and those who did not fare as well—the subsistence farmers and schoolteachers, the local Party officials who had fallen out of favor—were suddenly able to glimpse the kinds of material comforts they had lived without their whole lives. What's more, Deng's commendable efforts to loosen the household registration system, which had locked the Chinese peasantry in place, eventually unleashed a substantial internal migration and gave birth to a floating population of migrant workers that numbered in the tens of millions. The area around Fuzhou was flooded by eager odd-jobbers from the hinterland. For the local unskilled labor base, it became more and more difficult to find work.

For this frustrated, largely uneducated population (fewer than 10 percent of Fujianese completed high school), the United States developed an irresistible allure. They might have been excluded from the economic growth in China, but America was ripe with possibilities. Fantastical stories abounded about America and the wealth that could be had there. American markets sold a thousand types of bread, people said. The very tapwater tasted sweet—you could gain weight just by drinking it. Above all, America seemed to hold the promise of upward mobility. Not overnight mobility, by any means; it was understood that you went to America to work, and work hard, just as the gold rushers had done in California over a century earlier. But the promise was that the work would bear fruit—that your children would live an incrementally better life than you did; that one generation's toil would secure comfort for the next. "Here, they're working like slaves," a Chinatown journalist in New York explained. "But there is hope for them to change everything." But in Fujian, he went on, "you work like a slave, and there is no hope to change anything. For a fisherman? For a farmer with a little piece of land? They'll never change their life. Never."

Sister Ping believed in America as ardently as, if not more than, her fellow Fujianese. When she was a little girl, her father told her it was a great country, full of opportunity. By the time her father returned to China, she was twenty-eight and already a mother. In high school she had met a mild-mannered young man from a neighboring village, Cheung Yick Tak, and the two were married in 1969. Short and shy, with sloping shoulders, a high forehead, and nervous, heavily lidded eyes, Yick Tak had little of his young wife's intelligence, determination, or fire. But he was devoted to her, and seemed happy to defer decisions large and small to the more assertive Sister Ping. Their first daughter, Cheng Hui Mui, who would later adopt the name Monica, was born in 1973, and the following year the whole family relocated to Hong Kong. Many Fujianese were fleeing to Hong Kong during those years, some of them going so far as to swim across the Shenzhen River. With a free-market economy and British administration, Hong Kong was a tempting bastion of capitalism just a short way down the coast, and the ever entrepreneurial Fujianese moved there and thrived.

Sister Ping and her family moved into an apartment in a new high-rise on Hong Kong Island, overlooking Stonecutter Island and the skyline of Tsim Sha Tsui. It is not clear how Sister Ping first arrived there—it may have been through the good offices of her father—but she and Yick Tak promptly opened up a small variety shop nearby, on Des Voeux Road West. The Cantonese majority in Hong Kong looked down on the Fujianese, and the Fujianese tended to cluster together, in the neighborhood of North Point, on Hong Kong Island, and in small enclaves in the New Territories. Sister Ping catered to this expatriate community and soon became quite successful, selling cheap clothing, fabric, and calculators. The twin pillars of independence and an equity stake were enormously important to many Fujianese. Even if the business itself was modest, what mattered most was that you owned it. Better to be in front of a chicken, a Fujianese saying goes, than behind a cow. Sister Ping had a sharp, flinty mind and a good head for numbers, and before long the shop was doing well enough for her to begin to expand her business interests. In 1979 she opened a clothing factory in Shenzhen, just across the border in the People's Republic.

But for all her success in Hong Kong, Sister Ping was restless, and eager to get to America. Jimmy Carter and Deng Xiaoping had met in 1978 and agreed to some limited immigration between China and the United States. University students and scholars were permitted to participate in exchanges, and measures were taken to allow the estranged family members of Chinese in America to emigrate legally. But Sister Ping was no scholar; she had barely finished high school. And in a cruel twist, the new policy coincided with her father's forced repatriation to China. Because education in Fujian was so poor and so few of the Chinese who had settled in America were Fujianese, very few of her countrymen were eligible to make the trip. Chinese census bureau figures indicate that in the early 1980s, the Fujianese represented less than 2 percent of China's emigrant population. And those few who did go tended to follow the pattern Sister Ping's father had: the men left and then, if they prospered, sent for their families. "Every man in the town had to be in New York before one woman would come," a New York lawyer who represented Fujianese clients in Chinatown recalled.

Sister Ping's husband, Yick Tak, did make the trip to the United States first. Before their children were born, he followed her father's lead, joining the crew of a ship in Hong Kong and sailing to the United States, then jumping ship and finding work. But with a haplessness that would become his trademark, Yick Tak was arrested and deported by the INS after two short years. He returned to Hong Kong and settled in to his old life with his wife and her family. Sister Ping was curious about America and intrigued by the things her husband had to say. It was easy to survive there, Yick Tak told her. Food and living expenses were cheap; the dollar was a strong currency. Education was common; most children in America seemed to go to college.

One day in June 1981, Sister Ping strode into the American consulate in Hong Kong and applied for a visa to the United States. She spoke little English but said she intended to work as a domestic. She was an established businesswoman in Hong Kong by then. A consular officer asked: Why would she go to the United States just to become a servant?

"When I was young and attending school, I knew that the United States is a civilized country," Sister Ping explained. In the United States, "one could make a living." Besides, she added, with a flash of pride, "I would make a very fine servant." She explained that her hope was someday to take her children to the United States. "It is for the sake of my children's future that I am willing to be a servant," she said.

Chapter Three

Eighteen-Thousand-Dollar Woman

THOUGH SHE would eventually become known as the very avatar of illegal immigration, when Sister Ping initially entered the United States, she had a legal right to do so. Several months after her meeting at the American consulate in Hong Kong, she was granted a visa, for "needed skilled or unskilled" work, and on November 17, 1981, she flew to the United States. She entered via Anchorage, Alaska, and wasted no time moving to Chinatown in New York. "The reason most Fujianese came to New York first is it's the center of everything," one of her Fujianese contemporaries in the neighborhood explained. "There are lawyers here, doctors, people who speak your dialect. Even in Brooklyn, I cannot get the herbs I want at a reasonable price. Chinatown, New York, is really the starting place. You'll always come here first for herbs, advice, jobs. People come here, they make it, then they move on. The next wave of immigrants say, where can I go? Where will they speak my language? Where can I find a job? Where can I buy bok choy and roast duck?"

As soon as she had arrived in Chinatown and established herself, Sister Ping sent for Yick Tak and the children, and within a year the family was together again. In 1982 the great Fujianese influx was just beginning, and the family settled on Chinatown's grubby eastern frontier. They moved into a four-room subsidized apartment at 14 Monroe Street, in a sprawling housing compound encompassing two city blocks that sat wedged between the Brooklyn Bridge and the Manhattan

Bridge on the banks of the East River. The complex was known as Knickerbocker Village. When it was constructed in the thirties, it was the first housing project in New York City to receive federal funding. It had been home to ethnic strivers of many stripes, but mainly Eastern European Jews and Italians. Julius and Ethel Rosenberg had occupied an eleventh-floor apartment in the 1940s. Half of New York's Bonnano crime family had lived there at one point or another, and a few were still resident when Sister Ping and Yick Tak moved in.

Sister Ping liked New York City immediately. It was so much bigger than Fujian and Hong Kong, and so full of opportunity. She did not take a job as a maid, as she had said she would in her interview at the U.S. consulate. Instead, she and her husband obtained a lease on the tiny storefront at 145B Hester, a cramped, narrow retail space on the street level of a fading tenement. The rent was $1,000 a month, and they opened the Tak Shun Variety Store. When they applied for a business certificate for the shop, they translated Tak Shun as "reliable." The shop next door was owned by a family from Shengmei village, and Sister Ping and Yick Tak stocked the place with clothing and simple goods that would appeal to the local Chinese community but particularly to the homesick Fujianese, more and more of whom seemed to turn up in the neighborhood each day. When the shop opened, some kids from a local gang dropped by and demanded a red envelope full of protection money. Sister Ping gave them $100, but that night they came by the store anyway and vandalized the place, tearing down the sign she had carefully erected above the front door.

The nascent Fujianese neighborhood was in every way at odds with the entrenched Cantonese Chinatown, a ghetto within a ghetto. The Cantonese end of town was clean and full of tourists at lunchtime and on weekends, a thicket of garish billboards arrayed vertically over the street in the Hong Kong style, the glitzy storefronts festooned with gilt calligraphy, the restaurant windows lined with showcase fishtanks. The dividing line was the Bowery, the traditional eastern frontier of Chinatown, and the Fujianese settled in the warren of streets beyond it—

Eldridge and Allen, East Broadway, Henry, and Division, in the shadow of the gray slab masonry of the on-ramp to the Manhattan Bridge. The businesses in this end of Chinatown didn't cater to tourists so much as to fellow Chinese. The aesthetic of the restaurants was more utilitarian.

The Fujianese who arrived in those days went to work immediately, doing difficult jobs: working as seamstresses in garment sweatshops in Chinatown or Queens; washing dishes in restaurant kitchens because they didn't speak the requisite increment of English to work as waiters; doing bicycle delivery in rough neighborhoods in the Bronx, where Fujianese cooks prepared Cantonese specialties in claustrophobic kitchens behind thick panes of bulletproof Plexiglas. During the slow daytime hours, restaurant workers were dispatched throughout the city to slide takeout menus under the doors of apartments, sneaking past doormen when the buildings had them, hovering outside until some legitimate guest was buzzed in when they didn't.

They stayed in a range of decrepit accommodations: grimy flophouses and single-resident-occupancy hotels along the Bowery, rat-infested dwellings where men and women, segregated by floor, slept in windowless six-by-six-foot cells. They crammed into the century-old tenements of Allen Street, Essex, Chrystie, and Hester, chutes-and-ladders fire escapes of black wrought iron stenciling a zigzag geometry across the brick facades. The famous Fujianese entrepreneurialism has a tendency to feed on itself, so landlords who owned, say, a one- or two-bedroom apartment in the neighborhood realized that they could break up the space into bunk beds and sell it in shifts. Everybody won. New arrivals from Fuzhou could keep their housing costs to $90 a month, forfeiting their bed to other off-shift tenants for sixteen hours a day, and the landlords reaped the benefits of triple-booking the space.

Employment agencies, many of them Fujianese-owned, began to bridge the gap between New York employers looking for cheap, exploitable labor and hungry arrivals from Fuzhou. The agencies occupied simple, brightly lit spaces where jobs were announced over a microphone or posted on little scraps of paper pinned to the wall. You could spot the Fujianese, their eyes hungry but downcast, looking to avoid conversation, chain-smoking, eyeing the wall, milling around, waiting for the next job—delivery boy (must supply own bike), seamstress, construction, cook. It was a buyer's market: the Fujianese were often undocumented, and many of them owed money to whoever had brought them over. They needed work fast, and the kind of work that wouldn't require them to fill out a W-2 form. As such, the jobs tended to be menial and often backbreaking, with minimal pay and excruciatingly long hours. And when a job came through, it was the worker, not the employer, who owed the employment agency a fee. They usually paid a few cents on every dollar they made.

The scrappiness of the Fujianese was not lost on the existing Cantonese community, which had reigned in Chinatown for a hundred years. Nineteenth-century Cantonese had come east from California around the time of the exclusion act and established the neighborhood at the intersection of Mott Street and Pell. Their descendants looked down on the Fujianese arrivals as strivers and peasants, poorly educated and willing to sully themselves in untold squalor in order to make a buck. Sister Ping felt that the Cantonese did not show the Fujianese adequate respect. "Fujianese and Cantonese always seem like different people, not very alike," she observed. As a result, the Fujianese stuck to themselves. "We always did our own thing," she said. It must have been unsettling for the Cantonese to watch the traditional identity of Chinese America give way to a tidal wave of Fujianese. In 1960 there were 236,000 Chinese in America. By 1990 that number had swelled to 1.6 million. A large proportion of that growth was Fujianese, and for the vast majority of Fujianese emigrants, the first stop in America was New York City. Chinatown residents began referring to East Broadway as Fuzhou Street. They knew that most of the Fujianese arrivals were illegal and were still paying off their passage. They called them "eighteen-thousand-dollar men," after the going snakehead rate in the eighties.

But the fact remained that a dishwasher in Chinatown could make in a month what a farmer in Fuzhou made in a year, and the Fujianese kept coming. They were willing to take on the debt associated with the journey because of the promise that life in America held. It was an investment, and families pooled their resources to support each émigré. The criminologist Ko-lin Chin likens the logic of the Fujianese in those years to the decision of a college graduate to take out loans for Harvard Law School; a huge debt is accumulated, but one that will exponentially increase the earning power of the debtor.

A child born on American soil is an American citizen, whatever the legal status of its parents, and many young Fujianese had children. Work left little time to raise them, so they sent their babies back to China, to the very villages the parents had fled, to be brought up by their grandparents until they were old enough for school. Whole villages in the countryside around Fuzhou emptied of men of working age. The Fujianese called them "widow's villages," for all of the wives who were left behind. But soon the wives started going to New York as well, and the only residents left were the aged and infirm and a profusion of fresh-faced American-born babies. Before long this reverse migration—undocumented parents sending their U.S.-citizen children back to China—struck some enterprising Fujianese as an opportunity, and businesses devoted to sending babies back became a flourishing industry in their own right.

By working long hours and living frugally, the Fujianese managed to save. Because their labor was off the books, it was also tax-free, and most Fujianese arrivals were able to pay off their snakehead debt within a couple of years. Despite, or perhaps because of, the depredations, the Fujianese forged a strong, insular, ethnic enclave on the fringes of Chinatown. After six, or often as many as thirteen, consecutive days of work, most new arrivals took a day of rest, known as a "cigarette day," to shop, recreate, and gamble—to indulge in a few simple luxuries, like cigarettes. Monday is traditionally a slow day in the restaurant trade, and after a week of slicing broccoli or pushing a mop, young men would wend their way through the hurly-burly of East Broadway, past the fishmongers and video shops, the storefront grocers with their bushels of fruit, their plastic vats of dried mushrooms, their mountains of red lychees.

As often as not, they would end up at the Tak Shun Variety Store, on Hester Street, where Sister Ping presided, asking after family members, advising youngsters to learn English (though she wouldn't do so herself), and generally accumulating relationships, or *guanxi*, the Chinese expression that entails connections—the kind of interlocking favors and dependencies that bind a community together. Local Fujianese began to visit Sister Ping when they needed help or advice. A restaurant worker named Ming Wang, who had lost his job because of an injury and could expect no compensation from his employer, once visited Sister Ping and explained his predicament. "Little brother, take this," she said, handing him $2,000. "Pay me back when you can." Three times a year she made trips to Hong Kong to buy merchandise, and often she was accompanied on the plane by the American-born babies of undocumented Fujianese from the neighborhood. "These were parents that didn't have legal INS status in the U.S.A. and needed someone to bring their children to China," she explained. "I would do it for them free of charge."

Sister Ping ran the store and oversaw the books. She was the dominant partner, with Yick Tak always hovering in the background. Almost as soon as she arrived in Chinatown in 1981, it seemed, she became a well-known, well-respected figure, notable for working hours in her store that were long even by Chinatown standards, for demonstrating a distinctly Fujianese interest in and acumen for business, and for maintaining a modest demeanor and a simple, indulgence-free way of life even as she became an entrepreneurial success story. "I was credible," she would later say, when asked about her status in the neighborhood. "I had a conscience. I did things for free, as favors. I treated relatives and friends well. I know it's difficult for people to be in a foreign land with few acquaintances."

She also developed a reputation during these years as someone who could move people.

In 1984 a young man named Weng Yu Hui wanted to leave his village in Fujian, not far from Shengmei, and move to the United States. Weng was grim-faced and stocky, with black hair that he parted to one side and a hint of a double chin. He had left school in the third grade, during the Cultural Revolution, and farmed sweet potatoes and rice with his family before getting into construction work. Weng had a wife and child, and his reason for wanting to leave was simple: "To make more money. To improve my family's living condition." There were very few snakeheads operating in Fujian in 1984, but Weng's brother-in-law had recently paid a woman who went by the name Sister Ping to smuggle him to New York, and she had gotten him there successfully. Weng asked around and eventually tracked down a villager who had been Sister Ping's teacher in school. The man told Weng he would need to pay $2,000 up front, and that if he made it to the United States, he would owe a further $16,000. Weng would also need a guarantor: someone already in America who would agree to pay the balance of his fee when he arrived. Weng turned over the down payment and the telephone number of a nephew who lived in the United States. He called the nephew to warn him: "If someone named Cheng Chui Ping calls, you have to agree to the terms." Shortly thereafter, Weng received a letter that purported to be an invitation to visit relatives in Guatemala. (Because the coolie trade transported many thousands of Chinese to work the plantations of Central America and the Caribbean in the nineteenth century, this ruse was not altogether implausible; small Chinese communities are a feature of many cities in that part of the world.) Weng took the letter to the Public Security Bureau in Fuzhou, told them about his family in Guatemala, and applied for a permit to leave the country. They issued him a passport.

Passport in hand, Weng made his way to the port city of Shenzhen, just across the border from Hong Kong. There he was met by Sister Ping's younger sister, a short Fujianese woman named Cheng Tsui Wah, who also went by Susan. A dozen other Fujianese customers were already waiting in a Shenzhen hotel, and after several weeks Susan obtained entry visas for Hong Kong and accompanied Weng and a half-dozen others on the short trip into the city. It was the Chinese New Year, and the city was given over to fireworks, lion dances, and revelry. The problem was, Weng and the others were dressed like farmers, with their shopworn cotton clothing and country-bumpkin haircuts. Susan led her wide-eyed charges through the bustle of Hong Kong and enacted a hasty makeover: she outfitted them with Western-style suits and slacks, got their hair cut, bought them watches, toothbrushes, and toothpaste. Snakeheads occasionally refer to themselves as "tour guides," and that is unquestionably one component of the job.

When Susan was satisfied that her customers might pass for passport-holding international travelers, she escorted them to a two-bedroom apartment in Hong Kong. She said it belonged to her father, and had them all sleep on the floor in one bedroom while she occupied the other. The next day they went to Hong Kong's Kai Tak Airport and boarded a flight to Guatemala City.

Sister Ping's brother, Cheng Mei Yeung, met them when they arrived. A squat Fujianese man with nervous eyes and a receding chin, Mei Yeung escorted the group to a hotel where another dozen Chinese passengers were waiting, some of them people Weng had encountered at the hotel in Shenzhen. Eventually Sister Ping herself appeared. It was immediately clear from her demeanor that she was the boss of the operation; she was aloof with the customers, speaking only to her brother. But she did approach Weng. There was a "money matter" that needed to be resolved, she said. Weng's brother-in-law, whom she had recently smuggled, had failed to pay the balance of his debt upon arrival in America. Weng had better get on the telephone and make sure someone paid up, Sister Ping said, because if he didn't, she had no reason to believe that Weng would honor his own debt when the time came. She might be forced to leave him stranded in Guatemala.

Weng's brother-in-law eventually settled his debt, but Weng ended up spending a month in the hotel. Sister Ping would visit every so often, and many passengers seemed to pass through the hotel, some coming, some going; it appeared to be one way station in a complex logistical network. When Weng finally left, it was with a group of others who were transported overland to Tijuana. Sister Ping was waiting for them in Mexico when they arrived. She told them that they had reached the final leg of the journey, and that the group that preceded theirs had arrived safely. "Have faith," she said.

At daybreak the following morning, Weng and the others were loaded into the trunk of a taxi, which delivered them to a van. The van had a false bottom, and ten of them squeezed into it for the ride across the border. Eventually they arrived in Los Angeles, and once again Sister Ping was there to meet them, this time accompanied by her husband, Yick Tak. "Congratulations, everyone," she said. "You have arrived." She issued them all plane tickets, and the group boarded a flight from LAX to Newark. Sister Ping and Yick Tak were careful to sit a few rows apart from the customers, lest any of them be caught.

When they reached Manhattan, Sister Ping placed Weng and the others in an apartment on Market Street and started telephoning their relatives to demand the balance of her fee. One misconception about the snakehead business is that the smugglers will bring people over and then force them to work as indentured servants for years in order to pay off their debt. Such an arrangement would make very little sense from the smuggler's point of view. A busy smuggler like Sister Ping didn't want to keep track of scores of debtors at various stages of repayment, any of whom might skip town during the months, or more often years, that it took them to come up with $18,000. Instead, the smugglers would hold passengers once they arrived in the United States, giving them thirty-six or seventy-two hours to satisfy the debt. Such an arrangement might be unimaginable in any other ethnic community, but familial and communal ties among the Chinese in America were so strong that a new arrival could count on a guarantor cobbling together a five-figure fee by borrowing small amounts from many people—$1,000 here, $500 there. The immigrant was thus indentured not so much to the snakehead as to his own family.

Once Weng's nephew had assembled the money Sister Ping was owed, she let Weng leave the Market Street apartment and look for work. He found a job working in an American restaurant Monday through Friday, and Sister Ping introduced him to an uncle of hers who ran a Chinese takeout in the Bronx. Weng could work there on weekends to supplement his income, she said. Weng threw himself into paying off his debts, and on his occasional days off he would make his way to Sister Ping's shop and hang out. "She smuggled me here," he later observed. Between the snakehead and the customer there was a peculiar kind of bond.

One dilemma Weng soon faced, which was shared by other undocumented Fujianese in the neighborhood, was how to send money home. Few of them had bank accounts; they took their payment, and hoarded it, in cash. Western Union charged expensive commissions and didn't have outposts in the areas surrounding Fuzhou. The Bank of China's money remittance service was notoriously slow and paid out remittances in Chinese yuan, always at an unfavorable exchange rate.

In her early years in New York, Sister Ping observed this dilemma and saw a business opportunity. More and more Fujianese were coming to the city every day. Along the border between Mexico and California, precisely the stretch where Weng had crossed, apprehensions of undocumented Chinese increased by 500 percent in 1984 alone. The number of immigrants stopped was only a fraction of the number who got across, and when these Fujianese got to New York's Chinatown, they started sending money home. They sent money in such quantities, in fact, that one theory for why the Chinese government tended to turn a blind eye to the snakehead trade in the 1980s involves the enormous sums of American currency being pumped into the Fujianese economy by the overseas Chinese. The Fujianese city of Changle alone eventually received several hundred million dollars a year in remittances from America.

Drawing on the connections she had made in New York, in Hong Kong, and around Fuzhou, Sister Ping started offering a sideline service out of the Tak Shun Variety Store. For a commission that steeply undercut the Bank of China, she would remit U.S. currency to Fujian. A restaurant worker could take her his weekly pay on a Monday and receive a special code number, which he would relay over the phone to his mother in a remote village outside Fuzhou. Sister Ping would make a telephone call or send a fax to her contacts in China, and within a day a courier on a motorbike would arrive at the mother's door and, provided she supplied the code, turn over the money—in U.S. dollars, not yuan.

Various underground banking systems, sometimes known as *fei-ch'ien,* or "flying money," date back centuries in China, and probably came into existence when tea traders needed to be able to send money from place to place but did not want to run the risk of carrying large sums of currency on dangerous roads. The genius of Sister Ping's system was that the money itself did not actually move. "Sister Ping keeps stores of money in the United States as well as Hong Kong and the Fujian Province as a base for the crediting," an FBI investigative report would later explain. When migrants wanted to send money back to China, she would pay the money out of her reserves in China. When the families of new arrivals wanted to send money to America to satisfy a relative's snakehead debt, Sister Ping could pay that sum out of her reserves in New York. The only trick was balancing the books occasionally and correcting any disparities that might emerge between the currency reserves in one place or the other. Such periodic corrections were easily made, generally by bulk-carrying a suitcase full of cash from one place to the next.

The business thrived, in no small measure because Sister Ping's smuggling efforts were supplying a steady stream of new customers. Once Weng Yu Hui had paid off the various family members who covered his snakehead fee, he wanted to send his restaurant wages home to his wife and child and to his parents. "If I send money home through the bank, it has to be money that I have paid taxes on, or money that can see the sunlight," he explained. "With her, there is no need for any identification. All you need is the address and the name, and in two, three days, the money would be there." For every thousand dollars, Sister Ping charged a 3 percent commission. This was a good deal cheaper than the Bank of China, and more and more Fujianese made the switch to Sister Ping. "Her clients are extremely comfortable having their money in her hands, because she has such an impeccable reputation," a fellow Fujianese snakehead explained. "People know that she will never take the money and run." Soon the Bank of China was losing so much business that it took to running advertisements in the neighborhood's Chinese-language newspapers, reminding people that using underground banks was illegal. The bank announced raffles and special prizes for people who used its service. But it was of no use.

The remittance market was growing rapidly, almost exponentially. According to the Fujian Statistical Bureau, in 1990 the total foreign capital investment in the province amounted to $379 million. By 1995 it was $4.1 billion. With her snakehead fees and 3 percent commissions, Sister Ping soon became so successful that she and Yick Tak outgrew the Tak Shun and relocated to a handsome five-story brick tenement at 47 East Broadway, in 1990. The building's title was not in her name, and the price she paid for it was underreported in order to avoid taxes—a standard practice in Chinatown. But it was rumored in the neighborhood that she had paid $3 million for the building. It may have merely been a coincidence, but people did not fail to notice that she had established her new operation directly across East Broadway from the building that housed the Chinatown headquarters of her chief competitor, the Bank of China.

On the ground floor, the couple opened a larger version of the Tak Shun, calling it the New Hong Kong Variety Store, and in the basement they opened a restaurant, the Yeung Sun, which specialized in the simple staples of Fujianese cuisine. These businesses weren't fronts, exactly. To have a front business that wasn't turning a profit in its own right would be, to a Fujianese way of thinking, deeply wasteful. So the family members sold their fair share of seafood and clothing. But to the Fujianese in the neighborhood, there was no mistaking the dominant revenue streams. You could see it when a line stretched out the door on Chinese holidays, as people queued to send money home to their families. Weng would go in every couple of months and send $1,000 back to Fujian. Sister Ping would be at the counter, or Yick Tak, or sometimes their oldest daughter, Monica. "There were always people there sending money," Weng remembered.

Nor was it just the shop and the restaurant and the money transfer business and the human smuggling that Sister Ping and Yick Tak engaged in. They diversified, opening the Long Shine Travel and Trading Agency and the 47 East Broadway Realty Corp. In the waterfront neighborhood of Red Hook, Brooklyn, they opened a poultry shop, which sold live chickens and ducks and supplied the restaurant. They continued to operate the garment factory in Shenzhen, and they opened a video arcade and import-export business in Hong Kong. Because property transactions in Chinatown were often done in cash, no one knew the extent of the family's holdings. In the early 1980s, the immigration code was amended to allow foreigners who worked ninety days a year in agriculture to obtain green cards and remain in the United States. The measure was designed to guarantee a steady supply of cheap Latino labor in California. But it was rumored that Sister Ping had identified a loophole in the policy and developed an interest in several farms in New York and New Jersey. The farms would allow her to become a key supplier to the insular and profitable restaurant economy in Chinatown while providing jobs, and immigration cover, for each new wave of Fujianese she escorted into the country.

One thing was clear: Sister Ping's greatest advantage seemed to be the immigration policies of the United States government. On November 6, 1986, the Immigration Reform and Control Act, or IRCA, took effect. The act contained an amnesty provision, which stipulated that any undocumented person who could prove that he or she had been resident in the United States prior to January 1, 1982, was eligible for employment authorization, the right to leave the country and return, and, ultimately, a green card. The law created a burgeoning industry of document vendors in Chinatown, who could whip up backdated leases, bills, pay stubs, or employment records. It was no trick to persuade officials you had been working off the books in Chinatown since 1981, so in addition to spawning another lucrative sideline for immigration profiteers, the amnesty provision extended the promise of a green card to future potential customers, who left China in the care of snakeheads long after the legislation passed.

With her new wealth, Sister Ping poured money into Fujian, cultivating an image not just as a capable and successful businesswoman but as something of a philanthropist as well. In Shengmei she constructed one of the biggest houses in town, Number 398, a four-story yellow-and-white confection with a horseshoe-shaped front entrance, hand-painted tile walls, balconies on each floor, and a pagoda on the roof. Inside, she hung photographs of her parents above incense burners. On her visits to Fuzhou, she would often stay not in the house but in the nicest hotels, paying for one night what her Fujianese compatriots who had not yet left the country could expect to earn in a month. The main thoroughfare in the village was renamed Qiao Xing Lu, or Overseas Happiness Road. The Chinese state had actually coined a term for villages that had benefited from migration to other countries—*qiaoxiang,* "sojourning" or "overseas Chinese" town. It was an appellation the villages wore with pride. On either side of the ornamental archway leading into Shengmei, a verse read:

The sky is high so birds can fly
The seas are vast so fish can leap
My breast carries a patriotic feeling
My heart longs for my old hometown.

A cultural assumption was beginning to take hold around Fuzhou that any able-bodied young adult who hadn't made the journey to New

York must be lazy, or just exceedingly dumb, and Sister Ping did nothing to discourage this view. The abstemiousness of the Fujianese in New York was bankrolling unprecedented extravagance back home. When Fujianese villagers learned that a relative had arrived safely in the States, they would unspool red banners in front of the family home, invite the relevant snakeheads to a community banquet, and set off firecrackers to celebrate. As the remittance money flowed in, families constructed garish multistory houses with karaoke rooms and disco balls, polished wooden floors and shrines to their ancestors. These new money palaces rose incongruously from the rice paddies, monuments to the filial loyalty of the overseas Chinese. And in status-conscious small towns the process fed on itself, creating a fever to go abroad, to the point where many of those elaborate houses simply emptied out, becoming lavish, tenantless temples to the good life in America.

The first outward indications that Sister Ping and her family had established a criminal enterprise in Chinatown were evident almost as soon as they had settled in New York. But to American law enforcement these early warnings amounted to a series of confusing and apparently unrelated ciphers, and it was several years before the scope of the Chengs' operation became clear.

In the fall of 1983, a Fujianese man named Frankie Wong was arrested in New York City on a charge of alien smuggling. Wong was diminutive and gay, the owner of a travel agency on Canal Street. As part of a plea bargain, he gave authorities the names of several smugglers in Chinatown, who he said had been bringing people into the country via Toronto. One of those names was Cheng Chui Ping. At the time, no one followed up on the lead. Several years later Frankie Wong walked into the basement of a building on Catherine Street that was ostensibly a wholesale fish market but actually an after-hours gambling joint and was shot five times. (Sister Ping was never linked in any way with the murder.)

One day in February 1985, customs officers in New York were doing a routine inspection of incoming mail when they stumbled on a mysterious package. The sender, according to the return address, was one Calgada Melchoz O'Campo, of Cuahtemoc, Mexico. The recipient was Sister Ping's husband, Cheung Yick Tak, care of the Tak Shun Variety Store, at 145B Hester Street. The package contained six passports from the People's Republic of China. The customs officers decided to hold on to them and see if Mr. Cheung received any more curious international mail. Sure enough, another package soon arrived, again from O'Campo, again addressed to Cheung. This one contained eight Chinese passports. Customs alerted investigators at the New York district office of the INS. The INS in turn got the telephone company to turn over toll records for all international calls made to or from the shop on Hester Street. (This is a preliminary step in most investigations and does not require a warrant.)

What they found surprised them. The small mom-and-pop variety store run by a couple of unassuming Chinese immigrants seemed to be in regular, almost constant contact with a handful of far-flung telephone numbers. The investigators started assembling minutely detailed charts, by hand, on large pieces of paper, with "Tak Shun Variety Store" written in a circle at the center and a series of lines radiating outward like spokes from a hub, each terminating in a small circle representing a number that was frequently dialed. There were calls to California and to Mexico City, but also to Fujian Province and to Hong Kong, to Honduras, El Salvador, and Guatemala.

The following month a Coast Guard cutter patrolling the shoreline of Miami stopped a boat that was drifting 5 miles out to sea. On board, Coast Guard officers found a dozen undocumented Fujianese men on their way from the Bahamas to Florida. The boat was a lease, and when authorities scanned the toll records of the man who had leased it, they found that on the day of the voyage he had made a single telephone call to New York City. The number he dialed was the Tak Shun Variety Store.

As these leads converged, the INS launched an investigation into the proprietors of the Tak Shun. They called it Operation Hester, after the street on the eastern fringe of Chinatown where Sister Ping and Cheung Yick Tak had set up shop. Aware, perhaps, of the likelihood that American law enforcement might take an interest in her activities, Sister Ping had kept a decidedly low profile in New York. The family purchased a house in the Sheepshead Bay section of Brooklyn in the mid-eighties but held on to the Monroe Street apartment. For a time it seemed that the couple's biggest liability, and greatest risk of exposure, was the frustrating logistical chore of transporting the mammoth quantities of cash they were amassing. Given his role as second fiddle in the relationship, this task often fell to Cheung Yick Tak. In 1984 he was stopped by airport authorities in New Orleans for trying to carry $18,000 into the country from El Salvador without declaring it. (By law you must declare amounts above $10,000.) In 1986 he was caught bulk carrying money again, and again in 1989. This time he was arrested. Investigators had trouble fingerprinting him; the tips of his fingers were covered in scars. (One prosecutor speculated that he might have deliberately cut his fingertips in order to avoid easy detection by the government. But no definitive explanation for the affliction has ever emerged.) To the investigators who looked into him, Yick Tak always seemed to be a bit of a bumbler, definitely not the brains behind the operation. "He sorta married into a smuggling family," one of them said.

After customs alerted the INS to the Chinese passports being sent to Yick Tak from Mexico in 1985, the case was referred to the chief of the New York office's Anti-Smuggling Unit, or ASU, a short, bullish immigration agent named Joe Occhipinti. Occhipinti contacted immigration authorities in Hong Kong, thinking that perhaps they might have some information on the family. They did. Several years earlier they had debriefed a high-ranking document forger, who told them about a Fujianese family that was beginning to assume a major role in global human smuggling. Sister Ping's father was "the main arranger in Foochow," Occhipinti's Hong Kong contacts told him. He was "assisted by three daughters, two sons and a son-in-law in escorting the aliens from Hong Kong, Central and South America on to Mexico." They identified Sister Ping as "a daughter who travels extensively between Hong Kong, Mexico, and New York City. She and her husband, Cheung Yick Tak, collect the monies on arrival in New York from families of the smuggled Fukienese. The trip costs range between $12,000 and $18,000." It emerged that in January 1983, only fourteen months after Sister Ping had first arrived in the United States, she was questioned by officials in Hong Kong and admitted that she had fraudulently obtained two reentry permits from mainland China.

From the Hong Kong investigators Occhipinti learned about Sister Ping's brother Cheng Mei Yeung, who had met Weng Yu Hui in Guatemala and was believed to be establishing a West Coast stronghold for the family's operations, in Monterey Park, California. Susan, the younger sister who had taken Weng shopping in Hong Kong, was chiefly responsible for obtaining visas to Central America, they continued. She was married to a Fujianese man in his twenties named Cheng Wai Wei, who went by the name Peter and who was the son of one of their father's closest friends, a man with whom he had jumped ship back in the sixties. When Susan wasn't in Hong Kong securing documents, she often helped out at the Tak Shun Variety Store.

The previous spring Susan had been stopped on the Hong Kong–China border trying to smuggle twenty-nine Chinese passports into the colony. When investigators questioned her, she did something that her older sister, Ping, would never do throughout her criminal career: she confessed, unburdening herself to her interrogators and explaining, in surprising detail, the dynamics of the family's nascent smuggling operation. The passports she was carrying belonged to prospective migrants who were waiting to be smuggled to Central America, Susan explained. The way the system worked, she continued, was that her father would recruit migrants around Fuzhou and then forward their passports to her. The family had an important connection in Guatemala, a Taiwanese native whom Susan always telephoned at the Ritz Hotel in Guatemala City. He helped her secure Guatemalan visas for the passports, which could then be used to fly passengers legally to Central America.

Susan seems to have won clemency with her detailed confession; the authorities in Hong Kong eventually let her go. But they took down all the information she gave, and when Joe Occhipinti questioned them about Sister Ping's family, they dutifully passed the details along. The more Occhipinti looked into the complexity of the smuggling network, the more impressed he became. During one ten-month period in 1985, INS agents found Sister Ping's name on twenty airline manifests, linking her to 250 Chinese traveling from Latin America to the United States. Her name kept cropping up in various ways; she seemed to be behind everything. Occhipinti pored over the call charts his team had assembled, tracing the tendrils of Sister Ping's operation through her dozens of telephone contacts on three different continents. Given its resources, there was no way the INS could go after such an intricate worldwide enterprise, Occhipinti realized. He decided to propose a well-funded national task force. "The smuggling of ethnic Chinese represents the most sophisticated level of criminal activity which the [Immigration] Service encounters," he wrote in the proposal. "Approaching the problem on the basis of individual incidents without gathering intelligence and sharing information on an international basis has little impact on the overall smuggling enterprise."

Occhipinti put together all the information he could gather on Sister Ping and Yick Tak—the phone calls, the passports, the reports from Hong Kong immigration—and went to the FBI to make his case. He thought there was enough for an indictment. But this was 1985, and the FBI politely told him that its major concern was the Soviets and it didn't have the time or the resources to launch its own investigation into his Chinese shopkeepers. He took his Hester file to federal prosecutors in the Southern District of New York, and they accepted the case for possible criminal prosecution. But without the FBI, the prosecutors had to rely on the INS to develop information for the case, and Occhipinti's request for a national task force had gone nowhere. He had asked for $25,000, thinking he might be able to use it to smuggle an informant through the Cheng family ring. But INS headquarters in Washington wouldn't authorize the task force or grant the funds. Eventually the prosecutors let the initiative lapse. There was no grand jury investigation, and Project Hester slid into "pending-inactive" status.

Occhipinti kept pushing. In 1988 he proposed that the INS reopen the Hester case "as a proactive, inter-regional task force investigation," what he called "Hester (Phase II)." As it happened, the INS had just had great success in bringing the first-ever immigration case using the RICO racketeering statute. In a 1986 investigation called Operation Hydra, the agency had shut down a major Taiwanese prostitution ring operated by a middle-aged Queens woman known as Madame Shih. Madame Shih imported Taiwanese women on routes that took them from Hong Kong and Bangkok through Bolivia, El Salvador, and Guatemala, overland through Mexico, and eventually to New York. INS investigators believed that some of those women were smuggled through pipelines operated by Sister Ping. Madame Shih's son-in-law, a major figure in her ring, was a pimp named Hon Tok Lou, and when INS agents sent a wired informant into the Tak Shun Variety Store, Yick Tak said that he didn't know where Hon Tok Lou was but that he owed him money. (In fact, when Yick Tak was stopped in New Orleans with $18,000 in 1984, he told authorities the money wasn't his—he was carrying it for Hon Tok Lou.)

Thus, with the inadvertent cooperation of Yick Tak, the INS had brought down a criminal enterprise they believed was closely associated with the Chengs. But to go after the Chengs themselves would be more difficult. Whenever people asked Occhipinti about Sister Ping, he told a story that he thought demonstrated just how untouchable she had become. Early on, he had gone to see her at the apartment in Knickerbocker Village, on Monroe Street. He'd taken along another investigator and an interpreter. Occhipinti didn't have much to bust her on, but he made it clear to Sister Ping, through the interpreter, that he was on to her and he would get her eventually. To Occhipinti's surprise, Sister Ping wasn't fazed in the slightest. "You don't have the time to get me," he remembers her saying. "Or the resources." He made a note of the meeting, and it ended up in Sister Ping's file. It became part of her lore within the agency. But what always struck Occhipinti about the exchange wasn't just the arrogance of it, or the insult, so much as the fact that she was right.

Chapter Four

Dai Lo of the Fuk Ching

ONE AUTUMN day in 1991, an elderly Chinese man shuffled into a meeting with a Senate investigator in a federal building in New York City. The old man had an owlish look to him; he was portly and bespectacled. He walked with a cane and wore a hearing aid. He was eighty-four years old.

"My name Benny Ong," he said.

"Are you also sometimes called Uncle Seven?" the investigator asked, as a stenographer transcribed.

"They call me Uncle Seven," the old man said. Born the seventh of nine sons to a poor bricklayer in China in 1907, he had immigrated to New York's Chinatown in the early 1920s. Over the next seven decades he rose from an illiterate teenager working in a laundry on Pell Street to become one of Chinatown's most revered grandees. The name Uncle Seven, like Sister Ping, was both familiar and respectful, an honorific. Everyone knew Benny Ong, and people saw him strolling each morning from his walkup apartment to the Hong Shoon restaurant on Pell Street. The only sign of his influence was the young men who attended to him, carrying cell phones and walkie-talkies. He passed his days playing mahjong or pai gow and reading the Chinese newspapers. He was an august figure, a village elder, a pillar of the community.

"Is it true that you were convicted of a homicide sometime in the 1930s?"

The old man scrutinized the investigator. "Fifth Amendment," he said.

Upon arriving in Chinatown, Ong had joined the Hip Sing, one of two tongs that dominated what was in those days a tiny neighborhood, consisting of a mere handful of streets. The word *tong* means "assembly hall," and these organizations sprang up almost as soon as the Chinese began arriving in America in the nineteenth century. For an alienated and often reviled Chinese population in the United States, the tongs played several roles: they functioned as credit unions and job agencies, an indigenous dispute resolution system, and a mutual aid society. Tongs are occasionally likened to triads, the highly ritualized secret societies with a long history in China, but the Chinatown tongs were very specifically the creation of an expatriate community: they afforded a shield against the hazards of being an immigrant in America, and preserved cultural and familial bonds among displaced Chinese. They offered loans and legal help and a social refuge for the ragged diaspora—a slice not just of China, but of the very village you left behind, the soothing music of your mother tongue.

In addition to these laudable activities, the tongs served another function. Dating back to the nineteenth century, when the Chinese in America were mainly male sojourners, the tongs oversaw the vice industries: the brothels, the opium dens, and above all the gambling parlors. These activities were just another business interest, albeit an especially lucrative one, and to stay profitable and orderly they needed to be policed with a firm hand. The tongs did this, and did it well, and for tolerating and regulating the unsavory side of the local economy, they drew substantial commissions, which they funneled back into the community. In this manner these fraternal organizations became deeply entrenched in San Francisco and New York, welcoming migrants to the United States and accruing the loyalty of generations of new arrivals. They became a dominant fact in Chinatown's political and economic landscape—the bedrock of the local civil society. And before long they had history on their side. After all, the two oldest tongs in New York, the

On Leong and the Hip Sing, predated the Communist government in Beijing by half a century. When New York's tongs were first established, an emperor ruled China.

That history was not without friction, of course, and at the turn of the twentieth century, the On Leong and the Hip Sing went to war. Because the rackets they controlled were lucrative, the tongs were seized by a feudal preoccupation with territory, and their skirmishes were extraordinarily violent. In *The Gangs of New York,* Herbert Asbury's colorful, apocryphal account, the "fat, moon-faced" Hip Sing named Mock Duck wore a chain-mail shirt and dispatched On Leong members with two guns, "squatting on his haunches in the street with both eyes shut, and blazing away." The short elbow crook of Doyers Street became known as the Bloody Angle for the massacres that unfolded there. It was Chinatown's cleaver-wielding assassins during these years that gave us the expression *hatchet man.*

By the time the teenaged Benny Ong arrived from China, the worst of the tong wars were over. But clashes continued as the tongs jockeyed over control of one illicit enterprise or another, and in 1935 Ong was arrested along with several Hip Sing associates after they stuck up a gambling operation. The robbery had gone awry, and shots were fired. Ong was found guilty of murder and served seventeen years in an upstate prison.

"Is it true that you were convicted in the 1970s of bribery?" the investigator asked.

"Invoke the Fifth Amendment again," Ong said.

Upon his release in 1952, Ong was welcomed back to the Hip Sing and began a fast ascent through the organization. By 1977, when he was caught on a wiretap bragging about payments he made to an immigration official, he was the leader of the Hip Sing and had assumed the grandiose title he would hold for the rest of his days: adviser for life to the tong. Law enforcement had begun to refer to him as something else: the Godfather of Chinatown.

"Have you ever heard of a street gang called the Flying Dragons?"

"Fifth Amendment."

As leader of the Hip Sing, Ong oversaw both the licit and the illicit activities of the organization. But during the 1970s, perhaps in an effort to legitimize the tong, he pioneered a new model, which would soon be adopted by tongs throughout New York. He subcontracted the gambling rackets, debt collection, and other illegal activities to an enforcement cadre, in this case a street gang called the Flying Dragons. In order to remain viable as ostensibly legitimate organizations, the tongs needed some measure of plausible deniability when it came to some of their traditional revenue streams. So in a fiction designed more to avoid prosecution than to actually persuade anyone—because at least in Chinatown, the truth was never in doubt—the tongs began to distance themselves from the traditional vice crimes that had been their bread and butter for nearly a century. Despite his murder conviction and his racketeering, Ong reinvented himself as a legitimate businessman, the head of a prominent and powerful civic organization. The Flying Dragons did the dirty work in order to keep Ong and the organization clean. The rival On Leong association also sought legitimacy. Its head, Eddie Chan, invested in a jewelry store, a funeral parlor, and restaurants and reportedly hired a PR firm, all the while outsourcing the tong's criminal activity to his own affiliated gang, the Ghost Shadows.

It was an effective ambiguity. Inside the neighborhood, it was known that the tong's word in all things should be taken seriously, because it was backed by a roving gang of armed thugs. But on the occasions when violence did break out, the tong could simply deny the relationship. In 1982 an associate of Ong's left the Hip Sing and started a rival tong, whose members congregated at the Golden Star Tea Room, on East Broadway. One December night four masked gunmen burst into the restaurant and began firing indiscriminately, killing three customers, including a thirteen-year-old boy. Benny Ong denied any role in the shooting at the time and insisted that the Hip Sing and the Flying Dragons were separate entities. In a later interview with *New York* magazine, he was more candid about the incident: "Sixty year I build up respect," he said, "and he think he knock me down in one day?"

But to the Senate investigator from Washington, Benny Ong said nothing, invoking the Fifth Amendment again and again. Eventually the investigator lost patience. "Do you intend to invoke your Fifth Amendment rights in response to any further questions that we may have for you today about organized crime activity in New York?" he asked.

"Yes," the old man said. And with that, he shuffled out of the room.

When Ong died, just three years later, his funeral was the largest in Chinatown's history: over a hundred limousines lined the narrow streets around Mott and Mulberry; traffic backed up along Canal Street all the way to the East River. Thousands of mourners paid their respects before his solid bronze casket. The president of Taiwan sent a wreath. High above, on a terrace of the new courthouse at 500 Pearl Street, federal agents snapped photographs with a long lens.

Ong's funeral brought into uncomfortably close proximity the disparate power brokers in Chinatown: politicians mourning alongside teenage gunslingers, business leaders paying their respects under the gaze of the FBI. Ong's life captured the contradictory role played not just by the tongs but by the snakeheads as well. Ong defended the Chinatown community, and he exploited it. He nurtured it, and he devoured it. It was a fine balance, dependent in part on the tolerance of Chinatown's residents and a grudging cultural acceptance of corruption and extortion, but also on the reluctance of the local population to go to law enforcement. "The Chinese community is afraid of the tongs and the gangs more than they are afraid of the American police," a former Ghost Shadow once testified.

Tong leaders of Ong's generation kept their youth gangs in relatively tight check. The police referred to the gangs as the "youth wing" or "standing army" of the tongs. However much they denied it, the elders exercised command and control over these armed teenagers, and that control kept a lid on the neighborhood. But even as Ong talked with the

Senate investigator, the world that he had inhabited and helped to create was spinning out of control. A series of changes had uncoupled the street gangs from their tong masters and ushered in a decade of gang warfare unlike any Chinatown had seen since the fabled tong wars nearly a century earlier. "There are no norms anymore, no rules, no values," the Taiwanese American criminologist Ko-lin Chin observed in 1991. "The code has broken down."

The great Fujianese influx of the 1980s coincided with a series of developments that together would spark a severe crime epidemic in Lower Manhattan, although it went largely unnoticed outside the Chinatown community. Whereas the population in the neighborhood had remained somewhat constant during the middle decades of the twentieth century, Chinatown was flooded with new immigrants throughout the eighties. They came from Fujian, and also from Vietnam—refugees from the war, many of them ethnic Chinese who had grown up amid the brutality of the waning years of the conflict.

Meanwhile, Turkey had cracked down on poppy farming during the 1970s, and the French connection, which had supplied the majority of America's heroin, was dismantled. The center of gravity for global opiate production shifted to the Golden Triangle in Southeast Asia. The Italian Mob had traditionally controlled the drug trade in New York, but Asian gangs had easy access to China White (as the heroin from the Golden Triangle was known), and the population explosion in Chinatown combined with the profit opportunities associated with the drug trade led to a sudden profusion of gangs. Whereas traditionally a handful of Cantonese gangs, each affiliated with a major tong, had bickered over territory in the neighborhood, suddenly it seemed that a new gang started up every week. Nor was it ABCs, or American-born Chinese, starting the gangs; immigrants who had arrived mere months before hatched fledgling criminal enterprises. The 1960 census showed 20,000 Chinese living in New York City. By the mid-eighties, the population had swelled to more than 200,000, and Chinatown soon burst its boundaries. Along with the eastern expansion of the neighborhood by the Fujianese, satellite Chinatowns sprang up in Sunset Park, Brooklyn, and in Elmhurst and Flushing, Queens, in the low-rise, low-rent neighborhoods surrounding Shea Stadium, along the trajectory of the Number 7 train, which soon became known as the Orient Express. Competition for turf was so intense that entrepreneurial gangs laid claim to the tiniest of territories, sometimes waging all-out bloody war over a single city block. The Italian Mob, doomed by high-profile prosecutions, a low birthrate, and flight to the suburbs, found that whole blocks of the Lower East Side that had historically belonged to the Cosa Nostra were being swallowed up by ragtag bands of gun-toting Chinese teenagers. "You gotta be strong with the Chinese," one Gambino family capo exclaimed, a little defensively, on a wiretap. "You gotta push their skinny asses into a chair and stick your fingers in their face. 'Keep your fucking chopsticks outta my place, you little slant cocksucker. You savvy?' "

The new gangs were much more violent than their predecessors. Without adult supervision by the tongs, they fell into bloody feuds based not just on real estate but on the most petty of pretexts. An insufficiently deferential facial expression on a Friday night at a bowling alley could result in shots fired. The police often came to the aid of teenagers who had been beaten and stabbed on a busy sidewalk, only to learn that the victim had no gang connection and the whole incident was a case of mistaken identity: the assailants had thought he was somebody else. A gang of Vietnamese teenagers who, in a chilling appropriation of the stock phrase of American GIs, called themselves Born To Kill, or BTK, became known for upping the ante on indiscriminate brutality. They worked for various tongs, or even for other gangs, in a freelance capacity, when there was truly dirty work to be done. A BTK funeral at a cemetery in Linden, New Jersey, was interrupted once when several mourners dropped the flowers they had brought, produced automatic weapons, and sprayed the crowd with bullets, prompting some of the mourners to take cover by jumping into the open grave and others, who had come to the funeral armed, to fire back.

Because much of the gang violence was Chinese-on-Chinese, and many of the victims were undocumented immigrants who could disappear from the streets without anyone so much as filing a police report, it took some time before the authorities came to appreciate the extent of the brutal anarchy that had taken hold. On the Fourth of July, 1991, a twenty-six-year-old woman named Rhona Lantin came to New York City for a girls' night out with old friends from high school. Lantin lived in Maryland and worked as an economist at the Department of Agriculture in Washington. As a graduate student at the University of Maryland, she had met and fallen in love with a fellow student named Patrick, and the two were engaged to be married the following spring. It was a warm, beautiful night in the city, and Lantin and her friends watched the fireworks over New York Harbor, then all six of them piled into a Ford Explorer and drove to Chinatown for a late-night snack. The narrow streets and sidewalks were crowded with merrymakers, and the Explorer slowed to the halting pace of Chinatown traffic. Inching north along Mulberry, none of the passengers would have realized it, but they had entered the heart of Ghost Shadows territory. At around 11:30, as they reached the intersection with Bayard, several shots rang out and a single bullet pierced the windshield and struck Rhona Lantin in the head. It was a stray bullet in a gang shootout; the killer, a teenaged Ghost Shadow, would eventually be convicted of "depraved indifference" murder. The morning after the shooting, Lantin died in the hospital. For police and prosecutors in New York, the randomness of the killing—and the fact that the victim was not Chinese or Vietnamese, that she was a tourist—brought home the urgent realization that the violence of the Chinatown gangs was no longer purely indigenous or contained. It had become an epidemic.

Part of the unruliness of the gangs was simple immaturity. Many of the members had barely reached puberty—they were twelve, fourteen, sixteen. The snakehead trade and America's accommodating asylum policies meant that thousands of new children arrived in Chinatown every year. Many of them had been uprooted from a claustrophobic, sheltered childhood of agrarian poverty only to be thrust into the riotous urban scrum of Chinatown. They lived in cramped quarters with older relatives who were largely absent, working day and night to pay off snakehead debts or raise money to send for more relatives. They spoke little or no English and attended substandard schools. It was from these schools that the gangs plucked their recruits.

"I would have my kids go to a high school in Chinatown and look for the turkey right off the boat," David Chong recalled. Chong was a New York cop who infiltrated the Flying Dragons in the 1980s. He was so effective that he soon became a *dai lo,* "big brother," or leader, in the gang, running his own crew of twelve. "You want him in ninth or tenth grade, he can't speak English, he's got a stupid haircut. And when you find this kid, you go beat the shit out of him. Tease him, beat him up, knock him around. We isolate this kid; he's our target. What will happen, one day I'll make sure I'm around when this kid is getting beaten up, and I'll stop it with the snap of my finger. He'll look at me—he'll see that I have a fancy car, fancy girls, I'm wearing a beeper—and I'll turn around and say, 'Hey, kid, how come these people are beating on you?' I'm gonna be this kid's hero, this kid's guru—I'm gonna be his *dai lo.*"

One day in 1981, a slim, handsome Fujianese teenager with hard eyes, a square jaw, and a mop of black hair arrived in New York. His name was Guo Liang Qi, but he would become known by the nickname Ah Kay. Born to a humble family in 1965, in a village not far from Sister Ping's, Ah Kay was uncommonly intelligent, but quit school in the fifth grade. He hung around the village a few more years, but he was ambitious, and an uncle living in the United States paid a snakehead $12,000 to smuggle him over. Ah Kay traveled overland to Hong Kong and then by air to Bangkok. He had a ticket for Ecuador, with a layover in Los Angeles. But when he reached LAX he slipped out of the terminal, a quiet Chinese kid security wouldn't give a second look. He had no papers and didn't speak a word of English, but he managed to make his way to New Jersey, where he stayed with his uncle. He found an entry-level job at a steakhouse called Charlie Brown's. But Ah Kay had a taste for nightlife, and for gambling in particular, to say nothing of a series of innate leadership skills which, at Charlie Brown's, anyway, were going untapped. He left the steakhouse by the end of 1982 and moved to New York's Chinatown. There he joined a fledgling gang, the Fuk Ching, which was short for Fukien Chingnian, or Fujianese Youth.

In those early days, before the Fujianese boom had begun in earnest, the Fuk Ching (which is pronounced "Fook Ching") occupied a small stretch of Grand Street. The precise origins of the gang are murky, but by the time Ah Kay arrived in New York, it existed in loose form. It was founded by a man named Kin Fei Wong, who went by Foochow Paul. He was in his mid-twenties when he and a couple of associates established the gang, which made him an elder statesman next to teenage recruits like Ah Kay. Foochow Paul had a mullet and a mustache and a stylish way about him. He surrounded himself with loyal kids, paid them off, gave them apartments in which to crash, bailed them out when they got locked up. There were a few members who weren't Fujianese, but most of them were like Ah Kay: recent arrivals from the province, connected by myriad bonds from the country they had left behind and by a fierce entrepreneurial drive to muscle in on whatever business opportunity they could. They took to dressing in black jeans and black bomber jackets. They grew their hair into dramatic pompadours streaked with dyed strands of orange or red. They congregated in the restaurants and gambling parlors of Fujianese Chinatown, lounging on the stoops, giving hard looks to passersby, always seeming to venture out in clusters of three or four.

For all their violence, Chinatown gangs were first and foremost a business, and the Fuk Ching leadership tried to colonize the Fujianese territory north of Canal and east of the Bowery. They fanned out through the neighborhood and quickly excelled at the staple enterprise of the Chinatown gang: collecting extortion. Since the dawn of Chinatown, monthly payments of lucky money had been a fact of doing business in the neighborhood, and by the time Ah Kay started collecting protection money for the Fuk Ching the practice had developed its own long-standing and elaborate choreography. If you wanted to open a restaurant in the territory of some tong or gang, you would receive a visit from a contingent of gang members. They would roll into your place of business and often be extremely, almost ostentatiously polite. Provided the business owner was cooperative, the interaction was at least superficially courteous. The particular denomination was often negotiated over tea. The one-time payment to open a restaurant could be as high as $100,000, and bought you the privilege of turning over smaller monthly payments to the gang for the foreseeable future. These were delivered in ceremonial red envelopes, and everyone paid—not just the restaurateurs, but the manicurists and the lawyers, the herbalists and the bookies, the video rental guy and the madam. During the Moon Festival each September, the gangs went door to door selling moon cakes at extortionate prices—$108 or $208, always a denomination ending in 8, for prosperity. At the Chinese New Year they sold orange plants or fireworks, again with an extravagant markup. When they were hungry, they would stroll into restaurants and order up a feast, roughhouse and boast, then simply scrawl the name of the gang on the check, tapping an inexhaustible tab that would never come due.

This was lucrative grazing, and the right to graze in a certain corner of the neighborhood did not come uncontested. For each block they controlled, for each basement mahjong game or walk-up brothel, and above all for control of the local heroin trade, the Fuk Ching had to fight a rival, and in Ah Kay's early years as a foot soldier they regularly clashed with the Tung Ons and the Flying Dragons. Fuk Ching members fought with knives, machetes, and ballpeen hammers—anything that could shatter bone with one quick, lethal swing, then just as quickly be concealed. They had guns as well, but the male gang members rarely carried them because of the penalties if they were caught with one in a stop-and-frisk by the cops. Instead they gave the guns to their girlfriends, who were less likely to be searched and held them at the ready. Not unlike Mock Duck in the tong wars, who is said to have closed his eyes while he pulled the trigger, the Fuk Ching were terrible shots. It was not unusual for the FBI to descend on the scene of a noisy gang clash and discover thirty shell casings on the ground and not a single person wounded.

Nevertheless, the Fuk Ching eventually gained control of a series of streets around Eldridge, and in that grove of narrow seven-story brick tenements they established a home base. With their connections to China and Chinese communities throughout Southeast Asia, the gang moved into the heroin trade, and Foochow Paul is said to have become a multimillionaire during the 1980s. He bought an apartment in midtown and property in Fujian and Hong Kong.

From his early days in the gang, Ah Kay knew that he was smarter than most of his lughead, country-boy contemporaries, and he must have observed Foochow Paul's largesse with a combination of admiration and envy. He was unusually ambitious from the beginning, and excelled as an earner and enforcer. In the spring of 1984, a Fuk Ching member named Steven Lim was rumored to be defecting to the gang's sworn enemies, the Tung On. On Saint Patrick's Day, Ah Kay and a couple of associates let themselves into Lim's apartment. Lim walked out of the bedroom and Ah Kay and the others fired a volley of shots, killing him. As they stood in the hallway they heard a woman scream and realized that Lim was not alone: his girlfriend must be with him. Ah Kay opened the bedroom door and shot her. He didn't stick around to find out if she'd lived or died. The episode was Ah Kay's introduction to killing, and he performed the task with a cool-headed insouciance that would become his signature. To Ah Kay, the lives of his own countrymen were cheap and expendable; the authorities took no notice when it was expunged, and killing Fujianese made him not a pariah in the neighborhood, but a known comer, a young man on the rise. "You Fujianese?" he once observed. "You die? You die. No more than killing a dog or a cat." An absence of scruples and a steady hand helped him rise through the gang, and in no time he was anointed a *dai ma,* or lower leader—a deputy, with his own crew. His chief responsibility was overseeing the gang's extortion of Chinese-owned businesses in Chinatown and as far away as midtown.

For their own survival, traditional gangs in Chinatown had tended to exploit the most vulnerable members of the community and show a certain respect for the existing power structure. But the Fuk Ching distinguished itself early on by showing no such deference. By 1985 Sister Ping had already established herself as a major figure in Fujianese society. People treated her store as a second home. They paid her to bring family members to them and used her money transfer service to remit their savings back to China. They trusted her. But to Ah Kay, Sister Ping's stature in the neighborhood rendered her not less of a target but more of one: it meant that she was rich.

Bank accounts were uncommon in Chinatown in those days. The neighborhood functioned as a cash economy for the most part, and residents tucked away bills in shoeboxes, coffee jars, or the back of the sock drawer. The abundance of cash squirreled away in local apartments was not lost on the gangs, and armed robbery became a favorite sideline. One day in 1985, Ah Kay decided to rob Sister Ping. Cash was, in a very real sense, the product of her money transfer business. Perhaps she had it warehoused somewhere. He knew she had a house in Brooklyn but didn't know precisely where it was, so he dispatched his girlfriend to trail Sister Ping's daughter Monica one day when she took the subway home from school. The girlfriend reported that the family lived on Neck Road, in Sheepshead Bay. Ah Kay and several others followed Monica themselves one day, and as she was walking to her house from the subway they drove by in a van, opened the side door, and snatched her off the sidewalk. She sat facing Ah Kay. "Robbery," he said simply, pointing a gun at her. "Be cooperative."

Monica let the gangsters into the house, where they found her younger brothers but no adults. Ah Kay trained his gun on the children and told them to sit on the couch and stay quiet while the other Fuk Ching members ransacked the rooms in search of money. They managed to dig up a thousand dollars, but that was it, and eventually the gangsters departed, tying up the children and telling them that if anyone spoke to the police, they would return and kill the family.

The meager haul "was not ideal for us," Ah Kay concluded. So several months later he decided to rob Sister Ping again. This time he didn't go himself but sent his underlings, as he called them, to do it. In order to make sure that Sister Ping was home herself, one of Ah Kay's associates made an appointment with her, saying he had some business to discuss. Given that Sister Ping knew about the Fuk Ching robbery several months before, it is a mystery why she agreed to meet with one of the young gangsters at her own home. The particular business the two were meant to be discussing has never become clear. But in any event Sister Ping came to the door, and the gang pulled guns and forced their way into the house. The children were there, and again, one gang member kept a gun on them while the others searched the house. "Please do not scare my children," Sister Ping said. "Just point the gun at me." Eventually someone searched the refrigerator and found $20,000. (Years later a prosecutor would wonder aloud before a jury whether "a legitimate businesswoman keeps her profits in her refrigerator.")

When Luke Rettler first started hearing about Ah Kay, the tales of the ruthless Fuk Ching enforcer had a larger-than-life, almost mythical quality. Ah Kay seemed "untouchable," Rettler thought.

Rettler was a young prosecutor with the Manhattan district attorney's office. He had an athletic build and a quiet intensity about him, with short brown hair, blue eyes, and dimples. He had grown up on a dairy farm in Wisconsin in a big Catholic family. (Luke's four brothers were Peter, Paul, Mark, and John.) After graduating from University of

Wisconsin Law School, he wanted to become a prosecutor, and a professor told him the only place to do it was at the Manhattan DA's office.

Rettler joined the office in 1983, around the time Ah Kay joined the Fuk Ching. He found himself working in the trial bureau for a short, hard-charging attorney named Nancy Ryan, who had started prosecuting Asian gangs in New York and was known in Chinatown as "the Dragon Lady." Luke was detailed to the Jade Squad, the interagency Asian gang unit, where he worked with Dougie Lee, the young Cantonese American detective whose family had come to America from Hong Kong when he was a child. The crime wave was starting to sweep Chinatown, and Luke was beginning to believe that the community was growing unpoliceable, completely out of control. Extortion was rampant, and when the restaurant owners and convenience store clerks didn't pay the painstakingly polite gangsters who visited once a month, they would be dragged into the back room and beaten with a pipe. Some would show up for work the next day to find that their business had been burned to the ground. One problem with the extortion cases was that it was almost impossible to get victims to cooperate. Frightened merchants, many of them with dubious immigration status, were reluctant to go to the authorities. In China the police were corrupt, and there was no reason to believe that New York cops would be any different. The gangsters knew this, and preyed upon it. How do you explain to a terrified witness from a corrupt country the concept of posting bail? The gangster he has risked his life to inform the police about is locked up but makes bail and is released. How do you convey to a potential witness that the gangster has not simply bribed his way out?

Ah Kay was gradually becoming known to law enforcement. Fuk Ching members were clashing with the Tung On and shaking down people on the street. With his languid movements and wiry, muscular build, Ah Kay stood out naturally in a cluster of them as a leader. But he was hard to catch. Street cops would stop him occasionally, but nothing seemed to stick. Once when they patted him down they found he was carrying $50,000. They had to let him go—they had nothing to charge him with—but they held on to the money. Ah Kay hired a lawyer to get it back.

Still, everyone slips up eventually, and eventually Ah Kay did. In August 1985 Ah Kay tried to extort money from a restaurant owner named Charlie Kwok. Kwok didn't want to pay, and he went to the police. Dougie Lee headed to a condo on Henry Street where he knew Ah Kay was staying, and arrested him. Ah Kay pleaded guilty and served two and a half years in prison. He did not find prison to be too much of an impediment to business; from behind bars he continued to manage his gang responsibilities, deputizing work to one of his younger brothers, Ah Wong, who was then still a teenager.

When his sentence was served, Ah Kay was deported back to China, but he stayed only six months, then sneaked back into America, taking a typically circuitous route, from China to Hong Kong to Bangkok to Belize to Guatemala to Mexico. He was apprehended at the border in El Paso and held for twenty-four hours by the INS. They released him on bail and he returned to New York, but Dougie and the other cops who had sent him away heard he was back on the streets. They rearrested him for illegal entry, and for parole violations on top of that. Ah Kay pleaded guilty again and served eleven months. This time he was not deported immediately upon release. The massacres at Tiananmen Square had occurred while he was in jail, and he applied for political asylum in the United States, claiming that his pro-democracy politics would make him a target for persecution if he was forced to return to China. He was given a date for an administrative hearing of his claim. Until the hearing, which was months away, he was free to go.

By the time Ah Kay walked out of prison on March 25, 1990, he had become the *dai lo,* the undisputed leader of the Fuk Ching gang. Foochow Paul had left the Fuk Ching in 1986 and started a gang called the Green Dragons in Queens. After ordering the execution of a rival in 1989, he had fled to China, ahead of the authorities. During Ah Kay's time in prison and in China, his allies within the gang had laid the foundation for his ascendance, and that spring he took over an organization that had until recently been leaderless, awaiting his triumphant return. He was twenty-four years old.

Ah Kay took his leadership role seriously, not merely responding to events as they developed but looking to the outside world for models of what it means to be a leader. "Why did Bush step down? Because the economy was in bad shape," he remarked to one of his subordinates after Bill Clinton won the presidential election in 1992. "Why was President Reagan in power for eight years? Because he did a good job with the economy, so people supported him. The same thing here. A whole group of people follow me, and our life is the best."

Ah Kay had an older brother who had chosen a more legitimate path in life, entering the restaurant business. But Ah Kay enlisted his two younger brothers, Ah Wong and Ah Qun, to join the gang. As he assumed the mantle of *dai lo,* he was surrounded at all times by a coterie of loyal yes-men.

"If Ah Kay said, 'Go get me a cup of coffee,' would you run and get him a cup of coffee?" a prosecutor would later ask one Fuk Ching member, who had joined the gang at thirteen.

"Yes," the underling replied.

"If he said, 'Get me some videotapes,' would you go get some videotapes?"

"Yes."

"If he said, 'Go kill somebody,' would you go kill somebody? Take your time and think it over."

The underling thought it over. "At that time, I say yes."

Ah Kay was attended by two bodyguards, who were his principal deputies and confidants, a loyal but unintelligent assassin named Li Xing Hua, whose gang nickname was Stupid, and another killer named Song You Lin. Ronald Chau, an ethnic Chinese refugee from Vietnam who was known as China Man, ran street operations for the gang and oversaw extortions and assaults.

The most unlikely member of the gang was a six-foot-tall, half Chinese, half African American named Alan Tam. Tam had grown up in the United States, the son of a Chinese mother and an African American father. He was dimwitted even by the standards of the gang, and had a serious drug problem. ("If there was no crack, I smoke marijuana just to stop thinking about crack," he later explained.) But he served a number of important purposes. As a native English speaker, Tam could be the gang's point of contact with the outside world, renting cars and apartments, dealing with lawyers, bailing people out of jail. There was also the fact that even the most hardened Chinese gangster tended to get nervous in the presence of a big African American. Tam was actually a fairly peaceful guy, neither especially inclined to violence nor especially good at it. He was, in the words of one FBI agent who got to know him, "a big mush." And the gang generally had him drive the getaway car rather than carry out any serious crimes; he was too easy to pick out of a lineup. But whenever Ah Kay and his colleagues got in a tangle, their adversaries would immediately pile onto Alan Tam, figuring that their best strategy for success was to join forces against the big black guy. Tam's body was covered with craters and nicks from knife wounds sustained in these fights. As if to underline the point, his gang nickname was Ha Gwei, literally Black Ghost or Black Guy.

All the money the gang earned went to Ah Kay, and he in turn doled it out. He was not generous with this allowance—when he initially took over the gang, the underlings tended to make $150 to $200 a week—but he covered a variety of other expenses so that they would want for little: crash pads were paid for; meals tended to be free if eaten at a local restaurant; the gang members drove black BMWs that they forced local businessmen to rent for them, as a form of extortion.

In some respects the Fuk Ching kids were no different from any other indolent high school or college-aged American males. They hung out, got high, gambled, and watched videos. They preferred kung fu pictures or lurid tales of Hong Kong triads. Their biggest day-to-day responsibility was collecting extortion, or, as Tam once put it, in a typical malapropism, collecting "distortion." Their turf consisted of forty or fifty businesses, each of which had to be shaken down at least once a month. And they policed that turf vigilantly, erecting surveillance cameras along the length of Eldridge Street so they could monitor the arrival of police or trespassers.

The gang had operated a modest casino on Eldridge, but when Ah Kay assumed leadership in the spring of 1990, he decided that it was too small. He elected to open a bigger gambling parlor in the basement of a massive red-brick building at 125 East Broadway. Gang members oversaw the conversion of the space, insulating the casino with a succession of five locked doors and a series of closed-circuit television cameras. The choice of venue was deliberately provocative: that stretch of East Broadway was Tung On territory, and Ah Kay told his underlings to expect trouble.

The grand opening was scheduled for October 1, 1990, and that afternoon, as predicted, a posse of Tung On members sauntered up to the casino entrance. Ah Kay walked out of the building and asked what they wanted. The Tung Ons demanded lucky money. Ah Kay informed them that he would not be paying and held his ground. "If you want to fuck around here," he added, "I'll shoot your fucking ass." With that he turned his back on the Tung Ons and entered the casino. A phalanx of Fuk Ching members remained guarding the door, and with no further preamble both sides drew weapons and started shooting. Ah Kay's little brother Ah Wong took a bullet and was dragged into the vestibule as the Tung Ons ran down the crowded street, the Fuk Ching members still firing wildly after them.

The location of the casino in the basement of the fortresslike structure at 125 East Broadway was significant, because the building had recently become the headquarters of the Fukienese American Association, the FAA, a Fujianese answer to Chinatown's Cantonese tongs. The association had actually been around for decades, but with huge numbers of Fujianese arriving in the neighborhood every week, it had suddenly gained a new prominence. The FAA was run by a wealthy middle-aged businessman named Alan Man Sin Lau, and in many ways Lau seemed to be a Fujianese Benny Ong—a slippery operator, at ease both with the licit world of politics and commerce and with the shadier universe of gang warfare and extortion. Lau was an entrepreneur who invested heavily in China, constructing a twenty-story office tower in Fuzhou. Governor Mario Cuomo presented him with an award for being an "outstanding" Asian American. At the same time, Lau was under suspicion by law enforcement in the United States and Canada as a major human smuggler. In 1990, Toronto law enforcement officers uncovered apparent links between Lau and the snakeheads. According to investigators, wiretapped conversations revealed that he had promised to provide five hundred customers to the snakeheads and to help fund their trips.

"It is unfair to blacken the name of the Fukien American Association as a whole based on the behavior of some nonmember bad elements which are not under the control of the association," Lau said at a press conference, insisting that he and his organization were beyond reproach. He raised money from prominent members of the Fujianese community to cover the $1.6 million cost of the new headquarters. Cheung Yick Tak was honored as one of twenty donors who gave $10,000 or more. But from its opening the building served not just as a meeting place for new Fujianese arrivals, but as a kind of annex for the Fuk Ching gang. In 1991 and 1992 alone, police counted fourteen shootings in the vicinity of the building. In some instances Fuk Ching gunmen would flee a shooting and enter 125 East Broadway, and police would follow, only to become lost in a maze of passages and hidden doors within.

At the DA's office, Rettler began to suspect that the FAA's involvement in criminal activity surpassed even that of more established tongs like the On Leong and the Hip Sing. He wondered if perhaps the traditional relationship had been inverted somewhat, if maybe the tail was wagging the dog and the tong was taking orders from the gang rather than the other way around. A Senate subcommittee found in 1991 that "the tong is instrumental in assisting other ethnic Fukienese to immigrate to the United States," and seemed to be involved in the heroin trade as well. It outlined the close relationship between Alan Man Sin Lau and the Fuk Ching gang and determined that "the leader of the Fuk Ching gang is . . . 'Ah Kay.' "

On New Year's Eve 1990, several gang members walked into a Chinese restaurant on Third Avenue and kidnapped a Fujianese man named Fang Kin Wah. Fang had arrived in New York just a few months earlier, joining his wife and her brother, who owned the restaurant and had given him a job. The gangsters grabbed Fang and handed a beeper to his frightened wife. Fang still owed money on his snakehead debt, they said. The Fuk Ching was often employed by snakeheads as muscle, to hold migrants hostage until they paid up. But starting that fall gang members had begun demanding ransom money that far exceeded the cost of passage to the United States. They would telephone family members in China and threaten to kill the hostage unless they arranged to have money paid to the gang in New York. Law enforcement was confused by this development: a call would come in, directly to the NYPD or even to the Manhattan DA's office, saying that a kidnapping was taking place in New York. The terrified families wouldn't have much more information than that. But they could tell authorities where the gang members had told them to send the money, and as often as not it was 125 East Broadway. In many cases the cops would just accompany the family when they went to pay the ransom and arrest whoever showed up to receive it.

The Fuk Ching members took Fang to a second-floor apartment on Arthur Avenue, in a vestigial Italian neighborhood in the Bronx. There they beat him with a gun and a hammer. They paused to beep his wife and demand $30,000, then continued beating him. Fang's wife called the police, who easily traced the number the kidnappers had left on the beeper. When the cops arrived, they found Fang and over a dozen other frightened Fujianese hostages. The gang members had scrambled, leaving behind a small arsenal of weapons and a large pile of cash.

Shortly thereafter, the beating victim, Fang Kin Wah, was escorted into Luke Rettler's office at the district attorney's building on Centre Street, not far from Chinatown. Fang was frail and very frightened, and Rettler called in Dougie Lee to question him. Along with getting Chinese victims to cooperate, the major problem Rettler faced was language. The NYPD had only one Fujianese speaker during those years, and had started pulling cadets out of the academy if they spoke a little Chinese, to handle the multitude of gang cases. Rettler himself had started taking Chinese classes at New York University at night, but it was a difficult language, and in any event, NYU offered Mandarin, not Fujianese. On top of that, Rettler was reluctant to use Fujianese translators, or even Fujianese cops, to interpret. The area around Fuzhou was so small and tight-knit that any Fujianese speaker he could find in New York City would have family back in China, and that family would be vulnerable. There was also widespread fear within the police force that a Fujianese gang member might infiltrate the department.

So Rettler often ended up using Dougie for translation, and Dougie made do with his Cantonese and Mandarin. As Dougie sat with Fang, flipping through photographs of the twenty-four people arrested in the Arthur Avenue apartment, trying to determine which ones had been the kidnappers, Rettler could see that they were dealing with a terrified witness. He told Dougie to explain to Fang that the Fuk Ching kidnappers had been caught red-handed, that they would never go to trial. All Rettler had to do was take Fang before the grand jury in order to get an indictment. The grand jury proceedings were secret. The Fuk Ching would never know that Fang had talked. "Don't worry," Rettler said. "They'll plead guilty. You won't have to testify."

Fang reluctantly agreed to go before the grand jury, and he recounted the beating, the abuse, how the kidnappers had pointed a gun at his head and played Russian roulette. As Rettler predicted, the indictment came down and the culprits were charged. But they didn't plead guilty. They wanted to go to trial. Rettler and Dougie didn't know what to do. Their witness was panicked about retribution. They called Fang into the office, and Rettler told Dougie to translate. "Tell him they pleaded not guilty," Rettler said. "You're gonna have to testify."

Dougie relayed the news, and even before he had finished, Fang's eyes widened and the color drained from his face. He started shaking his head, and his body began to tremble and then convulse. Rettler thought Fang might be having a heart attack.

Then Fang began talking in Chinese, a mile a minute, a torrent of worried words. His whole body was shaking, and he was crying, and he talked and talked, his countenance hysterical, his expression seeming to plead with Dougie.

"What's he saying?" Rettler asked Dougie impatiently. "What's he saying?"

Dougie looked at their frantic witness, then looked up gamely at Rettler.

"Luke," Dougie said, "he says no problem. He'll do it."

They did end up persuading Fang to testify, and the case eventually went to trial. On the day of Fang's testimony, a column of black-clad, scowling members of the Fuk Ching filed into the courtroom. When Fang saw them, he panicked and darted into the jury room to hide. He told the judge he would not leave the room, much less testify. "They want to kill me," he said. "Dangerous men. Chinese men. Dangerous." The judge insisted that Fang leave the room and testify against his kidnappers, but Fang refused, and began crying and hyperventilating, having what Rettler described as "a complete meltdown." "I'm worried about my family," Fang said, sobbing. The court couldn't protect them from retribution, he said. "Who is going to believe in this U.S. law?" Eventually court officers had to physically drag Fang to the stand. "After I testify, I'll be dead," he shouted at the judge. "They will make sure I die." The judge ended up barring the Fuk Ching members from his courtroom. Fang testified against his captors, and the jury delivered a conviction.

After the police showed up at 125 East Broadway a number of times, the Fuk Ching stopped having ransoms delivered there. They diversified their locations. They had been using pay phones to make their ransom demands, but when the cops caught on to the phones they were using, they started using cell phones instead. When it proved too difficult to pick up a ransom in New York, they began instructing families in China to make payments to contacts in Fujian Province, so that no money changed hands in New York. Their associates in Fuzhou could then use a service like Sister Ping's to remit the money back to them in Chinatown, saving them the scrutiny of the police. The Fuk Ching were above all adaptable. Each time the landscape in Chinatown presented some new business opportunity, they pursued it. Each time law enforcement caught on to their modus operandi, they would innovate.

By the early 1990s, the gang was beginning to undertake an adaptation that was more decisive, and ultimately consequential, than any other. There was only so much money in shakedowns, burglaries, and kidnappings. The heroin trade was lucrative, but there was a lot of competition in a limited marketplace, and the criminal penalties for drug running were enough to put you away for life. Snakeheads, in contrast, seemed to enjoy a market so inexhaustible that there was less competition. And the criminal sentences for human smuggling amounted to a slap on the wrist. Ah Kay observed the kinds of profits that Sister Ping and other snakeheads were reaping and realized that for the truly enterprising criminal, the snakehead business represented an unparalleled opportunity. "It was a better business than drug trafficking," one Fujianese community leader recalled. "More profit. Less risk. You get caught and plead guilty right away, you only go to jail for six months. Another thing is, your merchandise can walk."

Chapter Five

Swiftwater

THE NIAGARA River is 34 miles long. It issues from Lake Erie and flows north, cataracting over the famous falls and culminating in Lake Ontario, the rush of its currents bringing hydroelectric power to the region and the general course of its trajectory tracing the national boundary between southern Ontario, in Canada, and western New York State. On January 3, 1989, the Niagara County Sheriff's Department responded to a call about "a floater." A local man had been walking along the banks of the Niagara when he discovered two nylon suitcases and, further on, a dead body floating facedown in the icy water by the riverbank. It was snowing when officers arrived at the scene that evening. They rolled the body over and saw that it was an Asian woman, with plump cheeks, full lips, and a tangle of black hair wreathing her head. Her eyes were firmly shut. She wore a coarse gray winter coat, wool pants, and a black shirt that rode up around her belly, which was distended from river water. Her right arm extended from her body at a crooked angle, her index finger taut and outstretched, as if she had been pointing to something just before she died. The river had been cold for days, with drifts of ice floating along it. The woman's body was frozen through; when the medical examiner cut her chest open for an autopsy, he had to wait for her internal organs to thaw.

Not far away, the officers found a cheap inflatable raft made of vinyl, the sort of thing, one investigator observed, "you might try to use in your backyard swimming pool." From the woman's luggage they retrieved a plastic bag of clothing: a winter coat, a green pullover, a pair of white-and-black-checked slacks. But when the officers examined the clothing, they found that the garments did not appear to fit the victim. She hadn't been alone on the raft.

Two days earlier, on New Year's Day, the Border Patrol at Niagara Falls had received an anonymous telephone call inquiring about whether by any chance they had apprehended a six-year-old girl in the area. They had not. Then a man named Steven Gleit telephoned and said he was a lawyer in New York City calling on behalf of a client whose six-year-old niece might have tried crossing the Niagara River by boat. He said the child should have been accompanied by three adults, including a Malaysian female. He said the little girl's name was Haw Wang.

When the woman's body was discovered two days later, a Niagara County investigator named Ed Garde took over the case. In the pants pocket of the woman on the riverbank Garde found a grocery receipt with a 212 telephone number scrawled across it. He dialed the number and spoke with a woman named Sue Chan. She wouldn't answer any questions, but she asked him if he knew anything about a little girl. She said he should call her back at work and gave a different number. It was the office number of the attorney Steven Gleit.

Ed Garde called Sue Chan again and learned that she was Gleit's secretary. The little girl, Haw Wang, was her niece. Haw Wang had been born in Fuzhou. Her mother, Sue's sister, was living illegally in New York City. The little girl had been accompanied by an uncle as far as Toronto, where she had been turned over to a group of people who would be transported across the river, including a nice middle-aged Malaysian woman, Cheah Fong Yew, who spoke Chinese and promised to take care of her. It was Cheah Fong Yew whom the investigators had found by the riverbank.

Dating back to the exclusion act, Chinese people had been crossing the Niagara to enter the United States. In 1904 the *Buffalo Times* reported that white smugglers were outfitting Chinese with "Indian garb" and baskets of sassafras and sending them rowing across the river. Through much of the twentieth century, Canada tended to have more permissive immigration policies, especially with respect to Asians, than the United States. Hong Kong residents didn't need a visa to visit Canada, so it became an appealing penultimate stop in the logistical networks devised by the snakeheads, a chilly alternative to the Guatemala route. By the time Haw Wang flew into Toronto with her uncle that winter, Canadian law enforcement had found that four out of ten refugee claimants entering Canada from China were subsequently smuggled into the United States. The previous July, three Chinese men had been stopped in Lewiston, New York, as they walked along the side of the road, their trousers soaked from the waist down. They admitted to Border Patrol agents that they had taken a raft across the river from Canada. By the end of August, nearly a dozen others had been caught in Lewiston alone, and because illegal immigration statistics are always a game of extrapolation, authorities surmised that a far greater number must be entering without getting caught.

On January 3, shortly after the discovery of the body, Ed Garde initiated an investigation, bringing together the Niagara County Sheriff's Office, the Niagara Regional Police, and the INS's Anti-Smuggling Unit in Buffalo. They called it Operation Swiftwater, after the merciless currents of the Niagara. And within days they had a significant lead. An INS informant divulged the names of two people who might have been involved in smuggling the raft across the river. One was a Vietnamese man who lived on the Canadian side of the river. The other was Sister Ping's husband, Cheung Yick Tak.

The Niagara investigators knew nothing of Operation Hester, Joe

Occhipinti's short-lived INS investigation in New York. But when they ran Yick Tak's name through Department of Motor Vehicles records, they found a car registered to the apartment at 14 Monroe Street. And when they found the phone number listed for that apartment, they made an interesting discovery: it matched a number that had been found in the possession of two different groups of "alien rafters" apprehended the previous summer. When they checked the phone tolls for the Monroe Street apartment, they found numerous calls to a number on the Canadian side of Niagara Falls, which was listed to a Vietnamese man named Minh Hoang. A search of *his* toll records revealed twenty-six calls to an American by the name of Richard Kephart.

Kephart was a cabdriver with a history of petty larceny. Ed Garde worked with INS investigators to assemble information on him, and before long they showed up at Kephart's door.

"You know what this is about?" they asked.

"I got a pretty good idea," Kephart said.

The investigators took Kephart to the INS office at the Whirlpool Bridge in Niagara Falls and proceeded to question him for ten hours. One evening the previous August, Kephart explained, he had been driving his taxi when he responded to a call to pick up a party outside a Lewiston bar called the Bucket of Blood. There he met three Asian men and three Asian women. They each carried one piece of luggage, except for a Vietnamese man in his twenties who introduced himself as Paul. The other passengers sat in wordless silence while Paul did the talking. He had a mustache and a confident, happy-go-lucky way about him, Kephart thought. Paul said their car had broken down; could Kephart drive them to the Buffalo airport? Kephart headed in that direction, but when they were halfway there, Paul abruptly changed his mind. How much would it cost to drive them all the way to New York City?

Eight hundred bucks, Kephart said.

Paul produced a stack of cash and paid up front. They drove

through the night, without talking, until they reached Manhattan. Kephart dropped them off in Chinatown, and Paul announced that he wanted to head straight back to Buffalo. Kephart said he'd drive him free of charge; he could use some company on the ride back, to keep him awake. When they reached Lewiston, Paul said he might be taking other groups of people down to the city in the future. He asked for Kephart's phone number.

The two men started working together, and established a routine. Paul was bringing people across the river from Canada in an inflatable rubber raft. At a prearranged time of night, Kephart would park his car on the New York side of the river. Paul would load several passengers and their luggage into a raft and paddle across. He was excellent on the water, proud of how quickly he could traverse the tricky slipstreams, zigzagging in an expert pattern through the crosscurrents to the other side. There he would deflate the raft, stuff it in a backpack, and load the passengers into Kephart's car for the long ride to New York City.

In New York, Paul introduced him to Cheung Yick Tak, whom Paul called Billy. When Kephart dropped people off in Chinatown, Yick Tak would meet him. "He'd come out and he'd open the door and let the illegal aliens out and pay me my money," he recalled. Yick Tak was businesslike. He might ask how the trip had been, just to be polite, but that was it. He called the passengers "clients." When they arrived, he would help unload their belongings for them, hustling suitcases out of the van and onto the sidewalk like a valet. He always passed Kephart his money in a brown paper bag.

Kephart started making trips every week or two. He met Yick Tak some fourteen times through that fall and early winter. There were so many people coming over that he gave up using his cab and rented a van instead. He recruited an old fishing buddy named James Dullan to help him. There seemed to be a lot of money in the business. Paul certainly spent a great deal of it. He gambled a lot; he once said he'd run up a $30,000 debt in a single day. He was a risk-taker, as evidenced by his masterful but hazardous piloting of the cheap rafts across the river (a stunt that Dullan maintained was "one step from suicide, in my opinion"). Paul's favorite expression was "Don't Worry, Be Happy," after the Bobby McFerrin song that was popular on the radio at that time. But he also had a callous side to him, a hardness. He told Dullan that when he met the customers on the Canadian side, he would keep them at his house or in a cheap motel and feed them only a gallon of milk and a loaf of bread. "Just throw them a loaf of bread and a gallon of milk and they're happy," he joked.

After a few trips Kephart and Dullan realized that Yick Tak wasn't working alone. He had a partner in New York, his brother-in-law Cheng Wai Wei, whom they called Peter. Just as Sister Ping's father had enlisted his children to assist him in the smuggling business, Sister Ping and her sister Susan both enlisted their husbands. Like Yick Tak, Peter seems to have married into a smuggling clan, and he took to the family business. In fact, as soon as Kephart and Dullan met Peter, it became clear that he, not Yick Tak, was running the operation. Peter was taller than Yick Tak, younger, more charismatic. It was Yick Tak who met Kephart and Dullan and took the immigrants and paid them, but Kephart gradually concluded that Yick Tak was just a flunky.

It also seemed as though Peter might be making more money. He had made "millions doing this here," Paul told Kephart.

"Are they bringing drugs across?" Kephart asked. They must be, he figured, to be making that kind of money.

No, Paul said. Just people.

Through the course of the fall Kephart and Dullan gradually came to realize that they were one small cog in a sophisticated operation. Kephart heard Yick Tak and Peter allude to a separate trick in which they sneaked people in coffins from a funeral parlor on the Canadian side over to Albany. Paul said that when the migrants arrived in Chinatown, Yick Tak and Peter could set them up with English lessons and jobs. He said Peter could get driver's licenses and even phony birth certificates for his customers. "They have somebody down there in New York that's a clerk or something that can take care of the paperwork," he explained. They got the impression that Peter paid off people in Chinatown as well. Once when they were double-parked in Chinatown, unloading passengers, they saw two police officers approaching. "Don't worry about the cops," Peter said. "I run Chinatown." Kephart and Dullan continued to unload people from the double-parked van. The cops approached and clearly saw what they were doing. But they kept on walking. The cabbies were impressed. Peter produced a thick roll of bills. "You guys do good," he said. "You can make this kind of money."

As fall became winter and the river began to freeze over, the men discussed an ambitious plan for the spring. Yick Tak and Peter would give Kephart and Dullan money to purchase a boat. Then the cabbies could get fishing licenses and start ferrying large numbers of customers across. Peter told them they could each make $40,000 to $60,000 a year. When they discussed the plan for spring, it seemed implicit that it would follow a hiatus during the coldest months of winter. But the hiatus didn't happen.

"The river is rough in the wintertime," Kephart said when Paul told him that there was a plan to bring a group across around New Year's. "You got ice and everything coming down through it." But Paul didn't worry. He never did.

On the night of December 30, Kephart and Dullan pulled a rented Ford van into their usual spot on the New York side of the river. The temperature outside was 30 degrees. The river was covered in drifting ice and flowing at 11 miles an hour. Kephart got out of the van and stood on the riverbank. The moon was in its last quarter and the sky was cloudy, but shortly after eight o'clock, several hundred yards away, Kephart saw a car pull over on the Canadian side. He could see the light from the trunk when Paul opened it to retrieve the luggage and the raft. Then the trunk light disappeared. It was cold, and Kephart got back in the van.

The radio was on, the volume low enough that above the music Kephart and Dullan could hear the squawk of gulls in the gorge below. They waited. Normally it took Paul less than twenty minutes to make the trip, deflate the raft, and tuck it into his backpack. But after half an hour there was no sign of him. They didn't worry. He had been late before, caught up in a current that washed him downstream, forcing him to walk the passengers back to the car. They kept waiting.

Then they heard something, a noise outside the van that wasn't the gulls. They both heard it. It sounded like a scream.

"That might have come from the river," Dullan said.

"Hell of a time for a cold bath," Kephart joked uncomfortably.

The two men sat in silence for a while.

"That raft goes over, man," Dullan said, "as cold as that water is, they got about three minutes before they freeze."

Kephart didn't say anything. But he started to worry. Dullan could tell by looking at his face.

They kept waiting, but they heard nothing more, and after an hour both men began to panic. They drove to a pay phone and called Paul's house on the Canadian side. Paul had gone down to the river, his wife said. He hadn't come home. They drove back to the riverbank and sat for another hour, but there was no sign of the raft, just the rushing of the water and the squawking of the gulls. Eventually Kephart dropped Dullan off and drove home. The next morning he woke early and used the van to drop his son off at school. Then he returned it to the dealership. Then he went home. Finally, that evening Paul telephoned.

"The raft overturned," he said matter-of-factly. "All the people drowned."

"What do you mean?" Kephart asked.

"They all drowned," Paul said again.

There had been four of them altogether: a young Malaysian man named Vincent Ooi; his girlfriend, Vasugee Krishan; the little Fujianese girl, Haw Wang; and the middle-aged Malaysian woman who was looking after her, Cheah Fong Yew. The four of them had been staying at a Hotel Ibis in Toronto. When Paul picked them up that night, they were dressed warmly: sweaters, overcoats, mittens. Cheah had tucked a towel around her neck as a scarf. Sometimes Paul used two rafts, one for the passengers and another, strung to the first with a length of rope, for their luggage. But this time he opted to pack them all in together. He inflated a blue-and-white raft and laid the suitcases on its floor. Then he instructed Cheah and Vasugee to sit in the middle, on top of the suitcases. He took up position in the back, with his wooden paddle. Vincent Ooi sat in the front of the raft, and in the very front sat Haw Wang. She was bundled up, to keep warm. She carried her belongings in a little yellow backpack.

They never made it more than 20 yards out. The night was dark and icy. The raft was overloaded with people and bags and the current was treacherous. The raft just flipped, throwing them all into the frigid water. Paul was a strong swimmer, and he immediately made his way to shore. He heard the others scream, saw hands flail, then disappear in the whirlpools of the Niagara. Then he went home. The following morning he went back to the riverbank, but he found no sign of anyone. Everything had been washed away. Paul relayed the news to Kephart. Then he hung up and left town, headed for Nova Scotia to lie low.

It didn't take the Niagara investigators long to realize that Cheung Yick Tak was married to Sister Ping. In fact, well before the drowning, a hard-nosed Buffalo INS agent named Patrick Devine had believed she was behind the sudden onslaught of Chinese coming over the border from Canada. Her name had started appearing in case after case, and eventually Devine drove down to New York and connected with Joe Occhipinti, who gave him all the information assembled on the Cheng family during the Hester investigation. Devine even stopped by the Tak Shun Variety Store. Yick Tak was there, minding the shop. Devine introduced himself and asked if he could look around. Yick Tak consented, in broken English, and Devine wandered through the shop. He didn't find anything objectionable, and eventually he left. But before he did, he approached Yick Tak. "We know what you're doing," he said. Yick Tak looked at him blankly. "We know you're smuggling. We're going to get you eventually."

Devine told the Swiftwater investigators that what they had stumbled on was actually an extensive and intricate criminal enterprise. Ed Garde thought the best approach was to flip Kephart and Dullan, and the cabbies were happy to cooperate; they seemed to realize they had gotten in a bit over their heads. Slowly Garde assembled information on Yick Tak and Peter. "The organization appears to be structured, utilizing travel routes and safehouses through Hong Kong; Vancouver, British Columbia; Toronto, Ontario; and New York City," one Swiftwater report concluded. "The organization has smuggled approximately 75 Chinese Nationals into the United States between August and December, 1988."

Then suddenly that spring there was an unexpected break in the case: Patrick Devine and the INS in Buffalo managed to capture Sister Ping. A Canadian deadbeat named Terry Honesburger had been working at a Chinese restaurant in Toronto when, like the cabbies, he was lured into the smuggling business by the promise of a quick buck. He started driving Chinese immigrants across the border in the trunk of his car, but he was caught almost immediately. A bearded Canadian Mountie named Larry Hay told Honesburger that the authorities would spare him, but only if he helped set up a sting. On March 28, 1989, Hay met with Honesburger and drove to the Toronto airport. They waited by a bank of pay phones in the arrivals area, and before long a short Chinese woman in a gray knit sports jacket approached them. It was Sister Ping. She looked impatient. "What took you?" she demanded in broken English. With her were four Chinese people: a man, a boy, a pregnant woman, and a teenage girl in a brown leather jacket.

"Are all four to go?" Hay asked her.

"No," she said, indicating the teenager. "This one is my daughter."

Sister Ping slid $340 into a newspaper and handed it to the Mountie, with the understanding that he would drive the passengers over the border. Then she and her daughter left, and Hay eventually delivered the three passengers to a bus station in Albany, where they were arrested. Several months later, with a warrant out for her arrest, Sister Ping arrived at the Vancouver airport and was about to board a flight to Mexico when the police caught up with her. After she was transferred to upstate New York and charged, Sister Ping posted $25,000 bail and immediately hired one of Buffalo's most elite and expensive criminal defense lawyers to handle her case. Patrick Devine didn't understand how this woman who had no education and spoke hardly any English managed to connect to a brand-name defense attorney, but he noted that money was apparently not much of a concern.

Sister Ping did not want to go to jail under any circumstances, and she expressed a willingness to plead guilty and cooperate with law enforcement if it might help her avoid incarceration. On several occasions she flew into Buffalo, accompanied by her daughter Monica, who had a better grasp of English, and met Devine at a Denny's to haggle over the terms of cooperation for a few hours before catching a flight back to New York. Devine was mystified by this gruff, brusque little woman. At one point she produced her passport to show it to him, and all sorts of carefully folded money that had been tucked between the pages scattered out onto the floor. Finally, on June 27, 1990, Sister Ping pleaded guilty, acknowledging that "I knew that if the three Chinese people go to the U.S. they would be illegal" and signing her confession in a slanted, looping script.

A few weeks later INS agents assembled outside 14 Monroe Street at 6:15 one morning, banged on the door of Apartment 7B, and arrested Cheung Yick Tak. Paul and his wife had already been captured in Canada. Peter had fled to Hong Kong, but he was eventually captured as well, as he tried to reenter the United States through a pedestrian line from Mexico. When Yick Tak was taken in, Patrick Devine went to see him. He was different from his wife, Devine thought. More evasive. He would just deny and deny, play dumb to the charges, beat the investigators with silence. Sister Ping was never linked to the rafting deaths in any definitive way. But many of the investigators who tracked the couple over the years believe that there wasn't anything Yick Tak did that she wasn't somehow behind. And Devine, for one, was convinced she had had a hand in it.

In September a Buffalo federal judge named Richard Arcara held a sentencing hearing for Sister Ping. He called her a "prime mover" in the illegal migrant business. "I am convinced you have been involved in smuggling aliens on a more extensive basis than you have admitted," he said.

Her lawyer, William Skretny, objected, insisting that Arcara sentence her "for what she did in this indictment and not, as may be alleged, [because] she is something akin to an empress of alien-smuggling."

"I knew what I did was wrong," Sister Ping said when it was her turn to speak. She said that the pregnant woman she had been smuggling was her cousin, who had fled from China with her husband and nephew to escape a forced abortion. (Government agents said that the abortion part of the story was true but that the two women were not related.) "With my Chinese cultural background, I have to put family considerations into top priority," she said. "When my cousin was pleading for me to help, how could I not?"

Arcara was unimpressed, and delivered the maximum sentence of six months. But Sister Ping was desperate not to serve. She volunteered again to give Devine information in exchange for leniency. She had conditions: she would not testify against associates or wear a wire or allow her telephone calls to be recorded, but she would supply information. She gave Devine the addresses of two apartments in Arizona, and when INS agents raided them, they found sixty undocumented Chinese. But as busts go, they were inconsequential. Devine wasn't after the passengers themselves; he was after the snakeheads. Part of him suspected that the Arizona loads might even be Sister Ping's own clients, whom she had sacrificed so that she could appear to be cooperating.

Nevertheless, the government recommended a reduction in Sister Ping's sentence, from six months down to four. She was not satisfied with that and had her lawyers argue that her sentence should be reduced to the two months she had already served. "I'm either the fourth or fifth attorney to represent Mrs. Cheng," a New York lawyer named Stephen Goldenberg told the judge in June 1991. Her habit of acquiring prominent counsel seemed to have backfired: two of the attorneys hired to represent her in Buffalo had to abandon Sister Ping because after taking on her case they had been appointed judges. Goldenberg pointed to the Arizona case as an example of Sister Ping's cooperation. "This smuggling route through Phoenix, Arizona, has been shut down," Goldenberg said. "In effect, the case which Mrs. Cheng assisted the Government with was a far larger and more significant prosecution than her own case."

The prosecutor objected. "We believe that we have identified, prosecuted, and convicted a person who may well be the single largest figure in Chinese alien smuggling in the United States," he said. "She stood in this court, addressing the Court through her attorneys, as if this incident for which she was convicted was an incident of aberrant conduct, and not something consistent with what we think to be her past history."

But the incident wasn't "an alien smuggling for profit type situation," Goldenberg insisted. He raised a nuanced distinction: Sister Ping may have known that she was breaking the law. But she did not think of herself as a criminal. "People from the area of China that she comes from assist one another in getting to the United States. They try to bring over their families. And in speaking to members of her family, they don't see it as a criminal enterprise, but almost as a duty to try to get family members in."

When her lawyers ascertained that there would be no further reduction in her sentence in exchange for cooperation, Sister Ping asked whether she might provide further information that could "go to my husband's credit." She might have wondered—because Cheung Yick Tak had been sold out by his own partner and brother-in-law, Peter. In March 1991, Peter was sentenced to three months in prison. He had obtained a reduction in his sentence because his lawyers claimed that he was in no way responsible for the deaths on the Niagara, that his only involvement in the scheme consisted of transporting the customers around New York City once they arrived. Peter was not the ringleader but the flunky, they argued. Yick Tak was the number-one man in the operation. And Peter was willing to cooperate and give them information about him.

Even so, Yick Tak somehow managed to avoid paying any serious dues. He pleaded guilty to conspiracy to smuggle illegal aliens and was initially sentenced to nine months, with the stipulation "that such incarceration will not commence until release of defendant's wife from current custody." But the sentencing kept getting pushed back. Finally, in February 1993, the prosecution and defense had a session with the judge. The records of this session are sealed, and the government has never offered any explanation, but according to the docket in the case, the upshot was that Yick Tack's "sentence is reduced to 0 incarceration." It seems clear that Yick Tak, like his wife, had offered the authorities some information or cooperation in exchange for leniency. But the precise nature or extent of his assistance remains a mystery.

Sister Ping did go to prison, in upstate New York. She hated it—hated the mushy Western food, hated being separated from her family, hated being in an environment where she didn't understand the language. She was bitter, because the couple she had helped at the airport in Toronto ended up obtaining asylum while she had to go to prison. She no doubt was also troubled by the opportunity costs of remaining in jail. Goldenberg had asked that she be permitted to serve her time in a halfway house in New York, arguing that she should be close to her four children, but also that if she was removed from her base of operations in Chinatown, "she would merely languish and her time would not be used profitably."

She did have one regular visitor, however. Five years after brushing off Joe Occhipinti's request for assistance on Operation Hester, the FBI was beginning to take an interest in human smuggling and Fujianese organized crime, and the New York field office dispatched a young Cantonese American special agent named Peter Lee to interview Sister Ping. Lee had been with the FBI only since 1989; he was a rookie, no match, perhaps, for so formidable an adversary. He was born in Hong Kong in 1959 and had come to the United States when he was ten. Lee would take along photo arrays of various underworld figures in Chinatown, and he and Sister Ping would page through them, photo by photo, as Sister Ping told Lee who was who and who was doing what. She was remarkably cooperative, feeding Lee information about the illegal activities of her various competitors. She liked Peter Lee. He was the kind of fed she could talk to.

Nor was implicating the opposition the only fruitful use Sister Ping found for her time behind bars. She could still communicate with Yick Tak and the rest of the family in New York City, and as her lawyer had observed, Sister Ping was eager to use her time profitably. The nature of the immigrant smuggling business, after all, is that there is a pipeline. It sometimes took months to move people from Fuzhou or Changle to Chinatown, so at any given moment there were numerous people at stations along the way: in Shenzhen or Hong Kong, Guatemala or Belize, Tijuana or California, Vancouver or Toronto. "Sister Ping had to keep working from prison," Patrick Devine explained. "Because when she went in, there were already dozens of people en route to the U.S."

Upon her release from prison, Sister Ping continued to meet occasionally with Peter Lee. Sometimes he would go to 47 East Broadway and they would sit in an upstairs room discussing various neighborhood personalities. They became so friendly that when her daughter Monica got married, Sister Ping and Yick Tak invited Lee to the wedding. (Worried about how that might look, Lee politely declined.) Then one day Lee was abruptly ordered by his superiors to terminate the relationship. In an affidavit written some time later, Lee acknowledged that he had "learned that the defendant was continuing to engage in illegal activities even while she purported to be cooperating with the FBI."

The Niagara runs deep in the area where the raft crossed that New

Year's, 85 or 90 feet in places, and sometimes the bodies of the dead just disappear. Throughout the Swiftwater case, the Niagara investigator Ed Garde felt haunted by the specter of Haw Wang, the six-year-old girl who drowned. Some bodies stay submerged for months in the river, popping up only when the water warms, petrified, fish-eaten, or decomposed. And long after Yick Tak's incarceration was reduced to zero, Garde waited for the day when someone would find the little girl's body, when some human remains might grace the whole bleak episode with a finality that the legal system couldn't. Garde waited. But she never washed ashore.

Chapter Six

Year of the Snake

BY THE time the squat green tanks of the People's Liberation Army rumbled into Beijing's Tiananmen Square in the early hours of June 4, 1989, tension had been building in the capital for months. Pro-democracy students had been staging sit-ins and hunger strikes since April, and several massive demonstrations had converged on the square. Party officials were concerned by the sheer numbers of people turning out for these events, and embarrassed by the spectacle; by the end of May, they had declared martial law.

But for all the complexity of the events at Tiananmen Square, the episode would be seared into the world's imagination in the form of a simple iconic image: a lone, unidentified man who stood on Chang'an Avenue, clad in dark pants and a white shirt, and faced down a column of tanks. This was the image that alerted newspaper readers around the planet to the turmoil inside China. The most widely reproduced version of the picture was taken by Jeff Widener, an Associated Press photographer who took the photograph from the sixth floor of the Beijing Hotel, about half a mile away. The clean staging of the photograph told a simple, angry story: a brave individual yearns for freedom in the face of an oppressive military dictatorship. It was a stark enactment of a certain dynamic, which would come to define the international community's reaction to China in the wake of Tiananmen.

On June 5, the day the photograph was taken, a top-secret State

Department summary describing the events circulated in Washington. It was titled "After the Bloodbath." The crackdown by the Chinese government created extraordinary pressure for President George H. W. Bush, who had been in office for less than six months. Bush had assumed the presidency with a goal of forging closer relations with China, a country with which he had some history. In 1974, Gerald Ford had offered Bush his choice of ambassadorships, raising prestige assignments like London and Paris. But Bush had something else in mind. "I asked him if he would send me to China—the big new challenge," he recalled. Richard Nixon had reestablished ties with China only two years earlier, creating liaison offices in the respective capitals. Formal diplomatic relations were not reinstated until 1979, but Bush spent over a year in China, learning about the people, the culture, and the history and attempting to establish allegiances with the leadership in Beijing. He and his wife, Barbara, purchased bicycles and pedaled around the city in the manner of the local Chinese.

As president, Bush worried that Tiananmen would undo whatever goodwill China had been able to develop in the West since 1972. "To many, it appeared that reform was merely a sham," he concluded, "that China was still the dictatorship it had always been." Bush was reluctant to alienate the Chinese leadership, or punish the Chinese population, by initiating broad economic sanctions, but on June 5 he authorized military sanctions, halting any sales of military equipment to the People's Liberation Army. He also announced that the administration would encourage a sympathetic review of any requests for visa extensions by Chinese students in the United States. He met with some of these students, in a gesture of solidarity.

What kinds of allowances the United States should make for those fleeing the carnage and repression on display in Beijing was a sensitive question from the beginning, and central to America's response to Tiananmen. Even as the crackdown unfolded, one well-known dissident, the Beijing astrophysicist Fang Lizhi, appeared at the gates of the U.S. embassy and asked for refuge. He had been a vocal critic of the government, and China put immediate pressure on the embassy to turn him over to authorities. But he stayed. "We have no choice but to take him in," Bush wrote in his diary on June 10, "but it's going to be a stick in the eye of the Chinese." The president was torn. "I want to preserve the relationship, but I must also make clear that the U.S. cannot condone this kind of human rights brutality."

What Bush did not realize in the summer of 1989 was that his tortured posture on whether and when the United States should offer refuge to those fleeing China would unwittingly facilitate the snakehead trade and set the stage for an epic influx of undocumented Chinese. Bush's commitment to harboring those fleeing political persecution by the Chinese government eventually found its way into a directive, Executive Order 12711, which would serve as a kind of founding document for the Fujianese community in America. Signed on April 11, 1990, and titled "Policy Implementation with Respect to Nationals of the People's Republic of China," the directive held that any Chinese citizen who was in the United States before the crackdown should not be forcefully removed by immigration. (There were roughly 80,000 Chinese students studying in the United States at the time, and the provision effectively offered them safe haven.)

But Bush's executive order contained another clause as well, one that had nothing to do with the events at Tiananmen Square. In the aftermath of the crackdown, Washington was seized by a broad antipathy toward the repressive Communist regime in Beijing, and one matter of particular concern to legislators was the sometimes brutal manner in which China was enforcing its one-child policy. Reports from inside the country indicated that in some rural areas a low birthrate was being achieved by forcibly sterilizing couples who had more than one child—and in some cases by compelling women to have late-term abortions. In the mid-eighties President Ronald Reagan had withdrawn American support for the United Nations Population Fund because of concerns that the fund was supporting Chinese programs that involved coercive sterilization and abortion. Republican legislators, pro-life groups, and the Catholic Church had been especially vocal in opposing China's use of draconian measures in its efforts to limit population growth. Following Tiananmen, members of Congress pushed to withdraw China's most-favored-nation trading status, but Bush refused. As a consolation, he included a significant provision in the executive order that dealt with China's population-control tactics. Bush directed the secretary of state and the attorney general to provide for "enhanced consideration" under the immigration laws for individuals "who express a fear of persecution upon return to their country related to that country's policy of forced abortion or coerced sterilization."

Though the executive order was prompted by the events at Tiananmen, the breadth of the provision led to the de facto result that any fertile Chinese person, whether a parent or not, suddenly became a potential political refugee in the United States. Snakeheads and the uneducated migrants who made up their clientele had always shown an ingenious knack for identifying loopholes in immigration law, but the 1990 directive was an unambiguous invitation: the Bush administration had announced a posture of deference to asylum claims brought by individuals fleeing a nationwide planned birth policy in the largest country in the world. Bush's effort to placate anti-China Republicans in Congress could amount, perversely, to a free pass to a fifth of the world's population. The effects of the order were unmistakable; in 1992 political asylum was granted to roughly 85 percent of the undocumented Chinese immigrants who requested it, a rate almost three times higher than for immigrants from other countries. "The Fujianese thank two people," a Chinatown real estate broker who emigrated in the 1980s observed. "One is Cheng Chui Ping. And one is George Bush the father."

Word of the change in American policy spread to the smallest villages of rural Fujian. If you could set foot on American soil, even if you had phony documents, or no documents at all, no matter how obvious it was that you had made the trip illegally, you were entitled to a hearing of your asylum claims. And if you uttered the words *one-child policy* and rehearsed a tale of woe—a tale the snakeheads began coaching their passengers to commit to memory and recite on command—there was a good chance the Americans would let you stay. The other word of choice was *democracy,* and many Fujianese who had never felt any particular commitment to democratic freedoms, who had never been to Tiananmen Square or even to Beijing, claimed that they or their friends or their family members had played some role in the protests. It was said in New York's Chinatown that some of the actual student leaders from Beijing, who had been offered asylum and prestigious fellowships at universities in the United States, would come to town from time to time to make a little money, charging would-be asylees a few hundred dollars to pose alongside them for Polaroid pictures, which could then be included in an application as proof of involvement in the democracy movement. The number of Chinese nationals arriving at JFK Airport in New York who requested asylum jumped from 205 in 1988 to 1,287 in 1990—an increase of over 500 percent—and continued to grow. The peculiar dynamics of America's abortion politics that created the loophole were of little interest to the emigrants. What mattered was getting to America and making your claim. The Fujianese countryside was suddenly gripped by a fever to leave, an epidemic of outmigration. "Everybody went crazy," a *Sing Tao Daily* journalist reported from Fuzhou in the mid-nineties. "The area was in a frenzy. Farmers put down their tools, students discarded their books, workers quit their jobs, and everybody was talking about nothing but going to America."

Over the past half-century, more refugees have found new homes in America than in any other country in the world. In the past thirty-five years alone the United States has welcomed some 2.6 million people fleeing famine, persecution, and upheaval. In fact, of the top thirteen countries accepting refugees in 2005, the United States took in two times as many refugees as the next twelve countries on the list combined. Haunted by the memory of the *St. Louis,* an ocean liner carrying nearly a thousand Jewish refugees that came within sight of Florida during the spring of 1939, only to be turned away by the United States and sent back to Europe, where many of the passengers subsequently perished in the Holocaust, the United States has at least in principle embraced the notion of asylum. But the system for determining who should or should not be granted refuge in the United States was codified only in 1980, when Congress passed a sweeping new refugee law in response to a surge of displaced people from around the world—Haitians, Soviet Jews, Southeast Asians unmoored by the wars in Cambodia and Vietnam. More people were seeking permanent resettlement outside their homelands in 1979 than at any time since the end of the Second World War. With the Refugee Act of 1980, Congress replaced a system that had been largely ad hoc and prone to favor refugees from some countries over others with a uniform test: anyone who could show a "well-founded fear" of persecution in the country they were fleeing would be eligible for resettlement in the United States.

Still, in drafting the new law, the legislators focused primarily on refugees outside the United States who might bring their claims to American embassies abroad. They were less concerned with asylum-seekers—people who have already managed to get to America and ask for legal refuge once they've arrived. The law envisioned admitting some 50,000 refugees per year, but it projected only 5,000 asylum cases. Almost immediately it became clear that this was an extreme underestimate. Just as the law came into force, the Mariel boat lift was transporting tens of thousands of Cubans to Miami in the spring and summer of 1980. That event alone generated 50,000 requests for asylum. Within three years authorities were contending with a backlog of 170,000 asylum applications from people from 53 different countries. By the time the Bush executive order made China's one-child policy a ground for asylum in the United States, America's immigration system was already flooded with nearly 100,000 new applications each year, and the accumulated backlog of unresolved asylum claims had reached a quarter of a million cases.

The backlog meant that new arrivals could not have their asylum applications processed immediately. If you showed up at an American airport in the early 1990s and explained that you didn't have a passport or visa but you wanted to apply for asylum, it took a minimum of four months before you actually had a preliminary hearing in front of a judge, and it was often over a year after that before the actual facts of your case were heard. Immigration officials didn't have the resources to detain asylum-seekers during this protracted process, so they issued undocumented arrivals with work authorization forms, asked them to report to a judge on a given date, and sent them on their way. Many of them never showed up to have their claims heard, walking out of the airport and disappearing into the underground economy.

The INS had historically been a kind of stepchild of American law enforcement—terminally understaffed and underfunded, painfully jealous of its sibling agency, Customs, which seemed flush with cash by comparison (because all those seizures actually *made* money), and generally embittered about the Sisyphean nature of the work it was asked to do. Gene McNary, who ran the INS from 1989 to 1993, described it as "the agency that nobody cared about—dumped on, dirty-faced kids." The INS was laughably unprepared for the sudden onrush of asylum-seekers. Where the smugglers ran sophisticated transnational operations, with ever-evolving distribution networks, transshipment points in corrupt Central American countries, savvy Fujianese strategists who studied and exploited American immigration law, and liaisons and brokers from Beijing to Bangkok to Boston, the INS was cash-strapped and plodding, hidebound and hierarchical. At an organizational level, the agency was the exact opposite of the snakeheads: in its focus, activities, and sphere of influence, it was a domestic law enforcement agency striving for relevance in a world of global migration flows. And above all it was slow to change, unable to adapt to circumstances as they evolved.

Bill Slattery, the INS's district director for New York, complained bitterly about America's asylum policies, arguing that the Chinese were taking advantage of a forgiving system. Like many immigration officials who encountered the surge of Chinese asylum-seekers at first hand, Slattery worried that Bush's executive order had created a magnet for illegal immigration—an opportunity so irresistible that it would lure potential migrants who might otherwise never have left China. When he took the job in New York, in 1990, he looked over the records for the previous year and was outraged to learn that of the four thousand "inadmissibles" intercepted at Kennedy Airport, only eighty-seven had ultimately been deported. "The aliens have taken control," he warned. "The Third World has packed its bag, and it's moving."

Slattery thought of the asylum seekers at JFK as a "swarm"—a calculated ensemble maneuver, designed to overwhelm the United States. He wanted to begin summarily excluding any asylum applicants from China who had come to America by way of a third country. After all, the snakehead routes often brought migrants through numerous cities in Asia, Europe, or South America before they reached the United States. If they were really fleeing tyranny in China, why not stay in one of those intermediate locations? "If I have someone from China who has been through six or seven countries before finally asking for asylum when they hit JFK, I don't see why I should have to admit them," he told a reporter in 1993.

If a certain xenophobia seemed to lurk around the edges of Slattery's public pronouncements during those years, it was also the case that he was panicked, and justifiably so, by the migration explosion he was witnessing and being asked to contain. At JFK, the fluorescent-lit lobbies and grubby linoleum floors were overrun with undocumented arrivals. Twelve million people passed through the airport every year, roughly half of them not U.S. citizens. Out of those, the INS identified some eight thousand illegal immigrants in 1991, or more than twenty each day. That was just the number they caught; there were surely many more who managed to slip by undetected. And by 1992 the number apprehended nearly doubled. Many of the Chinese who arrived did so with no documents at all, having trashed their passports and visas in the airplane bathroom, knowing that it would be harder for U.S. authorities to turn them away if they arrived without a passport denoting their country of origin or a visa for their destination. Immigration officials called them "flushers." Who could the United States return them to? "Prove to us that they're Chinese," Beijing would say when the INS tried to turn over inadmissibles from China. "There are ethnic Chinese all over the world. How do we know these come from China?" Each time an arrival was found to have improper documents or no documents at all, the airline that brought him was fined $3,000. In 1992 the United States fined airlines $20 million for delivering undocumented or badly documented passengers to U.S. airports. Half of those passengers came through JFK.

The airport had a small immigration detention facility, a bleak converted warehouse run by a private company, but the space had just over a hundred beds. So even inadmissibles who had clearly arrived illegally tended to be released pending resolution of their asylum claims. "It's not like they're trying to avoid apprehension," Slattery would complain. "They know they're going to be intercepted at the airport, and they also recognize that we're not going to be able to hold them." Someone could arrive at JFK without a passport, request political asylum, and be sent on his way, all within a matter of hours. The snakeheads knew this. They coached their customers to tear up their passports before they touched down in New York and to demand asylum at the airport. They were so confident in this routine that they would show up at the airport to meet the customers and brazenly hang out in the arrivals lounge of the international terminal. The snakeheads were easy to spot: they all carried cell phones, still an uncommon accoutrement in the early 1990s.

Immigration officials marveled at the tenacity and adaptability of the Fujianese; Mexican border-crossers, the traditional targets of the INS and the Border Patrol, looked hopelessly amateur by comparison. The Fujianese flew into JFK, into Toronto, into Vancouver, San Diego, San Francisco. When they couldn't fly directly to North America, they obtained visas, and often passports, from corrupt Central American way stations where the snakeheads had developed a stronghold—Belize,

Guatemala, Panama—and flew there, then crossed the border in Texas, Arizona, or California. One Hong Kong triad, the Sun Yee On, was said to have arranged an operation in which its members chartered jets and sent whole planeloads of illegal Chinese to Belize, from which they could continue overland through Mexico. Authorities referred to this operation as "the Chinese charter." INS agents often heard stories about Chinese migrants crossing the border from Mexico, but their apprehension rate of Chinese was always very low compared to that of the Mexicans they stopped every day. One reason for this, it emerged, was that snakeheads at the border were paying poor Mexicans to run across en masse as a diversionary tactic to tie up the authorities while the Fujianese migrants strolled across unnoticed. By the 1990s, the smuggling fee for Fujianese was $30,000; a few hundred dollars for the Mexicans, who were happy to take the money and get caught, only to be released back into Mexico and cross another day, was a sensible operational expense.

It is the nature of illicit economies that their numbers are incredibly imprecise, and it may be impossible to arrive at any reliable tabulation of the number of Fujianese who came to the United States illegally in the years after Tiananmen Square. But even the low estimates are extraordinary. In the midnineties, a federal working group on Chinese human smuggling concluded that some 50,000 Fujianese were coming illegally every year. But James Woolsey, who was director of the CIA at that time, told Congress that the number of Chinese being smuggled in each year was closer to 100,000. One senior immigration official said in the early nineties that "at any given time, thirty thousand Chinese are stashed away in safe houses around the world, waiting for entry" to the United States. Sources within China's own Public Security Bureau put that number at half a million: 15,000 in Ho Chi Minh City, 25,000 in Bangkok, 10,000 in Brazil, and so on. The NYPD estimated that in the New York area alone, some three hundred safe houses were holding recently arrived illegals. One expert on the snakehead trade told a Senate subcommittee that by the early nineties the business was bringing in

$3.2 billion a year. (That would make it roughly comparable to the Gap or Sun Microsystems during the same period.) Other estimates place the annual revenue from the snakehead trade much higher; some officials eventually suggested that the industry brought in as much as $7 billion a year. According to Peter Kwong, a leading scholar of American Chinatowns and the history of the Chinese in America, the largest number of illegal Chinese in history entered the United States between 1988 and 1993.

One beneficiary of America's new asylum policy toward the Chinese was Ah Kay. After he was deported to China and then returned to New York, authorities attempted to deport him again, in 1991. But he applied for political asylum on the grounds that he had somehow been affiliated with the pro-democracy movement in China, and remarkably, despite being a convicted felon who had already been deported once, he was released and permitted to stay in the country while the authorities evaluated his claims.

On his journey back to America after the first deportation, Ah Kay had traveled via Belize, where he encountered a Taiwanese smuggler named Lo Cho. Lo Cho's particular specialty was boats. It is not entirely clear when the snakeheads first started using boats to transport customers to the United States. Most people in New York's Chinatown date the advent of boat smuggling to the early 1990s, and the first boat that was apprehended by U.S. authorities was a Taiwanese fishing trawler, the *I-Mao No. 306,* which was captured off the coast of Southern California in 1991 with 118 Chinese on board. But an INS Anti-Smuggling Unit memo from 1985 indicated that even at that point migrants were traveling from China "by cargo ship to the western coast of Mexico."

To the snakeheads, humans were ultimately a form of cargo like any other, subject to the economies of scale. Sending passengers on planes meant paying for expensive tickets and for legitimate or fraudulent passports and visas. In some cases, a snakehead who charged $25,000 to send a customer by plane ended up netting only $5,000 after covering all the relevant expenses. When the snakeheads realized that Fujianese demand for passage to America was so insatiable that they could oblige their customers to forgo the comforts of economy class for conditions that better resembled freight and shift the business from a retail model to a wholesale one—without actually lowering the going $30,000 rate—they turned to boats. Specifically, to Taiwanese boats. Fishing vessels had been smuggling people and goods back and forth across the strait between Fujian and Taiwan for centuries, and the shift to maritime human smuggling was facilitated by a Taiwanese connection.

Nobody knows how organized or centralized the Taiwanese were, and rumors persist on the streets of Chinatown and in law enforcement circles about faceless, nameless Taiwanese kingpins who sent a flotilla of smuggling ships to the United States and pocketed a disproportionate share of the profits, but who were sophisticated and politically connected enough to avoid capture, or even identification, by authorities. What is clear is that while the boats may have flown different flags and found their way to ports around the world, most of them started life as fishing vessels in Taiwan. Some have connected the advent of boat smuggling to Taiwan's agreement in 1991 to a ban on drift-net fishing, which left a fleet of oceangoing vessels suddenly obsolete, unable to perform their traditional function and ripe for reassignment. The snakeheads called the boats "buckets," in a nod to the unadorned utility of the vessels they favored. To get a bucket, you saw the "bucket man." And the bucket men were all from Taiwan.

The year that the bucket business really took off was 1992, and while many snakeheads made the switch to ships for purely economic reasons, others were obliged to adapt their smuggling routes by using ships for a more pressing logistical reason: they could no longer get customers onto airplanes. During the years immediately following Tiananmen, snakeheads had relied on a great deal of official corruption at the international airport in Bangkok. Thailand is extravagantly corrupt even by the standards of Southeast Asia, and the snakeheads had no trouble finding officials at the airport who would turn a blind eye to travel documents that were obviously phony. The situation was somewhat comical: you could walk into the departures hall at Bangkok Airport and see eight ticket windows without any line at all and a long line of Chinese travellers waiting patiently at the ninth, where the official was on the take. By 1992, U.S. authorities were encountering so many fraudulent documents on incoming flights from Thailand that they dispatched additional personnel to Bangkok to monitor their counterparts. American officials would perform "operation disrupts," observing the Thai ticket-takers to make sure no fake passports were getting through and obliging the attendants to shuffle stations every twenty minutes so that snakeheads could not simply count on sending their customers to a designated window. American document experts worked alongside the Thais, examining any passport or visa that didn't look legitimate.

Until that point Bangkok had been a kind of gateway to America; if you could make it from China to Bangkok, you could make it to the United States. People undertook long journeys to reach the city, and would wait in fetid safe houses in Bangkok's Chinatown until they were able to board an airplane. But when authorities cracked down at the airport, a bottleneck developed. Many snakeheads had gone to great lengths to get people to Bangkok. The business was a pipeline, and there were always customers at different stages of the route. With the bottleneck suddenly clogged, the safe houses in Bangkok started filling up with people, sometimes as many as thirty, crammed into small spaces, waiting for their flight out.

The solution was boats. In the past, snakeheads had flown their customers to Central America and used boats to transfer them north, into the United States. But with thousands of passengers accumulating in Bangkok, the smugglers improvised and began using ships to undertake the entire journey. Between August 1991 and July 1993, thirty-four ships carrying as many as 5,300 Chinese were found in waters near Japan, Taiwan, Indonesia, Australia, Singapore, Haiti, Guatemala, El

Salvador, Honduras, and the United States. And those were the boats that were found; an untold number of others boarded passengers in the Gulf of Thailand and bore them around the world, releasing them, undetected, on U.S. shores.

It was typical of Ah Kay's entrepreneurial approach that when he moved the Fuk Ching gang into the smuggling business, he began not by offering customers anything resembling a full-service operation but by identifying and embracing a lucrative niche and offering his services as a subcontractor to more established snakeheads. Dating back to 1989, the gang had gone into business as hired muscle who could force derelict immigrants to pay their fees. But Ah Kay had watched Lo Cho running a boat smuggling operation from Belize, and he had spent the early months of the snakehead boom in prison, where he was able to contemplate the best manner in which to enter the industry. Sailing a ship full of undocumented migrants directly to the coast of the United States was a risky proposition: the ship would attract the attention of the Coast Guard; hundreds of Chinese people disembarking from a decrepit freighter at a crowded marina had a tendency to raise alarms. A more cautious approach was to sail to a point several hundred miles off the coast of the United States, in international waters, and transfer the passengers to smaller, less conspicuous fishing boats, which could ferry them to shore.

Ah Kay called the process "offloading," and after his release from prison he made contact with Vietnamese refugees who lived along the East Coast and had access to fishing boats. Then he put the word out in Chinatown, offering his services to snakeheads who had ships coming in. "We [would] send out fishing boats to make contact with the larger boat," Ah Kay later explained. "We would wait until the big wave rise and then, you know, the level of the fishing boat would come up, and at that moment the people from the big boat would jump over to the small boat." In the dark of night, in the open sea, it was a haphazard, often perilous exercise. Occasionally a passenger would jump over and fail to land securely on the smaller boat, clinging to the side as the two boats heaved and swayed, nearly getting crushed as their bows bashed together.

By the summer of 1992 the gang had successfully offloaded several ships for New York–based snakeheads. They had been paying the Vietnamese $200,000 for their help each time, and Ah Kay sent an underling to Florida to purchase a boat for the gang, so they could cut out the subcontractor and "control the business" up and down the East Coast. Ah Kay was ferociously ambitious, and in the snakehead business he sensed a perfect opportunity: a service that, while not uncomplicated, required only one or two high-IQ masterminds and a great deal of low-skilled labor; a potentially unlimited market of customers in China, who seemed happy to endure any hardship and promise any fee in exchange for a new life in America. His goal, he told one associate, was to make $100 million in the snakehead business. "I'm not boasting," he said. "It's already in progress. If I was boasting, I'd say this business will make a billion."

Ah Kay was living in an apartment on Hester Street, not far from the shop Sister Ping had used as her base of operations throughout the 1980s. One day in August 1992 he was visited by a man named Wang Kong Fu, who came from Yingyu village, where Ah Kay grew up. It was hot, and the two men went to the rooftop to talk. Wang said he had come on behalf of Sister Ping. She understood Ah Kay had been "successful with boats." She had a ship coming in and wanted Ah Kay to offload it.

Sister Ping's fortunes had not suffered, nor had her business slowed down, after her conviction in Buffalo. A month after the raft sank on the Niagara River, Ping and Yick Tak filed a new business certificate for their shop. This time they offered a different translation for the name: "Everything will come out fine." But one price Sister Ping paid for her encounter with law enforcement was publicity. She had long been known within New York's Chinatown and in the villages of Fujian as an especially capable snakehead, but she had enjoyed a certain obscurity when it came to the larger community in New York. In 1990 a Chinatown journalist named Ying Chan, who had worked for several of New York's Chinese-language dailies, coauthored an investigative series for the *Daily News* that exposed Sister Ping and her operation. Under the headline "Merchants of Misery," the story described Ping and Yick Tak. "The couple portray themselves as respected shop owners and devoted parents of four," the article suggested, but in reality they are "an efficient business team who managed to stay one step ahead of authorities." Chan traveled to Fujian and interviewed a local Communist Party official from a farming village near Shengmei, who told her he wanted Sister Ping to send his youngest son to America. "She's the best," the official said. "She delivers." The Fujianese Chan encountered had heard about Sister Ping's legal troubles, but their desire to hire her was undiminished; she had more customers than she could handle. The piece included a photograph of the family mansion in Shengmei, and another of Sister Ping dressed in a gaudy plaid blazer and a black skirt, one hand shielding her face from the camera.

Sister Ping was angered by the coverage. She had always worked hard to maintain a low profile, and she feared that she was being unfairly portrayed, not as a local entrepreneur who was helping out her family and fellow villagers but as a "devil woman." But there was nothing she could do. The world outside of Chinatown was becoming aware of her activities. By 1991 a Senate subcommittee investigating Asian organized crime named Sister Ping as a prominent snakehead in Chinatown and found that she was "alleged to have amassed a personal fortune of over $30 million from alien smuggling."

Shortly after Ah Kay and Wang Kong Fu met on the Chinatown rooftop, Sister Ping telephoned Ah Kay. The two had not interacted since the burglaries back in the eighties, and Ah Kay hastened to apologize. "Sorry, Sister Ping," he said. "Everyone has their past."

Remarkably, Ping didn't seem angry. "That's what happened in the past," she said. "We're talking business now."

Her boat was due to arrive soon, off the coast of Boston, she explained. She wanted to know if Ah Kay's method for offloading customers was safe. He told her it was. She agreed to pay the gang three quarters of a million dollars for the job.

A few weeks later Sister Ping called with a walkie-talkie number, so that the Fuk Ching could make contact directly with the crew of the ship. Again she asked for Ah Kay's assurances that the offloading would be safe. Money was not the issue, she explained. She could pay him more if necessary.

"No need," Ah Kay said.

On the night of September 21, 1992, Ah Kay's deputy Cho Yee Yeung boarded a fishing boat for the 200-mile trip into the North Atlantic. He took bread, water, and a gun. The sea was calm; there was no wind, and Cho had no trouble arriving at the rendezvous point, where a ship full of immigrants was waiting. The passengers were desperate, fighting to get off the ship and onto Cho's fishing boat. He fired his gun in the air and told them to be calm; "I did not want any accidents to happen," he would later say. There were over a hundred passengers, and Cho forced them at gunpoint into the fish hold of the smaller boat, a cramped, dark, smelly space. The journey back to shore took over twenty hours; the fish hold was not ventilated, and some of the passengers fainted in the heat. Cho splashed water on their faces to revive them.

The night after the pickup at sea, a security guard named John Marcelino was on duty at Homer's Wharf, an outcropping of wood-planked landings lined with fishing boats and yachts in the gritty former whaling port of New Bedford, Massachusetts. Shortly before midnight, Marcelino saw a fishing boat enter the harbor and come to a stop alongside several vessels tied up by the pier. Normally when a fishing boat came in, it was all commotion and noise—wives and girlfriends thronging the wharf, rowdy sailors happy to be home, the hasty effort to unload the fresh catch. But there was no one waiting onshore for this boat, and it floated there silently in the dark for forty-five minutes.

Then, as Marcelino watched, three U-Haul trucks approached the pier. Suddenly he saw activity on the fishing boat. Dark figures materialized on the deck—many of them—scrambling out of the fish hold, clambering onto the wharf, then disappearing into the U-Hauls. They each carried a piece of luggage. Marcelino called the police. But before they could arrive, the last of the people left the boat and boarded the trucks, and the three U-Hauls started their engines and left the wharf. Marcelino couldn't wait on the cops, so he decided to follow the trucks. He drove after them at a distance and saw that they were headed for the highway. He pursued them north on Route 18, then west on 195. The trucks were traveling fast, but not conspicuously so. The roads were nearly empty at that late hour, and as he followed on 195, Marcelino saw the trucks suddenly slow down. They must have spotted him on their tail. He kept his pace, pulling alongside one of the U-Hauls. Marcelino looked into the passenger-side window. Two Asian men stared straight back at him. Then, as Marcelino looked at them, the one on the passenger side lifted something up to the window. It was a submachine gun. Marcelino veered his car away and got off at the next exit.

The U-Hauls proceeded south, reaching New York around dawn. They drove to a warehouse in Greenpoint, Brooklyn, where Ah Kay was waiting for them. Various Fuk Ching members hurried the passengers out of the trucks and into the warehouse, and Ah Kay telephoned Sister Ping to inform her that the offloading had been successful. Sister Ping was pleased. She sent Yick Tak to the warehouse to meet the passengers. For Ah Kay she prepared a red envelope containing $38,000—a bonus for a job well done.

When the FBI began investigating Fujianese organized crime in the United States, they found that it differed in several fundamental ways from the paradigms they had developed over decades of studying the Sicilian Mafia. Chinese organized criminals did not adhere to any fixed hierarchies or organizational structures. The original Chinese triads had been steeped in secret ritual and byzantine codes of conduct and allegiance, but there were no blood oaths among the Asian gangs in America. Rather, Chinatown's heroin dealers and human smugglers, its racket men and pimps, thought of themselves as entrepreneurs and opportunists, driven above all by a mercenary sense of self-interest and by the exigencies of circumstance. Family loyalty may have been a deep and enduring bond among the Fujianese, but extrafamilial loyalties didn't make sense from a business point of view. Alliances and coalitions were fluid, ever-evolving. An assortment of underworld types might come together in a temporary joint venture in order to move a shipment full of migrants or China White, but then they would split up and go their separate ways, looking for the next promising opportunity. The flip side of this dynamic was that while loyalty was bad for business, grudges were as well. And that may in part explain how it was that Sister Ping found herself in business with Ah Kay, a violent youth who had robbed her twice and threatened the lives of her children.

Changing circumstances could mean changing loyalties, and after the success of the New Bedford ship, Sister Ping developed a complicated partnership with Ah Kay and the Fuk Ching gang. She would later claim that she had been a victim—that the gang terrorized Chinatown and that everyone was forced to make allowances for them and be tainted by their activities in ways large and small. But Sister Ping prized efficiency, and when Ah Kay performed capably and efficiently, she appears to have forgiven his past offenses—and the kinds of risks entailed in his high-profile, high-liability criminal behavior—in order to work with him. Prosecutors would later describe Ah Kay as her "hired gun," to suggest not that he killed on her behalf but that she could subcontract her muscle and logistics to him, that he was paid handsomely to do the snakehead's bidding. Before long she was offering Fuk Ching members a discounted rate for sending money back to China. As Ah Kay saw it, he and Sister Ping became "good friends."

Still, it must have seemed strange to Ah Kay that Sister Ping had so readily forgiven his transgressions. It must have seemed to him that Sister Ping's paramount devotion to her own business was what let him off the hook. She had ships coming in, and he could offload ships. Expediency can pardon a multitude of sins.

But expediency works in a number of ways. What Ah Kay did not know when he and Sister Ping went into business is that she had already enacted a quiet revenge. What none of Sister Ping's clients and associates in Chinatown realized, in fact, was that after her release from prison, she continued to meet with Peter Lee, the young Cantonese American FBI agent, in out-of-the-way coffee shops and restaurants in New York, and give him information. Lee eventually terminated the relationship, after realizing that she was anything but reformed. And the FBI has since downplayed the information Sister Ping provided, suggesting that she did not furnish its agents with anything of value. But it has also been suggested that she used the young and naive Lee, feeding him information on her rivals in the snakehead trade. During the period when Ah Kay was getting into the smuggling business, Sister Ping was meeting with Peter Lee. He would quiz her about Chinatown gangs and snakeheads and show her surveillance photographs, asking her to identify various figures captured in the glossy black-and-whites. And there was one explanation for Sister Ping's willingness to forgive Ah Kay—a little betrayal of her own, about which he would never know. Sister Ping was giving information about Ah Kay to the FBI.

Book II

Chapter Seven

Mombasa

SEAN CHEN stood in the scorching African sun and surveyed the port of Mombasa, Kenya. Everything about the place was exotic, every sight and smell different from the village outside Fuzhou where he had grown up. That stretch of East African coast had been a hub of Indian Ocean trade for the better part of a thousand years, frigates crisscrossing its waters, laden with ivory, gold, and slaves. The coastline was dominated by the sixteenth-century stone fortifications of Fort Jesus, a relic of the Portuguese, who had come, and ruled, and left. The skyline was punctuated by the minarets of mosques. Sean had come ashore with some friends briefly and wandered through the labyrinthine alleys of the old town, past the little stalls where black women sold basketware and jewelry, past buckets full of vegetables and dates, past solicitous hawkers rattling on in the strange cadences of Swahili and mysterious women swathed in black *abayas*. The air was ripe with the unfamiliar smells of spices from the spice shops, of Arab coffee, of samosas and kebabs. Sean wondered about his family. He hadn't seen them in over a year. It was January 1993. He was eighteen years old.

Sean was short and slight but carried himself like a larger man, strutting a little when he walked and projecting a certain toughness; he was a bruiser, with a temper, and he certainly wouldn't allow his diminutive stature to let anyone think otherwise. His head was ovular, like a snub-nosed bullet, and he had a strong, square jaw and dark eyes that were round and small. He grew up outside Fuzhou, in Changle, where his father taught at a local high school. Sean lived with his parents and two younger brothers in an apartment at the school. He was a rebellious child, stubborn and independent. In May 1989, when he was fourteen, he joined a cousin who was organizing pro-democracy students at Fuzhou University. The police investigated the group and branded Sean as a counterrevolutionary, which led to his expulsion from school. Sean's father was mild-mannered, and somewhat meek in the face of authority. His passivity angered his more voluble son. Because Sean's parents had violated the one-child policy twice over, local officials fined his father, dropping by the school periodically to demand payment from the family. Village cadres ruled with impunity in small-town China, and Sean's father paid and paid again, but there was nothing he could do to satisfy the debt; he was forced to keep paying each time the officials demanded it.

One day in 1991 a local education official visited the family and said that Sean's father owed 5,000 yuan. He didn't have the money, and Sean grew angry and shouted at the official. The official shouted back, and Sean grew angrier. Then, without knowing what he was doing, really, he lashed out, his right fist connecting with the official's face. The official staggered backward, startled—and then furious. He went after Sean, but Sean's father stood between them, apologizing profusely and preventing the official from striking his son. Eventually the official stormed off, but the family was in a panic. Sean had insulted a powerful man, and with three children in a one-child system, the family was already at the mercy of the local government.

Sean's father had taught a generation of children who had gone on to various jobs in the area, and after the incident with the official, a former student who now worked with the police paid the family a visit. He said that Sean was being targeted for arrest. There was no telling what he would be charged with or how long he would be held. His father might lose his job, and if Sean was locked up, there would be no one to support the family. It was decided: Sean would journey to America. The family made a down payment to a local snakehead. Sean's parents gave him 3,000 yuan; they didn't have any U.S. dollars. The snakehead told him they would travel overland through Burma to Thailand and then by plane from Bangkok to the United States. Sean placed some extra T-shirts and underwear in a small backpack; he had few belongings and wanted to travel light. Then he bid his parents farewell and set out for Yunnan Province, near the border with Burma. He embarked on the trip without any documents—no passport, no visas, not even a driver's license or ID of any sort. After several days he reached the southwestern city of Kunming. There he met with another group of snakeheads. The snake, as the route is sometimes called, is actually a long relay, in which customers are passed from hand to hand, escorted each step of the way by local subcontractors. Close to the border, Sean connected with several local snakeheads who shepherded him, along with several other Chinese customers, across the wire fences and into Burma.

Kunming was the great jumping-off point for Chinese fleeing the country in those days. In order to reach Thailand, migrants had to trek over the dense jungle-covered mountains of eastern Burma, through tangled undergrowth and malarial swamps, into remote stretches inhabited only by hill tribes and ultimately across the opium country of the Golden Triangle, where the borders of Burma, Thailand, and Laos converge. This was Burma's isolated Shan State, which was administered as a kind of renegade principality by Khun Sa, the fearsome warlord turned drug runner who was known as the Prince of Death. Khun Sa was nominally the world's most wanted man—American drug officials estimated that he produced 60 percent of the world's heroin. But he had little to fear. ("When the DEA gives the Thais money, they come and attack me," he once joked. "When I give them money, they go away again.") Khun Sa's army of 20,000 men roamed the countryside, and his mountain ponies formed a long caravan through the jungle, bearing opium and morphine base to refineries on the Thai border, where it could be converted into heroin.

Sean joined another clandestine caravan, of Chinese migrants headed for Thailand, who stole across the poppy fields by night, dodging the roving searchlights of Khun Sa. Burma was wild country, sweltering hot and humid during the day, then perishing cold at night, the air aswarm with mosquitoes, the soaring trees draped with thick curtains of tangled vines. The battering monsoon rains churned the ground into mud, and the path was unmarked by any kind of signage. Sean's group split up, with the older men taking a slower, less arduous route and the younger ones taking a more direct but difficult one. The local snakeheads in the area had developed some ingenious methods for getting their customers across the hostile terrain. When they had to traverse a treacherous river, they would send a scout across first, carrying a length of rope. When he reached the other side, they would thread the rope through the center of a length of bamboo, which the travelers could cling to as they went across the rapids. Still, it was not unusual for these small expeditionary groups to get lost, or to run out of water or provisions in the mountains. For many Chinese, the journey to the Golden Mountain ended before they had even made it to Thailand; they succumbed to exhaustion or malnutrition, malaria, or some other unnamed tropical malady. It was not uncommon for Fujianese trekkers making their way over the mountains to pass the bodies of others who had preceded them, laid out by the side of the jungle path, their corpses draped in banana leaves.

When they had been in Burma for less than a week, the group stopped at a small hill station buried deep in the jungle, because the snakeheads had not managed to get money to the Burmese guides. The station was ruled by a local warlord named Lian, who dressed and acted like a military man and ruled a small irregular army in the forest but had no loyalty to the Burmese army and operated the area as a personal fief. Lian took a liking to Sean and let him stay in his own wooden house, which was larger and more comfortable than the other accommodations in the camp. Lian was ethnic Chinese and spoke Mandarin but had lived in Burma his whole life. He never said as much, but Sean was certain he was running drugs. Lian had two older brothers in prison in Thailand for carrying heroin across the border, and in that corner of the world, with the porous jungle borders of China and Thailand so close, Sean figured there wasn't any way to make a living but to dabble in the drug trade.

The camp was so secluded that for weeks the snakeheads were unable to send money so that Sean and his companions could continue their journey. Lian did not seem to mind having them in the village. He had a sister a few years younger than Sean who was as yet unmarried. She had dark eyes and very pale, milky skin. Sean thought she was beautiful. Because it grew so cold at night and the camp had no electricity, everyone from the surrounding area would gather when dark fell and huddle around a big communal bonfire. Sean and Lian's sister would flirt and exchange glances across the flickering flames. He wondered what life would be like if he stayed in the camp, marrying Lian's sister and becoming a brother to him. But it was only a passing thought. Deep in the jungles of Burma, Sean knew he had only one destination: New York, a metropolis he could scarcely imagine, a world more remote from this jungle dwelling than any place on earth.

Eventually the money came and a new set of Burmese guides prepared to walk Sean and the others to the border with Thailand. Before Sean left, Lian summoned him to say farewell. He handed Sean a gun, for his safety. It was a small handgun of German make. Sean hid it in his backpack. They set out, traveling sometimes by foot, sometimes in the back of a covered truck. There were checkpoints along the road, but the guides knew where they were located. When the truck was a mile from a checkpoint, it would stop and Sean and the others would get out and make their way around the checkpoint in the jungle so the empty truck could pass through the inspection, only to pick up the travelers on the other side.

It took Sean and his companions over a month to get to Thailand. When they reached the border area, one of the Burmese guides demanded that they turn over more money, saying that the trip had taken longer than anticipated. Sean objected, angrily pointing out that they all had contracts with their snakeheads; any dispute over the fees should be raised not with the customers but with them. Besides, he added, none of the customers had any money. The guide shouted back, and the argument escalated until the guide suddenly pulled out a gun and pointed it at Sean's head. Just as quickly, Sean reached into his backpack, produced Lian's gun, and pointed it back at the guide. For a long, intense moment Sean and the guide stood there. Then the Thai smuggler who controlled the area intervened, separating the two of them and confiscating Sean's gun.

In the border town of Chiang Rai, wedged between Burma and Laos, they met a bus that drove them the final 500 miles to Bangkok. It was the biggest city Sean had ever seen. He thought that it looked like Hong Kong, or at any rate, the way he imagined Hong Kong looked. Some people in Changle and Fuzhou drove cars, but not many; most people still got around by bicycle. But Bangkok was one sprawling, snarling traffic jam—cars, buses, motorcycles, and *tuk-tuk* taxis, choking smog and blaring horns. Soaring high-rises glittered in the sun along the curling banks of the muddy Chao Phraya River. Among the elevated highways and the stolid apartment blocks of chipped concrete the occasional colorful temple would protrude, the glimmering gold curvature of its roof like a licking flame.

Sean was taken to a studio apartment in a high-rise building, which he was to share with three other people. Several other apartments in the building were leased by snakeheads; sometimes it seemed that the whole establishment was full of Chinese passengers waiting to go to America. It was February 1992, and the crackdown at the Bangkok Airport had just begun. The snakeheads informed Sean that they were experiencing delays and that it might be some time before they could get him on an airplane. To further complicate matters, they were having trouble finding phony documents for Sean, because he looked so young. The source of most black market passports was travelers who were in their twenties or older, and Sean looked younger even than the teenager he still was.

A more mature, responsible traveler might have become concerned at this point, and some of Sean's fellow passengers did grow uneasy as the prospect of the final flight to America became uncertain and they found themselves stranded in a foreign city with no way forward, no way home, and little money to spare. They had families to support, and every month they languished in Bangkok was a month they were not sending money back to Fujian. But Sean was a teenager with an independent streak who was away from home for the first time. He telephoned a cousin in the United States to get some money wired to him and decided to make the most of his time in the city. He didn't worry about his predicament; on the contrary, he felt excited, liberated, and thrilled to be young and exposed to Bangkok in all its vibrancy and sordid glitz. Some snakeheads kept a close watch on their customers, confining them to the safe houses for weeks at a stretch. Thai police officers demanded kickbacks in return for not reporting safe houses full of migrants, and when those payments were late the cops would launch a raid, throwing the Fujianese into filthy Thai jails, where they were held for weeks or months, suffering beatings and contracting contagious skin diseases from the other inmates in their cells. But Sean's snakeheads must have paid their bribes in a timely fashion, because he was not hassled by the police, and they permitted him to come and go as he pleased, knowing, perhaps, that he wanted above all to get to the United States, and that because he needed them in order to do that, he was unlikely to disappear. He ventured out and explored the city—the frantic street life, the Bacchic nightlife, the moneyed tourists from around the world. It may have been limbo, but to Sean it felt like a bizarre, extended vacation. He got hold of a Chinese-English dictionary and spent the days reading through it, learning the language he knew he would need in America. He made solitary trips to the movies.

Five months had passed in this manner, with the possibility of a flight out receding every day, when the snakeheads told Sean that there was another option. A ship was coming to the Gulf of Thailand. Chinese customers who were waiting to get on planes were all being offered the option of traveling to America by ship instead. It was a big ship, the snakeheads explained. The voyage would take a month at most. Sean didn't have to go, they told him. He could stay in Bangkok if he wanted. But they didn't know when they would be able to get him on a plane.

Sean needed little persuading. It sounded like an adventure. On the evening of July 16, 1992, he boarded a tour bus in Bangkok with dozens of other people—Chinese men and women of various ages, Fujianese like him, some looking about them curiously after months cooped up in a safe house, most toting a single item of luggage. The buses headed south, wending their way along an elevated highway until the apartment blocks and the high-rises fell away and they reached a palm-fringed stretch of beach on the Gulf of Thailand. There were other buses there, and hundreds of passengers—240 all together—assembled on the beach before a small fleet of fishing boats that bobbed quietly on the water. They boarded the boats and headed out to sea, where Sean saw a massive vessel awaiting them, a 370-foot ferry with two long decks wrapping around it. The ship's hull was painted red and bore a name in white letters: *Najd II.*

Many snakeheads were represented on the *Najd II.* Even the most successful smugglers could not arrange to transport and then collect fees from hundreds of passengers at a go, so when they smuggled by ship, they preferred to join forces, distributing both the expense of the voyage and the risk that something might go awry. But the chief snakehead behind the *Najd II* was Weng Yu Hui, the pudgy Fujianese man who had been an early client of Sister Ping's, back in 1984. Weng had worked in a restaurant to pay Sister Ping's fees. He got a green card in 1987, under the American amnesty for anyone who had been living in the country illegally since before 1981. (Weng had arrived in 1984, but he supplied fraudulent paperwork and became a legal permanent resident.) He got a job in construction for a while, and every week or two, whenever he had a day off, he would go and hang around Sister Ping's shop—first the little shop on Hester Street, then the bigger one on East Broadway.

Weng was curious about the snakehead business. When he saw Sister Ping he would ask her about it—who the big snakeheads were, how the business worked. Then in 1991, seeing the industry explode, with so much demand in mainland China that no amount of supply in the United States seemed able to satisfy it, Weng decided to enter the business himself. He had contacts in Thailand and arranged to start smuggling passengers by plane, supplying them with passports purchased on the black market. Weng needed to pay for these materials up front, and he assembled $30,000 and went to Sister Ping's store on East Broadway. Sister Ping was behind the counter, and Weng asked her to send the money to Bangkok. Weng had sent small amounts of money through Sister Ping for years, but never a sum like this. "Oh," she said jokingly as he handed over the cash, "now you're my competitor."

Weng's new business grew quickly, but when the bottleneck at Bangkok began, he was unable to get any of his passengers on planes. He was maintaining an apartment in Bangkok, and his customers accumulated there until there were thirty people waiting to make the last leg of their journey. This wasn't good for business. It was expensive to maintain customers in Bangkok—they had to be fed and guarded—and there was always the risk that a safe house would be raided, resulting in new bribes to officials in Thailand and the possible loss of lucrative clients, who might disappear into the Thai prison system and never pay the balance of their fees. It also looked bad, having customers stranded in Thailand for months at a time. Success in the snakehead trade was driven largely by word of mouth; Weng had studied Sister Ping's success, and it was her reputation for a safe, efficient service that drove customers to select her from among the many snakeheads now offering passage. So unmatched was Sister Ping's reputation, in fact, that some snakeheads had taken to claiming they were working on her behalf or were affiliated with her in some way, in an effort to lure customers. Weng had heard about the use of ships as an alternative to planes, and he decided to arrange for a ship to transport his passengers.

Sister Ping may have perceived Weng as her competitor, but he knew that she faced the same problem he did when it came to the backlog in Bangkok. Her younger brother was based in Bangkok at that time, representing her interests in the region, and Weng flew there to meet with him. It was a fateful meeting: the two men were joined by a third individual, a shadowy Taiwanese bucket man who was known as Mr. Charlie. Mr. Charlie said he could arrange to charter a ship large enough to carry several hundred passengers from Thailand to America, and seaworthy enough to endure the voyage. It was agreed that Weng, Sister Ping's brother, and a third snakehead, Lau Xing Bau, would work on recruiting passengers for the voyage and Mr. Charlie would provide the vessel. Weng would put the thirty passengers who had been in his Bangkok apartment on the ship, and Sister Ping's brother would arrange for twenty of her customers to board. The rest of the space they would lease to other snakeheads who had passengers stranded in Thailand. Mr. Charlie found a Saudi-owned, Singaporean-registered ship that had ferried cars between the north and south islands of New Zealand and borne Muslim pilgrims across the Red Sea to Mecca. The ship was the *Najd II*.

As smuggling ships went, the *Najd II* was comfortable. There were over a hundred small cabins running around the two main decks. Each cabin had two beds, and the passengers moved into these. When Sean walked into one of the cabins, he found it stuffy and claustrophobic. He moved on, exploring a big recreation room at the front of the ship. Couches and chairs were scattered about, and Sean claimed two couches, pushing them together to serve as a bed.

The ship sailed south to Singapore, but before long problems arose. They ran aground briefly off the coast of Malaysia, and the passengers began to realize that the *Najd II* was on its last legs. The ship was thirty years old; the decks reeked of diesel; the engine noise was deafening. They managed to make their way through the Strait of Malacca, between the Malaysian peninsula and the Indonesian island of Sumatra, and out into the Indian Ocean. But there the engine troubles intensified, and their westward journey slowed to a crawl.

In addition to chartering a substandard ship, the snakeheads had made a curious and fateful navigational decision. Up until that point, most snakehead ships bound for the United States had taken the shorter route directly across the Pacific to Mexico or California. But several ships had recently been interdicted in the Pacific, and U.S. authorities were monitoring the waters off the West Coast, so Mr. Charlie elected to send the ship the wrong way around the world—through the chokepoint at Malacca and into the Indian Ocean, south around the coast of Africa and then north from the Cape of Good Hope.

When Sean and the others boarded the ship in July, there was plenty of food—rice, flour, biscuits, and canned fruits and vegetables. But after a month at sea they had still not reached America; they hadn't even reached the coast of Africa. The Indian Ocean is a desolate expanse of some 28 million square miles—more than seven times the surface area of the United States. As the ship made its slow journey toward Africa the food supply began to dwindle, and the fuel supply as well. Each day Sean scanned the water, but the horizon was a maddening ring, unbroken by ship or shore. The passengers were beginning to panic: they had been told they would reach the United States before the end of August, but it was September now, and they hadn't seen land in weeks. Fights broke out over rations. Even the crew members, who were all Burmese, were beginning to show signs of alarm. There were no snakeheads on the ship, but they had chosen representatives, who ruled with an increasingly tyrannical bent as the situation threatened to spin out of control; they walked the decks with Glock handguns and beat passengers who got out of line.

Finally, on September 4, 1992, they spotted land. The ship had reached the tiny, isolated island of Mauritius, some 600 miles east of Madagascar. The *Najd II* hobbled into the harbor at Port Louis, and the captain, a skinny Australian man named William Appleton, sought permission for the ship to remain there while it resolved its engine troubles and refueled. But the port authorities in Mauritius were suspicious of the ship, and the local press somehow got word that its cargo was undocumented Chinese. Officials in Mauritius radioed the *Najd II* and said that it could not stay. At that point Captain Appleton abandoned his ship. (It would subsequently emerge that Appleton's certification to captain a ship had actually been revoked several years earlier.)

One of the ship's officers, an obese Filipino whom Sean disliked, took over and somehow arranged for the ship to be repaired and refueled, but it was becoming increasingly clear that the *Najd II* was in no shape to transport the passengers as far as the United States. After another grueling two weeks at sea, with supplies continuing to diminish and tension over food and the boat's course intensifying, Sean spotted land again: the minarets and coconut palms of Mombasa, swimming in the equatorial heat.

When the ship reached Mombasa, it had no more food or water or fuel, and the new captain requested permission to dock there. Kenya was already reeling from an influx of half a million refugees from Somalia, Ethiopia, and Sudan, and the port authorities asked about the nationality and legal status of the passengers on board. A few of the snakeheads' representatives spoke English and told the Kenyans that the passengers were all from Thailand. But when the ship entered Mombasa harbor and representatives from the Thai embassy in Nairobi came aboard, none of the passengers could speak any Thai. To compound matters, the new captain had done some math, figuring that there were some 300 passengers on board, each paying an average of $30,000. He had a $9 million cargo, he realized, and he demanded more money. The snakeheads refused, and the new captain abandoned the ship and disappeared into Mombasa.

A delegation from Mombasa's Missions to Seamen boarded the ship, accompanied by Kenyan police, and found a terrifying scene. The Burmese crewmen were so frightened of the enforcers on board that they had actually welded themselves into their accommodation. They came out of their quarters only when they saw the Kenyans, and would not let them leave the ship without taking all the Burmese with them. The delegation took them to the Missions to Seamen's building, where they laid out mattresses and sheets on the badminton court and allowed the Burmese to stay.

As the Kenyan authorities searched the cabins of the Chinese passengers, they found an extraordinary number of improvised weapons. Hidden in every room was a shiv or a knife that had been made by tearing away pieces of the ship's metal lining and sharpening them to a point. Some of the weapons were almost like swords or cutlasses, as long as three and a half feet. As the Kenyans made their way through the ship, a scrum of jumpy Fujianese followed them around, menacing them in broken English when they began collecting the weapons. None of the shivs appeared to have seen any use, but there was a prevailing dread on board the ship, a sense that whether stuck at sea with no food or fuel or stranded in a foreign port without a captain and without permission to stay, the passengers of the *Najd II* had spent weeks poised on the edge of anarchy, and in the event that survival actually became a matter of self-defense, they did not want to be unprepared.

A peculiar standoff ensued. The Kenyan government did not want to formally grant the ship permission to remain in Mombasa, but the ship was clearly in no position to leave. So the *Najd II* ended up at anchor in a mangrove swamp, where, according to the local authorities, the passengers were expected to stay. Enterprising Kenyan fishermen began appearing in the waters around the ship, their dhows slowly circling the *Najd* while the fishermen shouted sales pitches and offered their wares. The hungry Chinese would place whatever currency they had in a bucket and lower it to the fishermen with string, then the fishermen would fill the bucket with fresh fish and send it back up to the ship. Most of the passengers didn't have any money, so instead they bartered, trading watches, clothing, the few keepsakes they had bothered to take aboard. Sean offered his sneakers and his belt for sale; other passengers discovered that their life preservers fetched a decent price and quickly sold all the safety equipment on board.

After a few days the passengers grew bolder. Some constructed small rafts out of steel drums and plywood and went fishing for crabs in the tropical swamps around the ship. Everyone was desperate to get to shore and telephone family members. They had been unaccounted for during the months at sea, and they wanted to reassure relatives and send for money. On the voyage Sean had developed a problem with his knee; it had become swollen and painful, and he concluded that he needed to see a doctor. Accompanied by two friends from the ship, he made his way to shore and into the city. Mombasa was shockingly foreign to Sean, but he knew that no matter how far-flung or godforsaken the backwater, there are always almost certain to be Chinese there. In cities around the planet, under the most hostile of circumstances, even in times of war, the Chinese restaurant is an enduring feature. In Baghdad or Mogadishu or any number of other conflict zones, the Chinese restaurant is a fixture that seems always to survive, unperturbed by ethnic strife or occasional shelling or even outright war. There were troubled corners of the world where the state itself had collapsed but the local Chinese restaurant stayed standing. In peacetime Mombasa, Sean and his companions went looking for a Chinese restaurant, and before long they found one. The restaurant's owners were accommodating, and arranged for Sean to telephone his cousin in the United States and have him send $400, which could be wired directly to the restaurant. Sean and his friends found a cheap hotel in Mombasa's old town and decided to lie low for a couple of days. They bought flour and salt and made their own noodles. Slowly Sean's knee began to heal.

By the time Sean returned to the ship, many other passengers had managed to sneak onto shore. Dozens of people were collecting money at the Chinese restaurant and venturing into town. A few of the more carefree passengers headed directly for the Golden Key casino, figuring if they had time to kill in Mombasa, they might as well enjoy themselves. The local police were angered by the Chinese wandering around the streets, given that technically they were not allowed to be there. They sent a police launch out to the ship to try to stop people from leaving, but the Chinese on board ran to the edge of the deck and began pelting the officers below with anything they could find—plastic bottles, balled-up paper, the detritus of the months at sea. The police were furious and fired their machine guns in the air. Sean, still very much a teenager, doubled over with laughter.

The Kenyans continued to insist that the Chinese remain on the boat, but enforcement seems to have been somewhat ad hoc. Some of the passengers were arrested and locked up in town. But others spent weeks, even months, staying openly in local hotels and gambling at the Golden Key. It depended on how much money their families were able to send. Others still gave up, making their way to the Chinese embassy in Nairobi and asking permission to return. But China owed them nothing; they were paperless drifters in a busy East African port town; they could not prove that they were Chinese. Some of the passengers bribed Kenyan port officials to ferry them back and forth between ship and shore to purchase supplies. Eventually, many of them ended up staying at the Oceanic Hotel, a dingy establishment that merited the name "resort" only because it featured a restaurant and a casino. The restaurant specialized in Indian food, but shortly after the arrival of the *Najd* it went bust. Reluctant to pass up a business opportunity, however accidental or remote, several of the Fujianese from the *Najd* opened a Chinese restaurant in the space, which quickly became a success.

At one point a delegation from the United Nations high commissioner for refugees visited the ship and offered to relocate the passengers to one of the refugee camps near Mombasa; the passengers refused, pointing out that unlike the refugees from Somalia and other African countries, they were going to the United States. For a time there was a rumor that because the *Najd II* was a Saudi ship, the Saudi government might intervene. But it did not, and the ship languished in the port for months. The mood on board turned to despair. According to several people who were on the ship, some of the women were taken into the hold by the snakehead enforcers and raped.

But through it all, Sean Chen never thought about returning to China. He telephoned his parents in Changle and acknowledged that the situation looked grim. "If something happens to me," he said, "just pretend you never had a son." There were only two possible futures for him at that moment, he told them, "Either I'll die, or I'll get to the U.S."

In November, Weng flew to Mombasa with $30,000 to distribute among the passengers so they could sustain themselves. Sister Ping gave him $20,000 and instructed him to pass the money along to her twenty passengers—$1,000 each. (Sister Ping was upset that the ship had stalled in Mombasa, and it was probably in consideration of what this type of gaffe would do for her reputation in the marketplace that she provided such a generous allowance.) The customers were angry and anxious, but Weng told them not to worry. Mr. Charlie was going to purchase another boat, which would come and pick them up.

This was indeed Mr. Charlie's plan, and not long afterward he flew to New York City for a meeting. He had found a ship that could sail to Kenya and pick up the stranded passengers. But he didn't want to charter the ship this time, he wanted to buy it. For that, he needed an investor. He was looking for someone who could put up a large sum of money to purchase the ship, in exchange for an even larger sum of the passengers' fees once it arrived. Sister Ping and Weng were both big figures in the smuggling world, and they were both desperate to get their customers to the United States, for the $9 million bounty if nothing else. Mr. Charlie was looking for someone who was flush with cash and wanted to break into the business in a bigger way, to work with the likes of Sister Ping and Weng and own an equity stake in the voyage. One night in New York City, he and Weng arranged a dinner at a restaurant in Koreatown to meet with one such potential investor. The investor was Ah Kay.

Chapter Eight

The Phantom Ship

PATTAYA IS situated in the northeastern crook of the Gulf of Thailand. The town is only a couple of hours' drive from Bangkok, and as a low-rent resort destination, it retains some of Bangkok's grit. Pattaya Beach Road is lined with food stalls, massage parlors, and cheap hotels. In the evenings, alleys occupied by outdoor bars are clogged with drunken Europeans who brawl and sing, careening down the sidewalks. Before the Vietnam War, Pattaya was an unspoiled encampment of village fishermen and white sand beaches. But when the GIs descended, the town devolved into an R&R bacchanal, and the go-go bars and seediness only persisted and multiplied after the war, through decades of overdevelopment. Somewhere along the way Pattaya gained a reputation as a haven for sex tourists.

On the evening of February 14, 1993, a stocky Thai police officer named Pao Pong was patrolling a secluded line of beaches on the outskirts of town. Pao Pong was a member of the Tourist Police, an elite force responsible for interacting with the surge of visiting foreigners—keeping them safe, and keeping the local population safe from them. On the coast just north of the main town, a series of slightly spiffier modern hotels rose above a row of stunted cliffs overlooking the ocean. It was largely the clientele of these establishments, and the Thais who serviced them, who frequented the narrow ribbon of sandy beach below: holidaymakers lounging on foldout chairs beneath umbrellas, gazing at the sea; sunburned German men sprawled belly-up on the sand like beached whales, enjoying a fifty-cent massage. Thai children, dark-eyed and gangly, sold burnished conch shells to passersby.

As darkness fell the beach began to empty, but Pao Pong continued to survey the area. The Tourist Police had received an alert that a major human smuggling operation might be taking place in Pattaya. The precise details of the scheme were unknown, but earlier in the week there had been a report that a man was asking around town, looking to rent twelve speedboats for the evening of the fourteenth. The man had said he wanted to take a group of Chinese businessmen out on a cruise of the harbor islands and wanted the boats from eight to midnight. Pao Pong hadn't seen any signs of the boats yet, but he walked a beat among the hotels perched above the beach, keeping an eye out for anything unusual.

He was approaching the Cozy Beach Hotel when he noticed some activity in the big parking lot that adjoined it. It was dark now, but he could see that there were half a dozen vans in the parking lot, and as he watched, people were leaving the vans and making their way down a set of steep stone steps to the beach. Pao Pong looked out at the bay below, and there in the moonlight, bobbing where the water was shoulder-deep, he saw a cluster of sleek speedboats. There could be a perfectly normal explanation for this, Pao Pong thought. It was Valentine's Day. Sometimes tourists liked to take boat trips to Pattaya's offshore islands, several miles out, to do nature walks or stargaze. But even by the wholesale tourist group standards of Pattaya, this was a lot of people.

Pao Pong walked toward the parking lot, and as he approached the vans, he saw two official-looking men standing nearby, who seemed to be monitoring the dark figures as they climbed out of the vans and scrambled down to the seashore. As Pao Pong got closer, he could make out the men's uniforms. They were Thai military police; they'd be able to explain what was going on. Pao Pong greeted the policemen. But as he did, the policemen turned and ran away.

By the time Pao Pong had called for backup and started making arrests, the speedboats had already ferried large numbers of people out to sea. They couldn't have been going very far out into the gulf; the boats had time to make multiple trips. But the police rounded up sixty-eight people before they could board the boats, along with the two military policemen, and arrested them. The people were Chinese, and in Thailand illegally. It was obviously a smuggling operation, and Pao Pong and his colleagues wanted to take boats out into the gulf and apprehend the mother ship. But someone had warned the ship that there was trouble onshore, and it had disappeared.

That night Pao Pong made a call to Bangkok, to the office of an American immigration agent named Mark Riordan. Riordan worked for the INS. Before coming to Bangkok several months earlier, he had been stationed in Europe, the Philippines, and Hong Kong, where he spent two and a half years and witnessed the British colony's role as a hub of human smuggling. He had been transferred to Bangkok with the title "enforcement coordinator" and specific instructions to tackle the problem of Chinese migrant smuggling. Several weeks earlier Riordan had received some intelligence traffic from the U.S. embassy in Bangkok that a ship would be picking up a large number of Chinese nationals somewhere off the coast of Thailand. After consulting a map of the Gulf of Thailand, Riordan had concluded that if the passengers were being bused to the coast from Bangkok, Pattaya would be the ideal spot for a pickup. He had driven to Pattaya himself and briefed Pao Pong and his colleagues about the possibility that a major smuggling operation might be taking place.

The morning after the Tourist Police made their arrests, Riordan arrived at the police station in Pattaya. When he walked inside, the place was overrun by Chinese passengers, all standing around, uncertain what would become of them. When Riordan questioned them, they told him that they had come from Fujian Province, that they had entered Thailand from Burma at the bustling border checkpoint in Chiang Rai. One of the passengers was sitting at a desk talking to the Thai cops. He was a handsome young Chinese man with a part in his hair and a polite, businesslike demeanor. The officers told Riordan that the man was going to help them; he had a cell phone, and he was waiting for a call from the chief smuggler, a man named Mr. Charlie. The man with the cell phone had agreed to tell Mr. Charlie to come and meet them at some designated spot, at which point the Thais could apprehend him. As Riordan talked to the passengers, he kept hearing that name; the passengers didn't know what he looked like, but Mr. Charlie was clearly the boss, the name on everyone's lips.

While they waited for the call, Riordan sat down with Pao Pong. Riordan had noticed that Thais often smile and joke even about subjects that make them profoundly unhappy or uncomfortable. Pao Pong seemed somewhat forlorn, and Riordan asked why. "They're going to move me to the border after this," he said with a smile. Pao Pong explained that he had gathered enough information to glean that Mr. Charlie had set up the whole operation. But if Thai military policemen had been escorting the passengers, then powerful people were on the payroll of these smugglers, and for arresting those policemen and stopping sixty-eight passengers from boarding the ship—for doing his job—he would now be relocated to the sticks as punishment.

A few days later Riordan returned to the station, curious about the status of the investigation and of the undocumented Chinese. When he arrived, he was greeted only by the officers; the Chinese weren't there. "Where is everybody?" Riordan asked.

"They were all deported, to Cambodia and Laos," the officers told him. They were matter-of-fact about it, but Riordan knew that the Thais never expelled people that quickly. Thai justice was slow-moving—you could commit some minor violation and sit in jail for a week before anyone decided what to do with you. Someone powerful had wanted those passengers out of the country.

Riordan approached Pao Pong. What about the young guy who was going to help catch Charlie? he asked.

"The one with the telephone?" Pao Pong said. "That *was* Charlie. He had a passport from Laos. They moved him back across two nights ago."

Mr. Charlie's real name was Lee Peng Fei. He was born in Taiwan but styled himself as a globe-trotting businessman. He had an athletic build and a take-charge attitude; he was a sharp dresser and had a good singing voice. He fancied himself a bit of a crooner and was known to be excellent at karaoke. Mr. Charlie had started smuggling years before; he had been arrested on alien smuggling charges in California in 1986.

A week after meeting with Ah Kay in New York, Mr. Charlie and Weng flew to Thailand. The plan was that Ah Kay would front the funds for a new boat. Weng visited Sister Ping and told her that while the *Najd II* was still in Mombasa and couldn't continue, he and Mr. Charlie were assembling investors, including Ah Kay, and were going to arrange for another ship. Sister Ping was firm with Weng: she told him that regardless of which investors he was able to gather, her passengers must be put on the new boat and brought to America. Sister Ping still owed Ah Kay $300,000 from the New Bedford offloading, and it was agreed that she would wire that money to Bangkok so that Mr. Charlie could purchase a new boat.

Next Mr. Charlie summoned a protégé of his, a young ruffian in his twenties named Kin Sin Lee, who was Fujianese by birth but traveled on a Malaysian passport and had helped Charlie on smuggling operations in the past. In January 1993, Kin Sin Lee traveled to Singapore to purchase a boat. Through a shipping agent there, he acquired an aging, rust-eaten 150-foot coastal freighter with a Panamanian registry, the *Tong Sern*. The ship had been used to transport dry goods on short trips between Thailand, Cambodia, and Vietnam; it was not designed for transoceanic travel, but Kin Sin Lee showed no signs of being troubled by this.

In Singapore, Lee met the forty-four-year-old Sumatran ship's captain Amir Tobing. Tobing later insisted that when he signed on for the voyage, he was unaware of what the ship would be carrying, but as a general matter he was unencumbered by scruples and comfortable with the kinds of compromises occasioned by a life on the ungovernable seas. A prosecutor later described him as "a pirate," an itinerant mariner with a mercenary sensibility. Lee enlisted a crew, and the *Tong Sern* set sail for Bangkok. There he announced to Tobing and the crew that the ship would be carrying Chinese migrants. He offered them bonuses for taking part in the operation. Tobing would be paid $2,000 a month, and an additional $40,000 if the journey was successful.

As the ship sat in Bangkok harbor, Mr. Charlie and Kin Sin Lee made preparations for the voyage. They laid plywood planks across the steel struts that bisected the dank, cavernous hold of the ship, creating two levels of makeshift accommodation. Charlie purchased eight hundred blankets, which would serve as bedding for the passengers who came aboard. He gave Kin Sin Lee money to pay the crew's wages, and on February 14, Captain Tobing and Kin Sin Lee piloted the ship out of Bangkok harbor. Just before the *Tong Sern* was to leave, Sister Ping wired the smugglers an additional $20,000 and reiterated that when the ship reached Kenya, it was essential that her customers get a place on board—"no matter what."

Mr. Charlie and Weng Yu Hui were both experienced smugglers by this time, and particularly in the business of maritime smuggling, they tended to think of what they did as not very different from any other long-haul shipping operation. One mantra of successful cargo transporters, whether they use boats, planes, or trucks, is that you never travel with an empty cargo bay. It was decided, given the large numbers of Chinese in Bangkok awaiting passage to America, that even though the mission of the *Tong Sern* was to pick up the stranded migrants from Kenya, it would be wasteful to make the first leg of the trip empty. So Mr. Charlie headed overland to Pattaya, with a plan to load an additional 160 passengers on the ship. But the snakeheads had not counted on Pao Pong stumbling across the clandestine boarding process. When the passengers started arriving in speedboats and climbing aboard, Lee and Tobing received a call telling them that the Pattaya police on shore had disrupted the operation. Tobing set sail. They had already taken on ninety of the passengers; they would simply have to leave the remaining seventy behind, to be captured by the police. As the ship headed out into the South China Sea, Kin Sin Lee herded the excited passengers down a single ladder that led to the hold. The passengers were exhilarated by the late-night operation and the race to evade the police. "America! America!" they chanted.

Until the early twentieth century, there was generally some correlation between the home port or ownership of an oceangoing vessel and the nationality of the flag that it flew. But during Prohibition the American owners of two cruise ships, frustrated that they could not serve alcohol on board, were permitted to reregister their ships in Panama, despite the fact that neither the companies nor their ships, nor the routes that those ships took, had any special relationship with the Central American country. When, on December 5, 1922, the ships lowered their U.S. flags and raised the red, white, and blue flag of Panama, they ushered in a phenomenon that would become known as "flags of convenience," in which a ship can be registered in a country that has no relationship to its owners, its crew, its home port, or its destination.

For international shipping companies, flags of convenience represented an unprecedented opportunity: by allowing shipowners to shop around for the most obliging venue in which to register their vessels, the system provided a way to avoid registering in countries like the United States, which have high taxes, rigorous vessel inspection standards, and other cumbersome regulations. For the countries that opened their registries, the practice was also lucrative. In the years since those two cruise ships raised the Panamanian flag, Panama has become the single largest registry of ships in the world. By the time the Panamanian-registered *Tong Sern* picked up its passengers off the coast of Pattaya in 1993, the government of Panama was collecting some $50 million a year in ship registration fees and taxes, and the maritime lawyers, shipping agents, and inspectors of Panama City were making that same amount again. Everybody won: registration was easy for shipowners and a great source of revenue for Panama. Dozens of other countries had seen the income that could be gained by offering flags of convenience. The second largest flag-state for hire was Liberia, which was riven by civil war and could hardly be considered a coherent country at all, but which offered a robust and accommodating ship registry. Today ships are flagged in Cambodia, which offers online registration in twenty-four hours; in landlocked Luxembourg and Bolivia; in the Mongolian desert, a thousand miles from the nearest ocean.

But if this system worked for the larger, licit world of shippers in the global economy, it also held special appeal for outlaws, pirates, smugglers, and thieves. A transparent registration system means accountability. In principle, it should be easy to spot a ship's name, home port, and flag and trace it back to the people who own the ship and are responsible for putting it out to sea. But with flags of convenience, it became more difficult to trace a vessel's provenance. Because it was easy to flag and reflag ships in jurisdictions that did not insist on rigorous inspections, it became possible to continue sailing a ship long after it was no longer seaworthy. Negligent registries permitted ships with bad safety records, substandard crews, or no insurance to ply the seas. Smugglers could move a variety of goods—timber, plywood, frozen prawns, or palm oil—by the shipload without paying taxes. Gunrunners could flout arms embargoes and send weapons into conflict zones. Pirates could hijack tankers, rerouting a vessel and reflagging it in some lax jurisdiction, repainting its name at sea, and effectively enabling it to drop off the nautical map and disappear, becoming what is known as a phantom ship.

As the *Tong Sern* sailed through the South China Sea, the crew lowered the flag of Panama and raised the blue-and-white-striped flag of

Honduras. Two crewmen were slung over the side by ropes and began repainting the name on the stern of the ship. They replaced the words *Tong Sern* with a new set of white block letters: *Golden Venture.*

While the *Golden Venture* made its way across the Indian Ocean to Africa, Weng Yu Hui flew to Mombasa. He purchased oil and food and began to make arrangements for Sean Chen and the other passengers to be transported out to sea. Late on the night of April 2, 1993, a series of tugboats and dhows began silently taking on passengers from the *Najd II.* Of the three hundred or so passengers who had arrived in Mombasa in October, only about two hundred remained; many had grown tired of waiting and had devised other means of moving back to China or on to the United States. (Nor were they the only ones who didn't board; a group of passengers from the *Najd* had found so much success running the Chinese restaurant they had opened in the Oceanic Hotel that they decided not to take their chances on America but to stay put in Mombasa. They had a business to run.)

Weng loaded the passengers onto the smaller boats and then left Mombasa. He telephoned Sister Ping to tell her that he had personally put her twenty customers on the smaller boat. But several days later she called him back. "Out of those twenty people, only two people got on the *Golden Venture,"* she said. Eighteen of them had seen the boat and decided that it was too small—that it couldn't possibly make the voyage to America. Sister Ping was furious. "They refused to get on board!" she said. In a pattern that had repeated itself several times already in her career, her reputation as a perfectionist with a high standard of care had succeeded in expanding her business to a point where she could no longer handle every aspect of the passage to America herself, and she was obliged to delegate and outsource to lesser professionals. Weng had let her down.

Sean Chen was aboard one of the small boats leaving Mombasa harbor. He saw the *Golden Venture* looming before him, and he too thought it looked very small. It was much smaller than the *Najd II*, where he had been living for months, and when he got on board he realized that there were already nearly a hundred passengers there. Kin Sin Lee had selected several of the passengers to assist him as "managers," or onboard enforcers, and together they hustled the passengers into the hold.

Sean entered the hatch leading to the nether recesses of the ship and descended the rungs of the ladder into another world—a fetid 20-by-40-foot space divided into two floors made of loosely secured plywood planks. The space was windowless and smelly; the other passengers had already been aboard the ship for six weeks. Each passenger was allotted a patch of plywood, a 2-by-6 foot spot on the floor. They fit together like the pieces of a jigsaw, wedged into a grotesquely intimate interlocking network of knees and elbows, heads and toes. Sean had to pick his way among the bodies and belongings of the others in order to claim his spot, and tread gingerly so as not to step on anyone. The space was lit by a few naked electric bulbs, and in the dim interior the passengers who had already made a home there stared at him through a fog of cigarette smoke as he passed. It was not so much a ship he had entered as a floating cattle car.

Sean and the others filed into the cramped space, corralled by Kin Sin Lee and the onboard enforcers. Some of the passengers had been sailors back in China; they looked around and judged the boat altogether too small—too small for so many people, too small for so long a voyage. The passengers were divided roughly into the Kenyan group and the Thai group, and further segregated by the snakeheads who represented them. Sean put his things down in his space and did his best to make himself comfortable. But it was difficult. The hold was hot, and the roar of the engine was deafening, a persistent, unhealthy drone. There was no privacy anywhere, no patch of floor not crawling with irritable and frightened Fujianese. There was only one bathroom for use by the passengers, Sean learned, and that was reserved for the two dozen women on board. The men were obliged to urinate where they could—from the deck if the enforcers would allow them, belowdecks if they wouldn't. They shit into plastic bags and threw them overboard. The air grew thick with the earthy reek of excrement and sweat.

Captain Tobing, Kin Sin Lee, and the crew enjoyed cabins above deck and a kitchen and bathroom of their own. The passengers' food was prepared on hot plates on the floor in the hold. They ate rice, mainly, along with small amounts of peanuts or dried vegetables. The supply of fresh water was extremely limited, and the passengers relied instead on a water purification system. But the system grew rusty, and some days the rice they ate was stained red by the water it yielded. Each passenger was allotted a cup of water a day. Salt was everywhere. They brushed their teeth with saltwater. There was a saltwater shower above deck, which passengers who behaved themselves were allowed to use in rotation, once a week. Their skin broke out in rashes from washing with water from the sea.

The scarcity led to fights over food and water. A certain Darwinian logic took hold of the ship: the strong and the crafty managed a greater daily allotment than the weak. The weak would argue and beg or try to steal food. When they did, the passengers who had been assigned to enforce order would beat the offenders mercilessly. They had sticks and clubs as well as handcuffs, and especially rebellious passengers would be handcuffed for hours at a time. Kin Sin Lee was clearly fearful that anarchy could break out on board, and he kept it at bay by making frequent examples of those who stepped out of line. He vowed to throw unruly passengers into the sea.

At times the journey seemed so harrowingly unforgiving, so calculated to test and break the spirit and endurance of the passengers on board, that the *Golden Venture* took on the aspect not of a late-twentieth-century vessel bearing intrepid migrants to the promised land but of an aimlessly floating madhouse, its cargo an assemblage of lunatics and sadists, a Renaissance-era ship of fools. The surreal indignities of life in the hold and the fierce indifference of the sea seemed to haunt the passengers, to break them down. One man cried every time he had a bowel movement, which, owing to the meager rations, was only once a week. Another man brought on board a handheld video game he had purchased in Thailand and continued idly pressing the buttons long after the batteries had died. "I think it changed many people, being on that ship," one of Sean's fellow passengers would later say. And indeed, to this day many of the men and women who were aboard the *Golden Venture* refuse to discuss the particulars of what happened during the months at sea, some of them because of an enduring sense of shame about the dishonor they endured, others simply skeptical that anyone who did not experience the journey could ever understand.

As the *Golden Venture* neared South Africa, it was suddenly engulfed in a violent storm. Waves as high as 50 feet rocked the ship, and rain lashed the deck. The sky went the color of charcoal, and the horizon line contracted so that Captain Tobing and his crew could not see beyond the next towering swell. They thought the ship would capsize. In the hold Sean was tossed from side to side. He tried to sleep, but the ship would lurch, sending him tumbling onto the people around him. Many of the passengers were overwhelmed by seasickness; the sound of retching and the stench of vomit filled the hold. People were crying. Others were praying. Some put on their best suits, preparing for death. There were no lifeboats on board the ship, nor any life jackets. And what would happen if the ship rolled over, with Sean and nearly three hundred others trapped in its hold, and sank slowly to the bottom of the ocean? The *Golden Venture* was a ghost ship. It was a ship full of stowaways on an illicit voyage; the captain was not sharing its latest coordinates with authorities at the nearest port. The vessel would simply vanish forever, leaving no headstone to mark the precise spot where they had died, no record or memory upon the surface of the sea.

After two days the storm subsided, and the ship dropped anchor at Cape Infanta, in South Africa. Kin Sin Lee had arranged to take on another eighty passengers, who would board from South Africa, but Captain Tobing refused. There was just no more room in the hold.

Despite the adversity and the periodic terror of the voyage, or perhaps because of it, a kind of society emerged on board over the months at sea. Apart from the disproportionate ratio of men to women, the passengers on the *Golden Venture* formed a fairly representative cross-section of Fujianese society, and in coping with the hardship and inertia of the voyage, many of the passengers assumed the roles they had played in the villages they had left behind. A young man who had been a village doctor tended to the sick; a teenager became known for giving good massages. Natural jokers and raconteurs emerged and amused the others, recycling stories and skits—any diversion to break the monotony. People played endless games of cards and shared recollections of their homes and families and gossiped about the reputations of the various snakeheads who had put them on the ship. (By general agreement, Sister Ping was the best.) When the weather was nice and the ship was in international waters, Kin Sin Lee permitted the passengers to go on deck and stretch and see the sun. They fished with makeshift rods.

The ship rounded the Cape of Good Hope before the end of April, plying the same waters that De Gama had on his return from India to Portugal in the fifteenth century, that Magellan, circumnavigator of the globe, had a few years after that. It hugged the African coast for a while, then angled west in the direction of Brazil, charting a course for the cold waters of the North Atlantic, where Ah Kay's fishing boats would be waiting.

Chapter Nine

The Teaneck Massacre

FROM THE moment the *Golden Venture* departed from Thailand, it was Ah Kay's plan to offload it somewhere on the high seas in the Atlantic, as he had done with so many other ships by now. He would not participate in the actual offloading himself; as *dai lo*, Ah Kay saw his job as negotiating the deals and delegating to his underlings, then exercising a kind of loose supervision while they did the dirty work. On his identity card, which was issued by the Fukienese American Association, he listed his occupation simply as "manager." In that respect Ah Kay was a typical Mob boss: he rarely ventured to the actual scene of a crime.

Instead he relied on an assortment of deputies, some of whom had been working for him for years and would, and often did, risk their lives to do his bidding. But as the Fuk Ching gang expanded, it began to admit new members who felt less personal allegiance to Ah Kay. One of these newcomers was a reedy young man with an angular face and straight black hair that hung in a fringe just above his eyes. His name was Dan Xin Lin. He was twenty-eight and had come from Fujian five years earlier.

Dan Xin had been a member of the gang for a couple of years and had worked as Ah Kay's bodyguard. But he was slightly older than many of the gang members, and he was promoted quickly and given responsibility for the gang's burgeoning human smuggling business. He saw the large numbers of people the Fuk Ching was bringing to New York in boats and vans, and he knew the huge fees that Ah Kay received for this work and then doled out, at his own discretion, to his underlings. Ah Kay had become a multimillionaire in a short few years; but to oversee the most lucrative of his criminal enterprises, he was paying Dan Xin a paltry $500 a week.

Ah Kay was developing a reputation for stinginess, and he was gambling more—more often, and with ever larger sums of money on the table. He lost tens and sometimes hundreds of thousands of dollars at a sitting, but he continued gambling, in some measure, perhaps, because the sheer quantities of cash he was collecting allowed him to sustain the habit. Dan Xin was ambitious. He knew that he was more intelligent than the Fuk Ching rank and file, and he was not cowed by the reverence for Ah Kay that the longer-serving members of the gang seemed to share. He saw Ah Kay's greed and his wastefulness, and it rankled him that it was he and the other underlings who actually did most of the smuggling work, hiring the Vietnamese fishermen, traveling out to sea to meet the mother ships, transporting the passengers to safe houses, and so on.

By the early 1990s the sudden influx of Fujianese and the flourishing of the snakehead trade had created a boomtown vibe in underworld circles in Chinatown: it was not clear how long this gold rush would last, and there was a prevailing sense that you would be mad not to get a piece of it while the going was good. Dan Xin had contacts in China and wanted to go out on his own, shipping in his own customers and negotiating offloading contracts with other snakeheads. In the summer of 1992 he traveled to Washington, D.C., and met with a Fuk Ching affiliate there to discuss a smuggling venture independent of Ah Kay. When Ah Kay learned about the trip, he was furious that Dan Xin would conduct such a meeting without his permission.

Ah Kay was blessed with a kind of natural charisma that would become legendary both in Chinatown and in law enforcement circles. He was muscular and handsome, and he possessed a striking calm, an outward tranquillity that somehow also bespoke intensity and convinced others that he was always thinking one or two steps ahead. But Dan Xin's disloyalty worried him. It was good to be envied, but not by someone who might have the intelligence and leadership skills to supplant him. And there was no question that Dan Xin coveted Ah Kay's role. "Dan Xin wanted that spot," one prosecutor would later say. "He was real itchy for it."

After the incident in Washington, Dan Xin became more openly defiant and started trying to persuade other members of the gang to join his splinter faction. "He's no good," he would tell the young members of the Fuk Ching. "He's cheap." The rebellion enraged Ah Kay. Before long, Dan Xin had persuaded half a dozen gang members to defect, and he seems to have raised doubts in Ah Kay about the quality of his own leadership. "What are my shortcomings?" the *dai lo* asked several of his remaining allies, trying to persuade them to air any grievances rather than go to the other side. He particularly resented the suggestion that he was a miser. "I never say no," he complained. "When you guys are in trouble, I put out the bail for you. When you guys visit home, I give each three thousand dollars. And when it's your birthday, I wrap a thousand dollars as a gift. What else do you want from me?" He accused Dan Xin of gambling excessively. "The money he lost on the gambling tables, fuck! Unthinkable. He lost on the gambling tables and he wants *me* to pay for it?"

In late December, Dan Xin and several of his allies moved their belongings out of the Fuk Ching safe house where they had been staying, in New Jersey, and relocated to Pennsylvania. Ah Kay thought the move showed weakness, that Dan Xin was a "paper tiger," without enough support in Chinatown to weather a conflict. "Dan Xin, you want to fight me?" Ah Kay said when the two men spoke by phone. "That will be a job for the rest of your life. Either I die or you die." He warned Dan Xin not to come back to Chinatown, and if he did, to watch his back. Ah Kay didn't make such threats lightly; to other members of the Fuk Ching, he announced that he would pay anyone who killed Dan Xin $300,000.

For a few days around the New Year, Dan Xin was able to stay away. But on January 8, 1993, he returned to Chinatown to renew the contract for his beeper at an electronics store on Allen Street. Around three o'clock that afternoon, Ah Kay was at a friend's house when he got a call on his cell phone from Song You Lin, one of his closest deputies, telling him that Dan Xin had come back and asking if he should go through with the murder.

"Do it," Ah Kay told him. "Do a clean job."

"Dai lo, don't worry," Song replied. He packed a .380 automatic, and he and two Fuk Ching members walked along the bustling sidewalks of eastern Chinatown to Allen Street. They entered the beeper store, and one of them blocked the entrance while Song pulled his gun. They found Dan Xin standing with two bodyguards, disaffected former Fuk Ching members who had decided to join him. Song fired at Dan Xin, but Dan Xin ducked behind a pillar. One of the bullets came within an inch of his head, singeing his hair, but miraculously, none connected. One of Dan Xin's bodyguards rushed toward Song to stop him, and Song shot and killed him. Dan Xin's other ally pulled a gun of his own and fired at Song, and Song fired back, hitting him in the chest and then the head. With the other two out of the way Song raised his gun to finish Dan Xin, but it clicked empty—he had run out of bullets. Song dashed out of the store. Dan Xin checked on his two friends. One of them was dead on the floor. The other had managed to crash out onto the sidewalk, where he lay bleeding, beyond help. Dan Xin straightened and fled the scene.

A broad-daylight double homicide on a busy street in Chinatown was brazen, but not atypical for the Fuk Ching gang. It was perhaps a reflection of the level of violence in New York City at that time, and of the general disregard in the press for Chinese-on-Chinese crime, but none of New York's major English-language newspapers contained so much as a mention of the event. The police had heard enough about the tensions within the Fuk Ching to bring Ah Kay in for questioning, but he stonewalled them, saying he knew nothing about the incident. Chinatown's residents and small-business owners were terrified of the gangs; after an incident like this, no one wanted to risk helping the police. They had no witnesses and no cooperators who could explicate the internecine clash that explained Ah Kay's connection to the murders. They were forced to let him go.

Ah Kay was unhappy with Song for allowing Dan Xin to get away. He worried about the police investigation, and about Dan Xin, who had only just escaped what was obviously an assassination attempt engineered by Ah Kay. Worse, the deaths of Dan Xin's two associates had only added to Ah Kay's reputation as a careless leader with little regard for the younger members of the gang. He fell into a depression, which was tempered only by his fury at Dan Xin. "I'm going to wash my hands and close the business," he told one associate. "My brothers—fuck! My close brothers, they won't take this," he said. "I can just put out one million dollars and they will die for me." Because he knew there were no witnesses who would testify about the shootings, he developed a bizarre plan to oblige local people from the community to volunteer as witnesses and say they had seen the shootings and that Dan Xin himself had killed his two allies. "It boils down to who has the money to get a better lawyer," Ah Kay concluded. "One hundred thousand dollars or eighty thousand dollars will not be a problem for me . . . But Dan Xin, can he handle that? I bet he can't. That's not a problem of whether I underestimate him or not. That's a fact."

Ah Kay hid in an apartment in Flushing, Queens. He stayed there through at least the end of February, talking to his footsoldiers by phone, trying to persuade them not to leave the gang. But he continued to worry. Then one day he left New York altogether and returned to China, to Fujian, to the dirt lanes and ramshackle homes of Yingyu, the village of his birth.

When Ah Kay left, he handed authority to his younger brother, Guo Liang Wong, who was only twenty-five. Ah Wong, as he was known, was a tough kid with a square jaw, a small mouth, and the same fierce, intelligent eyes as his older brother. He was skinny, with a sinuous, muscular body and a tendency to flaunt his good fortune at being the kid brother of a neighborhood kingpin. He wore gold jewelry and drove around New York in an expensive Lexus.

Ah Kay instructed Ah Wong that he was to manage the offloading of the *Golden Venture*, and Ah Wong began preparing for the arrival of the ship, making phone calls to the various snakeheads associated with the voyage to check on its status. The ship was already overdue to arrive, and Sister Ping and the other snakeheads would be counting on Ah Wong to oversee the offloading of their customers. But apart from preparing for the ship's arrival, Ah Wong kept a low profile; law enforcement was still trying to solve the beeper-store murders, and Dan Xin Lin was still at large somewhere and no doubt eager for revenge. The Fuk Ching had numerous safe houses in the cities and suburbs around New York, and Ah Wong began shuttling from safe house to safe house, aware that living too conspicuously in Chinatown was risky. To rent these spaces Ah Wong relied on Alan Tam, the amiable half African American giant whose fluent English made him the gang's designated public face for any interactions with the outside world. Tam served not just as realtor for the group but as scheduler and legal secretary. He kept track of everyone's criminal cases, maintaining a stack of minutely detailed notebooks and calendars, telling people when they had to go to an arraignment or a bail hearing. When Luke Rettler at the Manhattan DA's office eventually saw Tam's records, he was amazed. They were as orderly as a clerk's docket. Tam found criminal lawyers for the gang when they needed them, and bailed people out of jail, and chauffeured them around in his Mustang. When Ah Kay had a daughter, Alan Tam baby-sat her. He also signed leases on safe houses, sometimes using the alias John Tam, and, less plausibly, John Stein.

The safe houses were rentals, usually in quiet residential neighborhoods without a big Chinese population. The gang often had to hold customers who had arrived in America but had not yet paid their snakehead debts. They coexisted with these customers in a strange relationship; they cooked and ate and talked with the new arrivals, who often came from the same villages in China that they did. Prosecutors sometimes referred to the practice of holding people until they had paid their fees as "hostage-taking." But most of the arrivals seemed to think of themselves as debtors who had not yet fulfilled their end of a contractual exchange. They weren't tied up or locked up; this was one of the advantages of having safe houses far from Chinatown. With no immigration status and no English, if these people fled, where could they go? At the same time, the customers were often beaten and threatened when they didn't pay; and they were forced to cohabit, often in large numbers, in the basement. Alan Tam always specified to real estate agents that he would need a space in which the basement was finished.

In the months after Ah Kay's departure, Ah Wong and a few supporters were switching safe houses every few days. They moved so frequently that Alan Tam often couldn't remember at the end of the day where they were supposed to be staying that night. In the safe houses themselves, life had its indolent, adolescent pleasures. For all the violence and intrigue that marked their lives, Ah Wong and his followers were college-aged kids with plenty of money and a lot of spare time. They treated the houses like crash pads. Various people cycled through—the gang members, their girlfriends, the occasional customer who hadn't paid a debt. The bathroom at a safe house might have eighteen different toothbrushes in it, accommodating a revolving door of regulars and passers-through.

They cooked and brought Chinese takeout home and drank Heineken in abundant quantities. None of them cleaned, and the trash had a tendency to pile up. They hooked up VCRs and watched Chinese movies on video. "We watch kung fu movies or drama," Tam would later explain. They played Nintendo games as well; "Streetfighter" was a favorite. At one of the houses, they strung up a punching bag in the backyard. Some of them listened to English lessons on tape. Neighbors might wonder at the young Asian men with moussed hair and black suits who seemed always to be entering or leaving the split-level down the block, but it was hard to distinguish the kids, to tell how many they were. People assumed that they worked for some local Chinese restaurant.

Both the FBI and the Manhattan district attorney's office were investigating the beeper-store murders, but the Fuk Ching's decision to go underground made it difficult. Then one day Dan Xin Lin walked in to the FBI office in Lower Manhattan and said he was willing to cooperate. Ray Kerr, an FBI agent who was working on the Asian gang problem, and Peter Lee, the special agent who had debriefed Sister Ping, met with Dan Xin. He seemed nothing like his outsized reputation in the neighborhood, the giant-slayer who had dared to challenge Ah Kay. On the contrary, he appeared thin and meek, almost delicate. But it was immediately clear why Dan Xin had come in: he was furious at Ah Kay. He wanted revenge. Kerr and Lee told him they would round up Ah Kay's gang and arrest them, but they needed his help. "You don't need to get revenge," Kerr told him. "In this country, that's what law enforcement does."

Dan Xin sat with the agents and looked through surveillance photos. He picked out Song You Lin, the man who had nearly killed him, and Ah Wong. The FBI agents could see what was happening; it wasn't unusual for criminals to cooperate primarily for the purpose of getting the other guy arrested. But Dan Xin said he could help them get the beeper-store assassin. From FBI headquarters he made a call to Song You Lin, saying he wanted to meet in Chinatown to discuss the conflict. Song agreed to a rendezvous. The proposed scenario, in which the men would sit down over noodles and have a cordial discussion about the recent incident in which one had tried to murder the other, was so unlikely that the meeting could take place only if both parties had ulterior motives. Dan Xin had no intention of meeting with Song; he just wanted to confirm a time and a place where the police could arrest him. And Song had no intention of discussing the conflict. He agreed to the meeting so that he could finish the job; when the police picked him up, they found a gun, hidden, after the Fuk Ching fashion, in the backpack his girlfriend was carrying.

The FBI coordinated with Luke Rettler at the Manhattan DA's office and arranged to take Dan Xin before a grand jury, where he could finger Song You Lin and another Fuk Ching member for the beeper-store shootings. They transported him to the grand jury room downtown under guard and closed the elevator bank so that he could travel up without being seen. On the way up in the elevator, Rettler noticed that Dan Xin was shaking slightly; he looked like a frightened kid.

Dan Xin may have been shaking less from fear than from indignation. He had grown obsessed with getting revenge on Ah Kay. Certainly testifying against his assailant in the beeper store would bring some satisfaction, but he was increasingly focusing his enmity on Ah Kay's brother, Ah Wong. He had provided the FBI with information about Ah Wong, but Ah Wong was not an immediate target in their investigation; they wanted to close the beeper-store killings. Having appealed to America's criminal justice system, Dan Xin now felt that it was not moving quickly enough. He instructed some of his allies to try to find out where Ah Wong was staying, to study his travel habits. But it was precisely this kind of pursuit that Ah Wong was seeking to thwart by moving around so frequently, and he was evasive enough that Dan Xin could not pin down his location.

There was one vulnerability in Ah Wong's routine, however, and it happened to be the individual more familiar with the logistics of safe-house life than any other, if only because it was his duty to oversee those logistics. Alan Tam was loyal to Ah Wong, and above all to Ah Kay, but he was also a drug addict, and something of a buffoon. That March and April, Dan Xin and his crew began socializing with Tam. They met up with him at a brothel on Fifty-fifth Street in Brooklyn and offered him crack cocaine. Dan Xin talked to him about Ah Kay and told him that Ah Kay was no friend of his. Tam had been so loyal to Ah Kay for so many years but had never really benefited from all the money that the *dai lo* was making. Dan Xin's deputy was a young gangster named Simon Lau, who had chubby cheeks and wore round spectacles. Everyone called him Four-Eyed Fish. He pulled out a gun and placed it on the table in front of Tam.

"Alan," he said, "are you with us?"

Tam was high, and confused, and conflict-shy by nature. He told them he was.

Dan Xin offered Four-Eyed Fish and five other associates $50,000 each to help him take revenge. They visited a gun dealer they knew, a young man with spiked hair and a black leather jacket who worked out of an apartment he shared with his mother, a garment factory worker. They bought five handguns and a Cobray Mac-11 assault pistol, which could shoot 1,200 rounds per minute. At times they seemed not like juvenile killers but like harmless truants, kids playing GI Joe. They all referred to the Mac-11, erroneously, as "the Uzi." They bought serrated hunting knives and called them "Rambo knives." The plan was to kill Ah Wong and then torch his safe house, burning it to the ground. They went to a gas station and filled two plastic water jugs with gasoline, then departed on a scouting mission. But they had neglected to seal the jugs securely, and before long they had to stop, because they had all gotten woozy from the fumes.

Tam could see what was going to happen. He told Dan Xin where Ah Wong was hiding out—a safe house in Teaneck, New Jersey, a quiet suburb on the other side of the George Washington Bridge. As the plotters made their preparations, a pile of weapons began to accumulate on a living room table at the Brooklyn brothel. Tam said he didn't want to take part in the killing. But Four-Eyed Fish threatened him. "Whoever doesn't go, we gotta do him," Four-Eye said. Tam reluctantly drew them a map of the safe house, diagramming the entrances and exits. He would later claim that he had deliberately misconstrued the layout of the house, but it was of little importance; Dan Xin had the address where Ah Wong was hiding. Tam had always had an insatiable appetite for drugs, and in the days leading up to the operation he took whatever he could, trying to incapacitate himself, or at least appear to.

On the evening of May 23, 1993, Dan Xin traveled to the parking lot of a motel near the entrance to the Holland Tunnel. It was the last time he would meet with his handlers at the FBI. Ray Kerr and Peter Lee could sense that he had become impatient. But so far as they knew, Dan Xin still didn't know how to locate Ah Wong. "Remember, if you find out where that safe house is, you don't do anything. You call Peter," Kerr told him. Dan Xin nodded.

The next afternoon Dan Xin and the others left Alan asleep at the brothel. There were seven of them altogether. They got into a light blue Dodge Caravan and an Audi that sputtered with a broken muffler. Then they drove north, in the direction of the George Washington Bridge.

Teaneck is a placid middle-class community of tranquil avenues and subdivisions lined with leafy trees, pruned hedges, swing sets, and small, carefully tended lawns. The house at 1326 Somerset Road was a modest two-story brick-and-shingle place set back from the street and surrounded by hedges and towering oak trees. Inside, a man named Chang Liang Lin was cooking rice in the kitchen. Chang had grown up in a village in Fujian and had left his wife and eight-year-old son and been smuggled from China to Los Angeles. He had arrived in New York only recently, and still owed $33,000 for the trip. Chang had been in the house for a week. He'd been beaten once, but on the whole it hadn't been so bad. The house was very comfortable by Chinese standards; to Chang, it looked like a mansion.

The house was unusually empty that afternoon; it was just Chang and Guo Liang Qun, Ah Kay's youngest brother, who was twenty-one and whom everyone called Ah Qun. The doorbell rang, and Ah Qun walked to the front of the house to see who it was. He opened the door, and several people pushed their way in. One of them was Dan Xin Lin, whom Chang knew slightly, because they had lived near each other back in China. Dan Xin looked angry, and he and Ah Qun began arguing and shouting at each other. Suddenly Dan Xin and the men with him pulled out guns, and one of them accidentally discharged, the bullet lodging itself in Ah Qun's leg. The boy howled with pain. Two of Dan Xin's men went into the kitchen and started beating Chang. They took him into the living room, where Ah Qun was screaming, and tied his hands and legs, and Ah Qun's hands and legs, with duct tape. Dan Xin leaned over them and taped their mouths shut, and the others forced them down into the basement.

The basement floor was cold. One of Dan Xin's underlings, a sallow twenty-two-year-old named Yun Lin, stayed with Chang and Ah Qun. Yun Lin had high cheekbones and delicate lips. He had just arrived from China himself, and he was kind to Chang. He found a blanket and wrapped it around Chang to keep him warm. He spoke to him and called him uncle, a gesture of affection and respect. Chang lay on the floor next to Ah Qun and wondered what would become of them.

After establishing that only Chang and Ah Qun were home, Dan Xin set out to search the rest of the house. He walked upstairs and began going through the bedrooms, looking for any weapons that might be hidden there. Then he heard the doorbell ring.

Ah Wong had spent the day in Chinatown, gambling with other members of the gang. As afternoon gave way to evening, he and three friends drove back over the George Washington Bridge to New Jersey and through the quiet streets of Teaneck. They pulled up in front of the house, got out of the car, and walked up the front path. Ah Wong rang the doorbell, but no one answered. He told two of his companions, Yu Ping Zhang and Guang Sheng Li, to go around to the back of the house.

They jimmied a window and climbed into the kitchen. The house was quiet; no one seemed to be home. They walked through the living room to the entry foyer in the front. Yu Ping Zhang was smoking a cigarette. He unlocked the front door, and his hand was on the knob and opening the door to let the others in when Dan Xin Lin came down the stairs, dressed in black and holding the Mac-11. Yu Ping Zhang was dead before he hit the floor, the cigarette still in his mouth. Before Guang Sheng Li could escape, the attackers were upon him, shooting him in the head and stabbing him repeatedly. Dan Xin may have taken a special satisfaction in this—Guang Sheng Li had been one of the men at the beeper store the day he had almost died.

On the front porch, Ah Wong and the man he was with, Ming Cheng, heard the shots. They turned and sprinted in opposite directions, but the killers burst out after them. They fired wildly at Ming Cheng but missed, and eventually lost track of him. Ah Wong dashed down Somerset Road and cut across a lawn at Wendell Place. But the lawn had recently been mowed, and he slid on the loose grass. The attackers caught up with him and stood above him, pumping bullets into his body as he squirmed on the ground.

Then the killers returned to the house to execute the two witnesses in the basement. Chang heard the shot that killed Ah Qun. But he hardly registered a thing when the men shot him in the head.

Akiva Fleischmann, who had just turned nine years old, was eating a dinner of takeout chicken with his family in the kitchen of their house on Mercedes Street when he heard what he thought must be fireworks. Akiva and his older brother, Shaya, ran into their backyard. When they reached the curb, Akiva saw several Chinese men galloping toward him. As they ran past, Akiva saw one of the men pause to throw something underneath a Cadillac parked in front of a neighbor's house. Suddenly a blue minivan came tearing up Mercedes Street from the other direction and pulled to a stop right in front of him. As Akiva and his brother stood there, frozen, on the sidewalk, the van's side door slid open, the Chinese men piled in, and in a screech of tires the van did a wild U-turn, then tore down the street and disappeared.

The Fleischmann boys were hardly the only ones to notice the shooting. It was a balmy May evening, and still light. A neighbor who lived nearby was mowing her lawn and saw the shooters sprint by. Another neighbor was watering his garden and heard the shots. Three local kids were riding their bicycles along the sidewalk when the shooters ran by. The police were receiving 911 calls before the shooting had even stopped. When officers arrived at Somerset Road, they found a terrifying scene: two men dead in the front foyer, two others bound, gagged, and shot in the head downstairs. In the basement they found a pool of blood that didn't correspond to either of the victims on the floor, and they realized that one of the men in the foyer above had been stabbed so aggressively that the knife had pierced the hardwood floor and blood was seeping through to the basement.

It was beginning to get dark as police officers cordoned off the area. The lights from their cruisers cast magic-lantern shadows across the foliage and facades. Akiva Fleischmann still didn't know what to make of the events he had just witnessed, and from the safe distance of his front lawn, he watched the officers work. Then he remembered seeing the man throw something under his neighbor's Cadillac. He approached the car and reached underneath it, still thinking it was some sort of firecracker. He pulled out a black Smith & Wesson 9-millimeter, sleek and cool and heavy, its grip pebbly in his palm. Holding it in front of him, Akiva approached a cop who stood nearby. "Do you guys want this?" he asked.

Ah Wong was still alive, sprawled on the freshly cut grass, when a member of the volunteer ambulance corps approached him and began scissoring the bloody clothes away from his body. As the medic worked, Ah Wong slowly reached into his pocket, withdrew a wad of crumpled money, and handed it to him. He died at the hospital three hours later. "Naked oriental male, black crew cut hair, five foot five, 120 pounds," the medical examiner wrote when Ah Wong lay dead on a gurney, medical tubes still coiling out of his mouth. He surveyed Ah Wong's small, hard body, a weathered butcher block of gouges and nicks, a contour map exposing the full topography of a gangland youth—the marks that his few brutal years had left upon him.

Each arm was sheathed in a multicolored 8-inch tattoo of a ferocious dragon. Another dragon, this one a foot tall and 7 or 8 inches wide, sprawled across his back. "On the victim's upper right arm, approximately one inch below the armpit, the victim has what appear to be two old bullet wounds. On the deceased's lower chest and abdomen are six old scars which appear to be old stab wounds." Ah Wong had been shot nine times that night. Seven of the bullets were plucked from his body; two more had passed clear through. A tenth bullet—a .380-caliber hollow point—was extracted from his leg, but it didn't match any of the ballistics at the scene. The medical examiner determined that it was from an old gunshot wound he had never had treated. Even Fujianese who weren't involved in criminal activity often tended to avoid the hospital; they rarely had insurance, and they didn't want to occasion any unnecessary checks into their immigration status. But the gunfighters of the Fuk Ching were especially inclined to stoicism in the face of injury if it meant they could avoid questioning by police. Ah Wong had been walking around with a bullet in his leg.

Four-Eyed Fish and another assailant, Shing Chung, had fled in the blue Audi. They headed north to the Tappan Zee Bridge and escaped. Four-Eye was eventually apprehended two years later, in Florida, where he was working as a dishwasher in a Chinese restaurant. Shing Chung has never been caught.

Dan Xin Lin was not so lucky. "Get out of here!" he shouted when the Dodge Caravan picked him up. "Get onto the highway and cross the bridge." It may simply have been the terror and exhilaration of the slaughter the boys had just participated in, and a kind of homing instinct that suddenly asserted itself, drawing them out of the unfamiliar suburban universe of subdivisions and safe houses and back to the cramped safety of Chinatown. But heading back to Chinatown was a mistake. The George Washington Bridge was the most obvious route back into Manhattan, and within minutes of the shootings an all-points bulletin had gone out to police in the area to look out for the blue Dodge van that had fled the scene. In nearby Fort Lee, a police officer was stationed by the entrance to the bridge and spotted the van approaching the tollbooths. He drew his gun, walked toward the van, and ordered the passengers to get out. Five Chinese men stepped onto the pavement. Their clothes were covered in blood.

Ray Kerr was asleep that night when he got a call from a colleague at the FBI telling him that Dan Xin Lin had killed four people in New Jersey. When Dan Xin was put in jail and permitted to make one telephone call, he contacted Peter Lee. The authorities were furious, and embarrassed, that their witness in the beeper-store case had taken matters into his own hands. The *Daily News* ran an article on the incident under the headline "FBI Informer Held in Massacre." Kerr cut it out and put it on his wall, as a reminder to himself and others of the risks they ran when dealing with people like Dan Xin Lin.

The killers were held as maximum-security prisoners at the Bergen County Jail. When a judge set Dan Xin's bail at $1 million, he had a distinctly Fujianese response. "If I come up with one million from relatives," he wondered, "can I go?" Ultimately, Dan Xin and his accomplices were convicted and given multiple life sentences. Chang, the Fujianese hostage who was being held in the house in Teaneck, ended up surviving, albeit with a bullet permanently lodged in his head—and testifying against his assailants. The prosecutor who put him on the stand referred to him, affectionately and out of earshot of the jury, as Bullet Head.

In New York, the small band of officers of the state and federal government who knew that the bloodshed in Teaneck was in fact an installment in the larger struggle between Ah Kay and Dan Xin Lin all had the same thought: the gravest acts of terror could only be yet to come, because somewhere in the world Ah Kay had no doubt learned of the deaths of his two younger brothers, and his wrath would soon be felt. Only then would the true significance of Teaneck be understood. Luke Rettler was sure of it. So were Ray Kerr and his colleagues at the FBI. The Fifth Precinct of the NYPD began augmenting security on the streets of Chinatown. Everyone braced for an all-out war.

But the officials were all tragically mistaken. To American law enforcement, Ah Kay may have seemed uncatchable and undeportable, an almost superhuman wanderer who could flit from one country to the next, completely unimpeded by the niceties of national boundaries. But as it happened, they badly overestimated him. For even as he mourned the deaths of his brothers, Ah Kay was confronted by a plan gone devastatingly awry. During the trial of the murderers at Teaneck, it emerged that while Dan Xin's desire for revenge had driven the killings, there was another motivation as well. "He said he was going to do Ah Wong because Ah Kay was in China," Alan Tam testified. "When they do Ah Wong, they going to take over the smuggling business." Dan Xin knew that Ah Wong was expecting a boat to arrive in the United States, with a $9 million bounty of Fujianese passengers. Because the Teaneck trial unfolded later, after the ship arrived in so spectacular a fashion, and there was a fear that any association between the defendants and that event might prejudice the jury, the judge instructed Tam and the other witnesses to refer to the vessel in question simply as "the boat" or "the ship" and not by its name, the *Golden Venture*. "From what I hear from Dan Xin," one of the killers said, "after we kill those people . . . we could get Wong's boat of people that's coming to the United States, and we could collect those money."

With Ah Kay stuck in China and Ah Wong and the others dead, the gang was in disarray. Even the resourceful Ah Kay would not be able to arrange a fleet of fishing boats to offload the ship in the Atlantic. And with Dan Xin and his accomplices locked up in a Bergen County jail, they would not be able to meet the ship either. It was not the arrival of Ah Kay that the authorities should have been worrying about in the days following the massacre at Teaneck, but the arrival of the *Golden Venture*.

Chapter Ten

Mutiny in the Atlantic

ONE WEEK before the killings at Teaneck, as Ah Wong and his allies were hiding out in the safe house and Dan Xin and his allies were preparing to kill them, the *Golden Venture* rumbled toward a prearranged set of nautical coordinates in the North Atlantic, five days' journey from the East Coast, where according to the plan it would rendezvous with fishing boats sent by the Fuk Ching. The ship's imminent arrival was well known in Chinatown. Sister Ping was expecting her two customers any day, and both Weng Yu Hui and Mr. Charlie had flown back to New York to supervise the offloading. They had supplied their onboard enforcer, Kin Sin Lee, with a radio frequency to contact the smaller boats. But when Kin Sin Lee tried to reach them, the smaller boats did not reply. When Lee was able to reach Weng and Mr. Charlie, they told him that there was a problem with the smaller boats, because with Ah Kay in China and his brothers in hiding, they had been unable to arrange a way to transport the passengers from ship to shore.

Kin Sin Lee was growing anxious. The passengers were restless: it had been over a month since they left Mombasa, and three months since the ship took on the original passengers at Pattaya. Supplies were dwindling, he told the snakeheads; the ship was running low on fuel. But this lament did not have the intended effect; rather than saying that they would send out the smaller boats immediately, Charlie and Weng suggested that if supplies were so low, Kin Sin Lee should turn the ship around and head back east across the Atlantic to the Portuguese archipelago of Madeira, some 400 miles off the coast of Morocco, where he could resupply before endeavoring another mid-Atlantic meeting.

Captain Tobing liked this new plan. The journey had taken much longer than he anticipated. He was also fearful of being arrested in the coastal waters of the United States. It may simply be that he felt more secure heading away from America's shoreline and into the unpoliced wilderness of the Atlantic; it may also be that he planned on abandoning the ship once it docked in Madeira, as the *Najd II*'s original captain had done in Mauritius. If the snakeheads sent an employee to Madeira to resupply the ship, the captain figured, perhaps he and his crew could take the employee hostage and demand that Weng and Mr. Charlie send smaller boats. But Kin Sin Lee didn't like this plan. The passengers were getting manic and edgy. If the captain turned the ship around, Lee was certain they would revolt.

Tobing was two decades older than Lee, physically sturdier, and far more experienced at sea, and he stubbornly insisted that the best course of action was to head to Madeira. But Lee was in no mood to defer to some ship's captain. He ordered Tobing to sail the *Golden Venture* to America. Tobing steadfastly refused, saying he would only take the ship east, toward Madeira. With the matter unresolved, Lee assembled his various allies from among the passengers and arrived at a whispered plan. He quietly distributed six knives, three wooden clubs, and a gun and explained that if the captain was going to be so unreasonable, they would simply have to depose him. He didn't call it a mutiny. He called it "kidnapping the boat."

The ship's Burmese first officer, a young man named Sam Lwin, was eating lunch in the galley off the bridge when the mutineers barged into the room. The captain and the chief engineer had been removed from power and handcuffed belowdecks, they announced. They escorted the nervous Lwin to see Kin Sin Lee. Lwin and Lee have different recollections of the ensuing conversation. According to Lee, he told the first officer that he did not have to help sail the ship if he didn't want to. "You can eat and sleep—nobody is going to hurt you," he reassured him. If Lwin wanted to continue working, however, and take the captain's place, he would receive an increase in his salary, and a bonus when the passengers were offloaded. In Lwin's account, Kin Sin Lee left him with less of a choice. "Now we are going to a new spot," Lwin says Lee told him. "You are going to drive the ship to that place, or you are going to die." Lwin was not a licensed captain, but he knew how to control and navigate the ship. That afternoon he assumed command of the *Golden Venture*.

With Tobing locked in his cabin, Lwin directed the ship to a second rendezvous point, this one some 70 nautical miles southeast of Nantucket. The slow approach to U.S. waters took nearly a week, and by the time the *Golden Venture* arrived at the prearranged destination it was June, and unknown to the people on board, the Teaneck massacre had occurred. Kin Sin Lee tried to reach Weng and Charlie on shore, but they were not responding on the radio. The ship floated there for several days until finally Lee was able to reach Weng. He was hoping to hear that the fishing boats were on their way, but instead Weng told him to steer the ship to yet another set of coordinates, this one off the coast of New Bedford. Lee did not know Weng all that well, and did not trust him. Weng seemed to be dissembling, and it was not at all clear that once the *Golden Venture* arrived at this new meeting point there would be anyone there to meet it. "I don't want to talk to you," he snapped. "Let Charlie talk to me." Then he heard Mr. Charlie's voice on the radio. Charlie was his mentor; the two men knew each other well, and the younger enforcer trusted the worldly and experienced snakehead, who never seemed to lose his cool. But Charlie would only reiterate Weng's instructions. He repeated the coordinates of the new destination and told Kin Sin Lee to go there. The smaller boats were already sailing in that direction, he said.

On the morning of June 4, as the *Golden Venture* sat in the sea southeast of Nantucket, a small airplane soared overhead. No one on board would have given it much notice. The passengers were all confined to the hold and likely wouldn't have heard the distant hum pass above them, and the enforcers and the crew had become accustomed to the occasional passing plane etching a line across the blue sky before vanishing over the horizon. But the pilot of the plane took note of the *Golden Venture.* He had taken off that day from the Coast Guard Air Station at Cape Cod, and when he returned to the station he duly reported having "sited the vessel DIW" (dead in the water) at 0805 hours.

In the months and years to come, the arrival of the *Golden Venture* would often be described as a "tragedy," a dreadful loss of life and a stunning challenge to the immigration and asylum policies of the United States. But missing in all the commentary on this sad chapter in American immigration history is a simple, undeniable fact: the *Golden Venture* incident, as we have come to think of it, could have been avoided. For months prior to the sudden appearance of the ship off the beach on the Rockaway Peninsula, the United States knew that it was coming. As early as October 1992, nine months before the Coast Guard plane spotted the *Golden Venture* near Nantucket, the American government had learned that the *Najd II* was in Mombasa with a cargo of undocumented Chinese emigrants and a plan to travel to the United States. As soon as the ship arrived, representatives from Mombasa's Missions to Seamen contacted the small U.S. consulate in the city and explained the situation. At least on paper, U.S. authorities had a strong preference for interdicting smuggling vessels before they reached American shores. The ships the snakeheads used were seldom seaworthy enough to safely complete the journeys they were making, and it was most prudent to stop them at the earliest possible moment. There was also the fact that stopping a smuggling ship at sea, or in a third country, rather than allowing it to reach the United States, meant that American officials were not bound to offer asylum hearings and a whole range of procedural protections to the passengers on board.

As it happened, in February 1993, around the time the *Golden Venture* was leaving Pattaya to pick up the passengers in Mombasa, U.S.

authorities had pioneered a more proactive approach to snakehead vessels when a black-hulled cargo ship called the *East Wood* was discovered floating 1,500 miles southwest of Hawaii with some 500 Chinese passengers on board. The U.S. Coast Guard boarded the *East Wood* at sea. But a tense diplomatic standoff ensued. The Coast Guard wanted to divert the ship to the Marshall Islands rather than allow it to reach the United States, but the government of the Marshall Islands initially refused, observing that there was no reason it should be forced to admit 500 undocumented Chinese. Then the United States turned to Hong Kong, asking the British colony to accept the ship. But Hong Kong refused. "I think Hong Kong has dealt with more than its fair share of boat people," a government representative said. "They are clearly the responsibility of China or the U.S." Because the ship was registered in Panama, the United States appealed to the Panamanian government to accept it and either offer sanctuary to the passengers on board or deport them to China. But the Panamanians in turn looked to the shipping company that operated the *East Wood*, which was based in Hong Kong. The *East Wood* had become a liability that no government wanted to handle, and after protracted negotiations, officials in Washington arranged to have representatives from the United Nations high commissioner for refugees board the ship and determine if the passengers had fled from China because of bona fide persecution or a well-founded fear of it or if they were simply economic migrants, and as such deportable.

The UN monitors ultimately concluded that there were no genuine refugees on board, and the United States arranged to deport the immigrants back to China. "The government of China has given assurances that no one will be prosecuted or persecuted for having left the country illegally," a State Department spokesman said. But no sooner had the *East Wood* passengers arrived back in Fuzhou than reports began to indicate that the Chinese government had reneged on its promise. In a series of stories, the *South China Morning Post* revealed that many of the passengers were thrown into detention centers upon their return and forced to pay punitive fines. Officials in Beijing denied the reports. But the taint was there—the suggestion that even if the passengers had not been politically persecuted before they left China, the very act of returning them in so public a fashion would engender persecution.

Washington's experience with the *East Wood* would form the backdrop for its handling of the *Golden Venture*, both before and after it landed in New York. It remains unclear whether the diplomatic fallout from the incident and the apparent lesson that interdiction and deportation are not always the most efficient—or the most moral—solution to boat smuggling from China were on the minds of U.S. officials who chose not to interdict the *Najd II* while they had the opportunity to do so. What is clear is that Washington was well aware of the presence in Mombasa harbor of another ship full of Chinese migrants and did nothing about it. From the consulate in Mombasa, word of the *Najd II* went to the U.S. embassy in Nairobi. But when embassy officials communicated the relevant facts to the State Department, their impression was that "Washington seemed uninterested."

The INS had always struggled with the fact that it was essentially a domestic law enforcement agency, with very little international presence. In 1993 there was only one foreign-based American immigration officer for the whole of Africa, a man named Don Monica. Monica was based in Nairobi. He made the short flight to Mombasa and met with the Burmese crewmen who had fled the *Najd* and were staying at the Missions to Seamen, and gathered intelligence about the ship. He reported his findings to his supervisors at the INS.

Some at the INS felt that the agency should be more proactive in these matters, employing techniques similar to those used by the Drug Enforcement Agency. Some recommended sending an undercover agent on one of the smuggling ships, but the fact that the vessels tended to be so rickety made the plan unsafe; the agency could not risk losing an agent on a sinking ship. One plan that was briefly discussed was to place some kind of transponder or beacon on the *Najd II*, so that the United States could track it as it crossed the Atlantic. A beacon presented less of a risk than an agent, but the challenge was how to get it onto the *Najd* undetected. And when an appeal was made to officials at the INS and the Department of Justice in Washington, they simply rejected the plan.

Don Monica was still trying to decide what could be done about the *Najd II* when he was informed one morning in April that all the passengers from the ship had disappeared, having been transported in the dead of night to another vessel that would take them to America. He went to the office of the British naval liaison and asked for a record of all the ships that had left the port around the time the passengers disappeared. They gave him a list of ships, one of which was a cargo vessel bound for Durban, which they told him was called the *Gold Future*. Monica informed INS headquarters in Washington, and the name *Gold Future* was reported through INS intelligence channels as belonging to a ship that was possibly smuggling Chinese people to America. He also telephoned the U.S. embassy in Pretoria, South Africa, to let officials know that the *Gold Future* was heading their way.

On April 15, 1993, the Department of Justice issued a confidential intelligence brief describing the various smuggling ships that were thought to be approaching the United States. The document reveals the ongoing confusion of U.S. authorities. One ship identified in the report is the *Tung Sheng*—the *Tong Sern,* as the *Golden Venture* was named before it was rechristened at sea. The document recounts the success of the Pattaya Tourist Police in stopping an additional sixty-eight passengers from boarding the ship and says that the *Tong Sern* is a "Panamanian-flagged vessel" and is "most likely bound for the United States." Then, in the same laundry list of smuggling ships but as a separate entry, the document continues, "In October 1992, a Thai ferry boat, identified as the *Najd II,* entered the harbor at Mombasa, Kenya, with 292 PRC nationals on board. Despite attempts to remove the aliens, the *Najd II* and her passengers remained in Mombasa. On or about April 7, 1993, Kenyan Port tugboats ferried most of the PRC nationals to a vessel several miles off the coast of Kenya. The vessel has tentatively been identified as the *Gold Future,* a Panamanian flagged cargo vessel," which was "currently at sea along the east coast of Africa."

No one knew that the *Tong Sern* had been renamed and reflagged at sea, so as far as U.S. authorities were concerned, the *Tong Sern* and the *Golden Venture* were two separate Panamanian-registered ships. Ironically enough, the officials could have gained a much better understanding of the situation if they had simply consulted the newspaper. On April 4, 1993, the *South China Morning Post* delivered a report that was more accurate than the U.S. intelligence briefing of eleven days later. "A ship carrying hundreds of illegal Chinese immigrants is on its way to the United States," the article announced, before detailing the midnight departure of the immigrants who had been stranded in Mombasa. The Hong Kong–based newspaper exhibited no confusion about the names of the ships or the sequence of events, and explained that the immigrants were now bound for the United States "aboard a Honduran-registered fishing trawler MV *Golden Venture.*"

If anyone in the American diplomatic corps in Hong Kong took notice of this article on April 4, they did not ensure that the valuable information it contained reached Washington in time to correct the intelligence report on April 15. Of course, even intelligence officers familiar with the different ships might not have been able to deduce that the *Tong Sern* and the *Golden Venture* were actually one ship. But they might have paused over the fact that the intelligence community was looking for a ship called the *Gold Future,* while the paper proclaimed that the vessel in question was the *Golden Venture.* That might have seemed like a minor difference—it could just be that when Don Monica visited the naval liaison at Mombasa someone said the name wrong or he heard it wrong, an inconsequential loss in translation. But there was also the fact that the intelligence brief said the ship in question was registered in Panama, while the article suggested it was registered in Honduras. These probably seemed like trivial distinctions, and it is a commonplace in intelligence and law enforcement circles that the word of the press is not to be trusted and is no substitute for solid investigative work.

On April 16, the South African Coast Guard received word that a ship that U.S. intelligence believed might be transporting illegal Chinese immigrants to America had just entered Durban harbor. The ship was registered in Panama. It had come from Mombasa and was allegedly carrying a load of jute. It was not clear how long it would stay at anchor in Durban, and South African officials hastily boarded it and inspected the cabins and the hold. But there was no sign of any Chinese migrants on board. There weren't even any Chinese crew members. This must have struck the South Africans as odd, because the ship's name, painted on its bow, was definitely *Gold Future*. The ship's captain was less than thrilled about the raid. "He expressed indignation at the implication that his ship was possibly carrying illegal aliens," a subsequent cable from the embassy in Pretoria to the State Department explained. He "demanded to know who had started such a rumor."

The snakeheads could not have created a better decoy if they had arranged it themselves. By some extraordinary coincidence, this ship, the *Gold Future,* had left Mombasa at about the same time the *Golden Venture* had, producing the erroneous tip to Don Monica. It then proceeded down the coast to South Africa, where it was stopped by the authorities. As officials in Washington read over the intelligence report and scratched their heads, wondering how it was that the captain of the *Gold Future* had made a cargo of three hundred illegal Chinese disappear, the *Golden Venture* had sailed clear of Durban, no longer at any risk of being identified by the South African authorities, and was making its way to America.

In Chinatown, Weng and Charlie were desperately trying to find someone capable of securing a number of fishing boats, taking them out to sea by night, connecting with the *Golden Venture*, and offloading the three hundred passengers. But for all the haphazardness of the particular technique developed by the Fuk Ching gang, it was skilled work, and the incident at Teaneck meant that everyone from the gang was either dead or in prison, in hiding, or in China. It appears that Ah Kay had succeeded so completely in his efforts to monopolize the offloading business up and down the East Coast that with the gang in disarray, there was literally nobody else who could do the job. The next time Kin Sin Lee radioed from the boat, Weng decided to level with him. "You guys don't have to wait," he said. "There's a problem."

There wouldn't be any fishing boats, Weng explained. The *Golden Venture* was going to have to deposit the passengers directly on shore. Mr. Charlie got on the radio and spoke slowly, trying to reassure Kin Sin Lee that the situation was under control. He told Lee to pull out a nautical chart of the New York coastal area. Then Charlie told him to look for the East River. Lee found it on the map. Charlie asked if he could see two bridges that spanned the river very close together—the Brooklyn Bridge and the Manhattan Bridge. Lee saw them. Go there, Charlie said. "Somebody will pick you up on the left bank." What Charlie had in mind was the low-slung piers just north of the Manhattan Bridge, a few blocks from the eastern edge of Chinatown and Sister Ping's apartment at Knickerbocker Village. It was an audacious plan. He wanted to bring the *Golden Venture* into New York Bay, under the Verrazzano Bridge, along Red Hook, Brooklyn, right past the Coast Guard station at Governor's Island and directly up to Manhattan, to drop the passengers in Chinatown—the snakehead equivalent of door-to-door service. But the first officer turned captain, Lwin, rejected the plan outright, reasoning that if they were going to try to bring the ship ashore, there were probably less conspicuous places to suddenly disgorge three hundred stunned and blinking illegal immigrants than the Lower East Side of Manhattan.

Weng suggested that they look up a part of New York called Rockaway. The area was on the outskirts of the city, and remote. It faced out into the Atlantic, and on the charts, at any rate, the beach looked sandy. If Lwin could run the *Golden Venture* aground at Rockaway, Weng said, he would send vans to the beach to pick up the passengers as they came ashore.

The following day, June 5, Mr. Charlie and Weng drove out to Rockaway to inspect the site. People come from all over the city to visit the beach, especially during the summer months. None of the locals would have given much thought to the Chinese men looking out to sea and taking note of the sand on the beach, the depth of the water, the force of the currents offshore. Satisfied with the location, the snakeheads reached Lee on the ship-to-shore. Charlie instructed him to slow the ship so it would arrive at Rockaway late that night, when the locals were sleeping and the beach was completely dark. When he approached the shore, Charlie continued, he should gun the ship at full speed and run it aground on the sandy beach. At Charlie's urging, Kin Sin Lee and the crew began destroying all the documents they could find on the boat: passenger lists, registration documents, Captain Tobing's log. They tore them up and threw them overboard.

Sean Chen was huddled in the hold, overtaken by excitement. Word had spread among the passengers that they would be landing soon. Some people claimed to have been above deck long enough to catch a fleeting glimpse of the lights of the United States. Then, around midday, the passengers whom Kin Sin Lee had deputized as his onboard enforcers clambered down the ladder and into the hold. *We will soon be landing in America,* they said. *When the ship lands, you will need to brace yourselves, because it will land hard. If you know how to swim, you should get off the ship first and swim to shore.*

According to some accounts, it was announced that those who did not know how to swim should stay on board and someone would arrange to pick them up later. But according to others, the passengers were told that even those who did not know how to swim should jump and try to swim for shore, because everyone who remained on board would be arrested.

It may never be clear how it was that the Coast Guard, which had spotted the *Golden Venture* and was monitoring the ship, ultimately failed to prevent the catastrophe that followed. It is a frequent refrain of those in the business of actually keeping track of ships that the ocean is a very big place, crisscrossed at any moment by all manner of craft large and small, and it is not as easy as it sounds to monitor a ship continuously. But the *Golden Venture* was quite close to shore, and as it approached New York its course took it on a trajectory that ran directly perpendicular to the shipping lanes in the area—a dangerous move, and one that might have attracted some notice. What we do know is that on that Saturday evening, as the *Golden Venture* followed its slow course toward Rockaway, the Coast Guard dispatched boats to intercept it. But they couldn't find it.

When the ship reached the water off Rockaway, at around 11 P.M., Kin Sin Lee tried calling Charlie, but he couldn't make contact. He instructed the crew members and onboard enforcers to take flashlights and start giving light signals to confirm that Weng and Charlie were waiting on shore and would be ready to transport the passengers. There were many lights along the shoreline: streetlights, house lights, the occasional headlights of passing cars. But nothing answered their signal. Shortly after midnight, Lee turned to Lwin. "Nobody is picking up," he said. "We have to go to shore."

They consulted the chart to try to identify a sandy portion of beach that they could use as a target.

"Do we really have to do this?" Lwin asked.

"Yes," Kin Sin Lee replied.

As darkness fell, the weather had grown stormy. The wind had picked up, and the waves were choppy now, and very rough. The aggressive tide was actually a good thing, Lwin said. As the ship approached the beach, the surge of the strong waves would push it farther up onto the shore. When Lwin had selected the appropriate angle for their final approach, Kin Sin Lee pulled a bell which sent a command to the engine room: *full speed ahead.*

"Let's do it," he told Lwin.

Overcome by adrenaline, Lwin hugged Lee. "God bless you," he said. Then, as the ship picked up speed, he instructed Lee to sit down and hold on tight.

"Let's give New York a surprise," he said.

In the last moments at sea, Sean could feel the *Golden Venture* pick up speed. They had been warned to brace themselves, and he had grown accustomed, during the months in the hold, to clutching his belongings and positioning his limbs in such a way that he did not roll helplessly with every undulation. The hold was electric with excitement and anticipation: it had all been worth it, the sacrifice, the danger, the hunger, seasickness, and storms; the treks through Burma, the lonely months in Bangkok, the terrors of the *Najd II*, and the hopeless interlude in Africa. It was over. They had triumphed. They were about to set foot on American soil.

A huge *thwump* sent a shudder through the hold as the bow plowed into a sandbar. Everyone around Sean was thrown by the impact, rolling and sprawling, then trying to get purchase on the plywood floor, grab their belongings, and get out of the hold. They mobbed the ladder leading to the deck. Sean joined the throng, eventually getting his hands on the ladder and climbing up and out into the night. The wind was strong, the air salty, the lights of New York a glimmer in the distance. The small deck of the ship was chaotic—people were shouting and screaming, gathering their few belongings and jumping overboard into the sea. Sean could swim. He wasn't a strong swimmer, but he had learned how to swim growing up and knew that if he kept moving all four limbs in the water, he would stay afloat. He made his way to the front of the *Golden Venture,* took off his T-shirt and his pants, summoned his nerve, put a leg over the edge, and jumped.

His first sensation was the severe, terrible coldness of the water, the kind of chill that saps any strength or energy you have, seeming literally to freeze your limbs, paralyzing you. Sean found the strength to move his arms and legs. He swam, eyes on the lights of the shore. He could have been in the water for ten minutes, or it could have been an hour—he didn't know. He just kept pushing against his exhaustion, buffeted by the surf, one arm over the other, until his feet hit sand. He half walked, half crawled the last remaining yards until he reached the beach, where others were coming ashore around him. Then he straightened, took a few more steps, and collapsed.

When he came to, he was lying in a bed in a brightly lit room. He was wearing an unfamiliar garment: a simple cotton shift, a hospital johnny. He looked around. He was in the hospital. There was a black man standing above him, in a uniform—a police officer. The officer was speaking to him in English.

Sean tried to remember the English he had learned from his dictionary in Bangkok and practiced over the months at sea with anyone who could speak it.

"Where am I?" he asked.

"You're in New York City," the cop replied.

Sean felt an enormous, almost overwhelming sense of relief. But the relief was tempered somewhat by one especially strange detail of his new surroundings. As Sean lay there in his johnny in the hospital with the police officer and slowly took it all in, he made an alarming discovery. He was handcuffed to the bed.

Chapter Eleven

A Well-founded Fear

FOR MUCH of its history the United States has suffered from a kind of bipolarity when it comes to matters of immigration. The country's growth has been fueled by successive waves of strivers from other shores, who helped animate the westward push across the continent, fuel the industrial revolution of the nineteenth century, and accelerate the high-tech boom of the late twentieth century. The notion that America is a "nation of immigrants" is an enduring cliché. Yet while a steady demand for cheap labor and a sense that the United States should welcome the downtrodden of the world have led to a generally liberal immigration policy, American history has also been punctuated by periods of acute xenophobia and hostility to outsiders, particularly during difficult economic times, and a recurrent suggestion that the American dream will remain attainable only so long as the country fends off the fortune-seeking hordes and limits the number of people who can obtain access to the opportunities the country has to offer.

Whether through some accident of history or because of the industriousness with which they have answered America's siren call, or perhaps because their foreignness is written so indelibly on their faces, the Chinese seem to have suffered more than other immigrant groups at the mercy of the pendulum swing of American attitudes toward immigration. One historian referred to the Chinese as "the indispensable enemy"—needed for the labor they can provide, but also feared—and it does seem that the history of the Chinese in America serves as an object lesson in the country's fickle indecision on the subject of immigration. The Chinese who had the misfortune to be lured with the promise of work in the gold mines or on the railroads in the mid-nineteenth century, only to arrive and experience anti-Chinese pogroms and the advent of Chinese exclusion, experienced (and perhaps precipitated) one of these moments of sharp nativist reaction. The passengers aboard the *Golden Venture* happened to arrive during another.

In the summer of 1993, the mood in the United States had shifted perceptibly against immigrants, and perhaps especially against those immigrants who came seeking asylum. Six months before the *Golden Venture* arrived, in January, a Pakistani named Mir Aimal Kasi had gone on a shooting spree outside the CIA headquarters in McLean, Virginia, after applying for political asylum and using his work authorization documents to obtain a driver's license and purchase an AK-47. In February, five months before the ship ran aground, the World Trade Center was bombed in an operation masterminded by Ramzi Yousef, who had entered the country without a visa the year before and applied for political asylum, and by the Blind Sheikh, Omar Abdel Rahman, whose own asylum case was pending at the time of the bombings. Connecting these sensational examples of murderers who slipped through the system with the uptick in asylum applications from China, the press sounded the alarm: the United States had an immigration problem, and it was growing out of control. In March the *New York Times* warned of "a new boomtide of political asylum seekers that is swamping the process."

One person who was feeding the hysteria, in frequent interviews with the press, was Bill Slattery, the brash, determined head of the INS office in New York. Slattery felt that America's immigration policies were encouraging illegal immigrants to undertake the journey. The asylum system was broken, in his view, and the backlog was making it impossible to process migrants once they arrived. He sounded dire warnings to reporters that fraudulent asylum-seekers were "taking control of U.S. borders away from the U.S. government."

Slattery was hard-nosed and not given to self-doubt. He had volunteered for the Marine Corps in 1965, while he was still in high school, hoping to be sent to Vietnam. Instead he was sent to a training command in Yuma, Arizona, where he became fascinated by the Border Patrol. America's schizophrenia about immigration plays out in the culture of immigration officials. Historically, in the INS, one side of the job was known as "benefits" and involved accepting people—who should be let into the country and under what circumstances, how long they can stay, whether they can send for their families. The other side of the job was "enforcement"—fighting to keep people out or to send them back where they came from. The benefits/enforcement dichotomy is a matter of professional specialization for immigration officials, but also, on a deeper level, of philosophy. And from his early years with the Border Patrol, when Slattery was assigned to an outstation in the town of Hebbronville, east of Laredo, in what he referred to as "the tit" of Texas, he regarded his relationship with Mexicans as essentially an adversarial one. He learned to "cut for sign," stalking groups of migrants through the brush, noting each disturbance in the undergrowth, judging the age of a footprint by whether dew had settled on it or it had been traversed by bugs. The illegals were determined to outsmart Slattery, and he didn't want to let them.

After stints in Philadelphia and Newark, Slattery joined the New York office, rising through the ranks until he was made district director. His appointment, in 1990, coincided with the snakehead boom, and he spent the early nineties contending with the overwhelming numbers of Chinese who began disembarking from planes at JFK Airport. Slattery complained to his superiors, and also to the press, that as long as he was obliged to release asylum-seekers pending resolution of their claims, people would abuse the system. He wanted the authority to detain undocumented immigrants when they arrived in New York and to hold them while their asylum applications made their way through the system. If they were deprived of the opportunity to get out and work, Slattery guessed, word of the policy would make its way to China, and there would be fewer asylum-seekers in the future.

Before dawn on June 6, 1993, the telephone rang in Slattery's house in New Jersey. Slattery answered, and couldn't believe what he was hearing. "A ship?" he said. "In Queens?" He hung up and dressed. A special agent was en route to pick him up and take him to Rockaway. As the reality of what had happened sank in, Slattery's temper began to flare. The smugglers had brought a ship full of Chinese directly to New York City and run it aground on a beach in Queens. This was a final, unmistakable *fuck you* from the smugglers to the United States government, and Slattery took it personally.

As the car sped through the empty streets to Queens, Slattery took a call from the White House. Since the inauguration of Bill Clinton six months earlier, the INS had been a headless operation; Clinton had not yet appointed a commissioner, and many of the top positions were still unfilled. On the phone was a young National Security Council official, Eric Schwartz, who some months earlier had been charged with managing the Chinese boat smuggling issue. Earlier in his career, Schwartz had been the Washington director of Asia Watch, a human rights organization, and Slattery regarded him suspiciously, as an "alien activist." Schwartz seemed concerned with how the event was going to play out on television, and also with the human rights of the people on the ship. But Slattery had made up his mind before he reached the beach. "I'm detaining them, Eric," he said. "I'm going to lock them all up."

Sean Chen and the other passengers aboard the *Golden Venture* had been told that when they reached the United States, they would be questioned and processed, then released. That had indeed been the practice in recent years. Later, there would be much speculation about who made the decision to detain the *Golden Venture* passengers, and when. But there was no doubt in Slattery's mind. Washington was terrified, paralyzed by its own indecision. There was no leadership to speak of at the INS. Slattery bestrode the bureaucratic void created by the interregnum in Washington and made a decision. "I led. Washington followed," he would later recall, adding, "Nobody in Washington ever told me *not* to detain them."

Slattery faced something of a logistical challenge, however: there were simply not enough beds in the immigration detention centers in the New York area to house all of the *Golden Venture* passengers. Initially Sean and the other passengers were bused to the small detention facility on Varick Street. But the space was already overcrowded, and it was clear to Slattery that if the government was going to continue to detain the passengers for any length of time, some alternative arrangement would have to be made. Another problem, from Slattery's point of view, was that all the publicity surrounding the arrival of the *Golden Venture* seemed to have brought out the city's bleeding-heart contingent. Attorneys were showing up at Varick Street, offering to represent the Chinese. "It's been our tradition to protect these people," one of the lawyers told a reporter, citing the text of the Emma Lazarus poem inscribed on the Statue of Liberty. "If you ever wanted to see a picture of 'huddled masses yearning to breathe free,' it was on the front page of today's *New York Times*."

Slattery was not so easily moved. It rankled him when people referred to the Chinese as "refugees." Why was it that undocumented migrants from Mexico or Guatemala who arrived by truck were invariably described as "illegal aliens," but Cubans or Chinese who arrived by boat merited the designation "refugees"? Did the manner in which they came to the United States really make such a difference? To Slattery, Sister Ping and the other snakeheads in New York City seemed capable of exploiting every aspect of the American system. Some snakeheads had been known to collaborate actively with immigration attorneys, hiring them to assist clients in preparing bogus asylum applications. It wasn't unheard of for whole boatloads of passengers to end up represented by the same immigration attorney, prompting exasperated officials in New York to observe that "they didn't all look on the same page in the Yellow Pages." At Varick Street, someone placed a sign on a bulletin board saying that until further notice, lawyers would not be permitted to see the detainees. "Attorneys are permitted access when they've actually been retained by the detainees," an INS spokesman explained. But the attorneys would not be allowed to enter the facility "in an attempt to solicit business."

If Slattery could not turn the ship around and send it back to China or put the passengers on a plane immediately, it was clear that the process of removing them was going to take some time, and during that time he did not want to release them onto the streets. If he did so, it would send a message to China that the United States was a lax and permissive nation that could happily absorb untold numbers of illegals. Perhaps worst of all, Slattery knew from past experience with snakeheads that if he released the *Golden Venture* passengers, they would immediately find work and start saving money so they could pay off the balance of their $30,000 fees. Setting them free would be tantamount to giving $9 million to organized crime. Before long a plan was devised to farm out the passengers to detention facilities across the country, away from the immigration lawyers and the media glare of New York. The attorneys had maintained their presence at Varick Street, trying to get in to represent the passengers. But within forty-eight hours of the ship's arrival, volunteers who went to the facility were told it was too late. All the Chinese had gone.

Sean Chen found himself on a bus, in a convoy of buses that made its way out of New York City. It was a long ride, and Sean was hungry. He was unaccustomed to American food and unimpressed by the flimsy ham-on-white sandwich he was offered for the ride. He gazed out the window as the great asphalt and concrete snare of New York fell away and the bus traversed the highways and toll plazas of New Jersey and eventually entered Pennsylvania, pushing west into countryside that was more and more rural, with great verdant trees and sloping pastures segmented by lengths of whitewashed fence, and eventually the buggies and barns and silos of Amish country. Central Pennsylvania was the greenest place Sean had ever seen. It was beautiful.

On the outskirts of York, a rust belt town on the banks of the Susquehanna River, the buses came to a halt before a complex of low-slung beige buildings, the York County Prison. Sean filed in with the others and was issued a prison jumpsuit, then led to his cell. There were over a hundred *Golden Venture* passengers at York, all of them men. (The women had been sent to a prison in New Orleans.) Sean had been frightened on a number of occasions on his journey to America—when he passed through the mountains in Burma, when the local guide pointed a gun at him on the Thai border, when the *Golden Venture* nearly capsized in the gale off the Cape of Good Hope. But as the reality began to sink in that he was now a prisoner in an American jail, in a remote part of the country, far from any Chinatown or immigration lawyer, a deep, chilling fear of a sort that he had not felt before began to set in.

The *Golden Venture* passengers were segregated from the general population, in a separate wing of the prison. On that first day they tried to acclimate themselves to their new surroundings. They played cards and watched television to pass the time. They were puzzled by the strange food the prison served: beef pot pie, coleslaw, applesauce. But Sean was beginning to wonder if the various tribulations he had been through were for naught, if the whole odyssey had been a gross miscalculation. He thought about his parents back in Changle and how he could ever explain his misfortune to them. He felt, for the first time, that he had failed.

On Friday, June 11, six days after the arrival of the ship, Bill Clinton convened a meeting in the Oval Office. Senior staffers from the National Security Council, the Domestic Policy Council, the Coast Guard, and the INS discussed the *Golden Venture* incident and the larger policy dilemmas associated with boat smuggling. One of the agenda items at the meeting was "detention of smuggled aliens who do not have credible claims." The snakehead business was being discussed not merely as an immigration issue but as a matter of national security. Before the *Golden Venture* even arrived, the press was heralding a "smuggler ship invasion." It emerged that the month before, another ship, the *Pai Sheng*, had dumped 250 passengers on a pier near Fort Point in San Francisco, and a decision had been made to detain those passengers as well. Before the Oval Office meeting, the associate attorney general, Web Hubbell, wrote a letter to the national security adviser, Anthony Lake, suggesting that according to U.S. intelligence, as many as fifty-four additional vessels might be en route to the United States.

"Alien smuggling is a shameful practice of unspeakable degradation and unspeakable exploitation," Clinton declared in a speech at the White House the following week. He announced a new plan to combat the snakehead trade through aggressive pursuit of the smugglers, stiffer criminal penalties for smuggling, and efforts to interdict and redirect ships. (No mention was made of the many opportunities the United States had been afforded to interdict the *Golden Venture* or the *Najd II*.)

Nor did Clinton discuss the decision to detain the *Golden Venture* passengers. But his message about the new arrivals was unmistakable. "It is a commonplace of American life that immigrants have made our country great," Clinton said. "But we also know that under the pressures that we face today, we can't afford to lose control of our own borders or to take on new financial burdens at a time when we are not adequately providing for the jobs, the health care, and the education of our own people."

As he concluded his remarks, the president announced the nomination of a new commissioner to head the INS, a fifty-one-year-old immigration expert named Doris Meissner, who had held posts in the Carter and Reagan administrations before becoming director of immigration policy at the Carnegie Endowment for International Peace.

Meissner had been informed when she was offered the job that halting abuse of the asylum system was her "first-order immigration imperative."

Deciding who should be entitled to refuge in a country and who should be turned away entails a truly awesome responsiblity. If the individual who stands before you is an economic migrant masquerading as a refugee and you should happen to see through the ruse and send him packing, the migrant may come to regret the misadventure, but you can safely send him home and sleep soundly, knowing that you have done your job. But what if you mistake a bona fide refugee for an economic migrant? What if her fear of persecution is indeed well founded, but because some element of her story aroused your skepticism she is sent home to certain persecution—to imprisonment, torture, even death?

In principle, grants of asylum should entail a minimum of discretion: if an individual has a well-founded fear of persecution, then his or her claim should be granted, and whether or not the fear is well founded should be an objective test, subject to empirical inquiry. But in practice the determination is rarely so simple. People leaving their homelands in a hurry, under cover of dark, and making their way around the world to the United States do not always have the relevant documentation to substantiate the claims they make in their asylum applications. Information about current conditions in the countries they have fled is not always readily available. And to make matters worse, even individuals with a genuine asylum claim are sometimes inclined to lie, or to exaggerate one element of their story over another, in an effort to secure safe harbor. Desperate people are driven to desperate actions. Even those who tell the truth do not always make the best witnesses—they may garble a time line, misremember some small detail, mumble, give a weak handshake, or avert their eyes.

In practice, the individual hearing the asylum claim, whether it is an immigration officer or an immigration judge, is forced to make a judgment about the credibility of the claimant, and with the introduction of discretion comes an enormous measure of disparity, luck, and chance for the asylum-seeker. During the cold war, the ostensible objectivity of the asylum process was warped by political ideology, and life-and-death determinations were made not on the basis of the facts of a specific case but on the larger geopolitics involved. If you were coming from Cuba, you had a good shot at asylum. If you were coming from Haiti, you didn't. If you were fleeing a Communist regime in Eastern Europe, the door was often open; if you were fleeing a right-wing dictator in Latin America, it was generally closed.

Throughout the 1990s, asylum caseloads were exploding, and immigration judges were often underresourced and overworked. As a result, this most solomonic determination—who should be saved and who should be sent back—became an arbitrary and erratic activity. Disparities began to emerge in the ways that similar asylum cases were treated in different places. If you are a Chinese asylum-seeker applying for asylum in San Francisco today, for instance, you have a 74 percent chance of success, as opposed to 18 percent if you apply in Newark. When your case is assigned to an immigration judge, the assignment is random—there is no way to select which judge will hear your claim. But enormous differences exist in the grant rates of individual judges. One immigration judge in Los Angeles grants asylum to roughly 81 percent of all Chinese applicants, while a colleague in the same court grants asylum to only 9 percent. (Interestingly, female judges are much more likely than males to grant asylum. If your case is randomly assigned to a female judge, you automatically have a 44 percent better chance of getting approved.) "Whether an asylum applicant is able to live safely in the United States or is deported to a country in which he claims to fear persecution is very seriously influenced by a spin of the wheel," one study concludes, "by a clerk's random assignment of an applicant's case to one asylum officer rather than another, or one immigration judge rather than another."

For no other nationality is the disparity between grant rates on asylum cases as high as it is for the Chinese. One reason for this is simply that by virtue of its huge population, China represents an area in which the principle-driven platitudes of asylum and refugee law inevitably collide with more pragmatic concerns. With one fifth of the world's population, some 900 million of whom are peasants, China has a way of dousing any humanitarian assumptions with a colder demographic reality. There is a famous story about Deng Xiaoping's visit to Washington in January 1979, when President Jimmy Carter scolded him about China's restrictions on the "freedom of departure"—the right to emigration—and suggested that more people should be permitted to leave China. According to the story, Deng fixed Carter with his slightly beady gaze and said, "Why, certainly, President Carter. How many millions would you like?"

China's population was one major factor bedeviling determinations of whether and when to grant asylum to people fleeing the country. The other major, and not unrelated, factor was China's one-child policy. One month before the massacre at Tiananmen Square, these issues came to a head in a landmark court case called *Matter of Chang*. Chang was a Fujianese migrant who had fled to the United States and requested asylum, saying that the authorities in China had wanted to sterilize him and his wife following the birth of their second child. Chang lost his bid for asylum before an immigration judge. Traditionally, asylum-seekers must demonstrate that they have been persecuted in the past, or might be in the future, on the basis of their race, religion, nationality, political opinion, or membership in a particular social group. Coerced sterilization may have been a brutal practice, but it did not fit neatly in the established categories of persecution. Shortly after Chang's claim was rejected, however, Ronald Reagan's attorney general, Edwin Meese, issued guidelines to the INS suggesting that asylum could be granted to applicants who expressed a well-founded fear of persecution based on China's family-planning policies. In Meese's view, if the emigrants had refused to have an abortion or be sterilized, that refusal could itself be construed "as an act of political defiance," and as such grounds for asylum in the United States.

Meese's guidelines seemed to offer Chang new hope, but when he appealed his case to the Board of Immigration Appeals, in Falls Church, Virginia, the board was reluctant to bow to a standard that would in principle make any fertile Chinese parent eligible for asylum in the United States. Instead, the board held that even if Chang or his wife faced possible sterilization by the government, that would not constitute "persecution," because it was not directed at them specifically. They weren't being singled out. The one-child policy applied to everyone. And they had violated it.

Matter of Chang was not a case that made headlines when it was decided. But for U.S. officials concerned about the number of asylum applicants coming from China, it served a valuable purpose. The opinion went on the books and could be pointed to by future immigration judges. Chang's attorney, a lanky Brooklyn-born immigration lawyer named Jules Coven, who represented many Fujianese clients, could see the impact the ruling would have: if *Matter of Chang* took hold as a precedent, it would allow the government to deny thousands of asylum applications by Chinese fleeing the harsh tactics of the population enforcement cadres. Coven wanted to challenge the decision in federal court. But when he met with the assistant U.S. attorney assigned to the case, he realized how important it was to the government that the precedent established by *Matter of Chang* remain uncontested. In something of a backroom deal, the government lawyer assured Coven that if he let the matter go and opted not to appeal the ruling, Chang himself would be quietly granted asylum. Coven knew the momentous impact that the ruling would have on the cases of his other clients, and it gave him pause. But as an attorney, his first duty of loyalty was to his client Chang. So he took the deal, and *Matter of Chang* established the precedent that a well-founded fear of forced abortion or sterilization under China's one-child policy was not an adequate ground for asylum in the United States.

One fascinating feature of America's ongoing debate over immigration is that it seldom tracks neatly along existing partisan predilections. *Matter of Chang* might have seemed like the sort of tough-on-illegal-immigration measure that would be embraced by conservative hardliners. But a vocal contingent of pro-life and anti-Communist Republicans in Congress objected to the decision. Tiananmen unfolded a month after the *Matter of Chang* decision, and in the wake of the massacre, Congress voted on the Emergency Chinese Immigration Relief Act of 1989, which included a provision that would effectively overrule *Matter of Chang,* conferring refugee status on the basis of the one-child policy. The bill passed both houses of Congress, but George H. W. Bush vetoed it. When he did so, however, he claimed that he could "accomplish the laudable objectives of Congress" through executive action.

The executive action he had in mind was the famous directive of April 1990, which instructed the secretary of state and the attorney general to give "enhanced consideration" to individuals fleeing coerced sterilization or abortion in China. In January 1993, in the final days of the Bush administration, the outgoing attorney general, William Barr, signed a rule stating that forced abortion and sterilization were grounds for asylum, and noted explicitly that "one effect of this rule is to supersede the Board in *Matter of Chang.*" But in order for a rule to take effect, it must be published in the *Federal Register.* Barr signed the rule and sent it to the register, and it was scheduled for publication on January 25. But on January 22, after Bill Clinton's inauguration, the new administration issued a directive prohibiting the publication of any new regulations before it had approved them. So Barr's rule never took effect.

As a consequence some uncertainty about whether a claim of persecution under the one-child policy was sufficient ground for asylum endured through the early months of the Clinton administration, and still hung over the immigration process when the *Golden Venture* arrived on June 6. When Clinton assembled his staff in the Oval Office on June 11, one prominent item on the agenda was "modifying Bush administration policy regarding enhanced consideration of asylum claims based on one-child policy in China."

Bill Clinton was something of a cipher when it came to immigration. On the campaign trail he had accused the Bush administration of "immoral" repatriation of boat people from Haiti, but having promised to reverse that policy, he found his own inauguration marred by reports of over 150,000 Haitians preparing to board rickety boats on stormy seas in order to arrive after he was sworn in. Not wanting to introduce a magnet policy of its own, the administration announced that it would "study" the policy of its predecessors—but not necessarily change it. Clinton was above all attuned to the political mood of the country. After his nomination of Zoë Baird for attorney general was derailed when it was revealed that she had hired undocumented immigrants as household help, and *Time* magazine ran a cover story on the botched nomination under the headline "His First Blunder," he might have felt especially sensitive on the immigration issue.

To Doris Meissner, Clinton's choice to run the INS, it seemed that something else was weighing on Clinton's mind as he evaluated how to address the influx of Chinese asylum-seekers. Clinton had lost only one election in his life, his bid for reelection as governor of Arkansas in 1980. The months leading up to the election had coincided with the Mariel boat lift from Cuba, and some 25,000 Cuban refugees had been transferred to Fort Chaffee, a facility in western Arkansas that had been used in the mid-seventies to house refugees from Vietnam. During the summer of 1980 the Cubans at Fort Chaffee rioted, and thousands of them escaped the installation. Some of the Marielitos had criminal records or mental instabilities, and there was a run on firearms in every gun store within 50 miles of the fort as local residents armed themselves, fearing that they might literally have to fight the Cubans off. As governor, Clinton had ordered the National Guard to assist state and local police in preventing the refugees from leaving the fort, but the panic engendered by the events at Fort Chaffee was enough to turn supporters against him, and he attributed the loss in November in no small measure to "the Cubans." Even after the *Golden Venture* landed in Queens, Meissner thought Clinton was still "very conscious of having been burned" by the Fort Chaffee incident, and highly attuned to the political vulnerabilities that an appearance of being soft on immigration can create.

Clinton's managerial style was, famously, to let his advisers pick positions and duke it out among themselves, engaging in a kind of protracted policy bull session that would eventually yield a solution. In the weeks and months after the *Golden Venture* arrived, the main arguments for taking a limited view of the kinds of allowances that should be made for the passengers was articulated primarily by the State Department. The fear among many officials in Washington was that America's asylum policies had become a magnet for Chinese immigrants, actually encouraging them to leave their homes, pay snakeheads, and undertake perilous voyages to the United States. Tim Wirth, the undersecretary of state for global affairs, complained that America's asylum posture toward the Chinese had become "the come on down" policy.

According to the State Department, many of the asylum applicants were lying about the conditions back in China. "The majority of the Chinese who are coming here illegally . . . are principally economic migrants," Wirth wrote in a letter to the deputy national security adviser, Sandy Berger. State Department officials had been told by Chinese authorities that "the magnet effect of our permissive asylum policies was primarily responsible for the massive outflow of Chinese illegal aliens into the U.S. over the past two years."

State prepared a report casting doubts on asylum applications brought by migrants from Fujian Province. Claims brought by Fujianese who cited involvement in the pro-democracy movement in 1989 should be treated with skepticism, the memo maintained. And as for the one-child policy, the implementation of population controls in Fujian was actually "more relaxed" than in other parts of China. Forced abortion and sterilization were not as common as the number of asylum applications would seem to indicate.

On the other side of the argument was the INS, and in particular the agency's general counsel, a holdover from the Bush administration named Grover Joseph Rees III. Rees was a courtly constitutional law professor from a prominent family in Breaux Bridge, Louisiana. He was wiry, with a sly smile and intelligent, slightly bloodshot eyes. Rees was the youngest of his parents' twelve children; he was also ardently pro-life. Some critics disparaged him as a fanatic, an "anti-abortion zealot." To Bill Slattery, Rees seemed like a single-issue person, a bureaucrat with an agenda.

But Rees's philosophical differences with Slattery involved more than simply his opposition to China's population-control problems. If Slattery was a quintessential enforcement guy, Rees was a quintessential benefits guy. Rees believed that the INS had lost track of its mission, which was to offer safe harbor to people; that the agency, and Washington more generally, had been hijacked by the enforcement mentality. Rees had always believed that those fleeing coerced abortion or sterilization should be able to find refuge in the United States. Following George Bush's executive order, he had sent a letter to all regional INS offices reiterating that "application of such coercive policies" does constitute persecution. He instructed INS personnel to "be just as diligent in searching for indications that the applicant or the applicant's evidence may be credible as for indications that it may not be."

In Rees's view, the only crime of the people aboard the *Golden Venture* was having escaped from one of the most dangerous countries in the world. He felt that the administration was dramatically overplaying the risk that the country would be swamped by asylum-seekers. At the same time he believed that the State Department was underestimating the amount of coercive birth control going on in China. Six weeks before the *Golden Venture* arrived, Nicholas Kristof, the *New York Times* correspondent in Beijing, wrote a front-page story revealing a crackdown on the birthrate in China that had commanded a couple of years earlier, at precisely the time when Chinese began leaving for America in substantial numbers. "Through compulsory sterilization and other measures, China has lowered fertility to by far its lowest level ever here," Kristof reported. Abortion was less common in China than it had been during the 1980s, the article suggested. (Figures from China's Ministry of Health, which are probably incomplete, record a peak of 14 million abortions in 1990.) But as a tactic it had been replaced by "compulsory, organized sterilization." "Typically, local cadres swoop down on each village once or twice a year, taking all the women who have already had children to a nearby clinic," Kristof wrote. There had been a 25 percent surge in the number of people sterilized in 1991, to 12.5 million. And women who would not voluntarily abort surplus children were sometimes fined hundreds or even thousands of dollars, at a time when the per capita income in the Chinese countryside was roughly $135 a year.

Rees found it scandalous that in the face of such reports, the United States would adopt a jaundiced, cynical view of the claims of asylum-seekers fleeing the one-child policy. He worried that because the passengers on the *Golden Venture* and other ships had been obliged to pay snakeheads to smuggle them into the United States, the government was viewing them not in their capacity as asylum-seekers but in their capacity as smuggled aliens. That was the "overwhelming spirit" in which Washington approached the *Golden Venture*, Rees thought.

The problem for the *Golden Venture* passengers was that everyone was watching to see how Washington would react. The first decision, made by Slattery within hours of the ship's arrival and endorsed by the White House in the coming days, was to detain the passengers. To release them as other undocumented Chinese had been released in the past would be untenable. In later years some would maintain that the *Golden Venture* passengers were not treated any differently from other undocumented arrivals from China. But the statements at the time make clear that it was the explicit intention of the administration to treat the passengers differently, in order to send a message. "We are making arrangements to hold them as long as we have to," Slattery explained to the press the day the ship arrived. "We intend to make an example of this group."

In a memo to Vice President Al Gore, three administration officials working on the *Golden Venture* case proposed the use of "detention as a disincentive to illegal entry into the U.S." A Justice Department document elaborated: "The usual goal of illegal migrants is to gain entry to the United States, establish residence, and enter the work force. If such persons are detained upon arrival, maintained in detention throughout the administrative hearing process, and ultimately removed from the United States without ever having been at large and able to work, illegal migration by others is discouraged."

But the decision to detain the *Golden Venture* passengers only raised a deeper policy dilemma. If, as Joseph Rees contended, there were credible asylum-seekers among the passengers, who had a well-founded fear of persecution back in China, then they should be entitled to the full range of procedural allowances when it came to examining the merit of their claims. But everyone knew that under the best circumstances, the asylum process took months, if not years. How could the administration maintain its policy of detention without jailing bona fide refugees indefinitely while their cases dragged through the system?

The solution was to expedite the *Golden Venture* cases, seeking to streamline and accelerate the traditional asylum application process in order to resolve the cases as quickly as possible. Within a week of the *Golden Venture*'s arrival it had been decided that a special schedule would be created for the passengers. Both the initial asylum hearing before an immigration judge and, if necessary, an appeal were to be completed within 120 days—a pace that was unheard of. The case files of the *Golden Venture* passengers were given a special marking so that they could fly through the system as quickly as possible. The idea was to take the painstaking, error-prone process of assessing the validity of asylum claims and do it against the clock, without losing any accuracy. "The *Golden Venture* is sort of a test case for trying to compress this process," one official explained.

After several days in the York County Prison, Sean received a visitor: a British woman named Ann Carr who had worked as a paralegal and recently passed the bar exam to become a lawyer. Carr had gotten Sean's name through the local bar association, and she brought an interpreter so the two could discuss whether Sean would request asylum in the United States. Carr was astonished by how young Sean seemed, and how frightened. His skin had a deathly pallor after months in the ship's hold. And he looked young, too young to be in a prison cell. (There were sixteen minors aboard the *Golden Venture*, who were released into foster care when the ship arrived because they were under eighteen. Sean was carrying no documents when he washed ashore in Queens, and he looked much younger than he was. If he had had the wherewithal to lie about his age, he probably would have been released.)

This kid shouldn't be in this situation, Carr thought. As they sat there in the prison, Sean related his ordeal. He told her the story of how he had been kicked out of school after authorities saw his name on a list of possible "counterrevolutionaries," because he had participated in a demonstration around the time of Tiananmen. (There had been many sympathy demonstrations in and around Fuzhou at the time.) Sean was no political dissident, but it did appear that the mood of suspicion and recrimination in China in the months following Tiananmen had thrust him into a position that he may not have chosen and radically diminished his options for a future in Changle. To Carr, that sounded promising as a ground for political asylum. In order to make her case, she was going to need some time to prepare and to get the necessary paperwork from China. But Sean's case was scheduled for two weeks away. Carr had worked on immigration cases in the past and had never had any trouble getting a postponement, so she telephoned the court in Baltimore that was handling the cases and requested one. The clerk told her that none of the *Golden Venture* cases were eligible for postponements and that at most she could delay the hearing by one week. Carr was flustered. She didn't know how she could possibly assemble and translate the necessary documentation from China in so little time. She asked who had issued this policy. The clerk told her that someone from the White House had called the court directly.

Carr returned to the prison and asked Sean if there was any paperwork that might prove his story. He told her that when he was expelled from school, the administrators gave him a letter informing him of the expulsion, explicitly citing his political activity. Carr arranged for Sean to telephone China and get a message to his family to see if they could get the letter to her. If she could just get her hands on that letter, it would be proof that Sean was not merely making up his story—that he was a credible asylum-seeker who had been forced out of high school because of a passing affiliation with pro-democracy protesters.

But the letter didn't arrive, and as the hearing date approached, Carr grew anxious. On the morning of the hearing there was still no sign of the letter, and Carr was in a panic. The preceding weeks had played out with a certain emergency atmosphere, an encroaching sense of dread that with such a breakneck schedule it would be impossible to demonstrate that the passengers should not be sent home. It seemed that they had become the victims of a stifling and high-speed administrative juggernaut—Kafka on fast-forward. Then, just as Carr was getting ready to leave for the hearing, a fax arrived from China. She clutched the fax and headed to the prison, where a makeshift courtroom had been assembled to hear the men's cases.

One problem remained: the fax was in Chinese. As Carr sat in an adjacent waiting room, with an hour or so before Sean's hearing, she spotted a Chinese man waiting by himself. By some miracle, he spoke English. Overcome with relief, Carr grabbed the document and approached him. "Could you please translate this for me?" she said. "Tell me what it says."

The man dictated his translation, and Carr wrote it out longhand. Sure enough, it was a letter from the school, asserting that Sean had been dismissed for his involvement in political activity. When they had completed the translation, the man signed it, indicating that Carr had taken down the words as he interpreted them.

Eventually Sean and Carr entered the courtroom, where an immigration judge was waiting for them. The judge was a Caucasian who was heavily overweight, fatter than people got in China; to Sean he looked monstrous, cartoonishly obese. It was stuffy and unbearably hot in the little room, and the hearing dragged on for hours, with the judge, laconic and unsympathetic, posing skeptical questions to Sean. The authorities had been charged with locating translators for the hearings, but because Fujianese was not widely spoken among Chinese in the United States, they had supplied a translator from Berlitz, who spoke only Cantonese and some Mandarin. Sean spoke some Mandarin as well, but with a thick provincial accent, and as the hearing unfolded, Carr could tell that certain things were getting mangled in translation. When Sean described his interest in politics, and particularly in democracy, and his childhood experience on the fringes of the pro-democracy movement in Fujian, the interpreter would tell the judge, "He had a problem with the government."

Carr tried asking Sean pointed questions about his upbringing and his views on politics, but the judge snapped that she was leading her client, trying to coach him.

When Sean described his expulsion, Carr triumphantly presented the letter and the translation. But the judge's attention was drawn to the school's official seal on the original letter, which was a stamp with the date written in the center of it. The man in the waiting room had never translated the seal or the date. "This isn't authenticated," the judge said dismissively, setting it aside. Carr tried to explain that it takes weeks to authenticate an official document in another language from a foreign country, that she had asked to postpone the hearing and been told it wasn't possible. The judge was unmoved.

After several hours the judge announced that he found elements of Sean's story credible. But if the events in question had unfolded in 1989, he wondered, why had Sean waited until 1991 to leave Fujian? Surely circumstances could not have been so dire as he was making them out to be if he chose to wait two years before leaving for America? The judge denied asylum, and Sean and Carr were ushered out of the room so that the next passenger could have his hearing.

It may have brought him little comfort at the time, but Sean was fortunate at least to be found credible. Many of the passengers presented themselves before their jailhouse judges and told stories of being forced to flee from China after they were compelled to have abortions (in the case of some of the women from the ship) or after they or their wives were threatened with sterilization. The stories shared common details: the local cadres come to sterilize the wife, but she is sick and insists that she cannot submit to the procedure, so the cadres turn on the husband; a family is penalized for adopting a female baby they discover abandoned by the side of the road by some rural couple who did not want to "waste" their one-child allotment on a girl. The stories took on a repetitious, almost incantatory quality, and surely part of the reason for that was that many of them were not true. There was a series of stock narratives, like the boilerplate plots of bad movies, which could be figured and refigured with only the slightest hint of improvisation or individual embellishment. The snakeheads and the villagers back home, and quite possibly the occasional asylum lawyer as well, had all come together and coached the passengers to tell certain stories calculated to secure asylum in the United States.

The immigration judges knew this, of course. The rate of asylum granted to Chinese immigrants tends to be lower in cities where more Chinese cases are brought, and one possible explanation for this disparity is that judges who hear a single horror story are inclined to be sympathetic, but judges who hear the same story over and over again begin to wonder whether what they're hearing is true. But the deck was stacked against the *Golden Venture* passengers from the beginning. The State Department had prepared a special memorandum for the immigration judges hearing the cases. "There are some elements of stories that have recurred in Fujian cases over a long time," the memo suggested. "Some of these statements, we believe, can bear importantly on applicants' credibility." The memo cited tales of zealous birth control officials imposing fines on couples who have more than one child, and of husbands being sterilized because their wives were too sick to undergo the procedure, of men fleeing from their villages after getting into physical fights with birth-control cadres, and of couples who made the mistake of "adopting a foundling, who the officials charged was the couple's natural child." Every conceivable scenario that the *Golden Venture* passengers might describe was accounted for in the memo from the State Department.

The memo conceded that "each of these types of events has occurred in China" but insisted that in Fujian Province they had not occurred "with anywhere near the frequency asserted by asylum applicants." To some extent the skepticism that greeted the *Golden Venture* passengers when they arrived was just shrewd governance. There was reason to be dubious of the claims, perhaps even a majority of the claims, and therefore it was a good thing that the judges were prepared to identify fraud when it came before them. And while the State Department's findings may have seemed to conflict with Nicholas Kristof's report in the *New York Times,* they did tend to dovetail with some independent scholarship that was being done by academics interested in the reasons that undocumented migrants left China. When the Rutgers criminologist Ko-lin Chin surveyed three hundred smuggled Chinese in New York City, the vast majority responded that their chief reason for coming to the United States was "U.S. dollars." Peter Kwong, a Hunter College professor and expert on Chinese immigration, maintained that the one-child policy was "honored more in the breach than the execution."

The problem was that while widespread fraud was one explanation for the repetition of the same stories among asylum-seekers, another reason that those stories were repeated, and that they were told in the first place, was that sometimes they were true. It may have been that the bulk of the *Golden Venture* passengers, the vast majority even, were simple economic migrants looking for a better job, a better life, and willing to tell a potted tale of woe in order to find new opportunities in America. It may have been that most of them were lying. But on the margins there were also genuine refugees who were fleeing horrific oppression at the hands of the family-planning cadres in China, and as the cases raced through the system, it was perhaps inevitable that the skepticism engendered by the repetitive stories, and by the State Department memo, would lead the judges to paint all of the asylum-seekers with the same brush.

Ultimately, even those who were telling the truth and could prove it would have trouble making their cases—because as the Clinton administration tried to determine how to handle the Bush administration's posture on asylum and the one-child policy, it had rediscovered *Matter of Chang*. During the fall of 1993, there was some question as to which position the administration would take on the issue: whether Clinton would bend to pressure from Republicans in Congress to continue allowing the one-child policy to serve as a ground for asylum, or whether he would definitively assert that, horrible though it might be, forced abortion or sterilization did not amount to "persecution" under U.S. law. Eventually the Board of Immigration Appeals took the latter view, maintaining that "our interpretation of the law regarding China's one-couple, one-child policy articulated in *Matter of Chang* is legally correct and consistent."

By September, 14 of the *Golden Venture* passengers had been granted asylum and 171 had been denied. Another 68 were still waiting to be told. (Of those who did succeed in obtaining asylum, a number were Christians from Fujian and from Wenzhou, both of which had historically been home to long-standing Christian minorities.)

But most of the passengers were rejected. The difference between a successful bid for asylum and a failed one meant more than just the life or livelihood of the individual in question; it could, in a very real sense, determine the future course of the lives of their families. Two cellmates from the *Golden Venture* could suddenly watch their trajectories diverge. The one who was granted asylum would eventually be able to send for his wife and children, if he had any. Those children could hope to attend American colleges, perhaps obtain advanced degrees, and eventually join the assimilated middle class. For the one who was rejected, the future was less certain. He could appeal the decision, but there was little reason to believe that his case would be more compelling to a dubious American establishment the second time around. When his appeals were exhausted, he could count on being sent home to China. There, after he suffered through whatever punishment lay in store for breaking the law and embarrassing Beijing, he might succeed in the lottery of the new Chinese economy. But there was a stronger likelihood that he would end up working in a factory, and that his children would grow up to work in a factory as well.

"It seems we were unlucky," one of the passengers at York told a reporter after his asylum claim on the basis of the one-child policy was rejected. "Other people with circumstances like mine have won before, I know that. I don't understand why I lost."

One of Sean's fellow inmates at York was a father of three named Y. C. Dong. In his asylum hearing, Dong told his judge that he left China because he had three children and he feared that the authorities would sterilize him. The judge denied Dong's claim, dismissing his fear of persecution under the one-child policy as "subjective." Sometime later, Dong was deported back to China. When he got there, he was arrested, then jailed, beaten, fined—and sterilized.

Chapter Twelve

The Fat Man

BROOKLYN'S GREEN-WOOD Cemetery was established in 1838 and sprawls over 500 acres of rolling hills and winding paths just west of Prospect Park. Around midday on Saturday, August 28, 1993, a funeral ceremony was under way at the crematorium. Scores of mourners had gathered to pay their final respects to a forty-three-year-old Fujianese man named Ai Cheung, who had been smuggled to America by Sister Ping the year before, arriving on the shipment to New Bedford. He had joined the Fuk Ching gang, and he must have developed enemies, because the week before the funeral a beachcomber had noticed a hand sticking out of the sand on Plum Beach, a stretch of Jamaica Bay just off the Belt Parkway in Brooklyn, which had become a favorite dumping ground for the many bodies felled by the city's Asian gangs. The hand was Ai Cheung's. He had been hog-tied, stabbed to death, and buried on the beach.

As the mourners lined up to pay their final respects, none of them gave much notice to a Nissan Pathfinder that was parked some distance away, where two FBI agents sat waiting. The agent in the passenger seat was a young man named Konrad Motyka, who was burly and broad-shouldered, with close-cropped brown hair and eyes that had a natural squint. Like the driver, his colleague David Shafer, Motyka was dressed in civilian clothes but wore a bulletproof vest and had a 9-millimeter pistol strapped to his leg. As it happened, the deceased had been named in a sprawling forty-five-count indictment that authorities in New York were preparing against the Fuk Ching gang, and when Motyka and his colleagues at the FBI learned about his funeral, they saw an opportunity: many of the other gang members named in the indictment would probably attend the ceremony, and the FBI could arrest them all at once. It would be a dazzling strike, but not without a certain danger: if the feds crashed the funeral with guns drawn, the cornered mourners might very well start shooting. Motyka remembered an incident three summers earlier, when an Asian gang funeral in Linden, New Jersey, had degenerated into a shootout. He did not discount the possibility that the same thing could happen today.

Motyka had grown up on Manhattan's Upper West Side. His father was first-generation Polish American and his mother was from Germany; they met on a ski trip. They were eager to see their son preserve a sense of European culture and tradition, and sent him to the Lycée Français on the Upper East Side, where he became fluent in French, and from there to Columbia University. But the more Motyka's parents endeavored to instill a European identity in their son, the more profoundly he insisted that he was a regular American kid. At Columbia he signed up for the football team. When he graduated, in 1985, and his classmates headed to law school or investment banks, Motyka joined the Marine Corps. The choice was driven by a sense of patriotism—a conviction that as an American he owed a duty to his country. But it didn't hurt that as a Marine he would get to see the world. He spent the next couple of years as an infantry officer in Norway, the Philippines, and Okinawa. Eventually he married his college girlfriend, who was working as a nurse for the Navy, and together they applied to the FBI.

After completing the academy at Quantico, Motyka was assigned to the Bureau's office in New York and spent several years working on cold war counterintelligence, pursuing spies embedded in the city's foreign consulates and UN missions. In 1989 the Bureau formed a new unit, known as C-6, to deal with what was referred to as "nontraditional" organized crime. C-6 was run by Ray Kerr, the agent who handled the Fuk

Ching gang defector Dan Xin Lin during his brief period of cooperation. Its mission was somewhat diffuse, touching on any ethnic organized crime that did not involve the Mafia. Kerr and his agents went after Jamaican groups and Greek groups before moving on to the new breed of Asian gangs that had begun to terrorize Chinatown. By the time Konrad Motyka was transferred to C-6 in 1992, the unit was developing a case against Ah Kay and the Fuk Ching gang.

Motyka and his colleagues had begun assembling information on the gang and watched in shock as the death toll escalated. There was the brazenness of Ah Kay's botched effort to have Dan Xin assassinated at the beeper store in January 1993; then there was Dan Xin's bloody revenge at Teaneck in May. But if each of those incidents was an incremental indication that the Fuk Ching and the snakehead trade were growing out of hand, the arrival of the *Golden Venture* on June 6 was something else altogether. Suddenly the Fuk Ching investigation took on a new urgency. The message from Washington was unequivocal: spare no time or expense in tracking the people who masterminded the voyage of the *Golden Venture*; take them down.

As Motyka and Shafer watched, the funeral ceremony appeared to be coming to an end. Mourners in black suits began to leave the crematorium and make their way toward a line of waiting limousines parked along the road. Motyka braced himself, and Shafer started the engine.

Nearly three months earlier, the day after the *Golden Venture* ran aground, the ship's captain, Amir Tobing, and the chief onboard enforcer, Kin Sin Lee, sat scowling at each other in a federal courtroom in Brooklyn. Tobing looked disheveled, his hair uncombed. He claimed that he was a victim—that it was only after the mutiny divested him of power that everything had gone awry. "He beat me and tortured me," he said, gesturing at Kin Sin Lee, who sat erect and motionless. "They cheated me out of my money."

Both men were ultimately charged with conspiracy and smuggling.

Because alien smuggling convictions still carried relatively light sentences, prosecutors took the unusual step of charging Kin Sin Lee under an antique statute that dealt with manslaughter at sea. The ten crew members were also charged, along with eight of the passengers who had assisted Kin Sin Lee during the voyage. All twenty of the perpetrators who had been on board the ship pleaded guilty. The judge, Reena Raggi, rejected a plea bargain offered by defense attorneys, observing that light sentences might run the risk of "trivializing" the severity of the crime committed. "The boat did not just run aground," she said, her voice rising. "It was deliberately run aground." For his role in the operation, Kin Sin Lee was sentenced to ten years. When he was asked what obligation he had felt for the safety of the passengers, he replied, "I never thought of that at the time." Sam Lwin, the first officer, received four and a half years. And despite his protests, Captain Tobing was sentenced to four years. "I am sorry," he told the court. "I promise not to do it again." (If he meant smuggling, this was not a promise he would keep. Several years after he was released and deported to Indonesia, Tobing resurfaced off the coast of Washington State, when the Coast Guard stopped a sailboat he was skippering, which contained five tons of Cambodian marijuana. "Why Smuggle Pot to NW?" the local press wondered. "Authorities Puzzled; There's Plenty Here.")

As investigators questioned perpetrators from the *Golden Venture*, names began to emerge—names of co-conspirators who were not on board. Along with Mr. Charlie, Weng Yu Hui had been the chief liaison for the ship, loading the stranded passengers from the *Najd II* onto the *Golden Venture* in early April and coordinating the crash landing in Queens over the ship-to-shore. On the morning the *Golden Venture* arrived, Weng had visited Sister Ping in her shop and found her watching the news coverage—the arrests, the deaths, people jumping from the ship and being rescued from the surf. "The government is definitely going to investigate the people behind the boat," Sister Ping said. She told Weng to leave town for a while. She had an apartment in New Jersey. Perhaps he could go there.

Weng did as she said, but he did not stay gone for long. The following month he was back in Chinatown and dropped by Sister Ping's store at 47 East Broadway. "How come you're still in New York?" Sister Ping asked angrily. "This is very dangerous."

Again Sister Ping volunteered a place for Weng to hide, but this time she did not think New Jersey would be far enough away. She proposed that he fly to South Africa, where she happened to own an ostrich farm. How it is that Sister Ping would own property in South Africa at all, much less an ostrich farm, is unclear. It may simply be that in order to manage a truly global smuggling network, she needed hideouts and way stations throughout the world. And indeed, after eighteen of her passengers in Mombasa refused to board the *Golden Venture*, she had arranged to have them transported to South Africa and put up at the farm until she could figure how to facilitate the next step in their journey. Weng could join them, she suggested.

But Weng lived a life of circumscribed horizons. He was a creature of habit, and could not stay away from Chinatown for long. He never made it to South Africa, and instead relocated temporarily to West Virginia. But he kept coming back to Chinatown. He had a girlfriend who lived in an apartment on Henry Street, and he drove to town to visit her from time to time. One day two INS agents were staking out the apartment when they saw Weng drive up and walk in the front door. They called for backup, and a team of agents raided the apartment. They found Weng cowering in a bedroom closet. He pleaded guilty and was sentenced to ten years.

Within hours of the *Golden Venture*'s arrival, authorities in New York had announced that Ah Kay was a chief suspect. Konrad Motyka was working with Luke Rettler, the prosecutor in the Manhattan DA's office, to prepare a case against the Fuk Ching, and evidence was being assembled to charge Ah Kay with a colorful litany of crimes: murder, attempted murder, conspiracy to commit murder, maiming, assault with a deadly weapon, assault resulting in severe bodily injury, threatening to commit a crime of violence. The problem for the law enforcement officers was that they did not want to round up the gang until they had captured Ah Kay. And Ah Kay was in China. After the Teaneck killings there had been some speculation that Ah Kay would return to America to avenge his brothers' deaths, but with the *Golden Venture* operation gone so devastatingly wrong, it seemed even Ah Kay would not dare to come back. Stories circulated in Chinatown about a walled mansion that Ah Kay was building in his home village in China. He was a famous rogue in his native region; everybody knew who he was. He was said to be surrounded by bodyguards at all times and to enjoy the protection of local officials.

But the FBI had one interesting advantage. In the chaos of the split in the Fuk Ching, the beeper-store killings, the Teaneck massacre, and the arrival of the *Golden Venture*, agents had been able to cultivate a few cooperators from the gang, chief among them Ah Kay's former errand boy, Alan Tam. After the killings at Teaneck, Tam had telephoned Ah Kay in China. It was an awkward conversation, with Ah Kay wondering if Tam had anything to do with the killings and Tam skirting the fact that he had supplied the address where Ah Kay's brothers were hiding and a floor plan of the house. If Ah Kay was devastated by the murders of his two younger brothers, he did not let it interfere with his ability to assess the situation in his capacity as the leader of the Fuk Ching gang. (Even in anger, Ah Kay displayed a cold, almost clinical rationality. When he was asked later how he felt about the fact that Dan Xin Lin paid others $50,000 to murder his brothers, Ah Kay replied, "I wouldn't kill someone for free.") Before Tam hung up, Ah Kay instructed him to go to New Jersey and try to find out more about what had happened. Tam did as he was instructed, but a half-black, half-Chinese giant loitering around the police station in Bergen County was nothing if not conspicuous, and within a few hours he was under arrest.

Tam proved to be a valuable source. He had always been a pushover—after all, with little more than peer pressure and drugs, Dan

Xin had persuaded him to assist in a quadruple homicide. The FBI easily convinced him to cooperate. In some respects he was a less than ideal informant; he was inarticulate to the point of incoherence sometimes, and his foot soldier's view of the world could never capture all the intricacies of Ah Kay's organization. But at the same time Tam had managed to be in the room or behind the wheel of the car during numerous important exchanges.

At considerable expense, the government paid to have a new identity created for Alan Tam. He was relocated and given a new name in order to avoid retribution from the gang. But like Weng Yu Hui, Tam seems to have found himself unable to thrive far from the Chinatown ecosystem where he had spent so many years. When Luke Rettler telephoned him at his new residence and made a point of asking to speak to him by his new name, Tam would grow confused. "What? Who?" he would say, before offering, "This is Alan."

One day a detective from the Fifth Precinct, in Chinatown, went to lunch at a Japanese and Chinese restaurant a block north of City Hall Park, near the federal buildings of downtown Manhattan and Luke Rettler's office on Centre Street and a five-minute walk from Chinatown. As she was eating her lunch, she looked up and saw a tall, half-black, half-Chinese man emerge from the kitchen and stand behind the counter. She thought he looked familiar. "Aren't you Alan Tam?" she asked. The man froze, then spun around and dashed into the kitchen.

The detective telephoned Luke Rettler. "Where's Alan Tam?" she asked.

"He's in witness protection," Rettler replied.

"Well, they can't be doing a very good job with the witness protection," the detective said. "Because I just saw him working in a restaurant about three blocks from Chinatown."

Motyka and his colleagues were interested in the information Tam could feed them about his former boss, but there was someone else they thought they could use in order to get to Ah Kay: his father. Ah Kay was already a fast-rising member of the Fuk Ching by the time his father immigrated from Fujian to New York in the late 1980s. When Ah Kay fled to China, he continued speaking with his father, who lived in an apartment on the third floor of the Fukienese American Association, at 125 East Broadway. The FBI set up a wiretap on the telephone, hoping to catch a conversation between father and son.

Of course Ah Kay had considered the possibility that the authorities might try to monitor his father's phone. When it comes to new technologies, criminals are often early adopters. Before the police and the FBI had beepers, the drug runners and gangsters did; by the time the authorities got their own beepers, the crooks had moved on to cellular phones. During the summer of 1993, it was possible for the FBI to monitor only fifteen different cell phones in the New York area at any given time. It was not unusual for an agent to go to the phone company, warrant in hand, only to be told that all the available taps were in use. Knowing that cell phones were more secure than landlines, Ah Kay had purchased one for his father and told him to use it whenever the two communicated.

But if anything, Ah Kay was too much of an early adopter. Or at any rate, he was an earlier adopter than his father was. The older man found the new telephone confusing and offputting. He couldn't work out how to make a call go through. After several failed experiments with the cell phone, he took to using a more traditional method: the landline in his apartment at 125 East Broadway.

"Are you on the cell phone?" Ah Kay would ask every time his father called.

"Yeah, yeah, I'm on the cell phone," the delighted agents would hear his father reply.

Ah Kay's father was concerned, because the young gangster's gambling problem appeared to be growing out of control. The members of the Fuk Ching gang had always loved to gamble. They played mahjong, thirteen-card poker, pai gow, fan tan, seven cards, high-low, anything they could bet money on. Like Mock Duck, the fabled tong war warrior before him, who was "known to wager his entire wealth on whether the number of seeds in an orange picked at random from a fruit cart was odd or even," Ah Kay gravitated to high-stakes games of chance.

Since the *Golden Venture* had run aground, Ah Kay had been hiding in Yingyu village with his most loyal lieutenant, Li Xing Hua. Li was happy. He was a country boy, content to be back in the village where he had grown up. He could have stayed there forever. But Ah Kay was restless. The village he had left as a child was a remote backwater, and even the nearby centers of Changle and Fuzhou seemed provincial in comparison to New York. There was gambling in Fujian Province, to be sure, but for paltry stakes, and with none of the heady splendor of the big city. Ah Kay had seen the world, made millions of dollars, and killed men; he was still in his mid-twenties, and the staid life of rural China bored him. So he started making trips to Hong Kong to gamble.

The stakes could get exceedingly high in Hong Kong, and before long Ah Kay was losing, and losing a lot. He ran up debts of hundreds of thousands of dollars, sometimes in a single evening. Ah Kay had always been cavalier about his losses, but his revenue stream had been severely curtailed when he went underground and stopped offloading ships. He turned to his father for help. One day in mid-August, he spoke with his father on the phone and asked the older man to have Sister Ping remit him $20,000 to satisfy a gambling debt.

"Don't do it anymore!" his father pleaded.

"It's not like I'm not paying people back," Ah Kay said defensively. "If there is no money, then say it's because there's no money."

His father promised to send the funds.

Under Title III of the Criminal Code, warrants for phone taps needed to be renewed with a judge every ten days, and Luke Rettler spent most of the summer frantically preparing applications to re-up the tap. Rettler had been cross-designated to work in the U.S. attorney's office, because the Fuk Ching case would be a federal prosecution. He was collaborating with an old friend, Chauncey Parker, a talented prosecutor who had worked with Rettler at the DA's office before moving over to the federal side. Parker's girlfriend's family had a big, beautiful house on the water in Rhode Island, and on Friday afternoons the two prosecutors would load a car full of legal materials, pick up Parker's girlfriend and Rettler's wife, and drive out to the beach house. The four of them would relax over dinner on Friday night. Then the next morning Rettler and Parker would wake up first thing and spend the day preparing progress reports in order to extend the wiretap.

When Ah Kay's telephone calls indicated that he was making trips to Hong Kong, it seemed that there might be an opportunity to catch him. Hong Kong was still under British control in 1993, and U.S. authorities had close working ties with their counterparts in the colony. The challenge would be determining when Ah Kay left China and traveled to Hong Kong, where he was staying, and what identity he was using, as he was almost certainly not traveling under his own name. In New York, Rettler was told that U.S. authorities had a secret informant in the Hong Kong underworld, a man who might be able to help them find Ah Kay. His identity was a closely guarded secret, so much so that Rettler never learned more than his code name: Four Star.

Standing six feet tall and possessing a considerable girth, Dickson Yao was an outsized, jovial figure with a confident swagger and a booming laugh. His manner of dress was ostentatiously expensive: he wore gold belt buckles, a sapphire ring, and a gold-and-diamond Rolex. He could stride into any restaurant or gambling den in Southeast Asia and act like he owned the place, and so complete was his cocksure insouciance that the other patrons tended to assume that he did.

Yao had been born in Shanghai. His father was a lieutenant general under Chiang Kai-shek, who sent him to navy school in Great Britain. He was still a teenager when he returned to China and became the skipper of an anti-smuggling patrol boat. On this first exposure to the world of smuggling, he began to blur the line between enforcement and transgression that he would continue to straddle for the rest of his life.

Under Dickson Yao the patrol boat became a kind of pirate ship: the crew would descend on a smuggling vessel, seize its cargo, sink it, and then sell the goods themselves. In Saigon during the Vietnam War, Yao met a U.S. Air Force colonel, and the two of them began using American pilots to smuggle materials around Southeast Asia. It started with wristwatches and bales of fabric, but soon they were moving morphine base from Bangkok to Hong Kong. In the 1980s Yao was arrested in Bangkok and thrown into jail. An American minister visited him in his cell, and Yao had a single request. He wanted to see an American narcotics agent; he was willing to cooperate.

It was the beginning of a decades-long relationship between Dickson Yao and U.S. authorities in Southeast Asia—a relationship in which Yao furnished enormous amounts of information not just about drug smuggling in the region but about human smuggling as well. To generations of U.S. agents in Bangkok and Hong Kong, Dickson Yao was an unreformable rogue, but also a reliable and well-connected source of intelligence. To Rettler and others working in New York, he was known as Four Star. But to the men who interacted with him in the bars and hotel restaurants of Southeast Asia, he was known by another, more evocative nickname. They all called him the Fat Man.

The Fat Man had marvelous *guanxi*—a web of relationships and acquaintances that encompassed the loose-knit cross-border criminal underworld of Asia and stretched as far away as the United States. He had superb connections everywhere he went, among them a beautiful young Chinese girlfriend who happened also to be the mistress of the prime minister of Thailand. He was so likable, and so credible in his role as a reprobate, that there were occasions when he would orchestrate a sting, setting up a big-ticket drug runner to be busted by the DEA, and then, some years later, approach the same drug runner to propose another buy and set him up again. The agents knew the Fat Man was a scoundrel, of course; by all indications, he continued to dabble in drug smuggling throughout his tenure as a DEA informant. But he seemed incorrigible, a man of epic appetites and infectious mirth, and if he indulged occasionally in the seamier side of the Southeast Asian economy, it was a small price to pay for the kind of access he provided.

The Fat Man had been working for the DEA for over a decade when the snakehead boom got under way in the early 1990s. As a general matter, agencies tend to hoard their most secret and valuable informants, but it was clear to the Fat Man's DEA handlers that their counterparts in the INS were overwhelmed by the sudden surge in smuggling activity in Hong Kong and Bangkok, and as a denizen of the underworld economy, the Fat Man knew a great deal about smuggling. He had spent some time in New York during the 1980s and gotten to know Sister Ping and Yick Tak, and Ah Kay as well. So the Fat Man's handler at DEA took an unusual step and loaned him to the INS.

Before long the Fat Man was meeting with the chief American immigration officer in Hong Kong, a man in his early forties named Jerry Stuchiner. Short and pugnacious, with a dark goatee and Coke-bottle glasses that exaggerated the size of his eyes, Stuchiner had a reputation among those who knew him as a bit of a Walter Mitty: he loved the drama and intrigue of the job and was always gunning to be the hero of the operation, the man kicking down the door. His parents had survived the Holocaust in Poland by pretending they were Roman Catholics, and had subsequently moved to Israel, where Stuchiner was born. Stuchiner told people he had been awarded a Bronze Star in Vietnam for his valor as a Marine Corps medic, though in reality he had never made it through boot camp. Like many of his INS colleagues, he spent some early years in the Border Patrol. He married the daughter of a Mexican landowner before transferring to San Francisco to work for the INS. Stuchiner was ambitious, and studied law at night. He applied for a job with the CIA but was rejected on account of his poor eyesight.

Still, in 1984 Stuchiner's hunger for intrigue was rewarded. He was transferred to Vienna, which had become a key hub in the effort to relocate Jews from the Soviet Union and Iran to Israel. Stuchiner told people it was dangerous work—that he had received death threats from

Islamic groups like Hezbollah. Eventually he was obliged to leave Vienna—because his work had made him too much of a target, he said—and the INS sent him to Hong Kong. He arrived in 1989, two months after Tiananmen. All sorts of dissidents were trying to escape from mainland China, and once again Stuchiner found himself in the role of shepherd to the persecuted, ushering student leaders and intellectuals into the colony and then on to the United States.

When it came to the snakeheads, Stuchiner felt that the INS should be far more aggressive than it was. He developed a habit of telephoning his colleagues without regard to the time difference, often reaching them at home in the middle of the night, and insisting that the agency take more rigorous action against the smugglers. He lambasted the bureaucrats at headquarters for being too soft, for holding him back. From the Fat Man he began acquiring fresh intelligence. The Fat Man's sources told him about the *Golden Venture* before the ship had even picked up passengers in Pattaya. (It was Stuchiner who helped tip off the INS in Bangkok, who in turn tipped off the Pattaya Tourist Police.) In the days after the *Golden Venture* ran aground, Stuchiner telephoned Washington repeatedly, painting a menacing picture of a veritable armada of smuggling ships sitting in Hong Kong harbor, destined for the United States.

The Fat Man told Stuchiner about the different smugglers—who the big players were, how they operated. He explained that Sister Ping was so successful because she guaranteed that her customers would arrive; if they were stopped en route to America and sent home, she would send them back again free of charge. Before long Stuchiner was paying 90 percent of his budget for informants to the Fat Man. With Hong Kong's changeover from British to Chinese authorities approaching in 1997, the Fat Man was eager to obtain American green cards for his family. (He had married a much younger woman and had three small children.) He thought that perhaps Stuchiner could work something out.

The Fat Man and Stuchiner made an unlikely pair, but the two became close friends. It is not unusual for a certain intimacy to develop between a confidential informant and his handler. Many people who find themselves in this situation are leery of it, reluctant to be beguiled by a temporary symmetry of interests into believing that the official and the criminal might share a more enduring bond. But the ambitious immigration agent and the Shanghainese rogue had no such reservations. They flouted official INS guidelines and began socializing together in their spare time. They even discussed going into business together, importing paintings from the People's Republic or sending Chinese guest workers to Israel.

One day in August 1993, the Fat Man telephoned Stuchiner. The hunt for Ah Kay was on; Stuchiner knew he was coming in and out of Hong Kong, but the Fat Man had more specific information. Ah Kay was staying at a hotel on the north side of Hong Kong Island, not far from where the Fat Man lived. He was traveling under an assumed name and carrying a fraudulent Hong Kong residence card.

Stuchiner was excited. He conferred with his colleagues in the U.S. consulate and told them he wanted to go and do surveillance in the area. They worried that he was too much of a cowboy—that a *gweilo,* or "white ghost," as the Cantonese called Caucasians, would stick out like a sore thumb and might alert Ah Kay that they had tracked him down. Besides, U.S. law enforcement had no jurisdiction to act on its own in the streets of Hong Kong; the most it could do was pass a request to the Royal Hong Kong Police.

Several days later the Fat Man supplied information that was even more concrete: the name of a restaurant where Ah Kay would be dining that night. Stuchiner wanted to stake out the restaurant himself. "Jerry, I'm a *gweilo,* you're a *gweilo,*" one of his colleagues said, trying to reason with him. "You're gonna walk into a restaurant full of Chinese and no one's gonna spot you?" Instead, the FBI took over the operation and fed the intelligence about the restaurant to its counterparts in the Royal Hong Kong Police, who sent a team of officers to the area.

During his time in Hong Kong, Ah Kay had developed something of a routine. He spent the days indoors, sleeping, and emerged only in the early evening, surrounded by a coterie of bodyguards. He would work out, eat dinner with his entourage at a restaurant, and then gamble through the night, often returning home at six or seven the next morning.

On Friday, August 27, he left the building at dusk, with Li Xing Hua and three other bodyguards. Ah Kay was dressed casually, in jeans and a cotton pullover. The four men strolled to the restaurant where they planned to eat, which was really just a food stall in a busy market. Suddenly they were surrounded by plainclothes detectives from the Triad Bureau of the Royal Hong Kong Police. Ah Kay surrendered peacefully. When the officers searched him, they found no weapons and only a few dollars. The sole hint of his fortune and infamy was his jewelry: several gold chains dangling around his neck and a large gold ring fashioned into the head of a dragon.

Jerry Stuchiner was furious. He and the Fat Man had effected Ah Kay's arrest, he felt, yet it had somehow become an FBI operation, and the INS wasn't getting any of the credit. For his part, the Fat Man had anticipated some monetary reward for his assistance in securing so high-profile a target, but he had no relationship with the FBI the way he did with the DEA and the INS and was disappointed when no payment came through.

As soon as Ah Kay was in custody, one of the FBI agents in Hong Kong made a phone call to New York and spoke with Konrad Motyka and his colleagues in the C-6 squad. It was time to move on the Fuk Ching gang.

The following day Motyka was sitting in the Pathfinder with David Shafer in the Green-Wood Cemetery when the funeral cortege started to leave the crematorium. A long column of black limousines began rolling at a slow, stately pace toward the exit of the cemetery. The agents were parked on a little road that fed onto the main road through the cemetery to the exit, and as the convoy approached, Shafer turned on the engine and drove onto the main road directly in front of the procession, effectively becoming the lead car. Motyka felt his adrenaline surge as they approached a predetermined spot on the road amid the steep green hills of the cemetery. Suddenly Shafer hit the brakes. The Pathfinder was clogging the road now, blocking the mourners' limousines from reaching the exit. Motyka and Shafer got out and dashed around to the front of the vehicle. They didn't know how the next few minutes would play out, but they suspected there might be shooting. In the movies, police officers always seemed to be taking cover behind car doors, but in reality a lot of bullets can pierce a car door. Motyka wanted as much steel as possible between him and whatever was about to ensue.

The limousines were being driven by hired chauffeurs, who must have been confused to see a car cut them off and two men in bulletproof vests scramble out and disappear behind the hood. But before any of the passengers could ponder what was happening, dozens of black-clad SWAT agents suddenly materialized, charging over the hills on either side of the road. Nearly forty SWAT members swarmed around the cars, shouting and pointing machine guns at the startled mourners. The drama and surprise of a SWAT operation is designed to shock and terrify the target, leaving him too stunned to contemplate resistance. The members of the Fuk Ching were overwhelmed, pulled from their vehicles, separated from their girlfriends, identified, cuffed, and arrested.

As Motyka rounded up the mourners who were on the indictment, federal agents were fanning across New York City, making arrests at other locations. They raided apartments in Coney Island and in Queens. A team stormed the Fukienese American Association at 125 East Broadway. They wrapped the whole building in police tape and arrested several gang members, along with Ah Kay's father, who feigned a heart attack and had to be taken away in an ambulance.

From a high-tech command center at One Police Plaza, Luke Rettler watched the coordinated takedown unfold on an array of video screens. Nineteen members of the Fuk Ching were arrested that day, and a grand jury would soon deliver the forty-five-count racketeering indictment against them and against Ah Kay. Piece by piece the authorities were taking down the major figures associated with the *Golden Venture*, and with the snakehead trade in general. Once the captain and the crew and the onboard enforcers and Kin Sin Lee had been captured, along with Ah Kay and the Fuk Ching gang and Weng Yu Hui, only two major targets would remain. One of them was a fugitive—the Taiwanese snakehead Mr. Charlie, who had escaped capture once when he pretended to be a passenger in Pattaya and again when he had slipped out of New York after the *Golden Venture* ran aground. The other target, who was not a fugitive, or at any rate not yet, was right in New York City—Sister Ping.

Several weeks after the roundup of the Fuk Ching, Motyka and the C-6 squad raided Sister Ping's building at 47 East Broadway. She was not there; she had flown to Johannesburg to visit her passengers on the ostrich farm. But in the basement restaurant and street-level shop, and in the apartments upstairs, the agents found a laminating machine and passports, driver's licenses, green cards, Social Security cards, and employment authorization cards, all in other people's names—what a prosecutor would later describe as the "tools of the alien smuggling trade." Peter Lee, the FBI agent who had been Sister Ping's handler during her brief period of cooperation, was there, and he went through the records of her money transfer business—hundreds of notes containing the names of intended recipients, the amount of money to be sent, and the addresses in the counties around Fuzhou where the funds should be delivered. On their own, these materials might have been enough for an indictment. But the authorities did not want to repeat the folly of the Buffalo case, in which Sister Ping was prosecuted on minor charges and not forced to answer for the scope of her criminal enterprise. Instead they continued to assemble evidence in order to make a broader case against the snakehead, which might actually result in substantial jail time.

Sister Ping returned to New York after the raid, but between the roundup of the Fuk Ching and the FBI search warrant, and perhaps especially the fact that so many of her former associates and colleagues were now being interrogated by law enforcement, she must have sensed that she was running a risk by staying in the city. In addition to worrying about the steady advances of the FBI, she was growing concerned about the Chinatown journalist Ying Chan, who had written a series of high-profile articles on the snakehead trade for the *Daily News* and was working, in the months after the *Golden Venture* arrived, on getting to the bottom of who had orchestrated the voyage. Chan visited Sister Ping in her shop and was solicitous. "I heard that you are a very capable woman," she said. But Sister Ping was leery of the reporter and angry that in her articles Chan had portrayed her as a villain and not as the hardworking and selfless immigrant success story she believed herself to be.

Early in 1994, Chan's investigative reporting on the snakehead trade was singled out for the prestigious George Polk Award, and some friends planned a banquet in Chinatown in her honor. But before the banquet one of Chan's sources in the Fujianese community told her that she should stay away from the neighborhood for a while. The source explained that Chan had angered Sister Ping, and that the snakehead had put a $50,000 contract on her head. It was somewhat strange that Sister Ping would bother. For all her international travel, she still moved in a more or less exclusively Chinese-language milieu; the world of the mainstream English-language press could not have been more remote. But Chan was a Chinese journalist working in Chinatown, which both heightened the apparent transgression of having disrespected the venerable Sister Ping and made Chan vulnerable in a neighborhood where dispatching another Chinese person was, as Ah Kay had put it, "like killing a dog or a cat." Chan reported the threat to the police, and the *Daily News* arranged for a twenty-four-hour bodyguard.

Dougie Lee, the Cantonese American detective from the Jade Squad, knew Sister Ping slightly. He would see her around the neighborhood, running errands or working the counter in her store. Through his own sources he heard about the contract on Ying Chan, and he understood that Sister Ping's stature in the community was such that if people thought she would be open to the idea, some ambitious upstart might kill Chan just to make a good impression. He sent word back through the community that the NYPD knew about the threat to Ying Chan's life, and if anything should happen, they would know where to look. Before long, the idea of killing Ying Chan was abandoned.

(Sister Ping denies that she offered money to have Chan killed but acknowledges that she disliked the press coverage she was receiving, and maintains that she was approached by a member of the Fuk Ching who *offered* to take care of Chan for $6,000. She declined the offer, she insists, telling the gang member, "It doesn't matter to me. Whatever they want to write, they can go ahead.")

What is clear is that by this time Sister Ping was beginning to feel besieged. With both Ah Kay and Weng Yu Hui arrested, she must have realized that one or both might start cooperating with the government and furnish them with evidence of her criminal activities. In recent years she had relied heavily on the young men of the Fuk Ching to offload her smuggling ships, and now several lesser figures from the gang were reportedly prepared to testify against her.

The FBI continued to monitor her activity throughout 1994. Its agents obtained a warrant to wiretap her telephones, and it appeared that her smuggling had continued uninterrupted after the *Golden Venture* fiasco. In March 1994 she arranged for a ship to transport over a hundred passengers to the New Jersey shore. The following month, investigators recorded a conversation in which a passenger who was being held after arriving in the United States told his family that if they didn't pay Sister Ping, his captors would amputate his feet. After months of painstaking investigation, a federal indictment was finally ready in December 1994, charging Sister Ping with kidnapping and with holding customers for ransom.

But by then she was already gone. Sister Ping had used her passport to fly to Hong Kong on September 20, 1994. It was the last time she would travel on her own documents. After that flight, one government lawyer would later observe, "Sister Ping, at least on paper, ceased to exist."

Chapter Thirteen

Freedom Birds

TO CRAIG Trebilcock, a rangy young litigator with a boyish face and a casual manner that belied a certain intensity, the small city of York, Pennsylvania, seemed like a throwback to America in the 1950s, in both positive and negative respects. By the time Craig moved to York to practice law in 1991, the city was suffering from factory closures and a steady erosion of the manufacturing base that had made it a boomtown in an earlier era. Many of the businesses in the handsome brick buildings of the historic town center were shuttered, and a certain sense hung in the air that the city's best days might be behind it. But York's residents were fiercely devoted to it, and to the particular, almost exaggerated sense of Norman Rockwell–style, small-town American life that the city more or less preserved. Peppermint Patties, which took their name from York, were no longer made in town, but the Harley-Davidson plant was still active, as was York International, which manufactured heating and air-conditioning systems, and many people in town still drew a living by punching a clock in a factory. When Trebilcock left his office at lunchtime, it sometimes seemed that half the people he passed in the span of a block or two were friends or colleagues or acquaintances, everyone smiling and wishing him well. Politically, the area was fairly conservative, with "values" voters determined to raise their families in a traditional Christian manner; potlucks and dinner parties invariably began with someone saying grace. York residents tended to share an abiding and deeply felt appreciation for the United States and all that it stood for. The Articles of Confederation were drafted in York, and many local businesses still bear the proud, if historically erroneous, name First Capital.

The flip side of all that tradition was that York could seem close-minded and claustrophobic at times, even retrograde. A local joke had it that the state was divided neatly into Western Pennsylvania on one side, Eastern Pennsylvania on the other, and Alabama in the middle. The town was home to a fairly active chapter of the Ku Klux Klan. When a local bookstore featured the works of Dr. Martin Luther King, Jr., in a display window, the proprietor received anonymous death threats.

One day in June 1993, a partner at Craig's firm asked the young associate to do him a favor. The *Golden Venture* incident several weeks earlier had made national news, and Craig was surprised to hear that nearly half of the passengers from the ship had been relocated to the county prison on the outskirts of York. The INS had contacted the local bar association, because the detainees were entitled to bring asylum cases before they were deported and they would need representation. The partner had signed up to volunteer his time, but now he had a scheduling conflict. Could Craig go in his place? Craig was already busy with work and wasn't exactly looking for some additional, time-consuming, pro bono commitment. *It will take you ten hours,* the partner assured him. *Nothing more.*

Craig knew nothing about immigration law, or about immigration as an issue, for that matter. There weren't many immigration lawyers in York; there weren't many immigrants. But the bar association arranged a training session, a three-hour crash course in asylum law. From what Craig could gather by talking to people at the session, representing the *Golden Venture* passengers would be a straightforward process consisting primarily of paperwork. The Chinese men would apply for asylum in America, citing their political activism or their resistance to the one-child policy; then they would be granted asylum, as Chinese asylum-seekers fleeing those conditions routinely were, and Craig could go back to working for billable clients.

As the session concluded, someone handed out a list with the names of the Chinese detainees on it and instructed each attorney to pick a name. When the list came to Craig, he peered at it with a mild sense of trepidation: everything seemed forbiddingly unpronounceable, a thicket of *X*s and *Q*s. He scanned the list for a name he could manage and finally spotted one: Pin Lin.

On his way out to the prison, Craig was curious to meet his new client, but also, preemptively, a little dubious. Before arriving in York he had been an Army lawyer, working as a defense attorney in courts-martial, and after a while he had developed a kind of hardwired skepticism, an abiding hunch that a lawyer can never trust his client 100 percent. At the training session, some of the other attorneys had told him that according to the INS, the Chinese had a tendency to lie in their asylum applications and the notion that the *Golden Venture* detainees at York County Prison were all political refugees was a sham. Craig would go in and hear what his client had to say, of course, but he considered himself warned. He was not going to let anyone dupe him that day.

Craig presented his credentials at the prison and was led to a small room where inmates can meet their attorneys. When he laid eyes on Pin Lin, the first thing that struck Craig was how frightened he seemed. He was shaking; his shoulders were hunched protectively; his face was downcast. Craig had brought a young interpreter, and he looked at the interpreter and looked at Pin Lin. Then Craig realized: *He's frightened of me*. Through the interpreter, Craig began to explain why he was there, why Pin Lin was in prison, the complex choreography of obtaining asylum. It was slow going, but over the course of several meetings, Pin told Craig a terrifying story. When his wife gave birth to their second child, he had been chased and beaten by the local family-planning cadres, he said. They had sterilized his wife and tried to sterilize him. He fought the men off physically and eventually went into hiding, before fleeing to Thailand and boarding the *Golden Venture* at Pattaya.

It was an awful story, and at first Craig was incredulous. As he and Pin Lin talked, he employed a number of techniques he had picked up as a defense attorney to determine whether a client was telling the truth. He began by suggesting, in effect, that Pin should sweeten the story, pointing out that hypothetically, had *this* or *that* happened, it might help Pin's chances of winning asylum.

"No!" Pin would interrupt impatiently. "That's not what happened!"

In his defense work, Craig had found that liars often have trouble repeating the same complicated lie, detail for detail, more than once. In his meetings with Pin, he would suggest that they revisit some portion of the story that they had discussed the day before, but Craig would adjust some minor detail of the narrative. Again Pin would interrupt him, reiterating each particular he had recounted the previous day.

At a certain point during these lengthy sessions in the cramped little room at the prison, Craig came to a surprising realization: he believed Pin Lin was telling the truth. It certainly bolstered the man's credibility that he seemed to pass every test Craig imposed and avoid the usual tells of a liar. But there was something else, something from Craig's own past, that made him believe Pin Lin.

Between 1988 and 1990, the Army had stationed Craig with the armored cavalry regiment overlooking the Fulda Gap, a key strategic stretch of the border between West Germany and East Germany during the cold war. From Observation Post Alpha, you could peer through binoculars at East Germany across a 300-yard stretch of no-man's-land. During those years Craig bore witness to the enormous sacrifices that regular East Germans undertook to flee a miserable life under communism. He knew of incidents where whole families rushed across the border, and incidents when, in full view of the American troops, East German guards would open fire and cut the runners down. At the foot of the American watchtower, a white birch cross commemorated an East German farmer who was fatally shot one Christmas while trying to escape with his son. To the thousands of Americans amassed there, that stretch of the border had become known as "the frontier of freedom."

Craig and his wife chose to live not on the base but in the nearby town of Fulda. They liked the community, liked their neighbors. Despite the cultural differences, they felt that the West Germans weren't so different from themselves: they seemed to harbor similar hopes and nurture similar plans. Craig knew that before the Iron Curtain had been erected a generation earlier, the area had been one more or less coherent community—that families and friends had been split asunder by the Wall. He had always assumed somehow that apart from the divergent political ideology that they might or might not subscribe to, the people on the other side of no-man's-land were probably much like his neighbors in Fulda.

But when the Wall came down late in 1989 and the East Germans began streaming into town, they looked different to Craig, on some fundamental level: they looked downtrodden, bereft of any hope. They seemed to have a sickly pallor. Curious to see what life was like on the other side, Craig ventured into the towns and villages across the border and was appalled at the grim disrepair he encountered. The houses were forlorn and unkempt, the churches darkened by soot. Many of the buildings still bore the scars of ordnance from World War II. And the people seemed universally dispirited. The more Craig pondered the circumstances on either side of the border, the more it seemed like a sort of psychological experiment, in which a single community had been roughly divided into two different systems in order to see how each might play out. To Craig the evidence was unambiguous. Whereas his West German neighbors were gregarious, relaxed, and generally optimistic, the East Germans seemed just to shuffle along, their eyes on their shoes, always a little fearful of what the future held in store.

Craig was not a political person and had never been given to the sort of reflexive anticommunism he had occasionally encountered growing up, but on an almost anthropological level, the countenance of the

East Germans he observed in 1989—that *look*—instilled in him an abiding conviction about the oppressive toll that a Communist system could have on the human spirit. And four years later, as he sat facing Pin Lin in the York County Prison, he recognized that look again.

In ways that he could not have predicted, Craig was moved by Pin's story, and despite the fact that he would have mere days to prepare the case, he became determined to prevent the government from sending Pin back to China. He made repeated visits to the prison and began studying asylum law and endeavoring to cull some corroborating material to bolster the case. Realizing that a man's life potentially hung in the balance, he let his other work slide. Craig had never argued an immigration case before, but when he and Pin appeared before the judge, he felt that it went pretty well.

But they lost. Like Sean Chen and so many other *Golden Venture* passengers, Pin learned that his claim had been denied. As word spread among the local lawyers who had taken on the asylum cases that *everyone* was losing and that all the Chinese men would be sent home, Craig came to an unpleasant realization: they had been set up. He had a naturally self-deprecating manner, and as various local lawyers answered the bar association's call and took on the asylum cases, Craig had found it funny that a group he jokingly described as "country lawyers" and "guys who write wills for a living" were suddenly boning up on current events in China and the finer nuances of the Refugee Act. But now it occurred to him that perhaps that was the point: the INS had hustled the Chinese passengers out of New York City, where legions of immigration specialists were on hand to represent them, and bused them to central Pennsylvania. The government had to at least appear to be offering the passengers some opportunity to make their claims, so the INS enlisted the pro bono lawyers in York, knowing full well that this was just a formality, that the game was rigged, that few if any of the claims would succeed.

Craig's secretary, Margo, was sitting at her desk when Craig suddenly burst into the office, angrier than she had ever seen him. "Get me NBC," he shouted. "Get me CBS. Get me ABC. Get me the fucking White House!"

About a month later, a Methodist minister named Joan Maruskin read an article in the *York Daily Record* about the *Golden Venture* detainees being held at the local prison. Maruskin has a wide, open face, a brassy laugh, and a feisty grin. She had long been engaged in social activism on a range of liberal causes, and she was moved by the account of the Chinese men who were being held in prison even though they were charged with no crime. The article quoted Craig Trebilcock, and Maruskin decided to telephone him and see if there was anything she could do. Craig told her that he and other local lawyers would be appealing the asylum decisions. But it would be good to publicize the case, he said, and to show some support for the men. Perhaps she could go to the prison?

On a Sunday morning in August, Maruskin drove out to the prison at seven o'clock. She had telephoned a number of friends and acquaintances from her church, as well as every reporter and news organization she could think of. About ten people showed up, including a reporter from the local paper. The York County Prison was unaccustomed to protesters or vigils of any description, and the warden must have grown somewhat alarmed, because as Maruskin and her little flock approached the prison grounds, a phalanx of two dozen guards emerged from the building holding rifles and stood in formation, monitoring the group. Maruskin was startled—but delighted. She had been wondering how she could publicize the vigil so that people in town would take notice, and a photo in the paper of a harmless prayer group staring down a team of armed guards was better publicity than she could ever have asked for. "God has a sense of humor," she liked to say.

From that morning forth, Maruskin and an ever-expanding band of supporters began holding vigils outside the York County Prison to show their solidarity with the passengers of the *Golden Venture*. For the first year they met every single morning at seven o'clock. Every morning for a year, Sean Chen and the other detainees could look out the narrow windows of their cells and see a knot of people praying and singing. When summer gave way to fall, they lit candles against the darkness. As fall turned to winter, the candles blew out in the brittle wind and the groups bundled up in heavy winter coats and stood close together to ward off the cold. Inside the prison, it sometimes felt as though there were no seasons: the temperature always the same, the light a headachy fluorescence. But through the windows the prisoners could watch the people who attended the vigils experience the seasons, standing knee-deep in snow in their colorful winter gear, then huddling under shared umbrellas as the spring rains fell. The York residents knew which wing of the prison the *Golden Venture* detainees were housed in, and they would wave to them. Sometimes they saw the Chinese men, silhouetted in the windows, waving back.

Over the months, and ultimately years, that the vigils took place in York, an extraordinarily odd and diverse cast of characters coalesced around the plight of the *Golden Venture* detainees. Along with Maruskin there was Beverly Church, a nurse and paralegal who was a grandmother, a gun owner, and a lifelong Republican. Bev, as everyone knew her, had always been suspicious of immigrants but had signed on to do some pro bono work through the bar association, thinking it would amount to a little light paperwork. *We don't need these people here,* she thought to herself, concluding that they would probably be sent home, and that wasn't such a bad thing. *Get them in and get them out.* She drove out to the prison in her big Cadillac and was introduced to Zheng Xin Bin, a forty-year-old Fujianese man whose wife had given birth to a son who was mentally disabled. Knowing that their son would not be able to care for them in their old age, the couple tried and tried again to have another son, but produced three daughters instead, enraging the local cadres. As she listened to Xin Bin's story, which he delivered in a flat, mournful manner, Bev found herself unaccountably moved. She kept thinking about her own grandfather, who had left Ireland and journeyed to America nearly a century earlier. He had come through Ellis Island; she didn't know what kind of paperwork he did or did not have. "This can't be happening in my country," she said. She resolved to do everything she could to get Xin Bin and the other passengers out of prison and help them remain in the United States.

There was Sterling Showers, a retired factory worker who was not a lawyer and could speak no Chinese, but who started visiting the *Golden Venture* passengers several times a week, talking to them through a glass partition and a formidable language barrier. He would stop by the local Chinese restaurant in York and collect any old Chinese newspapers the employees had finished reading, then take them to the prison to give to the detainees.

There was Lena Ngo, whose grandparents had fled the Communists in China in the 1950s and moved to South Vietnam, and whose parents had fled the Communists in Vietnam in 1975. As a girl she came to America as one of the Vietnamese boat people. She had been taken in by a family she met through a church in York, and she liked to joke that if America ever turned Communist, there would be no place else for her to go. As a former refugee whose grandparents had fled the country that the *Golden Venture* passengers were fleeing, she felt she should show solidarity with the detainees.

There was Rod Merrill, a high school teacher and retired Navy pilot who began composing songs about the detainees, about China, about freedom, and about immigration. He wrote a new Woodie Guthrie–style ditty for each vigil and would take his guitar and try to bolster people's spirits, eventually composing hundreds of songs and compiling a CD, *Where Is the Freedom?*

There was Demian Yumi, a New Agey singer and artist who corresponded with the detainees and developed a performance art piece in which she recited parts of their stories, explaining their reasons for leaving China. She eventually took the performance to the steps of the Capitol building in Washington, D.C.

There was Cindy Lobach, an ebullient archconservative who was the wife of one of the lead lawyers working on the asylum cases with Craig. Lobach was organized and energetic and began producing a weekly newsletter on bright colored paper, which she wrote, edited, published, and distributed herself, giving updates on the legal proceedings, quoting inspirational snippets of poems or scripture, and printing translated letters from the *Golden Venture* detainees. Lobach proudly self-identified as a "Rush Limbaugh dittohead conservative," and when she initially began attending the vigils, she expressed some reservations about keeping company with an aging hippie like Joan Maruskin, wondering, "How can I work on the same side of an issue with these crazy, left-wing, liberal wackos?" But on the issue of the Chinese asylum-seekers the two had found common cause. By mutual agreement, they steered clear of every other political issue, and before long they had become close friends.

To help them communicate with the men in the prison, the group found a young reference librarian from the local college named Zehao Zhou. Known to everyone in the group as ZZ, he had grown up in northern China and spent six years in a forced labor camp before obtaining a student visa to America in 1987. Alone among the group, he was somewhat dubious of the *Golden Venture* passengers' various claims about the one-child policy or political involvement in 1989. But ZZ was bitterly opposed to Beijing and felt that on some fundamental level the men had left for the same reason he had—a lack of opportunity, a sickening sense that tomorrow would not be any better than today.

The members of the group called themselves the People of the Golden Vision and adopted a line from Margaret Mead as their motto: "Never doubt that a small group of thoughtful, committed citizens can change the world. Indeed, it's the only thing that ever has." They found passages from the Bible that seemed to resonate with their feelings about the detainees. "When a stranger resides with you in your land, you shall not oppress the stranger," Leviticus reads. "The stranger who resides with you shall be to you as the citizen among you. You shall love the stranger as yourself, for you were strangers in the land of Egypt."

They courted the press. "The Bible is the ultimate immigration handbook," Joan Maruskin told the *Baltimore Sun*. "Moses was a criminal alien who came back to Egypt to lead a nation of aliens into the promised land. Jesus was an undocumented refugee. What would have happened to Christianity if they had put him in an INS prison?" They appealed not merely to people's sense of religion but to a deeply ingrained conception of the United States as a country in which the system retains some degree of fairness and transparency and even the most misbegotten can still expect a fair shake. People who had never been politically active in the past suddenly found themselves engaged in the most elemental, and perhaps quixotic, forms of civic expression. They telephoned their congressman and wrote impassioned personal letters to President Clinton. "It's injustice," Cindy Lobach told the *New York Times*. "It's a complete embarrassment to be an American when people are treated like this." The arrival of the men from the *Golden Venture* had awakened something in the people of York, something that none of them knew they were looking for. To Caryl Clarke, a local reporter who covered each development in the *Golden Venture* case and marveled at the way the event had galvanized people, it seemed that the Chinese men "have brought the world into our rather cloistered community."

To be sure, the people who rallied around the *Golden Venture* passengers were prompted by a wide range of motivations and personal, political, and above all religious predilections that in many instances had existed long before the arrival of the ship. The People of the Golden Vision counted Buddhists, Jews, agnostics, and atheists among their numbers, but the overwhelming spirit of the support they offered was unmistakably Christian. They came from different denominations, but the prayers intoned at the vigils were Christian prayers, and they tended to construe even the secular principles for which they were fighting in explicitly Christian terms. Joan Maruskin assembled a composite first-person narrative, drawn from the experiences of the Chinese detainees, called "In Search of a Better Hell," which acted as an appeal to members of the public, the press, and the political establishment. "You, the people of America, are my only hope," it read. "In this country I have learned about God. China is a godless country. In this country, I have learned about the love of Jesus Christ through the actions and love of his followers."

Maruskin insisted that she had no intention of converting any of the detainees, but the same could not be said of the chaplain at the York County Prison, a fervent evangelical who launched an aggressive effort to have the men from the *Golden Venture* baptized. He confided in Maruskin that it was his belief that the Chinese men had been sent to him by God so that he could convert them to Christianity and then deport them back to China, where they could spread God's word.

One particular animating issue for many of the York supporters was the notion that the detainees had fled from China in order to avoid forced abortion or sterilization. The group had ardent pro-choicers and pro-lifers, and Craig Trebilcock wryly observed that forced abortion and sterilization might actually be one issue upon which the two groups could agree. But Craig had moments when he grew cynical about the outpouring of support for the *Golden Venture* passengers, and he wondered to what degree they had simply become the latest front in the long-standing abortion wars of the United States—to what degree, indeed, the pro-life lobby might be using the detainees for the publicity they generated and the issues they appeared to symbolize. At one point Craig filed a brief in which he used the expression "reproductive freedom" in a strictly neutral, descriptive sense. He received a furious telephone call from a representative of a prominent Catholic group that had been supporting the effort, who accused him of employing the phrase as a coded pro-choice message. Still, Craig was a pragmatist. He was happy to have whatever support he could find.

The two dozen women who had arrived on the *Golden Venture* proved to be an especially significant cause for pro-life groups. The women were housed in a detention facility in New Orleans, where Joan Maruskin and an assortment of York supporters went to visit them. Many of the women told harrowing stories about the birth-control tactics employed by the cadres in China. In the summer of 1995, the conservative New Jersey congressman Chris Smith held a hearing on Capitol Hill and invited several of the women to testify about their experiences. Craig and the York supporters drove to Washington to attend the hearing, and the women were escorted into the Capitol building in shackles. "The cadres of the local government were trying to catch women," a soft-spoken detainee named Chen Yun Fei recalled. "So you could hear the sound of crying, you know, everywhere. And they used the tractors to put on this big loudspeaker to tell people that those people who are pregnant, you have to go to have it born immature."

Chen Yun Fei recounted how she was compelled to have a late-term abortion at the hands of an inexperienced medical student, which led to an infection. After the abortion, she found an abandoned baby girl by the side of the road, she continued. The baby was crying and hungry. She took it home, which angered the cadres, and she was forced to flee. She hid in the countryside, she said, subsisting on sorghum and maize. But when she returned to her village, the cadres captured her and sterilized her.

The other women's stories were equally horrific. "The crimes that have been committed against you and against the women of China are no less serious than the crimes that were committed by the Nazis," Representative Smith said. "It is even more appalling when we realize that the Clinton administration wants to send you back to your oppressors."

But because of the altered posture on claims of persecution under the one-child policy, the women were unable to secure asylum, and when their legal options were exhausted, they were transferred from New Orleans to a facility in Bakersfield, California, as preparations were undertaken to deport them back to China. In Bakersfield they caught the attention of Tim and Terri Palmquist, who ran a local anti-abortion group, Life Savers Ministries. Twice a week Terri Palmquist walked the sidewalk in front of a local abortion clinic; the family's Dodge Caravan bore a bumper sticker reading "Abortion: One Dead, One Wounded." When they learned that the women were being held in Bakersfield and would soon be returned to China, the Palmquists began organizing prayer vigils like the ones in York. They broadcast news about the women on the local Christian radio station.

On February 29, 1996, when the women marked their thousandth day of confinement, the Palmquists led a 13-mile walk from a replica of the Liberty Bell in downtown Bakersfield to the Lerdo Detention Facility, where the women were being held. Terri did the walk dressed as the Statue of Liberty. Six months later, with the women still detained and their future uncertain, Tim Palmquist announced that five of them had converted to Christianity. A visitor had explained the differences between Buddhism and Christianity to the women, Palmquist said. The detainees had begun attending Mandarin-language chapel services and had each been given a Chinese Bible.

Just as it appeared that the women would be deported, they found help from a most unlikely corner. Word of their predicament had spread around the world and reached the Vatican, where the Office of Resettlement suddenly took an interest. By some accounts, the decision to help the women went as high as Pope John Paul II. They could not remain in American jails, but neither could they return to China, so the Vatican persuaded Ecuador to take the women in. In order to secure the deal, Ecuador needed a guarantee of financial support for the women. In three weeks of outreach among local supporters, the Palmquists raised $50,000.

The women were flown to Quito. "They have a well-founded fear of practices that are contrary to their moral convictions and their religious beliefs," an Ecuadorian official said. The church helped the women settle in their unfamiliar new surroundings, and before long three of them had opened a restaurant. Another three aimed to start their own boutique.

With the expedited schedule that had been imposed on the asylum proceedings of the *Golden Venture* passengers, it was only a matter of months before Craig Trebilcock and the network of forty or so lawyers in York and around the country who were representing the detainees had learned that very few of the appeals filed before the Board of Immigration Appeals were successful. There was one last option available to prevent, or at least forestall, the deportation of Sean Chen and Pin Lin and the other passengers: they could sue the Clinton administration in federal court. It would be a daunting undertaking, as Craig and his colleagues endeavored to argue that because of the highly publicized arrival of the *Golden Venture*, a decision had been made in Washington to make an example of the passengers, denying them the kinds of procedural protections that had been available to Chinese asylum-seekers in the past, detaining them, expediting their cases, and adopting a presumption against granting them asylum. The suit was procedurally complex, and ultimately unsuccessful. But it represented one last opportunity to keep the passengers in the country, and it armored Craig with the power to depose officials from the Clinton administration and question them about the decision-making process in the hours and days after the arrival of the ship.

Occasionally the hopes of the People of the Golden Vision were bolstered by the release of a man here or there—the lucky ones whose asylum cases or appeals were so persuasive that they prevailed. Those detainees who were released often found themselves ejected by prison guards in the middle of the night, with no money, no civilian clothes, no directions, and just the few words of English they had managed to pick up in prison.

On these occasions, Beverly Church or Joan Maruskin would often receive a call. "You want a Chinese guy?" Maruskin asked the retired factory worker Sterling Showers after one of these calls. "Sure," Showers replied.

The two of them drove to New York City, where a few of the men were still being held at the Varick Street facility. They picked up two *Golden Venture* passengers who had taken on American names: Ben and Rocky. The men carried their belongings in paper bags, which they loaded into the trunk. Then they climbed into the backseat for the long ride to York.

Several hours later they stopped to fill up the gas tank at a station by the side of the highway. Maruskin turned and saw Rocky fast asleep. Ben was wide awake. He watched her as she looked at Rocky and then looked back at him.

"Ben no sleep," he said in English. "Ben sleep in prison. Ben free."

Stories like Ben's were the exception, however, and as the months became years in York County Prison, Sean Chen and the other detainees were insulated, somewhat, from the daily victories and setbacks of the legal maneuverings and public lobbying being undertaken on their behalf. Many of the men succumbed to despair; they had families struggling in desperate poverty back in China, families that had gone into debt to send them to America and were counting on their remittances. Several of the passengers went on a hunger strike for a week, until their supporters in York pleaded with them to stop. A prison guard caught one of the men trying to hang himself with a bedsheet in the middle of the night. Sixteen others vowed to commit suicide rather than return to China. The inmates were given paper shirts and trousers, because guards feared they would fashion nooses from their clothing. Without access to proper medical care, some of the passengers suffered from dangerous conditions that remained untreated. One man developed a tumor on his liver and began to vomit blood. Another was diagnosed with stomach cancer, and was released to the care of his extended family in New York only when it became clear that he was dying.

As seemed so often to be the case, Sean Chen's youth and independence allowed him to make the most of the situation. He spent his time in prison trying to learn English and study for his GED. He was excited to be able to take classes again; since his expulsion from school four years earlier, he had felt robbed of an education. "Just pretend you're still in school," one of his cousins suggested in a letter, and he did his best to heed that advice.

To Craig Trebilcock, Sean always seemed a little brash, a little overconfident—he had none of the mournful humility of older passengers, like Craig's client, Pin Lin. But different people process incarceration in different ways, and Sean may simply have been unready to give up hope. Nor did he lose sight of the fact that dreadful though it might have been, the men's imprisonment was on some fundamental level voluntary. They could submit to deportation any day. Of course there would be fines to pay, and possibly prison, or worse, in China. The *Golden Venture* episode had badly embarrassed Beijing, and any returnees would no doubt be made to suffer for the slight. One of the passengers was able to make a telephone call home and learned that another passenger, who had accepted deportation, had been thrown into prison upon his return. The authorities broke both of his legs, saying, "He won't run away again, will he?" That story made the rounds in the prison, hardening the resolve of many of the men to stick out their indefinite jail sentence in America rather than take their chances by going home.

But perhaps the most extraordinary testament to the motivation the *Golden Venture* passengers had to forge a life in the United States was the experience of the men who accepted deportation, after the months it had taken to get as far as Bangkok, the months stuck in Mombasa, the months aboard the *Golden Venture*, and the months in an American jail, only to reach China and begin the process all over again, endeavoring once more to reach America. One of the York detainees, a skinny forty-year-old named Wang Wu Dong, agreed to be deported to China in 1996, after three years behind bars. His asylum claim, under the one-child policy, had failed. ("You knew that if you . . . attempted to have another child and you already had two, most likely you would have to be sterilized or be punished?" his judge asked. "That's not persecution. That's punishment for not obeying the law.")

When local officials learned that Wang would be returning to his village in Fujian, it seemed likely that he and his wife, who was still there, raising their two children, might try to have a third child. While Wang was being held in detention in the nearby town of Fuqing, the cadres hauled his wife to a birth-control clinic, administered an epidural anesthetic, and removed her uterus. Wang was devastated when he returned home and learned what had happened. He was consumed by shame and wept for days. But he still owed over $10,000 to his snakeheads; Sister Ping might have had a satisfaction guarantee for her customers, but less scrupulous smugglers demanded payment even after a catastrophe like the *Golden Venture*. The family's small plot of land, on which they cultivated rice, beans, and sweet potatoes, would never generate enough income to cover the debts.

Wang had been home for less than two months when he and his wife made the desperate decision to turn to the snakeheads once again. From a loan shark they borrowed $5,000 and made a down payment. With the snakeheads' help, Wang obtained a false passport and boarded a flight to Surinam, the former Dutch colony on the Atlantic coast of South America, which had become a minor hub for snakeheads. For months Wang waited in Surinam, until finally local snakeheads loaded him onto a fishing trawler bound for the United States.

Some days later, the snakeheads aboard the trawler offloaded their passengers to a 30-foot speedboat, which made its way toward the shore near Bay Head, New Jersey. But as the speedboat approached, it was enveloped in a dense fog, and, tragic and improbable though it might seem, the boat ran aground. The passengers scattered, and all of them,

Wang included, were arrested by the police. "Sent Back to China, Man Washes Up Again," the *New York Times* marveled, in an article that noted the "cruelly flippant aptness" of the name of the speedboat Wang arrived on: *Oops II*.

The INS immediately moved to deport Wang once again. But in one final, merciful twist to the story, a federal judge in New Jersey ended up granting Wang "withholding" status, a rarely invoked designation that enabled him to live and work in the United States (though not to become a permanent resident or citizen, or to sponsor his wife or children to come to America). It may have been a limited freedom, but it would enable Wang to send money home in order to cover his family's debts and in time, perhaps, to pay snakeheads to bring his family to America as well.

While a green card and the legal right to petition to bring family members to America was obviously preferable to an undocumented life for the passengers who arrived on the *Golden Venture*, there was among them a sense that even an illegal existence in the United States was better than a legal existence anywhere else.

This was nowhere more evident than in the case of the women of the *Golden Venture*, whom the Vatican had gone to such trouble to relocate in South America. Within a couple of years, every single one of them had abandoned Ecuador and returned to live illegally in the United States.

One day in York County Prison a tall, slightly taciturn detainee named Yang You Yi took a magazine he was reading and began tearing the glossy pages and folding them into little paper triangles. He made more and more of the triangles, until he had an impressive pile. Then he started interlocking them and assembling the bound configurations that resulted in a larger sculpture. What emerged, after hours of work, was a rough, corrugated shape that was recognizably a pineapple, replete with a spiky stem. Some of the other men had gathered around Yang, watching as he worked, and in the ensuing days they copied his steps, producing a variety of pineapples of their own.

The men were painfully bored in the prison, and desperate for a way to busy themselves, and the introduction of this colorful, ambitious origami initiated a craze. Soon it was not just pineapples they were creating but paper bowls, vases, birds, and a menagerie of other creatures. The tools they had at their disposal were simple: newspaper, yellow legal pads, and old magazines discarded by the prison guards or donated by the People of the Golden Vision. But some of the men were quite artistically inclined—they had worked as carpenters and stonemasons, architects and weavers, kite makers and set designers before leaving China—and soon they were improvising new techniques. Someone realized that by mixing toilet paper, water, and toothpaste, they could produce a pasty papier-mâché, which could then be molded with a plastic spoon and colored with a magic marker until it acquired a porcelain sheen.

As the sculptures grew less experimental and more impressive, the men began sending them out to their attorneys and to the supporters attending the vigils, as humble gifts and tokens of thanks. The York residents were astonished that the men could have produced anything so beautiful from a prison cell. They negotiated with prison administrators to send in jugs of Elmer's Glue, blunt children's scissors, and Sharpie markers. As more and more of the men started spending their days on the artwork, the results got bigger and more impressive. They sculpted turkeys, cranes, and storks by the dozen; a family of squat, moon-faced owls; dragons and Buddhas; a muscular warrior astride a horse, his skin smooth and shiny as lacquer. They presented Bev Church with a twin-engine propeller plane made entirely of folded legal paper, the word *Hope* inscribed in green felt marker on its nose.

Before long the detainees were going through so much prison-issue toilet paper that the warden complained, and the People of the Golden Vision took to visiting the prison with wholesale bales of Charmin. The men developed an assembly line, so that the less experienced artisans could work on folding small components and the artists among them could assemble these pieces into ever more impressive creations.

As word spread through the community about the artworks the men were creating, they became collector's items, and people began inquiring about whether it was possible to purchase the sculptures. Cindy Lobach obtained permission to visit the men once a week and cart out the works as they produced them. She held a sale at the local YWCA to help defray some of the costs of the men's legal defense, and before long the sales were a regular event, and the People of the Golden Vision held cultural nights, with Chinese food, artwork by the detainees, and impassioned discussions of immigration and asylum in America.

The art was a sensation. Soon the proprietor of a New York gallery specializing in American folk art got in touch and began selling the sculptures. The press started to take note. *Life* ran an article about the *Golden Venture* immigrants with a portfolio of photos of the sculptures. The art seemed emblematic of both the work ethic and the talent of the men, who wanted nothing more than to leave prison and become productive members of the American workforce. It was a perfect calling card for those lobbying to set them free. "There's some intelligent people here," Bev Church told a reporter. "They're not just some peasants who fell off a rice paddy."

The detainees at York ultimately produced 16,000 sculptures and, through Cindy Lobach's sales, earned $135,000. Pieces ended up in the collections of Dan Rather, Peter Jennings, and other notable personalities who took an interest in the case. A traveling exhibit of the sculptures was featured in museums and galleries around the country, including the Smithsonian in Washington, D.C. Several of the most talented sculptors were eventually released from prison and granted special visas for "aliens of extraordinary ability in the arts."

One of the most striking aspects of the artwork the men produced during their years in York County Prison, and surely one of the reasons for the attention and enthusiasm it garnered, was the preponderance in the designs they selected of Americana. The red, white, and blue of the

American flag became a recurring color scheme. The men clipped the "Made in America" stamps from Wal-Mart ads and affixed them to their work. They loved birds, especially birds of prey, and American bald eagles in particular. After one of the men created a papier-mâché eagle alighting on a white branch and inscribed the words *Fly to Freedom* on the branch in English and Chinese, the supporters in York began calling the sculptures Freedom Birds. There were birds in midflight, their fearsome talons clutching the air in front of them, and birds standing sentry, in repose. Many of the paper birds were captive, locked up in ornamental cages.

The sculptures that the men produced behind bars and sent to the outside world served as a form of prison letter, less articulate than those of Gramsci or Martin Luther King, perhaps, but no less eloquent. There was a kind of rough-hewn poetry to a sculpture of the Statue of Liberty that was made entirely of toilet paper and had taken a detainee three days to construct. To some extent all this was surely calculated, designed to play on the sentimentality of Americans on the outside who might be in a position to help. But at the same time the sculptures provided a kind of testimony, suggesting that for the men at York County Prison, for whom the reality of the United States had proved to be such an unmitigated nightmare, the *idea* of America—that beautiful idea that had launched the *Mayflower* and the *Golden Venture* and ten thousand other ships—remained miraculously unsullied.

Book III

Chapter Fourteen

The Goldfish and the Great Wall

AS THE *Golden Venture* passengers produced their prison art, American law enforcement was systematically tracking down and prosecuting the various perpetrators of the voyage. By 1995 only two figures remained at large. One was Sister Ping, who was thought to be hiding in China. The other was Mr. Charlie, the Taiwanese snakehead who along with Ah Kay and Weng Yu Hui had arranged to purchase the ship and had been one of the chief architects of the operation.

Mark Riordan, the Bangkok-based INS officer who came so close to capturing Mr. Charlie after he was arrested by the Thai Tourist Police in Pattaya in February 1993, was still on the lookout for the smuggler. But even after Weng Yu Hui had been captured and interrogated about his shadowy accomplice, Mr. Charlie remained a mysterious figure about whom little was known. After his escape from Pattaya, the Tourist Police had given Riordan a copy of the passport Mr. Charlie was carrying, which was from Laos. Riordan ran the information through the INS database and found a match: a Thai passport and a U.S. immigration file. The file contained a photograph of the handsome snakehead, and fingerprints. It also noted that Mr. Charlie had been arrested in San Francisco for alien smuggling in 1986.

Riordan took a copy of the Thai passport to the Thai police, along with the fingerprints. But they said they had no information on the smuggler, and there the trail ran cold. Nobody knew anything about

Mr. Charlie: where he was from, who he worked with, where he was hiding out, what he was up to now. Over the next two years, Riordan made a point of mentioning the *Golden Venture* incident and the name Mr. Charlie whenever he was meeting with contacts in Thailand, to see whether anyone knew anything about the elusive smuggler. But no one ever did. Riordan began to conclude that Charlie had protection at a very high level; that was the only explanation for his ability to escape the prison in Pattaya and be released to Laos, and it was the only way he could disappear so comprehensively from the scene, leaving behind only a maddening series of nicknames and aliases, none of which ever seemed to ring a bell with the corrupt denizens of the local constabulary. It was beginning to seem that Mr. Charlie was a ghost, that he had simply evaporated and might never reappear.

Then one evening in the fall of 1995, Riordan met an attaché from the Taiwanese embassy in Bangkok for tea. Riordan liked the attaché; he had an unguarded, chatty manner. As the conversation was winding down, Riordan paused, as was his custom, and withdrew from his pocket a worn list of names. The names on the list belonged to various smugglers and fugitives and other local disreputables he was seeking information on. He ran down the list to see if any of the names might spark a reaction in the attaché. He wasn't especially optimistic; this was a wish list, the names that no one knew anything about. But he had found that in a convivial and often corrupt place like Thailand, it never hurts to keep asking. When he read Mr. Charlie's name, the attaché stopped him. "I'm having dinner with him Thursday night," he said.

Riordan felt his heart skip.

The attaché told him that Mr. Charlie's real name was Lee Peng Fei, though he went by Mr. Charlie and Charlie and Char Lee and sometimes Ma Lee. He had been a snakehead for some time and had become very wealthy. He had a wife and child at home, but he was known for enjoying Bangkok's nightlife. He liked to spend the evenings in clubs, singing karaoke. "He's a good singer," the attaché said, with evident admiration. "He's a *great* singer."

"Is he Thai?" Riordan asked.

"No. He's Taiwanese," the attaché said. "I'll give you a copy of his military record."

Riordan was flabbergasted. Mr. Charlie had been in Bangkok all along. On a muggy day not long afterward, a team of Royal Thai Police officers assembled and headed to a high-end condominium complex near Bangkok Airport. When they arrived at the building, they found Mr. Charlie standing outside polishing a brand-new forest green Mercedes, which glistened in the tropical sun.

In Thailand it is not uncommon for criminals with wealth to pay poor surrogates to serve jail sentences in their place, and when Mark Riordan heard that Mr. Charlie had been arrested, he wanted to see the man in person to be certain it was him. The smuggler had managed to slip out of police custody in Pattaya, and Riordan didn't want to see it happen again. When he entered the room where Mr. Charlie was being held, he immediately recognized the well-groomed, slightly sporty young man who had appeared to be so helpful in the police station in Pattaya nearly three years before. Riordan asked Mr. Charlie how he had managed to get some two hundred passengers onto the *Golden Venture* before the Tourist Police stopped the operation. The smuggler responded, very casually, that in that particular instance he had enjoyed the assistance of the Royal Thai Navy. Riordan asked about the *Golden Venture*'s arrival in Rockaway, and Charlie said that he had been standing on the beach, waiting for the ship to come in. What he couldn't understand was how anyone could blame him for the deaths of people who decided by themselves to jump overboard.

Mr. Charlie was eventually extradited to the United States, where he admitted that he had given the order to run the *Golden Venture* aground and pleaded guilty to charges of alien smuggling and manslaughter at sea. He was sentenced to the maximum, twenty years in prison. It was a major triumph for American law enforcement. Mr. Charlie was the twenty-second person charged in relation to the voyage, and the one who had played the most important role in the botched logistics that led to the deaths at Rockaway. "This case demonstrates our resolve to strike at the very heart of international alien smuggling," Attorney General Janet Reno announced. At the same time, however, a suggestion endured that Mr. Charlie's capture might not signify the absolute conclusion of the *Golden Venture* investigation. "He is not a general but a top lieutenant," Mr. Charlie's protégé, the onboard enforcer Kin Sin Lee, had told investigators. There was a lingering suggestion that the case was not yet closed, that some elusive twenty-third suspect might still be at large.

Sister Ping's movements during these years remain somewhat mysterious, but it is known that when she left New York and flew to Hong Kong in 1994, she continued on to Beijing for an anniversary celebration of the Communist Party, where she was to be honored, along with other notable overseas Fujianese. But when she arrived in Beijing, she was arrested. She was not held for long; she managed to bribe her way out of custody. But it was clear at that point that with the FBI's investigation of the *Golden Venture* intensifying in New York, it was only a matter of time before the agents ascertained that it had been she who helped finance the purchase of the ship by wiring Ah Kay's money to Thailand, and that one of the ten dead passengers was a customer she had put on board. She could not return to the United States.

Instead, just as federal prosecutors in New York prepared to indict her, Sister Ping returned to her native village of Shengmei and took up residence once again in the palatial house she had constructed at Number 398. During the thirteen years she had been living in the United States, the village had prospered, as she had facilitated the passage of more and more of her neighbors to New York City. Other grand houses had sprung up in the area, some of them even dwarfing her own. Another side effect of Sister Ping's successful relocation of so many of her fellow villagers was that the area had grown conspicuously quiet. The narrow alleyways were empty, save for the occasional grandparent walking hand-in-hand with an American-born toddler. Eventually the village saw the introduction of what was by Chinese standards a novelty: an old folk's home. So many of the young and middle-aged residents of Shengmei had left the village that there was no one left behind to take care of the older generation. A placard in the lobby heralded the various New York–based Fujianese whose contributions had underwritten the construction.

In the wake of the *Golden Venture* incident and the negative publicity it generated for Beijing, the Fujianese authorities launched a far-reaching anti-snakehead campaign, vowing to hunt down and prosecute the smugglers and discourage local people from leaving illegally. "Illegal Emigration Is a Crime," banners in Fuzhou read. "Resolutely Clamp Down on the Crime of Snakehead Activities." In Sister Ping's village, officials erected a sign that said, "It seriously damages the reputation of our party and our country, undermines border security, destroys public stability, and ruins the general social atmosphere."

But in reality the campaign and its placards amounted to so much lip service. For the Fujianese who could now afford refrigerators and televisions, who could purchase cars or throw decadent wedding banquets or build new homes, no amount of propaganda or persuasion could diminish the widely held conviction that the snakehead trade was a fundamental social good—that it had enabled hundreds of thousands of people to pull themselves out of poverty and indulge in material comforts that would have been unimaginable to the generation before them. At a major intersection in downtown Changle, an imposing monument was erected, which dispelled any ambiguity about the role of outmigration from the region. The monument was a gleaming, soaring sail, from the base of which sprouted a set of angular wings, like the wings of an airplane. It was built to symbolize the debt that Changle owed to the people who had left the city on boats and planes.

As long as Sister Ping wanted to stay in the village of Shengmei, she had nothing to fear. Her *guanxi* penetrated deep into the local bureaucracy, where officials would ensure that no harm befell her, and in the popular mythology of the region she was regarded as a kind of saint. Like some homegrown Chinese Vito Corleone, Sister Ping had spent a lifetime accumulating favors owed, and the result was that in China, at any rate, she was untouchable. Everyone knew where she was during those years, recalled a local police officer who was charged with working specifically on the snakehead problem. But in order to take any action against Sister Ping, the authorities needed something to charge her with—a witness, a complaint. And no one was willing to come forward. "This is a different era from Mao Zedong's time," the cop observed. "If you're going to lock someone up, you need evidence."

At the FBI in New York, evidence was not the problem. Investigators had plenty of evidence on Sister Ping; they had an indictment that was beginning to gather dust. Their informants in Chinatown told them that Sister Ping was living out in the open, that she held meetings in hotels in Fuzhou, that she owned property throughout the region. But when the agents passed the information along, their Chinese counterparts simply refused to cooperate. When they tried to "follow the money" by tracing the international flow of Sister Ping's funds, lack of cooperation from the authorities in China amounted to a kind of wall, behind which assets and capital flows were simply beyond their investigative reach. "There's this giant black line, which is the border of China, and that is the end of the trail," one FBI agent explained. "There was money that we could have followed for a while, into Hong Kong and Thailand and places like that. But eventually all roads led back to China, and that's the end of the road."

It cannot have helped that Sister Ping was a hometown hero in Fujian, but there was another key reason that the authorities in China would not cooperate with the FBI. At any given time, the Bureau had a list of twenty wanted fugitives who were hiding in China and whom the Chinese government would not help them catch. China and the United

States do not have an extradition treaty, which would facilitate the process. But the real problem was a famous episode from the recent past that was still fresh in the minds of members of China's People's Security Bureau. While the incident never drew much press coverage in the United States, it was painfully familiar to the members of America's various three-letter agencies, and in the minds of many, it was the event that irrevocably soured relations between law enforcement agencies in the United States and China. It was known as the Goldfish Case.

In the spring of 1988, customs officers in San Francisco seized seven pounds of heroin that had been stuffed into condoms and sewn into the bellies of sixty-nine dead ornamental goldfish in a crate shipped from Hong Kong to a local pet store. As the Drug Enforcement Agency began investigating, its agents went to great lengths to cooperate with their counterparts in China's People's Security Bureau. Several suspects were arrested for the scheme: the Americans picked up two co-conspirators, Andrew and Chico Wong, in San Francisco, and in Shanghai the People's Security Bureau brought in a young man named Wang Zong Xiao. The Chinese held their suspect in Shanghai from March 1988 to December 1989, while federal prosecutors in the United States developed their case against the Wong brothers. An assistant U.S. attorney named Eric Swenson was hoping that in a highly unusual step, he could use the Shanghai suspect as a witness in his case, obliging the Chinese to lend him their suspect long enough for Wang to fly to San Francisco and testify against his former accomplices. In May 1988, Swenson flew to Shanghai and tried to persuade Chinese officials that there would be "no downside" to sending Wang to America to testify. Technically, China would not be extraditing Wang, because he faced no charges in the United States; he was China's suspect, to be dealt with by the Chinese criminal justice system. But he would make a valuable star witness against the American-based drug smugglers, and after a series of meetings in which Swenson and representatives from the DEA made their case, the Chinese agreed to fly Wang to San Francisco, under close Chinese custody, and allow him to testify in the trial before flying back to China to face his own punishment.

In late December 1989, Wang flew to San Francisco along with five handlers from the Chinese police. The trial began in January, and after several weeks of testimony, Eric Swenson called his witness to the stand. The courtroom was full as Wang was led in; both Washington and Beijing were carefully monitoring the unprecedented experiment that was about to unfold. If Wang could point the finger at the San Francisco smugglers and help convict them, it might cement a new level of cooperation and trust between law enforcement in the two countries. It might even lay the foundation for a mutual legal assistance treaty some day.

Wang took the stand and was sworn in, and Swenson began to question him. But in his testimony Wang meandered, changing his story and then changing it again. He couldn't keep his account straight, and became flustered and increasingly frightened. After a brief recess, he returned to the stand and continued to dissemble for a while before finally breaking down and announcing that the People's Security Bureau had encouraged him to lie on the stand in order to indicate that the source of the goldfish heroin was not Shanghai but Hong Kong. He said that during his confinement in China he had been tortured with a cattle prod, and that the handlers who accompanied him said that if he erred on the stand, he would be shot.

Then Wang asked for political asylum.

Chaos ensued. A mistrial was declared, the judge barred Wang from being returned to China before his asylum claim could be resolved, and the handlers from the People's Security Bureau hastily left the country. It emerged that the prosecutor, Eric Swenson, had ample evidence that Wang might have been tortured in China but had chosen to overlook it. The Justice Department's Office of Professional Responsibility investigated and found that Swenson had acted "with reckless disregard of his obligations as a prosecutor," and the judge in the case, William Orrick, ultimately issued a blistering 131-page opinion in which he chastised U.S. officials for telling "outrageous lies."

In his application for asylum, Wang reported that he had been imprisoned during the Tiananmen crackdown and had seen pro-democracy students and newspaper reporters beaten and tortured. His request was denied, but Judge Orrick permanently enjoined U.S. authorities from returning him to China.

Officials in Beijing were irate. They blasted the United States for "utter defiance of basic international laws and norms governing international relations." The judge's actions represented a "wanton violation of China's judicial sovereignty in an attempt to grant political asylum." (Wang remained in the United States until one night in 2003 when he and his girlfriend were leaving a nightclub in Flushing, Queens, and two men approached them in the parking lot and hacked Wang to death with a machete. The killing was initially unsolved but later linked by authorities to an international drug syndicate involved in the Ecstasy trade.)

The Goldfish Case raised significant issues about prosecutorial misconduct, confessions elicited under torture, and witnesses being pressured to perjure themselves. But the most damaging legacy of the case was an abrupt and enduring chill in the relations between law enforcement authorities in the two countries, just as the snakehead boom was beginning and on the eve of Sister Ping's escape from the United States. When Judge Orrick declared a mistrial in the case, he maintained that it was "proof positive you can't meld the legal system in the People's Republic of China with the legal system in the United States."

The memory of the Goldfish Case was still fresh when Sister Ping fled New York, so American officials could count on no assistance from China in their efforts to catch her. But they did find a willing source of help in a place they were not expecting it. During a blizzard in February 1994, Luke Rettler boarded a plane with the federal prosecutor

Chauncey Parker and two FBI agents, Tom Trautman and Peter Lee. When they touched down in balmy Hong Kong, they made their way to a maximum-security prison in Kowloon. The prison was a grim, frightening place. As Rettler walked in, he wondered for a moment whether or not he would be walking out in one piece. The Americans were ushered into a tiny room inside the prison, where they sat and waited. Then the door opened, and Ah Kay entered the room.

It was the first time Rettler had actually laid eyes on the legendary gangster. In the eighteen months he had been incarcerated, Ah Kay had been lifting weights and had bulked up his wiry frame. But his demeanor was not hostile; on the contrary, he was quiet and polite, not the least bit defiant. To Rettler, Ah Kay seemed subdued, almost relieved. His two brothers had been murdered. His father had been arrested. He had been on the run from law enforcement on two continents. And while his hated rival, Dan Xin Lin, would be spending the rest of his life behind bars in the United States, he still had contacts in Hong Kong and in China, and he might yet try to have Ah Kay killed. There was an expression Ah Kay had used occasionally while he was running the Fuk Ching gang: A big tree catches the wind. So many violent winds seemed to have gathered around Ah Kay in recent years that it occurred to Rettler, as it no doubt had to Ah Kay, that the young gangster was probably safer in prison than he would be anyplace else.

For all his ruthless violence, Ah Kay was by and large a rational actor, and there were signs that even before his arrest he had entertained plans, unrealistic though they may have been, to give up the criminal life. "I feel like a failure," he confided in an associate in the spring of 1993. "I'm thinking of running the business for another year."

"You're quite okay," the associate reassured him. "Living a dream."

"Not a dream life at all," Ah Kay replied. "To earn a living in gangster society is . . . you know, is like leading toward a dead end."

For his meeting with Luke Rettler in Hong Kong, Ah Kay had summoned Gerry Shargel, a bearded and intense attorney who had won John Gotti a surprise acquittal in 1990 and who represented numerous other members of the Gambino crime family. Shargel was an elegant dresser and a shrewd tactician who listened to recordings of Martin Luther King's speeches and borrowed their rousing cadences for his summations. He was thought to be perhaps the finest criminal defense attorney in New York City.

Rettler was impressed—impressed that Ah Kay had flown Shargel to Hong Kong to do his negotiating, and impressed by Shargel. The purpose of the meeting was to discuss whether Ah Kay might waive extradition and return voluntarily to the United States. Shargel had insisted that his client would do so only if the government offered him an attractive deal in exchange for his willingness to cooperate with authorities. Rettler and his associates were eager to hear what kind of information Ah Kay might be willing to provide them with, and this was one of the key subjects of the meeting in the Kowloon jail. Over the course of several days, Rettler, Parker, Trautman, and Lee would join Ah Kay, Shargel, a local Hong Kong lawyer Ah Kay had hired, and a guard in the little room. Rettler marveled at Shargel's skill in these negotiations; he always seemed to be five steps ahead of Rettler and his colleagues. Rettler found it telling that whereas he would return to his hotel room after a long day of negotiations to prepare his bargaining tactics for the following day, Shargel would head to his Hong Kong tailor to get fitted for a suit.

There was a reason for Shargel's calm. Cooperation from Chinese, and especially Fujianese, gangsters was somewhat unusual in those days. But through an interpreter, Ah Kay explained that he was willing to assist the government. He wanted a more lenient sentence for his father, and he wanted some lenience for himself. But in exchange he was prepared to return to America and help the FBI. He would tell them everything he knew about the Fuk Ching, about other gangs, about the snakehead trade. As Ah Kay described his proffer, outlining the kind of information he could furnish, Rettler was surprised and impressed by his intelligence. Ah Kay would arrive at their meetings with yellow legal pads on which he had outlined and bullet-pointed the information he could supply. He quickly caught on to the potential evidentiary value of different types of information—what could and could not be used in court. The cream rises to the top, Rettler thought, even in gangs. Having Ah Kay as a cooperator would be like having a good Fujianese FBI agent on the case. So central was Ah Kay's role for so many years that if he switched sides and began helping law enforcement, he would offer a kind of Rosetta Stone for apprehending all the outstanding mysteries of Fujianese organized crime. He had information about the Fuk Ching gang, about the Teaneck killings, and about the *Golden Venture.* He said he would testify in court. Perhaps most significantly, Ah Kay was willing to help the FBI try to capture Sister Ping.

Chapter Fifteen

Parole

ON SEPTEMBER 30, 1996, President Clinton signed a major new piece of immigration legislation, the Illegal Immigration Reform and Immigrant Responsibility Act. The law was a response to the immigration woes of the early years of the Clinton administration—the onslaught of boats from Haiti, Cuba, and China—as well as the Republican sweep of Congress in 1994 and the growing mood of hostility toward immigrants that had taken hold across the country. It introduced a host of tough new measures to curb illegal immigration: expedited removal of immigrants who did not have a persuasive asylum claim, stiffer punishments for snakeheads and other immigrant smugglers, and a reduction in the rights of immigrants to have their asylum cases reviewed in federal courts. Bill Clinton had been forced by circumstance to make immigration reform a major policy initiative of his first administration, and he had taken important steps to revitalize the INS, doubling the agency's budget at a time when other federal agencies were seeing their budgets slashed, and augmenting the number of Border Patrol guards by 45 percent. The service deported 25,000 more illegal immigrants in fiscal year 1996 than it had in 1993, and the new legislation seemed to signify that the administration and the Republican Congress were in agreement on the need for a tough immigration policy.

Still, while Republican lawmakers like the Texas congressman Lamar Smith and the Wyoming senator Alan Simpson led the charge for more restrictions not just on illegal immigration but on *legal* immigration as well, other powerful Republicans, like Congressman Chris Smith of New Jersey and Senator Jesse Helms of North Carolina, were pushing for a special exception to the stiff new immigration posture for those escaping forced abortion or sterilization. Before the bill was passed, an amendment was added that changed the statutory definition of *persecution* so that someone who was fleeing forced abortion or sterilization, or a well-founded fear of it, would be eligible for asylum. The bill's sponsors arrived at a curious accommodation between the principled notion that anyone subjected to such treatment in China should be afforded a safe haven in the United States and the pragmatic fear that the country would be flooded by Chinese asylum-seekers. They imposed a numerical ceiling of one thousand people who could be eligible for this kind of asylum each year. While clearly designed as a compromise, the provision suggested the perverse possibility that an individual's likelihood of receiving asylum might be determined not by the objective conditions she was fleeing but by the moment in the calendar year when she arrived. Would the one thousand and first person simply be deported? No one was especially happy with the measure. An attorney for the Lawyers Committee for Human Rights called it "an unprincipled way of standing on principle," while a lawyer with the anti-immigration Center for Immigration Studies deemed it "a broad and promiscuous granting of asylum."

One group of people who might have celebrated the new law was the *Golden Venture* passengers who were still being held in jail. By the end of 1996, most of the passengers had been deported to China or transferred to third countries, but fifty-five remained in York and other prisons, where it sometimes seemed that the nation had forgotten about them. "Dear President Clinton," they said in a handwritten letter to the White House:

> On behalf of all of the Chinese people of the *Golden Venture* ship we wish to thank you in advance for your consideration in

granting freedom to us. We shall be good citizens and we shall contribute much to America. We have been in prison for more than three years. We have committed no crime. We come from a land where exit documents are almost impossible to receive. We fled to America the only way we could. Please help us President Clinton. We will never forget you.

Very sincerely,
The Remaining Passengers

The detainees were exhausted. They had grown resigned to life in prison. When their lawyers and other supporters in York visited to deliver the exciting news about the new law and to suggest that it might be possible to have their asylum claims reconsidered, few of the detainees could muster the energy to share in the enthusiasm. They had grown cynical about the American system and the likelihood that it would produce any results for them. One by one, they had given up hope. At a certain point they stopped making the paper sculptures.

Then, quite suddenly, things began to happen. On February 3, 1997, the *New York Times* ran a front-page story under the headline "Dozens of Chinese from 1993 Voyage Still in Jail." The story, by Celia Dugger, explained that a third of the passengers had been released or resettled in Latin America, but that ninety-nine had been deported to China and a further fifty-five still remained in American prisons, thirty-eight of them in York. It noted, pointedly, that many of the passengers would have won asylum "had they come ashore a year earlier—when George Bush was President," and cited a Clinton administration official saying that no one in the government had ever contemplated the possibility that the passengers would be detained for three and a half years. The article quoted Bev Church saying, "Shame on this country."

The day after the article appeared, Bill Clinton was scheduled to deliver the first State of the Union address of his second term. In the audience on Capitol Hill was a sixty-nine-year-old former school superintendent named Bill Goodling, who since 1974 had been the Republican congressman for York, Pennsylvania. After the speech, as Clinton slowly made his way out of the House chamber, shaking hands and having short conversations with the legislators lining the aisles, Goodling stepped in front of him.

"Mr. President," Goodling said, "you still have thirty-eight *Golden Venture* Chinese in my York County prison."

"Yes, that makes me angry," Clinton said. "I just read about it in the *New York Times*."

Just over a week later, Clinton received Goodling in the Oval Office for a discussion of Clinton's education plans (Goodling was chairman of the Education and Workforce Committee). Goodling took two of the sculptures with him, an eagle made of folded paper and a papier-mâché tree. He presented them to the president.

"They're beautiful," Clinton marveled.

"They've had four years to sit in prison and do that," Goodling replied.

Clinton looked at the sculptures. "Four years is an awfully long time," he said.

The following day Clinton telephoned Goodling. "I've made my decision," he said. "They'll be released from prison." Clinton told Goodling that his administration was not "unanimous" in supporting his decision. But he proceeded with it, signing an executive order on Valentine's Day 1997, four years to the day after the passengers boarded the *Golden Venture* off the beach in Pattaya.

Beverly Church was at the prison visiting the men when she heard the news. She dropped to her knees, banging one of them so hard that she bruised it. Joan Maruskin received a call from Goodling and immediately went about informing the others. When the news reached Craig Trebilcock, he was at Fort Benning, Georgia, preparing to deploy for a tour of National Guard duty in Bosnia. Craig stood under a pine tree by an old barracks that dated to World War II and wondered at the fateful twists his life had taken in the years since he agreed to volunteer ten hours to represent Pin Lin. The irony had never been lost on Craig that he was an Army man who had ended up suing the government of the United States. And now, as he prepared to don the uniform of his country once again, he could scarcely believe that after nearly four years the men of the *Golden Venture* would finally be set free.

On February 26, 1997, the People of the Golden Vision assembled at a local church. They had stood vigil for 183 consecutive Sundays, waiting for the men to be released, and now, finally, the day had come. Across the country *Golden Venture* detainees were being set free in Bakersfield, California, in Winchester, Virginia, and in New Orleans. But most of the remaining passengers were in York, and as the men entered the church, their supporters erupted in cheers. Beverly Church had dressed up in a black suit with gold earrings and a gold necklace, offset by bright red lipstick. Joan Maruskin captured the men on a camcorder as they filed through the door. They had blocky prison haircuts and blinked shyly at the camera. The supporters in York had initiated a clothing drive, and the men showed off their ill-fitting outfits: sweatshirts and sweaters and stone-washed jeans, double-breasted blazers that fell below the knee.

It was a jubilant scene. Each man was given a shopping bag, and they wandered among a set of tables piled high with donated clothing. Each was also given a plastic crate with toiletries and a towel, and several hundred dollars from the proceeds that had been pooled from the final artwork sales. (There had been a run on the sculptures when it was announced that the men would soon be released.) Someone had brought large containers of chicken and rice from a local restaurant, Hunan East, and for the first time since arriving in the United States, the men ate Chinese food. For dessert there was a red, white, and blue cake with an inscription made of icing: "Welcome to America." The atmosphere was warm and triumphant, though not without a certain awkwardness. For nearly four years the Americans in York had related to the Chinese men only within the strictly enforced parameters established by the prison for visiting hours. Suddenly finding themselves face-to-face in the outside world, they stumbled toward a more unfettered mode of friendship and communication, everyone overcome by a surge of deep emotion. They all prayed and embraced, and the men stood together, stifling tears and smiles, and sang "We Shall Overcome," in Chinese and then in English.

A local couple, Harriet and Ray Miller, had arranged for each man to be released to a family in the area. There had been reports about snakeheads going to the prison in order to collect their fees or kidnap recently released detainees, so some effort was made to keep the precise addresses where the men were staying a secret. At the end of the evening, the men walked out into a chill rain in the dark parking lot and were greeted by camera flashes: the media had been barred from the church during the event, but reporters and cameramen had assembled outside and wanted interviews and photos. The men walked hurriedly by, smiling politely but apologetically at the cameras. "They're learning English," Bev Church told the reporters. "They just learned to say, 'No comment.' " One by one the men climbed into the waiting cars, clutching their new belongings in trash bags. As the cars bore them off to the townhouses and split-levels of their sponsors, it marked the first time each man had been physically separated from all the others since they first assembled in the hold of the *Golden Venture* in 1993.

The first few weeks of freedom were strange for the *Golden Venture* men. They telephoned their families back in China to tell them the news, ate abundant quantities of Chinese noodles, and took long walks through the gray and alien terrain of the Pennsylvania woods. Their adoptive families were eager to take them out and about, to show them the grocery store, to introduce them to people at church, to take them to Wal-Mart. The whole community in York and the surrounding area knew about the saga of the *Golden Venture*, and there was some resistance to having any of the passengers settle in the neighborhood. As the men wandered, awestruck, through the local supermarket, they received strange, curious, and sometimes hostile looks from the people they encountered. The families sponsoring them noticed, but the men hardly did, so great was their sense of wonderment at the sheer cornucopia of meat and produce and colorfully packaged consumer goods all laid out on display.

A local woman named Ann Wolcott, whose son had been killed in an ambush in Vietnam nearly three decades earlier, signed on to sponsor one of the younger detainees, a sweet-natured boy in his early twenties with a basketball obsession and a toothy smile, named Zheng. When Zheng had been at her home for a day or so, Wolcott decided that he needed a decent pair of shoes. Together they drove to the Galleria Mall and went to a shoe store. Wolcott prompted Zheng to select a pair that he liked, and after some deliberation the two made their way to the cash register. As they did, a woman Wolcott had never met approached them.

"Is he one of those *Golden Venture* people? From the prison?" the woman asked.

Wolcott was prepared for hostility and held her ground. "Yes," she replied. "He is."

The woman looked at Zheng. "I would like to buy his shoes," she said.

In generations past, the men might have headed directly to one Chinatown or another, in Philadelphia or Boston or New York, and a few of the *Golden Venture* passengers did just that. But even as the men had passed the years in prison, the Fujianese sense of adventure was bringing about a major shift in the way in which the Chinese settled in America. For many of the most ambitious Fujianese, especially those who wound up in the restaurant business—which the overwhelming majority of them did—remaining in Chinatown for a generation, or even a year, seemed self-defeating. Of course there was some comfort in being surrounded by fellow Fujianese, and there were a host of risks associated with venturing out of the cities and into suburban America, beyond the reach of the support networks other Fujianese had labored so long to establish. But there were benefits as well. For restaurateurs, costs were often lower outside the major cities, and, more important, there was less competition: why open a Chinese restaurant on a block full of Chinese restaurants in Manhattan or San Francisco in the hopes that passersby will stumble into yours, when you could go to some strip mall or small town in Virginia or Iowa or Texas and operate the only Chinese restaurant for miles around?

By the time the last of the *Golden Venture* passengers were released, America's first-generation Chinese had become mobile to a degree that they had not been at any other time in history. The Fujianese had come all the way to America to find work; there was no reason they could not travel an additional 100 or 300 or 1,200 miles to find a job that paid a few more dollars each month. For the *Golden Venture* passengers, who had paid so traumatic a price for availing themselves of the services of snakeheads, there was an additional reason to travel far from Chinatown: it remained unclear whether the snakeheads would come calling. "If I can leave here, I'll just run away," Sean Chen told a reporter while he was still in prison. "I won't go to New York, won't go to any Chinese place. I'll just find a job in some small town. It doesn't matter what the job is. If we stay away from Chinatowns, we'll be okay."

Toward the end of the 1990s, local entrepreneurs in Chinatown, many of them Fujianese, were beginning to realize that the labor market in Chinese restaurants in Boston and New York was very fluid—that demand seemed to fluctuate not just seasonally but weekly, and owners could never predict in advance how many people they would need to wait on tables or fire the woks. Soon a no-frills passenger van was shuttling restaurant workers from New York to Boston and back again for a few dollars each way, allowing undocumented busboys and dishwashers to save on the cost of a ticket and avoid having to navigate their way from Port Authority or South Station to their ultimate destination. The Chinatown bus, as it came to be called, formed a direct transit link from one Chinatown to the other, from the ornamental arch on Harrison Avenue in Boston to Confucius Plaza or the foot of the Manhattan Bridge.

The Fujianese are great imitators of business ideas that seem to work, and before long there were multiple Chinese-owned minivans tearing along the highways between New York and Boston, and new routes were devised to the Chinatowns in Philadelphia and Washington, D.C. The proprietors invested in full-sized, air-conditioned coaches and gave their companies names like Fung Wah Transport Vans, New Century, Dragon Coach, and TravelPack. A price war between several of the companies drove the cost of a ticket lower and lower, until even on the larger buses the one-way fare to Boston was a mere $10—a 200-mile journey for the price of a cross-town cab. As word spread of the cheap new bus route that managed so dramatically to undercut Greyhound and Peter Pan, college kids began entering Chinatown and queuing with their Walkmen and backpacks to join the restaurant workers for the trip.

In no time the major bus lines were seeing their numbers dip and realizing that they were being undercut by the scrappy upstarts in Chinatown. Some pointed out, correctly, that the Chinatown buses seemed quite frequently to get into accidents: a bus hit a woman on a busy street, a bus rolled over on the highway, a bus's engine spontaneously burst into flames. At least initially the Chinatown bus market had been somewhat unregulated, and even after the larger services began obtaining licenses and submitting to inspections, they still obliged their drivers to work typically Fujianese shifts; it seemed inevitable that someone suffering from acute exhaustion and piloting a many-ton bus would occasionally slip up. There were other reasons the cautious passenger might steer clear of the Chinatown buses: some of the bus lines were controlled by organized crime, and before long the price wars became literal physical clashes, with the occasional bus owner shooting or stabbing a rival. Even so, the buses became more and more popular as the years went by. Eventually mighty Greyhound was obliged to slash its prices on routes where it was competing with the Chinatown bus.

The buses facilitated the explorations of a generation of Fujianese restaurant workers. Soon Chinatown buses were making trips to cities that didn't have Chinatowns and depositing restaurant workers in Richmond, in Pittsburgh, in Nashville. Any place that a quorum of ticket-buyers was willing to go became a viable destination, and the bus companies hired touts to stand on the street corner at Eldridge and East Broadway in New York and try to entice random pedestrians to abandon whatever plans they might have had that day and take an impromptu eighteen-hour bus trip. It was not uncommon to stroll through Chinatown at any hour of the day or night and pass flush-faced Fujianese women, fanny packs cinching their puffy winter coats, who would spot you and gamely shout, "Hey, boy, you want go Ohio?"

In Chinatown buses and in cars, the *Golden Venture* passengers spread out across the country. They ended up in Salem, New Hampshire, and Normal, Illinois. They went to work in Dublin, Ohio, and Independence, Missouri. They put down roots in small towns in Massachusetts and in Florida, and most of them went into the restaurant business in one form or another. In fact, the relative success of the *Golden Venture* passengers can be measured to some extent along the continuum from dishwasher or deliveryman to restaurant manager or proprietor. Michael Chen, one of the most ambitious passengers released from York in 1997, went on to own his own restaurant in an upscale strip mall outside Columbus. Less successful was Dong Xu Zhi, a mild-mannered Christian who moved into a cramped two-room apartment that he shared with several other people on the Lower East Side, and worked as a deliveryman for a Chinese restaurant in a rough part of the Bronx.

Not all of the men went into the restaurant business, and not all of them left York, Pennsylvania. Yang You Yi, the detainee who first folded a paper pineapple in prison, had run a weaving company in China, using old looms to manufacture mosquito nets. Through Joan Maruskin and Sterling Showers, he was introduced to a local man named David Kline, a gentle weaver with an Amish-style beard who had worked in mills most of his life and operated a company, Family Heir Loom Weavers, in a small town near York called Red Lion. Kline agreed to meet with Yang and said he could offer him work.

"How much will you pay?" Yang wondered.

"Seven dollars an hour," Kline replied.

As they were talking, Yang knelt down and picked up a length of thread from the floor. He toyed with it for a moment, then skillfully tied a weaver's knot.

"Okay," Kline said. "Eight dollars an hour."

In the coming years, Kline and his family essentially adopted Yang, allowing him to live rent-free in a room in an old cigar factory that they had converted into a weaving mill. Yang worked sixty hours a week at nine looms, bringing an extraordinary degree of dexterity and skill to his weaving and increasing the output of the mill by 50 percent over his first three years. He made garments for Civil War reenactors and upholstery fabric and period drapery for historic residences; the mill produced materials that would be used in the restored houses of nine former presidents. When the movie *Cold Mountain* needed hundreds of authentic-looking costumes and uniforms from the American Civil War era, it was Yang You Yi who produced the fabric. Yang called David Kline "Dad-Boss," and Kline credited him with turning the business around. Kline decided that when he retired, he would sell Yang half the company.

When the first thrill of freedom had worn off and the men had begun to adjust to their new American lives, paying taxes on their income, clipping coupons and shopping at Wal-Mart, and beginning to think about saving some money for a lease to open their own business or for a down payment on a house, they also began wondering about whether and when they could send for their family members. Many of them had left behind wives and children in China, family they had not seen, in some cases, since 1991. But in the general euphoria and exhausted relief that had attended the final release from prison, the men and their supporters had effectively failed to read the fine print. Immigration policy seems always to entail compromise, and when President Clinton signed the order to set the *Golden Venture* passengers free, the gesture included a subtle wrinkle that would seriously curtail their abilities to live full lives in the United States. Clinton had used his power to parole the passengers out of prison, which meant that they were free to live in America, to work, pay taxes, and own property. But technically they had no ironclad right to remain in the country, nor any of the rights that come along with a green card or naturalization. They were not allowed to petition for family members to join them. They had to check in with an immigration officer, who functioned in more or less the manner that a criminal parole officer would. And they could remain only at the whim of the United States. If some official in some future administration decided, during a period of alarm over immigration, to deport them, they would have no procedural defenses. Worst of all, parole operates as a kind of limbo: there is no graduation from parole to legal status. It is a nebulous state, but a permanent one.

Still, some of the men found ways, both legal and illegal, of arranging for their family members to join them. As husbands were reunited with their wives and fathers with their children, they struggled to reconstruct the families they had left behind. When Yang You Yi's wife was finally able to bring his three children to Pennsylvania in 2002, it had been a decade since the children had seen their father. He worried that he would not recognize them when they got off the plane. Yang had purchased a new home in Red Lion, installing soft blue carpeting upstairs and down. After a joyful reunion at the airport, he took his family home. But in the ensuing weeks and months he found that his children did not always heed the father who had been absent for so many years. In the village in Fujian they had enjoyed a certain autonomy, walking wherever they needed to go. But in suburban America they relied on their father to drive them, and soon, like any other American kids, they were hounding Yang for rides. The children "give me a lot of headaches," Yang said. "They don't listen."

For some of the older *Golden Venture* passengers, the sons and daughters who arrived in America and proved so much more adept at the tricky process of cultural assimilation eventually became a kind of crutch, helping their parents navigate an English-speaking world. Beverly Church remained close to the shy, middle-aged cook Zheng Xin Bin. While he was detained in York, Xin Bin had charmed Bev, and the two had become good friends. "We don't take any skinny people here," she would tell him, worried by the weight he had lost in prison. "You have to eat, to stay strong, so you can work hard." Xin Bin was released when President Clinton issued the pardon, and Bev drove him into Philadelphia to obtain his working permit, a laminated card the size of a driver's license. Finally released from detention and in a position to repay the kindness Bev had shown him, Xin Bin was a gentleman, always insisting on picking up the tab after a meal and volunteering to pay the highway toll anytime the two were driving. "Car hungry," he would joke, offering a $20 bill.

Xin Bin had left a wife and a young son and daughter behind when he boarded the *Golden Venture*, and in August 2000 he was finally able to send for them. The family settled in Washington, D.C., and his thirteen-year-old daughter, Xianjuan, enrolled in a local school and quickly established herself as a star: she learned English with ease and became an A student. She adapted more quickly than her older brother to American life and became a sort of manager for the family, a liaison to the outside world: she paid the bills, oversaw the banking, and handled the family's credit cards. By 2005 she was an eighteen-year-old senior at Northwestern High School and had decided to apply to college and study law. Xin Bin was fifty years old. He was reunited with his family, and the horrors of the voyage and the years in prison were beginning to recede. He and his wife were dependent on Xianjuan to assist them in their everyday affairs, and to some extent, by allowing them to continue functioning in a primarily Mandarin idiom, she may have served as a kind of buffer between the two of them and the English-speaking world, an impediment to their own assimilation. But at the same time she was in a very real sense the literal embodiment of their commitment to a life and a future in the United States. They were enormously proud of her.

Xin Bin was working as a cook at a nondescript Chinese restaurant in a strip mall in a rough corner of Washington. One evening his children came to pick him up at work. It was after ten o'clock, near the end of his shift, and Xianjuan filled a cup with seafood soup and went outside to wait for her father in front of the restaurant. As she sipped her soup, a car entered the parking lot, and two men got out. They walked toward Xianjuan. Then one of them pulled out a gun and shot her twice in the head.

"All of a sudden I heard *pang, pang*—two gunshots—and I went outside," Xin Bin said through tears not long afterward. "Ayah, my daughter had fallen there."

She lay by a blue mailbox, dead. Xin Bin collapsed on the ground beside her, his body convulsed by sobs. "I only have this one daughter," he said later. "She was so beautiful. She was such a good student."

No suspects were ever apprehended; the crime remained unsolved. Police speculated that it may have been a botched robbery, or a case of mistaken identity. Xin Bin was distraught, and his wife was even more so. She had a breakdown and remained in the house for weeks, catatonic with grief. Without Xianjuan the family became isolated from the outside world, and their despair deepened. Eventually Xin Bin's wife announced that she wanted to return to China. "She wants nothing to do with America," Bev said. "They killed her baby."

Before Xianjuan died, Xin Bin had been trying to obtain a green card for her. After her murder, he tried to explain to the people from Citizenship and Immigration Services that they should discontinue the application, because his daughter was no longer alive. But without Xianjuan to act as interpreter, he struggled to make himself clear, and for over a year after her death the agency continued sending him notices and forms, insisting that the family send them information that was necessary for Xianjuan to become a permanent resident of the United States.

Sean Chen had been luckier than the other detainees at York. He had walked out of the prison over a year before the other men did, after his lawyer, Ann Carr, managed to persuade a federal judge with a complex legal argument over whether or not the men who jumped off the *Golden Venture* had technically succeeded in entering the United States. If, as Carr contended, the passengers had indeed managed to enter the country, then there was a time limit on how long the government could keep them in jail (whereas if they had been caught before formally entering, they were "exclusion" cases and could be detained more or less indefinitely). The judge's ruling was ultimately reversed by an appeals court, but not before Sean had a chance to telephone relatives in China and the United States and assemble the $10,000 he needed for bail. On the day he was set free, Bev Church went to the prison. She had always admired Sean's fearless swagger, and she took him a pair of sunglasses as a gift. He wore them as he walked out.

Despite his suggestion in prison that he would avoid Chinatown at all costs, Sean moved to Philadelphia and found work in the Chinese community there. He owed his bail money to the various family members he had borrowed from, and needed to start earning in a hurry, so he found a job as a delivery boy for a Chinese restaurant. Next he worked at a garbage processing center, which paid him $8 an hour, and at a parking lot. Sean traveled light—he always had—and he was always in search of a new experience and a better paycheck. Through a Fujianese employment agency he found a job in New York City working as a busboy in a Chinese restaurant on Forty-ninth Street. He moved to New York and took the job, but he lasted there only one month before he relocated to the Bronx and found work as a cashier at a takeout restaurant. He didn't like that job either, and after another month or so he received a call from a cousin who owned a Chinese restaurant in Hartford, Connecticut. She needed a cashier, so Sean moved once again.

Sean liked Hartford. He helped wait on tables at the restaurant and slowly began accruing more and more experience in the business. He figured if he could work as a chef, cashier, delivery boy, busboy, waiter, bartender, and manager, he would become a kind of indispensable jack-of-all-trades in the Chinese restaurant world. He enrolled in bartending school and found that he loved tending bar: he was a naturally outgoing, gregarious person, and he liked practicing his English with customers. He liked having regulars. He liked having friends.

Still, the fact that he was not technically a legal immigrant rankled Sean. He still had to check in with an immigration officer on a regular basis, an imposition that he began to resent. He had been in the United States for years. He was working hard, paying taxes, making decent money. Why was he still being treated like a criminal?

When he wanted to start his own restaurant in Hartford, there was an additional challenge: because borrowing and lending money are so ingrained in Fujianese culture and contracts and debts tend to be honored, Fujianese people are a decent credit risk. But undocumented immigrants are not, and it is difficult for a parolee, who could be deported next year or next week, to obtain a loan from a bank. Instead Sean borrowed from friends and relatives and made the mistake of running up debts on credit cards in order to open his own place. For a while it seemed he had achieved that first crucial milestone for the Fujianese: he owned his own business. But before long the restaurant folded. Sean had borrowed so heavily from everyone he knew that when he failed to find customers and cover his bills, he was forced to close the place. He was devastated, and felt like a failure. He spoke with his parents in China. "Son, it's okay," his father reassured him. He tried to put Sean's trials in perspective. "You've been through so much," he said. "So much more than I have."

But the worst aspect of Sean's quasi-legal life was feeling like a man without a country. Eventually his parents and siblings moved to Taiwan, and he had no immediate family left in China. He had no Chinese passport, no Chinese identity papers. He felt that there was less and less connecting him to the country every day. When he spoke with his mother on the telephone, she complained that his Fujianese had become corrupted by English and by Cantonese, which he was obliged to pick up in the Chinese restaurant trade. Apart from his parents and Beverly Church, whom he still telephoned once a week, no one ever called him by his Chinese name, Chung Sing Chao, anymore. He was Sean Chen now; it was how others thought of him, and how he thought of himself. But he suffered from a gnawing anguish at the thought that he might be sent back to the country he had left in 1991, despite the fact that like generations of foreign people with foreign names from all over the world who had peopled the United States and made it what it was, Sean Chen had become, unmistakably and irreversibly, American.

Chapter Sixteen

Snakeheads International

ONE SUMMER day in 1995 a yellow school bus tore along the potholed surface of Highway 8 in Honduras, en route to the Guatemalan border. The bus held fourteen Sikhs who had paid to be smuggled from India into the United States. They were customers of one of Sister Ping's chief competitors, a Peruvian woman named Gloria Canales, who now worked out of Costa Rica. Canales transported migrants from India and China to Central America, then on to the United States. She was not accompanying the Sikhs herself; like Sister Ping, she had long since subcontracted her operational logistics. Instead, a hired driver was guiding the Sikhs to Guatemala so that they could rendezvous with *coyotes*, as Mexican human smugglers are known, and steal across the border.

Earlier in the day the bus had been tailed by a car containing immigration agents, but the driver seemed to have lost the pursuers on the back roads, and the agents were stymied when their government-issue radios stopped working. The transmitter at the airport had been mysteriously switched off, quite possibly by someone hoping the Sikhs would make it to Guatemala unmolested.

When the bus was 70 miles from the Guatemalan border, the driver needed to relieve his bladder. He pulled over to the side of the road and jumped out of the bus. As he did, a car appeared out of nowhere on the road behind him and raced up alongside the bus. Two men climbed out. One was a Honduran immigration official. The other was Jerry

Stuchiner, the goateed INS agent from Hong Kong who had worked with the Fat Man to locate Ah Kay.

Shortly after Ah Kay's arrest, Stuchiner had been transferred to the Honduran capital of Tegucigalpa. He was not happy with the move. He had loved the glamour and intrigue of Hong Kong; with just over a million people, the mountainous city of Tegucigalpa was a provincial backwater by comparison. The city had none of Hong Kong's cosmopolitan glitz. The people lived in sprawling shantytowns. Stuchiner's residence had no hot water or electricity. Worse still, he was deprived, at least initially, of that sense, so palpable in Hong Kong, of being at the heart of things professionally—an immigration agent in a den of human smugglers.

Still, Stuchiner did his best to stay close to the action. He explored the possibility of doing business deals on the side—exporting shark fins to Asia, perhaps, or fish stomachs. He kept in touch with the Fat Man, who visited him occasionally in Honduras. The two men would take steam baths and talk business. Stuchiner had a friend in Tegucigalpa, a Honduran of Jewish origin named Herbie Weizenblut, who Stuchiner thought would make a good Honduran consul in Hong Kong. Stuchiner thought of Weizenblut as "a coreligionist, and a lost soul," and wanted to help him out. In a decidedly unconventional move that was indicative of Stuchiner's deep friendship with the Fat Man, and of the Fat Man's willingness to buck propriety and indulge the occasionally shady side of government activity, the two men were able to persuade the Honduran government to make Weizenblut its new consul in Hong Kong, but only after the Fat Man committed to personally cover half of Weizenblut's expenses while he was on the job—a sum of $15,000 a month.

For Stuchiner, the saving grace of his new Central American home was that in its own way, little backward Honduras was emerging, along with nearby countries like Panama, Belize, and Guatemala, as a major regional hub in the global snakehead trade. Just as Stuchiner was arriving in the country, rumors were beginning to circulate about "Chinazo," a major scandal in which it emerged that in 1991 the Honduran National Assembly had passed a law that was nominally designed to attract foreign investment but actually amounted to a cash-for-citizenship scheme. A sophisticated ring of corrupt officials made nearly $20 million selling Honduran passports to the Chinese. Few of these newly minted Chinese Hondurans actually settled in Honduras. Instead, using their Honduran passports, they booked flights to Tegucigalpa that stopped over in the United States. Then they would destroy the costly passports on the airplane and request asylum at the first American airport they hit.

The case was emblematic of a deep culture of corruption in Honduras, and in Central America more generally, a culture that, along with the region's physical proximity to the United States, made it immensely appealing for smugglers. One seldom-remarked irony of globalization is that while the increased interknittedness of the world undoubtedly facilitated a plethora of useful innovations for consumers and governments, the unfettered flow of goods, people, capital, and ideas that so characterized the 1990s also presented major opportunities for the enterprising cross-border criminal. Any international effort to regulate clandestine international trade, whether of drugs, guns, or people, will be only as good as the least vigilant nation in the system. If the community of nations relies on official documents issued by countries to denote who is entitled to travel where, it takes only one spoiler country, like Honduras, to undo the whole thing. What's more, the better the rest of the system works—the more harmonized and efficient the international regulatory architecture is—the higher the rewards will be for the one country willing to cheat, offering an illicit back door.

Just as Bangkok functioned as a hub in the smuggling networks because snakeheads could put passengers on planes, Central America was emerging as a new hub. Official corruption is the oxygen that any kind of global smuggling requires to thrive, and the kind of corruption evident in the Chinazo case was pervasive in the region. In 1995 alone, the immigration directors of Panama, Belize, and Guatemala were all fired for accepting bribes from smugglers. That year a federal working group on alien smuggling reported that the growth of human smuggling was "made possible by staggering levels of official corruption" and a sense in many transit countries that the activity was fundamentally a "victimless crime."

When Stuchiner cracked the Canales ring, it was heralded as a great success in Washington, not just because one major smuggler had been removed from power, but because it seemed to promise a new, more dynamic approach to pursuing smugglers. Stuchiner recognized that in order to fight an international adversary, American authorities had to adopt a more international approach themselves. When a new head of Honduran immigration, Angelina Ulloa, took office, vowing to stamp out the corruption that had plagued her predecessors, Stuchiner began working closely with her. Their main target was Canales, and they devised a bold plan, involving the use of an undercover agent to set up the deal with the Sikhs. At that time Honduras was the only country in the region where human smuggling was actually a prosecutable crime, so Stuchiner tried to lure Canales to Honduras. It was the type of audacious scheme that Stuchiner's colleagues in Hong Kong had complained about. And it also seemed typical of Stuchiner's gift for self-mythologizing that rumors were soon circulating in Tegucigalpa that Canales had sent a henchman to town to assassinate him. It may have been that the rumors were true, but it was also the case that tales of assassination attempts against him were a staple in Stuchiner's conversational repertoire dating back to his days in Vienna during the 1980s.

Nevertheless, Stuchiner's tactics, however unorthodox, were delivering results. When he couldn't lure Canales to Honduras, he helped persuade Ecuador to arrest her and extradite her to Tegucigalpa. Against the odds, he seemed to have devised a manner of using the international system against the very international crime syndicates that exploited it. When Canales arrived in Honduras and was awaiting trial, she was accompanied by over a dozen guards, not so much to prevent her from escaping as to prevent her from being assassinated on behalf of the many powerful political figures with an interest in keeping her quiet.

"If this isthmus was closed off, there is no way they could get to the U.S.," Stuchiner told the press, flush with his victory over Canales. "You would force them to use air routes, which are easier to control." If Stuchiner was going to continue his crusade to shut down the snakehead trade in Central America, and was going to do it by finding a few clean officials in the various regional governments and forming alliances with people he could trust, it was only a matter of time before he would start to target another prominent smuggler who had recently intensified her operations in the area: Sister Ping.

These new international criminals are very mobile," a Senate investigator remarked in the mid-1990s. "For the first time in criminal history, they are able to establish and control on a day-to-day basis operations in foreign countries far from their home port. Law enforcement by and large stops at the border, and we're just in the first stumbling steps in trying to get better coordination internationally. These crooks are way ahead of the cops."

He could have been describing Sister Ping. After the wreck of the *Golden Venture* and her hasty flight to China in 1994, she did not curtail her smuggling activities. By the late nineties, an estimated 30,000 people from Tingjiang, the area surrounding her village, had made the trip to the United States. Many of these people faced the same predicament as the *Golden Venture* passengers released by President Clinton: without green cards, they could not petition for their family members to come to the United States legally. So instead they were forced to turn to snakeheads, and above all to Sister Ping.

It was no longer feasible to send smuggling ships directly to the coastal waters of the United States. After the *Golden Venture*, the U.S. Coast Guard had become very active in monitoring American shores, and numerous ships were turned back in the open seas. But neither did it make business sense to abandon boat smuggling altogether and revert to the expensive and piecemeal process of obtaining phony documents and sending passengers by plane. Throughout the 1990s, snakeheads everywhere were diversifying, evolving new routes to take customers to new places, and always adapting so that they stayed a step or two ahead of law enforcement. Even a partial listing of the routes that law enforcement discovered during those years reads like the bizarre itinerary for some madcap world tour: Fuzhou—Hong Kong—Bangkok—Moscow—Havana—Managua—Tucson; Fuzhou—Hong Kong—Bangkok—Kuala Lumpur—Singapore—Dubai—Frankfurt—Washington. When snakeheads discovered that it was relatively easy to obtain visas for Chinese passengers to visit Russia, a new route developed, with passengers flying into Moscow, then trekking over the loosely patrolled border into Ukraine and then Slovakia, from Slovakia in a minivan to Prague, and from Prague to points west—the Netherlands, Belgium, Italy, France, and Britain. New Chinatowns popped up in cities from São Paolo to Dubai. After sanctions were imposed on Yugoslavia in 1993, Slobodan Milošević began cultivating the Chinese leadership in Beijing and lifted visa requirements for Chinese citizens to travel to Serbia. The snakeheads wasted no time sending their customers to Belgrade by the planeload, knowing full well that from there they could make their way into Western Europe and on to Canada or the United States. (Milošević's sudden hospitality toward the Chinese may have been driven by the same intuition.)

All the snakeheads needed was a way station or staging post where authorities were willing to look the other way, what one observer described as a "geopolitical black hole" in the regulatory system. Some of these black holes were far from the United States. Others were closer to home. A handful of snakeheads saw potential in the Native American reservations that straddle the border between the United States and Canada and function as sovereign Native American territory. In a two-year period in the late 1990s, a sophisticated network of Fujianese snakeheads and Mohawk Indians smuggled thousands of undocumented Chinese into the United States through a reservation in upstate New York. Before the ring was dismantled by authorities, it made $170 million.

As the snakehead business boomed internationally, it began to attract a more ruthless element. Snakeheads started sending their clients not in the holds of ships but in cargo containers, a mode of transportation that actually managed to be more hazardous than the *Golden Venture*. Throughout the late 1990s stowaways were discovered in shipping containers entering the ports of Los Angeles or Seattle nearly every week. A young Fujianese woman emerged as one of the most dominant snakeheads in Europe and adopted the moniker Little Sister Ping, in a nod both to her own diminutive stature and to her much more famous namesake. Little Sister Ping worked out of a Chinese restaurant in Rotterdam, but there the similarities end. Whereas Big Sister Ping shunned any form of ostentation, invested her money in real estate, and scrupulously maintained a low profile, Little Sister Ping had a fleet of cars, wore expensive designer clothes, and favored vacations in Italy and Greece. In 2000 she was responsible for a notorious tragedy in which fifty-eight Fujianese who had crossed Europe and were headed for London ended up suffocating to death in the airtight back of a truck. A single air vent had been closed from the outside, and as the passengers began running out of air, they screamed and clawed at the vent and slammed the walls of the truck with their shoes. But the driver did not hear, and eventually the passengers died there in the dark, their bodies discovered only when customs officers stopped the truck at Dover.

From her village in Fujian Province, Big Sister Ping was believed to have been one of the pioneers of the snakehead route through Milošević's Serbia, and there is no doubt that she maintained an eclectic array of routes and way stations. But as she continued her boat smuggling operations during the late 1990s, she found that one particularly effective strategy was to send ships from Asia directly to the coast of Central America and then transport passengers overland to the United States. Honduras had the law against alien smuggling, which despite the general lack of enforcement made it a less than ideal location. But Sister Ping found a perfect logistical base in Guatemala. With stretches of coastline on both the Atlantic and the Pacific and a long and largely unpoliced border with Mexico, Guatemala was well situated as a transition point for passengers disembarking from fishing trawlers and preparing for the long journey overland. Sister Ping was hardly the only smuggler to see the virtues of the place; most of the Colombian cocaine that enters the United States passes through Guatemala first, and an astonishing 10 percent of Guatemala's population would ultimately emigrate to the United States. The country was deeply corrupt, and with a thriving informal economy, money laundering was a routine and fairly easy activity. (During the period when Sister Ping was operating there, the off-the-books economy in Guatemala generated over 40 percent of the country's gross domestic product.)

In some ways Sister Ping's organization was less like the Mafia than it was like a multinational corporation that seeks an optimal economic and regulatory environment in which to do business. Just as the state of Delaware offers a series of enticements to lure businesses to incorporate there, Guatemala offered Sister Ping a favorable location vis-à-vis China and the United States, a permissive government whose officials could easily be bought, an underground economy so extensive that it nearly engulfed the licit economy and made it more or less impossible to disentangle dirty money from clean, and a small but robust Chinese and Taiwanese population, which could be a source of safe houses, middlemen, and couriers. On top of everything else, Sister Ping could arrange for the Guatemalan navy to help facilitate the offloading of her ships, at the reasonable price of $50,000 a pop.

So after the *Golden Venture* debacle, Sister Ping began routing her ships through Guatemala. She had connections in the country dating at least as far back as 1984, when she smuggled Weng Yu Hui to the United States via Guatemala, and her family obtained visas from the mysterious Taiwanese man at the Guatemala City Ritz. But as more ships dropped off customers there, Guatemala became a crucial hub for

Sister Ping. If you drew a map of the many routes Sister Ping's customers took, a disproportionate number of them would converge on Guatemala, much as a map of flights by Continental Airlines would reveal the carrier's hub at the airport in Houston.

Of course, Sister Ping herself did not have to be present in Guatemala very often. Provided she had someone she could trust, to whom she could outsource the actual work of collecting passengers from ships, holding them in safe houses, and transporting them to Mexico, she could effectively telecommute, working from her home in Shengmei village, or from a hotel suite in Fuzhou, or from an apartment that she owned in Hong Kong. Sister Ping's man in Guatemala City, whom she found eminently reliable, was a Taiwanese-born smuggler named Kenny Feng. Feng spoke Spanish. Like so many others, he had become involved in the snakehead business when the boom was just starting, in 1990. He and Sister Ping had met in 1992, before the voyage of the *Golden Venture*; they collaborated on several successful shiploads of passengers that year, and they had continued to work together ever since.

Guatemala was so corrupt that at times it seemed the job of actually smuggling people was secondary to simply paying officials the gratuities they had come to expect. The officials were fairly shameless in this regard. In 1991 Guatemala's consul general had to be removed because of allegations that he had been selling visas to Chinese citizens. The industry was generating so much largesse that everyone needed to wet his beak. Occasionally Sister Ping would send her brother to Guatemala City with a suitcase containing $400,000, just to pay people off.

It was a fruitful operation. But boat smuggling is by its very nature a somewhat perilous activity, and there were mishaps from time to time, some of which were fatal. One morning in May 1998, a body washed ashore on a beach near Escuintla, on Guatemala's Pacific Coast. More corpses washed ashore throughout the day; fourteen were recovered in all. Sister Ping was in China, but she spoke with Kenny Feng on the phone and explained that one of her ships had sunk, and the survivors were stranded. She needed Feng to pick them up. If he could collect them and transfer them to another group of snakeheads at the Mexican border, she would pay him $10,000 for each customer who made it to the United States. Before she hung up, she instructed Feng to look after the bodies of the dead. They should be buried at a Chinese cemetery in Guatemala City, she said. She would cover the expenses.

Under slightly different circumstances, the deaths of the fourteen passengers in Guatemala might have signaled the end of the road for Sister Ping. A woman she had smuggled to Guatemala, who went by the name Sandy, had moved in with Kenny Feng and was living with him in the apartment in Guatemala City. (When Sandy arrived, Feng told her that her fee for the full trip to the United States would be some $20,000 more than what she had been told before leaving China, and she had no way to pay.) Feng tired of Sandy eventually, however, and sold her to some Mexican *coyotes*, who ended up holding her captive in a safe house in Brownsville, Texas. Desperate to escape, she jumped out a second-story window and broke her back when she hit the ground. From her hospital bed, she described her ordeal to the police, and eventually Kenny Feng was arrested.

It seemed that Sister Ping might be arrested as well. Jerry Stuchiner knew that she was operating out of Latin America, and he was still in regular contact with the Fat Man, who knew all about Sister Ping and her activities. Stuchiner was the INS's man in the region. He had managed to lock up Gloria Canales, and in the course of things it would have been only natural for him to move on to pursuing Sister Ping.

But by the time the ship went down off Guatemala in 1998, Jerry Stuchiner was gone. He had been unhappy in the months after the Canales arrest. He and his wife had quarreled. One day in July 1996 he boarded a plane bound for Hong Kong, accompanied by his Salvadoran mistress. He had altered his appearance somewhat, shaving his trademark goatee and dyeing his dark hair blond. The couple flew business class, and as the plane finally angled low over the bright lights of Hong Kong, Stuchiner grew excited: he was back on his own turf.

Stuchiner and his girlfriend exited the plane at Kai Tak Airport and queued at customs. Stuchiner flashed his black diplomatic passport, even though this was not technically an official visit. But as he was leaving the airport, he suddenly found himself surrounded by a team of Hong Kong Police officers, who placed him under arrest. He had not realized it during the long flight, but an undercover agent had been sitting a few rows behind him in the business-class cabin, watching his every move. Security agents began rifling through Stuchiner's belongings, and in his briefcase they found what they were looking for: five blank Honduran passports. According to the investigators, it had been Stuchiner's intention to sell the passports for $30,000 apiece to Chinese immigrants bound for the United States.

The Fat Man was standing in the airport arrivals lobby waiting to greet Stuchiner when he too was arrested. Herbie Weizenblut, the friend Stuchiner and the Fat Man had installed as Honduras's consul general in Hong Kong, was detained by the police as well, but he claimed diplomatic immunity from arrest and was released. He immediately left the colony, traveling first to Macau and from there to Kuala Lumpur, where authorities lost track of him. As details emerged about the immigration scam that Stuchiner had operated with the Fat Man and Weizenblut, Honduras's foreign minister was investigated for having permitted the Fat Man to pay Weizenblut's expenses during his time in Hong Kong. "I am very sad and very disappointed," said Angelina Ulloa, the anti-corruption crusader who as head of immigration in Honduras had worked with Stuchiner to crack the Canales case. She added that she had considered Stuchiner a friend. (She was subsequently suspended and investigated for corruption herself, though she insisted that she was innocent.)

Stuchiner pleaded guilty to passport fraud and was imprisoned in Hong Kong's Lai Chi Kok prison. But as the July 1, 1997, deadline for Great Britain to return Hong Kong to the People's Republic of China approached, Stuchiner, the great embellisher of stories and lover of international intrigue, outlined one last cloak-and-dagger scenario. He began to hint to the press that it might be shortsighted for U.S. authorities to allow him to serve out his sentence in a Chinese jail. He had been a senior federal agent for many years, and had been exposed to untold reams of sensitive intelligence. What if he was forced, under interrogation or even torture, to share those secrets with the Chinese?

The gambit succeeded, and on the eve of the handover, Hong Kong authorities commuted Stuchiner's sentence. For reasons that were never explained, the INS never conducted any sort of thorough investigation after learning that during the chief years of the human smuggling boom, one of its top anti-smuggling operatives had been dabbling in the business himself. But it did fire Stuchiner. He returned to the United States, and was never prosecuted for corruption. He moved to Nevada, where, extraordinary though it may seem, he is currently an attorney and a member of the bar. He practices law in Las Vegas. Immigration law is a particular specialty.

No one but Stuchiner will ever know the full extent of his corruption during the snakehead boom. No investigation ever conclusively determined whether the passports were an isolated incident or whether Stuchiner had colluded with the smugglers in other ways as well. Some speculated that he had gone after Canales with such fire simply in order to eliminate a competitor. Others wondered if the *Golden Venture* tragedy might have been prevented if the INS's chief anti-smuggling officer in Hong Kong had not had some vested interest in seeing the snakehead trade continue.

But whatever the extent of Stuchiner's corruption, it seems undeniable that his downfall represented yet another squandered opportunity to capture Sister Ping. He would have been the right person in the right place at the right time to bring her down, but instead he was selling blank Honduran passports, then sitting in a Hong Kong jail. To the immigration and law enforcement officials who were determined to capture Sister Ping, the arrest of Jerry Stuchiner brought home an unpalatable truth: the greatest adversary they faced, and their greatest disadvantage, was the pervasive, corrosive, endemic power of greed and official corruption. They had lamented the phenomenon in the two-bit backwater governments of Southeast Asia and Central America, but now they were forced to concede that the lucrative side of the snakehead trade had corrupted their own government as well. And while the boat that sank in the waters off Guatemala was a tragedy, some speculated that there must have been other boats that went down and remained unreported, minor catastrophes in which rickety vessels simply gave in to the sea, too far from dry land for the screams to be heard or the bodies to wash ashore. "The only person who really knows how many of those boats actually went down is Sister Ping," one of Stuchiner's colleagues said.

Chapter Seventeen

Catching Lilly Zhang

WHEN AH Kay returned to New York City late one night in the spring of 1994, the press was waiting for him, assembled at JFK Airport to photograph the gang leader and murderer who had authored the *Golden Venture* debacle. Ah Kay gazed directly into the television cameras. He looked small; he barely reached the shoulders of the officials escorting him. But he wore a cool, unapologetic expression on his face. If it is possible to strut while you have your hands cuffed behind your back and two burly federal agents fishhooking your elbows and dragging you between them, Ah Kay strutted.

By agreeing to cooperate with the FBI, Ah Kay had succeeded in reducing his father's sentence to eighteen months. Because the gang leader had worked over the years with so many criminal figures in Chinatown and China, Konrad Motyka and the C-6 squad had an endless list of questions for him. They installed him at the Metropolitan Correctional Center, or MCC, a hulking facility in downtown Manhattan adjacent to a clutch of courthouses and federal buildings that forms a kind of criminal justice complex on the southern edge of Chinatown. The MCC generally houses inmates on a short-term basis while a trial or some other proceeding is pending, but Ah Kay would prove to be so useful to authorities that he stayed in the prison for years, while a steady stream of interlocutors from the FBI and immigration went to pick his brain. He made himself at home, and became widely liked by both his fellow inmates and the prison staff. Ah Kay had always possessed a natural gift for leadership, and before long his handlers at the FBI noticed that even behind bars he had been able to cultivate a loyal coterie of followers.

"I'm benching three hundred," Ah Kay told an agent who went to visit him one day.

"No, you're not," the agent scoffed. Ah Kay did look conspicuously muscular and fit, but officials at the MCC had removed all the weights from the building years ago; there was nothing left to bench-press.

"I get a table," Ah Kay explained, "and two hundred-and-fifty-pound guys."

Once he made the decision to cooperate, Ah Kay committed to it with the same sort of thoroughness he had devoted to his criminal life, and it occasionally seemed that just debriefing him was a full-time job. Like the Fat Man before him, he had an excellent memory for detail, and he would patiently explicate the confusing dynamics of the tongs, the gangs, the triads, and the snakeheads. He made no effort to diminish his own culpability in the eyes of his interrogators, admitting fully to the murders he had committed, the beatings he had initiated, the parasitic patterns of Chinatown extortion. He detailed the history of the *Najd II* and the *Golden Venture*: the cooperation of Weng Yu Hui and Mr. Charlie, the interlude in Mombasa, the decision to purchase a second ship, the appeal to Sister Ping to wire the funds to Thailand. When Mr. Charlie was captured in Thailand, it was in part the fact that Ah Kay was on U.S. soil and willing to testify against him that persuaded him to plead guilty rather than risk a trial.

Ah Kay admitted that he had ordered the killings at the beeper store in January 1993, and described the price he had paid for it with the murder of his brothers in Teaneck. When Dan Xin Lin and the other murderers were tried in a courtroom in New Jersey, the prosecutor wanted background on the case and dutifully made the pilgrimage to the MCC to visit Ah Kay.

Nor did Ah Kay merely assist with cases in which he had personally played some role. He volunteered information on cases that hadn't even *been* cases—the buried bodies of nameless Chinese Americans who had run afoul of one gang or the other and disappeared, unnoticed, from the city's streets. He spent hours shuffling through surveillance photos, explaining who was who, correlating birth names with nicknames, and volunteering capsule histories of the criminal careers of a generation of thugs. He still had sources in China, and when he didn't know something, he would make a few phone calls back to Fujian Province to learn the answer. So extensive was this proactive intelligence-gathering that from behind bars Ah Kay ran up $60,000 in long-distance charges making international phone calls on behalf of the FBI. "The one thing about Ah Kay was that when he decided to cooperate, he cooperated one hundred percent," one of his handlers at the Bureau said. "He was probably the best cooperator that any of us have ever dealt with."

Over the years Ah Kay assisted in fifteen different federal cases, including a major investigation that resulted in an indictment against thirty-five members of another Chinatown gang, the Fukienese Flying Dragons. What's more, because he was such a notorious figure in the demimonde of Chinatown crime, the fact of his cooperation paid dividends far beyond the valuable information that he furnished. When word spread on the street that Ah Kay was talking, everyone who had ever done business with him was forced to consider whether he or she might be indicted next. The result was the criminal equivalent of a run on the banks. In the past, federal agents had struggled to persuade Chinatown criminals to turn their backs on the community and entrust their lives to the authorities by cooperating. But when Ah Kay became an informant, suddenly everyone seemed to want to come in and cut a deal. In the crude game theory of American organized crime, nobody wants to be the last one to rat. Before long, Luke Rettler joked that he had a line of Asian gangsters stretching out his door.

Upon his return to the United States, Ah Kay had agreed to plead guilty to murder and racketeering charges. But since his willingness to assist the FBI was driven at least in part by a desire to mitigate his own punishment, there was no sense in actually sentencing him for his crimes until he had been given an opportunity to help. So for several years Ah Kay's sentencing was postponed. Finally one day in 1998 he appeared before a federal judge, accompanied by his attorney, Gerry Shargel. Ah Kay had worked "virtually full time for five years doing what he could to improve his situation," Shargel told the judge. The government agreed. The federal prosecutor Chauncey Parker, who had spent the summer of 1993 working with Luke Rettler to re-up the wiretap on Ah Kay's father, maintained that the "unprecedented" level of assistance Ah Kay had extended was worthy of a lenient sentence.

Neither Ah Kay nor Shargel mentioned it during the proceedings, but if there was a model they were contemplating in their bid for a diminished sentence, it was surely the recent, highly publicized case of the former Gambino family underboss Sammy "the Bull" Gravano, who had turned state's evidence in 1991 and testified against his former employer, the Gambino crime boss John Gotti. After confessing to involvement in nineteen murders, Gravano was sentenced in 1994 to a mere five years. The prosecutors in that case had argued that a minimal sentence for Gravano might drive other criminals to cooperate with law enforcement in the future, and both Ah Kay and Shargel were acutely aware of the precedent established by Gravano's good fortune. (Shargel was perhaps especially so, as he had represented Gotti.)

"In these five years, I have felt the pain of two younger brothers and their suffering," Ah Kay told the judge. "I have felt regretful about all the unforgivable crimes that I have committed in the past."

But the judge, John Martin, was not swayed, and it was immediately apparent that Ah Kay would not be getting off quite so easily as Sammy the Bull. "There are five people dead directly because of this defendant," Martin said. "This defendant was the symbol of terror in the community where he lived, where his gang terrorized merchants, killed innocent people." He sentenced Ah Kay to twenty years in prison, and he said that he worried even that might not be sufficient. "That community is going to look on this sentence and be puzzled as to why a court would only give this man twenty years," the judge concluded.

The first thing Ah Kay did once the sentence was delivered was to fire Gerry Shargel. Another convict might simply have given up, resigning himself to the sentence and quietly serving his time. At the very least one might expect someone in Ah Kay's position to swear off helping the government. But after his sentencing Ah Kay continued to assist his handlers at the FBI, because there was still one narrow possibility that he could secure his freedom. The authorities had used Ah Kay to dismantle, in a fairly systematic manner, several major pillars of the criminal universe in Chinatown. But they were still holding out for one big case. Sister Ping was one of the first people Ah Kay had supplied information on when he originally came in. By 1998 she had been a fugitive for four years and was the FBI's most wanted Asian organized crime figure. Ah Kay had volunteered detailed information about her history and her various criminal activities, and he had made it clear that if the opportunity ever presented itself, he would be willing to testify against her—to stand in court and point the finger, the way Sam Gravano had pointed at John Gotti. If that day ever came, he might have the opportunity to do one final service for the government, to hand them the human smuggler they had been pursuing on and off since Operation Hester back in 1984. As Ah Kay sat in the Metropolitan Correctional Center, he could only hope that somehow someone could capture Sister Ping. "That's what he was waiting for," one of Sister Ping's lawyers would later remark. "She was his ticket out."

During the years that she had been in China, Sister Ping had seemed maddeningly elusive to the men at the FBI who were pursuing her. Konrad Motyka was still working on the case, and he was joined by Bill McMurry, a handsome young special agent from New Jersey, who had a quiet, almost laconic manner and began to immerse himself in the Bureau's extensive file on Sister Ping. McMurry was patient. He could appreciate the difficulty of conducting an international hunt for a woman who had so excelled over decades at the clandestine movement of people across borders. If Sister Ping had succeeded in making whole villages of people disappear from the countryside in China, only to reappear in the tenement blocks of Lower Manhattan, then surely she would have no trouble with the final vanishing act of eluding detection herself. By the late 1990s the FBI had developed many sources within the Fujianese community in Chinatown, far more than they had had when the *Golden Venture* ran aground. The informers came in from the streets and told McMurry and Motyka that Sister Ping was living openly in Fujian and that she was, if anything, more successful as a snakehead than she had been in the past. It sometimes seemed that she was simply invincible, impossible to catch.

Eventually Motyka and McMurry concluded that they could not count on China. Instead their plan would be to sit back and hope that at some point Sister Ping might leave China and travel to some jurisdiction where the authorities cooperated with the United States. Because Ah Kay had an interest in seeing Sister Ping captured, he proved happy to assist in this approach. Sister Ping was something of a celebrity in her home country, and little details like her whereabouts at a given time had a way of becoming public knowledge in the close-knit communities around Fuzhou. Ah Kay kept in touch with his sources in China, and when Sister Ping left town, he would hear about it and pass the information on to the FBI. Occasionally Motyka and McMurry would know not just that Sister Ping had left town for a few days, but that she was destined for Thailand or the Philippines. When they contacted the authorities in Bangkok or Manila, however, they would learn that there was no record of any Cheng Chui Ping entering or leaving the airports. Sister Ping might have been traveling, but she wasn't doing so under her own name.

One solution was for the FBI to persuade informants who knew Sister Ping to try to lure her out of China, enabling the local authorities in a friendly country to set up a sting. On one occasion the FBI arranged for an associate of Sister Ping's to try to interest her in a business deal. She initially agreed, and it was decided that she would meet the informant in Hong Kong. The FBI requested a provisional arrest warrant from Hong Kong authorities, and on the appointed day the Royal Hong Kong Police assembled and prepared to arrest Sister Ping. But something must have aroused her suspicions and she never appeared.

What the FBI did not know, and could not have known, was that Sister Ping was not simply making the occasional business trip during these years to attend to her smuggling operations in Hong Kong, Bangkok, and Guatemala. She was moving almost constantly. In fact, in an especially bold move she actually traveled to the United States. Because she had a range of assumed identities, it is impossible to say when and how often Sister Ping came to America during the years she was in hiding, but McMurry and Motyka were eventually able to confirm that in January 2000 the snakehead had flown into Miami International Airport. She passed in and out of the country like a ghost.

More present, if no less mysterious, was Sister Ping's husband, Cheung Yick Tak. He was not given to the same amount of international travel as his wife, and he seems to have led a more sedentary existence, not accompanying her on her many trips around the world. Indeed, it was rumored in Chinatown and among the FBI agents working the case that Sister Ping had fallen in love with her longtime smuggling associate Wang Kong Fu, who had introduced her to Ah Kay years earlier and who continued to work with her in Fuzhou. Yick Tak did not like Wang Kong Fu, and in later years he would blame the smuggler for encouraging Sister Ping to expand her operations too quickly. If Yick Tak was a cuckold, it would fit with his general persona—the hapless second fiddle to his fiery and intelligent wife. But it may also be that during these years, Sister Ping's husband, who had shown such subservient fealty to his domineering spouse, had secretly committed a small betrayal of his own.

The original criminal complaint against Sister Ping and Yick Tak was dated December 16, 1994. Sister Ping had already escaped to China by then, but on that date an arrest warrant was made out for Yick Tak. It was nearly three years before he was arrested, however. According to the FBI, its agents were unable to locate Yick Tak until 1997, when an informant walked in off the street and told them that they could find him in the restaurant at 47 East Broadway. Bill McMurry and another agent, Carlos Koo, headed to Chinatown and found Yick Tak at the restaurant. He put up no resistance when they arrested him.

But this account raises a few significant questions, primarily because according to Yick Tak, he had not just returned to Chinatown when the FBI captured him in 1997; he had never left town in the first place. "Since 1993, I have been working every day at the restaurant," he would later say to a judge. With Sister Ping back in China, "the restaurant needs me to run and operate it." His lawyer said the same, pointing out that Yick Tak "was not arrested on this complaint for a number of years, although the government was aware of the conduct and they were aware of where he was and he was easy to find. For whatever reason, they took their time in making this arrest."

If indeed Yick Tak was in Chinatown between the time the warrant for his arrest was issued in 1994 and the day three years later when Bill McMurry picked him up, it remains a mystery why the FBI either did not know he was in town or knew and did not arrest him. But if anything, Yick Tak's legal history grew more interesting after the arrest. On January 16, 1998, he was arraigned and pleaded not guilty. Two months later he suddenly changed his mind and pleaded guilty. He was not sentenced after the guilty plea, however. Instead, just like Ah Kay, Yick Tak found that his sentence was postponed. In the spring of 1999, the judge in the case gave an order allowing him to travel to Puerto Rico for four days. Generally a long delay in sentencing fits a certain profile, and it would seem that like Ah Kay, Yick Tak had found ways in which he could be helpful to the government. The special trip to Puerto Rico might simply have been a short vacation, but if that were the case, it is unlikely that the judge would have granted him permission to leave. A more realistic explanation is that it was a working holiday—that Yick Tak traveled to Puerto Rico in his capacity as a government informant. According to one prosecutor familiar with the case, the circumstances of the Puerto Rico trip indicate that "they were probably working him."

But the biggest mystery surrounding Sister Ping's husband is that on May 25, 1996, at a time when there was an active warrant out for his arrest, and when in the eyes of the FBI he was "out of pocket"—a wanted fugitive—Cheung Yick Tak was naturalized in New York City and became a full-fledged citizen of the United States. Under normal circumstances, immigration authorities cannot naturalize someone without first sending his fingerprints to the FBI. The Bureau checks the fingerprints and returns a report on whether the individual has any criminal history. Yick Tak may not have served any time for the deaths of the four people in the rubber raft on the Niagara, but he did plead guilty to a felony, which should have raised red flags. Yet the FBI maintains that it did not know he was even present in New York during these years. Either Yick Tak managed to slip through the system somehow, because of some miscommunication between immigration and the FBI, or he paid off someone at the INS—a possibility that several current and former immigration officials insist should not be discounted. The third possibility is that he cooperated with the government to such an extent that someone was willing to bend the rules for him as a reward.

There is no question that Yick Tak cooperated after his arrest. When he was finally sentenced, his lawyer, Stephen Goldenberg, said, "Mr. Cheung has provided a vast amount of information to law enforcement agencies." But along with both his defense attorney and the prosecutors, the judge in the case, Deborah Batts, refused to unseal the relevant court documents describing the nature and extent of his cooperation. Bill McMurry and Konrad Motyka acknowledge that Yick Tak came in and provided the FBI with information after his arrest. They say that none of the information was especially valuable, but they also confirm that during these years—years when he may well have assumed that his wife was untouchable, that the FBI would never be able to track her down—one of the people that Cheung Yick Tak gave them information about was Sister Ping.

Once McMurry and Motyka had concluded that Sister Ping was traveling widely but never using her own passport, they arrived at a key intuition: Sister Ping might be invisible, but her immediate family was not. Her husband was in New York, working in the restaurant and cooperating with the FBI. Her daughter Monica worked in the restaurant as well, and when her sons traveled, they seemed to do so on their own passports. If Sister Ping had an Achilles heel, it might just be her unstinting devotion to family. The agents had distributed Sister Ping's name to airports around the planet years ago, but now they assembled and circulated a family tree, laying out the names, nationalities, and passport numbers of Sister Ping's closest kin.

One day in early 2000, an American consular officer in Hong Kong was going through a stack of applications from people who had lost their green cards and were requesting a replacement copy. He paused over one of the forms, unable to figure out why the name of the applicant looked familiar. The officer ran a records check on the name. It was Sister Ping's son. He conferred with his colleagues, and it was decided that if Sister Ping's son was in Hong Kong and Sister Ping had herself been known to pass through the city in recent years, there was some small chance that the two might meet and she could be arrested.

It was decided that the U.S. consulate should contact the son, citing some pretense having to do with his green card application. They did so, and the young man dutifully appeared and tended to the paperwork they put in front of him. But when he left the building and several U.S. agents made an effort to follow him, they quickly lost him in the congested streets and sidewalks of Hong Kong.

The team at the consulate had not issued the replacement green card, and they came up with an alternative plan. Rather than supply the new card right away, they would say that there had been a routine bureaucratic delay but that if Sister Ping's son needed to fly to the United States, they could issue him a "boarding letter," which he could use in lieu of a green card. The catch, they would tell him, was that in order to issue the letter, they needed to know the precise details of his flight out of the country. It was a long shot, but perhaps his mother would drive him to the airport.

On April 11, 2000, a team of several dozen armed officers from the Hong Kong Police descended on the sleek departures terminal at Hong Kong International Airport and staked out the Korean Airlines desk. Just after 11:00 in the morning a short Chinese woman with wide-set eyes approached the counter and lingered there. She appeared to be waiting for someone. Another woman and a man who looked like he might be Sister Ping's son appeared, and the three of them went to the counter to check in. When the detectives were certain it was Sister Ping, they made their move.

They approached Sister Ping and asked if her name was Cheng Chui Ping. She did not reply. They asked for identification. But she wouldn't produce any. She just stood there.

The detectives led her to a nearby office. They proceeded to fingerprint her, and it was only then that she admitted who she was. The detectives searched her purse and found a Belizean passport that belonged to someone else and an array of loose passport pictures of other people. They found some Hong Kong currency, some Chinese currency, and $31,000 wrapped in newspaper and divided into three neat stacks.

When she was asked where she resided in Hong Kong, Sister Ping supplied the address of an apartment tower on Connaught Road West, in the same waterfront district where she had lived and worked in the late 1970s, before she left for the United States. It emerged that Sister Ping had maintained her residence in Hong Kong and had been living there on and off during the entire period that U.S. authorities had been searching for her. The detectives rushed to the building, noting, perhaps, in passing that the complex in which Sister Ping had been hiding was located one block from a major police station. Inside the twenty-second-floor apartment they encountered a Chinese couple, both carrying Belizean passports, who appeared to be customers and had just arrived in Hong Kong. They also found plane tickets—from Los Angeles to San Salvador, from San Salvador to Belize, from Hong Kong to Singapore, and so on. The plane tickets had been booked under the name Lilly Zhang, and in the apartment investigators recovered an authentic Belizean passport for a woman named Lilly Zhang, whose date of birth was listed as December 14, 1951. The photograph in the passport was of Sister Ping. There was another passport there as well, this one from Taiwan and in Sister Ping's own name. But it appeared that in recent months, at least, Lilly Zhang had been her default false identity. The passport had been issued just three months earlier, in January 2000. But it was covered in a welter of stamps. Under "occupation," Sister Ping had listed "housewife." But the passport bore visas for Honduras, Mexico, Mongolia, and numerous other places. In three months, Sister Ping had made fifty trips to foreign countries.

Bill McMurry and Konrad Motyka were elated when news of the arrest reached New York. When they found out about the passport, they were not surprised. Belize has a program that it euphemistically terms "economic citizenship," whereby a passport can essentially be purchased for a fee. If Sister Ping was traveling on a legitimate Belizean passport under someone else's name, there was almost no way that the FBI or Interpol or any foreign government might have succeeded in spotting her at an airport, unless they had someone on hand who actually recognized her face. When the agents contacted the authorities in Belize to try to get a copy of the passport application Sister Ping had filed, they were informed that it had been lost in a fire.

"It was lost in a lighter accident," Motyka joked.

"A very small fire," McMurry added with a smile.

But perhaps the most interesting thing that the Hong Kong investigators recovered from Sister Ping was a little black book full of names and phone numbers. There on the pages of the book, etched in Sister Ping's hasty, artless calligraphy, was a rendering of the extraordinary global web of contacts she had grown to rely on over a two-decade career. It was a singular document, a blueprint of her *guanxi* and her global operations. There were entries for an "Immigration Friend" in Thailand and immigration officials in Malaysia, Moscow, and Belize. There were associates in Mexico, Guatemala, Cuba, Singapore, Hong Kong, China, Mongolia, Canada, and, naturally, the United States.

Sister Ping was transported to prison in Hong Kong, and the United States announced that it would seek her extradition. "The arrest of Cheng Chui Ping after several years of diligent detective work demonstrates once again our common determination to bring to justice those who engage in the reprehensible and deadly practice of human smuggling," announced Michael Klosson, the U.S. consul general in Hong Kong, before noting—appropriately, if perhaps erroneously—that Sister Ping was "one of the masterminds" of the *Golden Venture* incident.

Chapter Eighteen

The Mother of All Snakeheads

ON MAY 16, 2005, Sister Ping was escorted into a courtroom in the federal courthouse on Pearl Street in downtown New York City. It had been over a decade since she fled from the neighborhood to take refuge in China, and she was visibly older: her face was still unlined, but her hair, which had grown long, was streaked with gray. She wore a smart black pantsuit, the professional garb of an inoffensive businesswoman. It was a canny choice of uniform: a businesswoman, Sister Ping would maintain throughout the trial, was all that she had ever been. The courtroom was filled with press, and with dozens of supporters and relatives from Chinatown. There was a measure of cruel irony in the location of the courthouse, in a cluster of imposing municipal buildings that abuts the southwestern corner of Chinatown. The restaurants and funeral parlors of Mott and Mulberry were a mere block away, and beyond those the safety and comfort of East Broadway, which even now people called Fuzhou Street, and the restaurant Sister Ping still owned at Number 47. If life had turned out differently, Sister Ping could have walked out of the building, strolled across Worth Street, and entered Columbus Park, where every day that summer the elderly men and women of Chinatown gathered to do slow, deliberate tai chi in the mornings and to pass the humid afternoons playing cards at concrete tables in the shade of the mulberry trees. She could have joined the spry Fujianese grandmothers who gathered there, women who were in their fifties, as she was, or older, and were finally slowing down after a lifetime of grueling work. They came from the same place she did, and had the same education. They had lived the type of life that, under different circumstances, she might have lived herself. She could have sat beside these women, their contemporary in every way, taken her shoes off, as they did, and fanned her face.

But Sister Ping had chosen a different life, and while she would continue to insist that she was simply a small businesswoman from Chinatown who had lived a hard and humble existence, the prospect of a leisurely retirement was looking increasingly unlikely. For Bill McMurry, who with Konrad Motyka had worked to pursue her around the world, and who sat in the back of the courtroom alongside the contingent of supporters from Chinatown every day of the trial, finally laying eyes on Sister Ping had come as something of a shock. "She's just a little old woman," McMurry marveled. "You wouldn't look at her twice on the street."

Sister Ping had always been a fighter, dismissive of the system of laws but more than ready to hire high-priced attorneys when it suited her. After her arrest in April 2000, the United States had announced that it would attempt to extradite her to face charges in New York. From a cell in an overcrowded maximum-security prison in the New Territories, she arranged to be represented by a leading barrister who was an expert on extradition law. She would argue that the Hong Kong government should not turn her over to the United States because so much time had elapsed since the crimes spelled out in the indictment against her that prosecution was barred by the statute of limitations. This gambit seemed animated by a curiously naive notion that if a criminal simply goes on the lam and stays away for long enough, her crimes will be forgiven.

When a Hong Kong court ruled against her, Sister Ping tried another argument, suggesting that Hong Kong's own Department of Justice had a conflict of interest, because in its handling of her case it had consulted with the American Justice Department and thus was representing the interests of the United States. She sued the government, saying she was being unlawfully detained and naming the United States and the prison where she was being held as defendants. Amid this flurry of legal activity, she was reportedly hospitalized for depression, which further delayed the proceedings. (Whether she was genuinely clinically depressed or merely stalling for time remains unclear.)

In December 2002, Sister Ping presented herself to the Court of Appeals in Hong Kong. By that time she had fired her attorney and in a bizarre move had chosen to represent herself. There is no question that Sister Ping was an exceptionally shrewd and intelligent entrepreneur, but she was no legal scholar, and after years of deference and reinforcement from those around her, she had developed a somewhat elliptical and highly self-referential style of conversation that produced comic results in the courtroom. She began by telling the court that she wanted to quote from a Mandarin television series, *Honorable Judge,* which she had enjoyed during her years on the mainland. "In the execution of law, not only had the judge to understand fully what the law says," she solemnly intoned, "but how the system deals with the cases and the general complexities of the case."

Sister Ping told the court that the Public Security Bureau in China had frozen her assets. She explained that she simply wanted to return to America and continue running her restaurant on East Broadway, which she had been forced to leave in the care of family and friends. "But if I go back," she added, "I would like to go back with the proper status."

The appeal was unsuccessful, and on Friday, June 6, 2003, a decade to the day after the *Golden Venture* ran aground in Queens, her final appeal was rejected as well. After three years of fighting, Sister Ping was out of options. A young FBI agent named Becky Chan flew to Hong Kong to escort her back to America. On the flight home the two women sat side by side in the back of the plane. Sister Ping wore plastic flexicuffs over a Rolex watch. She was adamant that she had done nothing wrong and that as soon as they touched down in New York she would be released and reunited with her family. Chan could see the determination in Sister Ping's eyes. "I'm going to beat this," her countenance seemed to say. "I'm going to get let out."

It was only when the plane touched down in San Francisco and Sister Ping caught sight of the media photographers waiting there that her confidence began to slip. She asked if she could telephone her husband. Becky Chan said that she could, but that they could not speak in their native dialect, which Chan did not understand. They had to speak in Mandarin.

When Sister Ping had exchanged a few words with Yick Tak, the women changed flights, retracing the route east across the United States that Sister Ping had made on so many occasions with Fujianese customers who had entered the country from Tijuana. When they arrived at Newark Airport, Bill McMurry and Konrad Motyka were waiting there to meet them.

By choosing to fight extradition, Sister Ping had actually made a significant mistake. Before her capture in 2000, Motyka and McMurry had struggled to persuade the FBI to invest resources in building a case against the snakehead. The 1994 indictment was beginning to feel somewhat stale, but given that she was a fugitive and it looked unlikely that she would ever be captured, the agents had trouble justifying the devotion of further investigative resources to tracking down witnesses and assembling evidence for a prosecution that might never come to pass. Once Sister Ping was in custody, however, Motyka and McMurry began reaching out to their counterparts in the INS and other agencies. By resisting extradition, Sister Ping had simply given them three additional years in which to refine the case against her.

There were five counts against Sister Ping. Count one was a conspiracy charge, alleging that she had conspired to commit the crimes of alien smuggling, hostage-taking, money laundering, and trafficking in ransom proceeds. Count two charged her with hostage-taking, with specific reference to one of the Boston boats she had hired the Fuk Ching gang to offload. "Hostage-taking and alien smuggling go hand in hand," one of the prosecutors observed. The third and fourth counts charged Sister Ping with money laundering—for the money she had sent to Bangkok so that Weng Yu Hui could start his own human smuggling business in 1991, and for the funds she sent on behalf of Ah Kay to help purchase the *Golden Venture*. The fifth count involved trafficking in ransom proceeds.

In a way, the indictment seemed to underline just how minimal Sister Ping's role in the *Golden Venture* operation had been. She had sent twenty clients aboard the *Najd II*, but only two of them had ended up on the *Golden Venture*. It was true that one of those two had died in the water off Rockaway, but Sister Ping was not charged with any crime related to that death. She had helped finance the ship, but technically the money she sent to Thailand so the boat could be purchased was not her own money; it was money that she owed to Ah Kay. "Cheng Chui Ping had nothing to do with the *Golden Venture*," her lawyer, Larry Hochheiser, said. Hochheiser was a rumpled criminal defense attorney with fluffy white hair, a bushy mustache, and a kind smile. He was a seasoned litigator who had spent years representing the Westies, a violent Irish American gang based in Hell's Kitchen. Hochheiser paced the courtroom with a slow gait and argued that Sister Ping had been an underground banker in an immigrant community, and that was the extent of her crimes. "It wasn't Cheng Chui Ping who created the idea of the *Golden Venture*," Hochheiser said. "No one claims that, except maybe the newspapers. The government doesn't claim that. Even their witnesses can't claim that. Ah Kay *was* the *Golden Venture*." The tail was wagging the dog, Hochheiser argued. "This is a credit union. This is a money business that is being used to tie Cheng Chui Ping to the alien smuggling business."

Nevertheless, the impression hung heavy in the courtroom that whatever the charges against Sister Ping, her trial would represent the final, definitive account of the tragic voyage of the *Golden Venture*. The judge in the case was Michael Mukasey, a stern, bespectacled conservative who in later years would become the attorney general of the United States. Mukasey had heard cases brought by *Golden Venture* passengers in the past; he had more than a passing familiarity with the tragic details of the voyage. The government lawyers, a team of three young assistant U.S. attorneys, spent an inordinate amount of trial time examining and reexamining Sister Ping's role in the *Golden Venture*. Their aim was not to convict her for any of the particulars of the voyage or the deaths, but to establish in as much detail as possible that she was not merely a shopkeeper or banker but a snakehead, and a major one at that.

"This is a case about the brutal business of smuggling human beings into the United States for profit, and about one woman, the defendant, Cheng Chui Ping, who rose to become one of the most powerful and most successful alien smugglers of our time," one of the prosecutors, David Burns, declared.

To make its case, the government produced a devastatingly comprehensive array of former criminal associates. Weng Yu Hui appeared in the courtroom and described how Sister Ping smuggled him to America in 1984; how she gave him money to take to her passengers when they were stranded in Mombasa; how the day the *Golden Venture* arrived, she had told him to get out of town. "She said that she had bad feelings and she was afraid," Weng recalled. "She was worried about her two customers." Various former underlings from the Fuk Ching detailed Sister Ping's complicated history with the gang. Larry Hay, the undercover Canadian Mountie who had executed the sting at the Buffalo airport leading to Sister Ping's first conviction, testified. Kenny Feng, the Taiwanese snakehead from Guatemala, recounted the tragedy of the boat that had overturned in 1998. A Fujianese woman whom Sister Ping had charged $43,000 for the journey to the United States explained that she was willing to commit to such a considerable fee because she knew Sister Ping's name and trusted her reputation.

But the most damning witness was the man who had been living in a temporary jail cell since 1994, the man whose decidedly complicated history with Sister Ping was about to undergo one final twist. After receiving his twenty-year sentence in 1998, Ah Kay had been waiting for the opportunity to do one last service for the government. When he strode into the courtroom and was sworn in, the jury could not perhaps appreciate the sense in which for Ah Kay, this was the culmination of his years of cooperation, what Konrad Motyka called his "final part to play."

Ah Kay was still a youth at the time of his arrest, but when he appeared in the courtroom, wearing an orange prison jumpsuit, he looked older, calmer, and more sensible, his hair shorn close to the scalp, his demeanor precise and free of hostility. Ah Kay was middle-aged. He had always been a quick study, and as a government witness he did not disappoint. For three days he testified about Sister Ping's role in the community, about his decision to rob her house in Brooklyn in the 1980s, and about how readily she had forgiven him when she needed him to offload her customers at sea. He was matter-of-fact about his own crimes, acknowledging his role as the Fuk Ching's *dai lo* and describing the murders he had committed and the mayhem for which he was responsible. He admitted that he had personally smuggled as many as a thousand people into the United States, and that in addition he had helped snakeheads like Sister Ping offload their ships and collect their fees. When he was asked whether this entailed violence, he replied, "Of course violence was used."

With impressive recall, Ah Kay revisited each detail of the decision to purchase the *Golden Venture* and send it to Africa to retrieve the passengers from the *Najd II*. He described asking Sister Ping to wire the funds for the ship to Thailand. "I told her that she still owed me three hundred thousand dollars," he recalled. "I said I would invest the money in that *Golden Venture* boat. She said, 'No problem.' " Ah Kay was direct and unflappable. He made a perfect witness, which should perhaps be no surprise; he had been preparing for this moment for ten years.

Sister Ping sat quietly through the testimony, listening through headphones to a simultaneous translation and occasionally taking notes.

Hochheiser hammered at the credibility of the government's witness. "Who are these people?" he asked. "What is the quality and character of the people that are giving you information?" Despite the fact that Weng, who was one of the government's lead witnesses, had already served his sentence and was a free man by the time he took the stand, Hochheiser suggested not only that the men testifying against Sister Ping were mendacious criminals, but that they had all been induced to testify with the promise of lesser sentences. "Murderers were hired to give you testimony in this case, and they were paid with a commodity worth a great deal more than simply money," he told the jury. "Their cooperation, we euphemistically call it, was bought and paid for with life—with freedom from serving years in jail."

"Make no mistake, ladies and gentlemen. These men *are* killers," the government lawyer David Burns conceded. "But they're killers she hired."

If Sister Ping was furious that her former associates were now lining up to betray her, she might have found some comfort in the fact that one person was not called upon to take the stand. After his arrest in 1997, her husband, Cheung Yick Tak, had his sentencing postponed and postponed again. It was as if the authorities were waiting to assess the full measure of Yick Tak's cooperation before delivering his sentence—as if, like Ah Kay, he still had one final part to play. Prior to Sister Ping's trial, two different attorneys who represented her expressed concerns that one of the government's witnesses against the snakehead might ultimately be her own husband.

The prosecution never called upon Yick Tak, but again there is some evidence, however circumstantial, that he may have already played a role in the government's efforts to apprehend Sister Ping. After pleading guilty to two counts of conspiracy in 1998, Yick Tak was not sentenced until July 14, 2003, which happened to be two weeks after the FBI agent Becky Chan escorted Sister Ping back to the United States. Was Yick Tak somehow instrumental in securing the extradition and prosecution of Sister Ping? Did he trade his wife's freedom for his own? The answer may never be known: everyone involved in the case, including the judge who delivered Yick Tak's sentence, is adamant that the nature of his cooperation must never be disclosed. But having been named in the original indictment with Sister Ping back in 1994, and having worked with her as a cash courier and junior partner throughout her criminal career, Yick Tak got off with a conspicuously light sentence of eighteen months. In Bill McMurry's view, Yick Tak "got a very good deal."

The trial took four weeks. "Sister Ping sat atop a smuggling empire that she herself had built over the course of almost two decades from the ground up," Leslie Brown, one of the government lawyers, said in her summation. "By the end of her long run, Sister Ping was at the apex of an international empire, a conglomerate built upon misery and greed."

In his closing arguments, Hochheiser invoked the Arthur Miller play *The Crucible*, about the witch trials in Salem. Most of his indignation seemed to be directed at Ah Kay. "He ordered murders," Hochheiser catalogued. "One beating that we heard about, ten ordered beatings, ten to twenty robberies, forty to fifty extortions, two arsons, a thousand alien smugglings, one racketeering, one gun possession, one parole violation, tax evasion, and fake passports." Hochheiser was a veteran defense attorney, but even he seemed sincerely impressed by the length of Ah Kay's rap sheet. "That's one of your main witnesses!" he exclaimed.

On June 22, after five days of deliberation, the jury members sent a note to Judge Mukasey saying that they had "come to an impasse" on count two, the hostage-taking charge. Hochheiser promptly requested a mistrial on that count, suggesting that Mukasey not resubmit it to the jury. He feared that when the jurors left the courthouse each day, they were being exposed to a barrage of negative publicity surrounding the case. It was true that the local newspapers in New York were painting an unflattering portrait of Sister Ping and suggesting that she had somehow been the ringleader behind the *Golden Venture* incident. It could not have helped that during the trial, in an unrelated incident, a restaurant worker from New Jersey had been gunned down at Sister Ping's restaurant on East Broadway.

Hochheiser was especially troubled by a front-page story and accompanying editorial in the *Daily News*, which, he noted, "may be the most popular paper in the city."

"They will be relieved to hear that," Judge Mukasey deadpanned.

The headline in the *News* was "Evil Incarnate."

But if Sister Ping was demonized in the mainstream New York press, she was lionized in Chinatown. Copies of the city's Chinese-language dailies sold out at newsstands throughout the trial. There was a great upswell of sympathy in the neighborhood, where Sister Ping was widely regarded as someone who had provided a service, lifting a generation of people out of dead-end lives of rural poverty. The *World Journal* reported that in Sister Ping's home village of Shengmei, people were volunteering to do jail time on her behalf. They described her as a "living Buddha." Ninety percent of the villagers now lived overseas and had managed to leave China through the good offices of Sister Ping. The remaining residents prepared a petition to send to Judge Mukasey, requesting lenience in her case.

To be sure, there was diversity of opinion among Fujianese in both China and the United States on the subject of the famous snakehead, but the prevailing attitude in Chinatown was that while she may have broken laws, her crimes were essentially victimless, and were ultimately justified in terms of the prosperity they created for her customers. "My sister was just thinking of helping others," the snakehead's younger sister, Susan, said from her home in New Jersey. "How would she know it would get her in trouble?" Chinatown residents made frequent, if somewhat inapt, comparisons between Sister Ping and Robin Hood. "She is even better than Robin Hood," one supporter said. "Sister Ping never stole anything, and still helped the poor. She is a good person."

After spending so many years pursuing Sister Ping, Konrad Motyka and Bill McMurry were frustrated that the Fujianese in Chinatown could not appreciate the extent to which the snakehead had exploited them. When the agents went into the community to talk to potential witnesses about testifying against her, they met with a great deal of resistance. "I don't want to be known as the one person who testified against Sister Ping," people would tell them. "It's going to hurt my business. It's going to hurt my family." It wasn't simply that people feared revenge from Sister Ping; they feared the kind of social stigma that would attach to anyone who turned on so popular an icon of the Fujianese community.

"There are people who are going to say, 'Sister Ping is the greatest thing in the world, because she brought me here,' " Motyka said. " 'I've been able to support my family. I now own my own restaurant. This is my version of the American dream.' But there's an equal number of people who drowned in the surf, or women who were raped by the gangs, or people who were shot in the head. Those people aren't going to have as positive a view of her." To the Robin Hood comparison, Motyka and McMurry replied, almost in unison, "Robin Hood never made forty million dollars."

For Justin Yu, a Chinatown journalist who covered both the legal proceedings and the response in the neighborhood and went on to write a book in Chinese about Sister Ping, the two different pictures of the snakehead represented a much deeper philosophical rift that separated those who grew up in China during the twentieth century and those who were born in the United States. What you thought about Sister Ping depended at least in part on the value you attached to a single human life and on how that value factored into a larger calculation of possible benefits and possible risks. "In China, a human's life isn't worth ten pennies," Yu remarked. "Ten thousand people come and one hundred people die? Bad luck. If they make it, their families get rich. Their *villages* get rich."

So for American-born prosecutors and members of the press to focus on the ten dead from the *Golden Venture*, or on the hazards and depredations of the journey, was to miss the point, and to indulge in a conception of the preciousness of human life and the primacy of physical comforts that would be foreign to the Fujianese because it would render almost any risk untenable. Sister Ping's business was inherently risky, and her clients understood those risks and accepted them. The key to understanding the snakehead trade was the concept of "acceptable risk," Yu concluded. "Acceptable risk, acceptable cruelty, acceptable lousy treatment, acceptable long trip, there's no toilet. It's *acceptable*. Because of the comparison: the life there, and the life here."

After several days of further deliberation, the jury returned a verdict. They found Sister Ping guilty of conspiracy, trafficking in ransom proceeds, and one count of money laundering. The jurors remained hung on the hostage-taking charge. As the verdict was read, Sister Ping betrayed no emotion, her face expressionless. But she may have been masking her surprise. Throughout the trial she had been housed at a prison in Brooklyn, and according to other inmates who met her there, she would sometimes gather her belongings and announce that she was preparing to return home, because any day she would be free.

The press took little notice of it, but the jury acquitted Sister Ping of count four, the money-laundering charge related to her wiring the funds for the purchase of the *Golden Venture*. She was cleared of the only charge that actually linked her to the ship. But it made little difference. The name and face of Sister Ping would always be synonymous with the voyage.

From their homes in cities and small towns around the country, the passengers of the *Golden Venture* followed the news of Sister Ping's conviction with a kind of detached interest. Despite the government's best efforts, the vast majority of the original migrants now lived in the United States, including nearly all of the hundred or so who had been deported. Still enamored of the elusive promise that America seemed to hold, they had returned in a variety of ways, some of them legal, some of them not, and many of them were too busy to take much notice of the Sister Ping case. Those who did take an interest felt sympathy for Sister Ping. The only snakehead toward whom any of them displayed ill will was Ah Kay, and the fear and hostility that his name still managed to awaken in them seemed driven more by his predatory relationship with the Chinatown community than by his role in the voyage of the *Golden Venture*.

Of more concern to the passengers was a conspicuous shift in the mood of the country—the return of a deep-seated panic on the issue of immigration. After the terrorist attacks of September 11, 2001, the kind of periodic hysteria that had occasionally gripped the nation throughout its history returned, but with a heightened element of fear. In 2003 the two sides of INS work, benefits and enforcement, were officially disaggregated, with the benefits side becoming a new agency, Citizenship and Immigration Services, and the enforcement side joining customs to become Immigration and Customs Enforcement, or ICE. If any doubt remained about which of the competing instincts behind immigration work would prevail, the instinct to admit people to the country or the instinct to shut them out, it was surely telling that both of these new agencies were absorbed into the Department of Homeland Security. As the bureaucratic reorganization took hold, one message was unmistakable: immigration would henceforth be regarded first and foremost as a matter of national security.

Nearly a decade after the last of the *Golden Venture* detainees had been released from York County Prison, the former prisoners were still on parole. ICE had begun launching impromptu raids on restaurants and garment factories across the country and rounding up undocumented people; numerous cities and municipalities were beginning to pass their own strict anti-immigrant ordinances. Some of the *Golden Venture* passengers began to fear that in such a hostile climate, they themselves might be deported. They had purchased property and opened businesses. Many of them had sent for their families, or met and married people in America. They had American-born children enrolled in elementary school. Yet in 2004 one of the men who had been pardoned by President Clinton, Zeng Hua Zheng, received a deportation order at his home in Aurora, Colorado. He was instructed to gather his belongings into 44 pounds of luggage and report on a certain date for his flight back to China.

As their fears grew, passengers all across the country started making telephone calls to York. Some of the original People of the Golden Vision had fallen out of touch with the passengers, but many had stayed in close contact, telephoning them at Christmas and the Chinese New Year and attending their weddings and the weddings of their children. Craig Trebilcock had just returned from a year spent with an Army civil affairs unit in Iraq, and he and Beverly Church began lobbying members of Congress to introduce a piece of private legislation that would finally put an end to the uncertainty and fear in which the *Golden Venture* passengers had lived for a decade, by granting them permanent resident status.

"They're picking them off one by one," Bev said. She was still working as a paralegal, but in her spare time, in the evenings and on weekends, she began compiling binders full of information on each of the passengers and sending them to legislators in Washington, hoping to persuade them to vote on the private bill. The catch with a private bill is that it can be approved only by a unanimous vote in Congress, and particularly on the matter of immigration, there would always be a few hardliners who would refuse to find sympathy for the men. But as long as the bill was pending before Congress, the passengers could not be deported. So at the beginning of each congressional term, Bev would work with allies in the House of Representatives to introduce the bill, and when it did not pass by the end of that term, she would make sure that it was reintroduced in the next one. "They paid the penalty but never got final status," Todd Platts, the Pennsylvania congressman who sponsored the bill, said of the *Golden Venture* passengers. "We want immigrants to be willing to work hard and provide for themselves. These individuals have shown that they do." Bev continued lobbying other members of Congress, and when her earnest letters received no reply, she would drive to Capitol Hill herself and doorstep the legislators in their offices. "You should see it," Craig joked. "They scurry into the nearest men's room as soon as they hear her heels coming down the hall."

In the spring of 2006, a documentary about the *Golden Venture* by the filmmaker Peter Cohn premiered at the Tribeca Film Festival in New York. Bev and Craig thought it might be an ideal PR opportunity, so they persuaded the passengers whose names were on the private bill to take a rare day off work and travel by bus and car to New York. It was a happy reunion for the men, who smiled and joked and exchanged family news and baby pictures. "When we saw these gentlemen on TV, on the shores of New York State, we took these gentlemen to be heroes, not liabilities to the country," Craig said at a crowded press conference in Chinatown. "They are the bravest men I have ever met."

"We almost died trying to get to America, and then we were in jail for four years," one of the passengers, the slight, bespectacled Ohio restaurant owner Michael Chen, told the newspaper reporters assembled in the room. With fluent English and a businesslike demeanor, Chen looked every bit the modern American professional, and had become something of a spokesman for the group. "We have been out of jail for almost a decade," he continued. "We have started businesses and families, paid taxes and been good citizens. But still we are not fully legal. It's hard for us to buy homes, get jobs, or even get driver's licenses. We live in fear that we will be sent back to China. We ask President Bush to recognize that we have already paid a very high price to find freedom in America, and to finally grant us legal status."

Standing among his fellow passengers, dressed in a black suit with the collar of his button-down shirt splayed over the lapels *Saturday Night Fever*–style, was Sean Chen. He had come from Philadelphia, where he had been living since 2002. He spent his days working as a manager and bartender at a Japanese restaurant and his nights tending bar at an Irish pub. He had bought his own place, a small brick townhouse on the outskirts of the city, and he was engaged to a beautiful

Fujianese woman named Dana, who was tall and had flawless skin and a giddy, infectious laugh. Dana had her green card, and she and Sean had met when she went to work at the Japanese restaurant as a cashier. On their first date, Sean took her to lunch at TGI Friday's, then to watch the New England Patriots play the Philadelphia Eagles at a Super Bowl party at a friend's house.

About a year after the press conference in New York City, Dana gave birth to their first child, a son, whom they named Brian. The baby was several weeks old before Sean's mother, who was living in Taiwan, insisted on giving him a Chinese name. In the excitement of the birth and those first few days of fatherhood, Sean had not gotten around to it.

On a lovely, crisp morning in March 2006, Judge Michael Mukasey's courtroom filled once again with members of the press and law enforcement officers, and with the many friends and relatives of Sister Ping. She entered, wearing a prison-issue gray T-shirt and blue pants, her long hair falling down her back. The casual clothing made the snakehead seem especially small; the T-shirt was too big for her, dropping almost to her knees. She turned to acknowledge her family, then put on her headphones so that she could hear the translation.

After perfunctory statements by the prosecution and defense, Judge Mukasey went through the standard practice of offering the convicted an opportunity to address the court. When defendants choose to make these statements, they tend to involve brief apologies to victims or their families, some sort of show of contrition, and a request for leniency in the sentencing.

Hochheiser stood and said that he had advised Sister Ping not to speak. "She is not a lawyer, aware of the legal issues," he said. "Having said that, I have told her that if she wishes to make a statement to the court, she may."

Mukasey turned to Sister Ping. "Is there anything you want to tell me before I impose sentence?" he asked.

For a moment Sister Ping was silent, sitting straight-backed behind the defense table. Then, slowly, she rose. She gestured to her interpreter, a slim Chinese woman with short hair who sat several feet away. Then she spoke.

"I cried once in court," she began. "That was when Ah Kay robbed my home twice and I was too afraid to report it to the police . . . The witnesses against me have all gone home, and they have received a light sentence as a result of testifying against me," she continued. "I'm happy for them. The way that I lead my life and also my personality is that I wish the best for people. I was a small businesswoman in Chinatown. If Ah Kay had come and robbed my home twice, you can imagine how many other people took advantage of me."

What followed was an extraordinary hour-long monologue as Sister Ping expounded and free-associated on her personal history and the events and personalities that had arisen in the trial. Everyone in the courtroom except her family members, who had perhaps been exposed to such feats of digressive oratory in the past, sat rapt, amazed that the woman who had waited so silently over the course of the proceedings had suddenly hijacked an opportunity to sound a few words of regret and was instead delivering a stump speech. "Everybody can tell you that Mrs. Ping was working in the store every day, especially people from my hometown," she continued. "I am not the kind of person that they depicted me and charged me with being." She pointed to the fact that for years other snakeheads had claimed to be associated with her and done business "using my name"; she seemed to be implying that some of her alleged associates were not associates at all, that she was merely the victim of guilt by association.

"Do you think that Mrs. Ping has some kind of psychological—some abnormality? That wasn't the case. It wasn't as if I didn't have any money. And the things that people have said, is it . . . is it logical?"

She quickened her pace, speaking so rapidly that the interpreter struggled to keep up, the words tumbling out, her indignation rising, pausing only to jot a character on a piece of paper from time to time to clarify her meaning. She retold each event that had come up at trial, but from a different vantage point, in which she was the victim of the narrative. When she was arrested in Buffalo, she had merely been helping a pregnant relative in need. She said she had always known Weng Yu Hui was trouble, that he was "too wily." She complained that the Fuk Ching gang had exploited her, robbed her, demanded extortion. "I am deathly afraid of these people," she said. She maintained that the evidence against her had been manufactured.

One reason an attorney might not want his client to speak freely in court is that she could make the mistake of alluding to crimes for which she has not been charged, and sure enough, despite the fact that government lawyers had made no mention of the contract on the journalist Ying Chan, Sister Ping brought the incident up, saying that the Fuk Ching had approached her and suggested that they take care of the writer for a fee.

Relentlessly she portrayed herself as a victim, a hardworking small-business owner who had wanted nothing more than to look after her family. "Everyone can tell you I work fourteen hours in the restaurant every day," she said. She pointed to her relatives in the back rows. "Every single one of my relatives, when they arrived, they borrowed the whole sum from me in order to pay the snakeheads." She would not admit to having smuggled the family members herself, but there was no mistaking the responsibility and pride she felt when it came to the presence in this country of so many of her kin. "It was my choice to bring them over—all of them—to the United States," she said.

It was not entirely clear whether Sister Ping actually believed any of what she was saying—whether she was delusional and had persuaded herself of her own martyrdom or whether the whole thing was a misguided charade, a last-ditch effort to persuade authorities to buy the cover she had been so assiduously cultivating for so many years. At one point she seemed to accept the idea that she would have to serve time in jail and began describing the role that someone like her could play there. "In jail I can help people," Sister Ping said. "People who are ill, people who just arrived, people who are in a bad state of mind . . . As a fellow passenger, I can lift their mood . . . because new arrivals usually do not have a happy state of mind. And I can also buy clothes, as well as daily supplies, for people who are poor, who have no money, and I can help those who are ill, who are pregnant." It was an extraordinary image, a creative adaptation of the mythology that surrounded Sister Ping. In her rendering, prison was just another Chinatown, a hard-luck ghetto in which Big Sister Ping could minister to the disenfranchised and the displaced. "My life remains valuable," she said defiantly. "It remains valuable."

But no sooner had she seemed to accept the idea of a life in prison than she changed course, blasting the FBI. "The FBI should be helping me," she exclaimed. "I was taken advantage of a lot in Chinatown." She seemed obliquely to suggest that she might be willing to cooperate. "I would like to speak privately with the prosecutors and with the FBI," she said. In particular, she expressed an interest in talking with her erstwhile handler from the Bureau, Peter Lee.

Few of the spectators in the courtroom would have known who Peter Lee was or had any inkling what Sister Ping was talking about, but this apparent offer to cooperate with the government once again raised an interesting question: why hadn't the FBI simply flipped her, turning her into a government witness? In the early 1990s, in meetings with Peter Lee, Sister Ping had given information on Ah Kay and other rivals and adversaries to the FBI. Dan Xin Lin had informed on Ah Kay and his brothers, and when Ah Kay was in hiding in Hong Kong, the Fat Man told INS agents where they could find him. Ah Kay had informed on seemingly everyone he had ever done business with, including Sister Ping, and Sister Ping's own husband had fed information to the FBI about his wife. One constant through the length of the whole sordid saga was that at decisive moments, each of the major players seemed willing to sacrifice loyalty for pragmatism and self-preservation and betray his or her closest associates. So why wouldn't Sister Ping cooperate? When she was captured, she had her little black book noting immigration contacts all over the world. "The potential if she had cooperated with us for uncovering international corruption would have been tremendous," Bill McMurry said. But when the FBI raised the possibility, she did not take it. In McMurry's view, the decision was driven by the knowledge that if she maintained her silence, her reputation would remain intact and her family would have nothing to fear. "Her family, I'm sure, is very welcome in Fujian," McMurry said. "If she had cooperated, all of that probably would have come to a screeching halt."

There may have been rewards for those who refused to cooperate, but there were rewards for those who agreed to cooperate as well. Shortly after Sister Ping's conviction, Ah Kay appeared before Judge Mukasey. He had served twelve years in prison and played a decisive role in the government's case against Sister Ping. Prosecutorial calculus can occasionally yield perverse results, and Ah Kay's cooperation was now considered so valuable that despite his criminal history, despite the fact that one of the prosecutors who had put him on the stand called him "an incredibly violent man with zero regard for human life," the government, along with Ah Kay's defense counsel, was now recommending that he be set free.

"I'll be candid with you," Mukasey told Lisa Scolari, Ah Kay's new attorney. "It is extraordinary. It is colossally extraordinary . . . Your client had been directly responsible for ending a lot of lives and a lot of worlds." Scolari insisted that Ah Kay was a changed man, that the murder of his brothers marked "a turning point in his life."

Then Ah Kay spoke. "I am close to forty years old now," he said. "The long-term incarcerations have taught me to be mature, have taught me to be a steady person." He said that he had found religious belief and that he regretted the pain he had caused his community and his family. "I have wasted half my life and have accomplished nothing," he said. "I swear that the next half of my life I will change thoroughly." He suggested that he would like to work with young people so that they might learn the lessons he had learned, to keep them out of gangs.

Ah Kay had not lost his charisma during the years in prison, his ability to mesmerize and persuade. Somehow, within the span of an hour-long hearing, Mukasey was won over. "I'm going to grant the motion to a far greater extent than I intended to," he said. "Mr. Guo, my hope is that the story that you wanted to tell youngsters gets out to youngsters, because in my view, that's really the only good that can still come of this."

And with that, Ah Kay's sentence was reduced, and shortly thereafter he was quietly released. Because of his many betrayals, the FBI assumed that Ah Kay would not be safe if he returned to Chinatown, so they created a new identity for him and placed him in the witness protection program. Today the *dai lo* of the Fuk Ching has a humdrum job in a humdrum town somewhere in America.

"He's serving pizzas in Idaho," Konrad Motyka said with a laugh.

As Sister Ping's speech dragged on, the spectators in the courtroom were beginning to shift uncomfortably in their seats, the way guests at a dinner party might when someone's story goes on a bit too long. In the back rows, where her family and supporters were sitting, an adolescent boy in a Nautica jacket, who might have been a nephew, was nodding off to sleep. Again and again in her remarks, Sister Ping returned to the concept of family, so important to the Fujianese, as the overriding explanation for her deeds and for her life. One of the prosecutors, Leslie Brown, was heavily pregnant. Sister Ping turned and addressed her directly. "Ms. Brown, you are about to be a mother," she murmured in an icy tone. "I congratulate you for being a mother. Once you become a mother, you will understand me."

To Judge Mukasey she said, "Your Honor may have noticed that when the trial began, there was a white-haired old man who came every day. That was my father." During the course of the trial, the old ship jumper who decades earlier had taught his daughter the snakehead trade had died. "I feel very sorrowful," Sister Ping said. "When I remember that my father instructed me how to conduct my life, I feel no regrets. I feel I have a clear conscience. I have lived up to my father's will."

Sister Ping sat, and Judge Mukasey, who had grown more visibly irritated the longer she spoke, fixed her in his gaze. "Ms. Ping, it is not my practice to deliver sermons at the time I impose sentence," he said. "But the words that you spoke . . . are bound to be reported in places other than this courtroom, and it may be that people will get the idea, reading those words and having no familiarity with your case, that you somehow were the victim of an unjust prosecution." Mukasey called her remarks a "lengthy exercise in self-justification" and pointed out that the statements of the various witnesses against her had been corroborated by phone records and other evidence. He was unmoved by her account of being robbed by the Fuk Ching and suggested that those initial encounters had "established, in a way, their credentials from your standpoint."

"You say that you love the United States," Mukasey continued. "I can't speak to that. But what the evidence in this case did show is that you were willing to take advantage of the attraction of the United States for the reasons that you described—in that you can lead a decent, honorable life by working hard. You took that attraction for many, many hundreds of other people, thousands of other people, and turned it to your own financial advantage."

Then Mukasey delivered the maximum sentence. For count one, she would receive five years; for count three, twenty years; for count five, ten years. The sentences would be served consecutively; she would be incarcerated for thirty-five years. Sister Ping was nearly sixty years old. This meant that she would very likely die in jail. As Mukasey tallied the counts, Cheung Yick Tak listened, his eyes wide, his mouth slightly ajar. He added up the numbers on a little piece of paper on his knee.

Bill McMurry was thrilled when he heard the sentence. "It gets the message out to the community that it doesn't matter how big you get or if you flee the country. It doesn't matter where you go. We're gonna get you," he concluded. "I don't know if we'll ever see a smuggler of the notoriety of Sister Ping again. There will be smugglers. But no smuggler will dominate the industry in the way that she did."

Everyone stood up. The Fujianese family and supporters who filled four benches in the rear of the room looked shell-shocked. Some of them began to whisper among themselves, shaking their heads. Others looked straight ahead in mournful resignation. Others still expressed confusion, unable to fathom what kind of system could bestow so merciless a punishment on the woman they had revered as both an agent and an embodiment of the American dream. Judge Mukasey left the courtroom through a door behind his bench, and the marshals began to escort Sister Ping away. As she was being ushered out a side door, she turned suddenly to face her family in the back of the room. She gave a kind of schoolgirl wave, an awkward gesture that seemed poignantly at odds with the gravity of the moment. Then she walked out of the courtroom, a strange smile on her face.

Epilogue

The smuggler [is] a person who, though no doubt highly blamable for violating the laws of the country, is frequently incapable of violating those of natural justice, and would have been, in every respect, an excellent citizen had not the laws of his country made that a crime which nature never meant to be so.

—ADAM SMITH
The Wealth of Nations

AFTER PRESIDENT George W. Bush delivered his State of the Union address to Congress in January 2003, the Democratic Party was afforded, in accordance with tradition, an opportunity to respond. The speaker the party selected to deliver its rebuttal that evening was Gary Locke, who since 1997 had served as the governor of Washington and who had the distinction of being the first individual of Chinese ancestry in American history to be elected governor of a state. Locke's grandfather had come from Canton at the turn of the twentieth century and worked as a houseboy in Olympia; Locke's father had joined the United States Army and stormed the beach at Normandy. Locke himself was raised speaking Chinese until he attended kindergarten. He went to public schools and was a scholarship kid at Yale before moving on to law school and a career in politics. "My grandfather came to this country from China nearly a century ago and worked as a servant," he said in his address that evening. "Now I serve as governor just one mile from where my grandfather worked. It took our family one hundred years to travel that mile. It was a voyage we could only make in America."

The Snakehead is the story of that mile. Migration scholars and refugee advocates tend to overlook the business of human smuggling, out of an understandable fear that the illicit means through which many immigrants reach the United States might further stigmatize the estimated 12 million undocumented people who live in the country today. But the business of human smuggling is now a pervasive and sophisticated reality—a $20 billion criminal industry, by some estimates, second only to the global trade in drugs. To ignore it is impossible, and irresponsible as well. The greatest favor we can do for the Fujianese and other migrant groups is to comprehend the complex and often misunderstood networks that bear them from one country to another. Doing so can shed light on how best to combat the trade, but also on the extraordinary sacrifices that many of these men and women have undertaken to find a new life in another country.

In the minds of many of the Fujianese I spoke to over the past three years, the ultimate success or failure of a single act of emigration can be measured only in generations: if the individual who transplants herself or her family to the United States undertakes extraordinary, even irresponsible risks in order to do so, or commits some crime or other along the way, those lapses will eventually be justified by the upward mobility of her children and their children, and the notion that some later generation will be born in America and have no solid grasp of how it was precisely that their grandmother or great-grandmother first crossed the oceans but simply know that she did. For all the extraordinary freedom and comfort and opportunity that being born in America entails, it will seem to that later generation like some happy accident of geography or fate, not a circumstance for which some forebear broke the law or risked her life.

If, as Balzac had it, behind every great fortune there is a crime, there might also be a sense in which many an immigration story begins with some transgression, large or small. Surely many American-born citizens can trace their personal genealogies back a generation or three or five and declare with conviction that at some long-ago juncture in history, no ancestor stole across a border or used a phony document. But many, many others cannot. In some ways it is the birthright of those who are born on American soil not to worry about such details, and for one ethnic group after another the story has been the same: those tenements on the Lower East Side that once housed the first-generation Italians and the Jews of Eastern Europe and today house the first-generation Fujianese will no doubt house some other scrappy flock in the years to come, as the revolving door of American immigration and assimilation continues and the Fujianese move on to bigger apartments and to houses, to the suburbs, perhaps even, one day, to the governor's mansion.

If one takes the generational model, there might be some sense in which Sister Ping could be absolved of her guilt by the good fortune of her grandchildren and the grandchildren of the many thousands of people she helped to make a new life in America. More than once while I was writing the book I thought of that moment in *The Godfather* where the dying Don Corleone utters a quiet lament that his son Michael has joined the family's criminal business rather than pursue a more legitimate career as a senator or a governor. "It wasn't enough time, Michael," he says. "It wasn't enough time."

"We'll get there, Pop," his son replies. "We'll get there."

It also seems possible to find a measure of sympathy for Sister Ping when one considers the extraordinarily high price that federal prosecutors were willing to pay to put her behind bars—the price of setting Ah Kay free. If the various personalities whose lives converged around the voyage of the *Golden Venture* can be measured on an ethical continuum, with undocumented passengers like Sean Chen at the least culpable extreme and Sister Ping somewhere in the middle, Ah Kay occupies the opposite pole. Whatever remorse he may have felt in later years, the fact remains that Ah Kay was a bandit and a killer, and while he may have done the right thing eventually, by assisting the FBI, he did so only at a time when he stood to gain his freedom through cooperation. It may be that Ah Kay is completely rehabilitated today and will melt into whatever environment the authorities have selected for his witness relocation and live a peaceful and productive life. But Ah Kay is still a young man—a young man with "zero regard for human life," in the words of the prosecutor who put him on the stand. Should the day ever come when his violent personality reasserts itself, the government will struggle to justify its decision to return a mass murderer to the streets in a trade for an aging snakehead.

This is not to suggest, by any stretch, that Sister Ping did not deserve to be incarcerated for her crimes. It might be tempting to draw some moral equivalence between the hopes and aspirations of Sister Ping and those of her clients, because they were all engaged in the same illegal enterprise. But to do so would be to overlook the fact that Sister Ping's business thrived because of her willingness to exploit the dreams and desperation of her fellow Fujianese. To this day, if you raise the name Sister Ping in any restaurant on the Fujianese side of Chinatown, you are likely to hear encomiums to her work ethic and generosity. She has become part of the folklore of the neighborhood—a latter-day Harriet Tubman who risked imprisonment to shepherd her countrymen to freedom. But the notion of Sister Ping as some sort of heroic figure is a fantasy, and these accounts tend to elide the vast quantities of money she charged for her services, the homicidal thugs she hired, and the many nameless dead who perished as a direct result of her reckless devotion to the economies of scale. There may be some respects in which Sister Ping is a morally complicated person. She may even be a person who has managed, however incidentally, to do a lot of good. But she is not a good person.

After her sentencing Sister Ping was transferred to a minimum-security federal women's prison in Danbury, Connecticut. Having been so explicit during the hearing about her conviction that the welfare of her family superseded the niceties of American law, she opted nonetheless to avail herself of every appeal that the legal system afforded her, and a procession of brand-name New York defense attorneys made the 70-mile pilgrimage to Danbury to meet the famous snakehead. The man she selected, Scott Tulman, was a former assistant district attorney in Queens who had become a criminal lawyer and opened an office on Market Street in Chinatown. The "notable cases" section of his firm's Web site featured such entries as "Blood and Bullet Found in the Car—Client Confesses—Case Dismissed" and "Caught in the Act with 27 Pounds of Cocaine in the Car—Client Confesses—Case Dismissed."

Tulman prepared an appeal that focused on Weng Yu Hui's testimony about asking Sister Ping to transfer money to Thailand when he got started in the snakehead business. On the stand, Weng had recalled Sister Ping joking, "Now you're my competitor." For Sister Ping to be found guilty of money laundering, Tulman argued, it should have been clear to the jury not only that she transferred the money but that she knew that Weng was going to use the money for alien smuggling for financial gain. Sister Ping might have suspected as much, Tulman conceded. She might even have tried to confirm her suspicions by suggesting, in jest, that Weng was her competitor. But he never replied to the joke. "Weng's silence at the time left her without knowledge of his purpose" in sending the money, Tulman maintained. He derided the government's evidence in the case as "reed thin" and implored the appeals court to overturn the conviction on the money-laundering and ransom proceeds charges. But the court wasted little time in upholding the conviction, observing that "the record at trial was replete with evidence that these smuggling rings were operated as commercial enterprises."

At the prison in Danbury, Sister Ping fell into a depression when she heard the news. She had her own explanation for why the conviction was upheld, and it had nothing to do with the technical details of the money-laundering charge. Between her sentencing and her appeal, the judge in her case, Michael Mukasey, had been nominated by President Bush to become the attorney general of the United States. For Sister Ping there was no mistaking what was going on: the appeals court judges could not overturn Mukasey's decision now, because to do so would represent an insult to a very powerful man—an unforgivable loss of face.

During the years after Sister Ping's arrest in 2000, China continued its astonishing economic transformation. When I met with a police officer in Bangkok in the spring of 2007 and announced that I was working on a book about Chinese human smuggling, he replied, "People trying to get *into* China? For jobs? Yes, it's a problem." In 2008 I traveled to Fujian: to Fuzhou and Changle; to Sister Ping's hometown, Shengmei, where the family mansion still stands; and to Ah Kay's village nearby. Throughout the region textile factories were springing up and roads were being built at a frantic pace. Armies of manual laborers from Sichuan had to be trucked in to build new shopping malls and office towers, because most of the low-skilled Fujianese men had long since departed for the United States.

As of 2007, some Chinese estimates still maintained that between 30,000 and 50,000 Fujianese continue to leave the province illegally every year. But at this point most of the Fujianese who want to leave have left, and the center of outmigration has shifted to other areas, like the city of Wenzhou, farther up the coast. As I spoke with people around Fuzhou, a consensus emerged that the dynamics of emigration have changed as well. Throughout the 1980s and 1990s, it was the most ambitious and adventurous Fujianese who took the risk of leaving for America. But today the fee for passage can reach as high as $70,000, and Fujian's best and brightest see little point in going into debt and risking their lives to become an undocumented dishwasher on the margins of American society. Much better to stay in China and start a business. "The people going away now are the ones who aren't doing that well," a young entrepreneur in Changle told me. "If you can do *anything* here, you stay."

If China has changed, Chinatown has as well. Strolling along East

Broadway, it is difficult to imagine the dark days of the 1990s, when a daylight double homicide in a beeper store on Allen Street would not occasion so much as a one-line notice in the *Daily News*. In 2002, for the first time in memory, the NYPD's Fifth Precinct did not register a single homicide. A few gangs are still active in the neighborhood, and extortion, graft, and other forms of exploitation persist. But the open criminality has receded from the sidewalks, and Chinatown is once again a vibrant bustle of schoolkids and tourists, hawkers and vendors, young professionals, and the elderly out for a stroll.

Still, even now the snakeheads are in business, and the undocumented migrants come. "The smuggling's never going to go away," Billy McMurry told me one afternoon at the FBI.

"It's too lucrative," Konrad Motyka chimed in.

"It's too lucrative," McMurry continued. "And our country's laws are never going to get restrictive enough where you're going to completely stop it." He paused. "Which is probably a good thing as well," he added. "It's what this country's based on."

New snakeheads have emerged to take Sister Ping's place. "Sister Ping got into the smuggling business early when few others were aware of it," a snakehead in Fuzhou observed. "But her reputation was inflated beyond her actual capability. She was successful for a while in the early 1990s, but her days are gone. I know people in Fuzhou who are far more successful than Sister Ping."

A short walk from FBI headquarters, not far from Sister Ping's restaurant, a modest white structure on Allen Street houses the Church of Grace for the Fujianese. I stopped by the church and spoke with the pastor, a man named Matthew Ding. Every Sunday during services, Ding takes a moment to welcome new arrivals to the city, he told me. And every Sunday another five or ten stand up.

What lessons can we learn from the saga of Sister Ping? There are roughly 200 million migrants in the world today, some 30 to 40 million of whom are undocumented. This transnational global underclass with a population larger than Canada's is on the move, in search of better opportunities, and just as the Gold Mountain of America held a special appeal for the Fujianese, these migrants are anything but random in their choice of destination. Seventy-five percent of all of the world's migrants end up in only 12 percent of the countries; they tend to venture from the preindustrial to the industrial, from the third world to the first. And in something of a paradox for immigration authorities, intensified enforcement along the border often has the perverse effect of bolstering the human smuggling trade, because when it becomes difficult for individuals to smuggle themselves into a country, they are obliged to turn to the experts. Human smuggling is one of the fastest-growing international crimes in the world today, and even as the boats from Asia may have stopped arriving on American shores, they continue to come ashore in Central and South America; boats still leave Cuba and Haiti overloaded with passengers desperate to reach the beaches of Florida, and in Europe the boats arrive as well, crude wooden fishing vessels and rust-speckled trawlers ferrying Africans from Morocco to the south of Spain or from Libya to the Italian island of Lampedusa. Afghans are smuggled to Indonesia, then loaded onto boats bound for Australia, and more than a quarter of a million Ecuadorans have boarded fishing boats bound for Mexico, from which they then cross into the United States.

In any boatload of migrants there will be those fleeing oppression and those fleeing demoralizing poverty and those who are not fleeing anything at all—those who have simply heard that in some distant city or town there are dishes that need washing or strawberries that need picking or bathrooms that need cleaning, and that in these jobs they might actually make enough money to send some of it home.

The story of the *Golden Venture* is a particular one, but the questions it raises have relevance throughout the world. How can governments combat the growth of organized human smuggling? How should individual countries handle the influx of undocumented migrants seeking work? How can an asylum policy be both efficient and fair without becoming a magnet that actually induces poor people to leave their homes and risk their lives in the expectation that if they can survive the journey, they will receive asylum once they arrive?

On the matter of law enforcement, it seems clear that purely domestic solutions will never be effective. International cooperation is essential in combating global criminal networks like Sister Ping's. In 2003 a new agreement, the United Nations Convention Against Transnational Organized Crime, went into force. This sort of legal instrument offers a promising framework for international cooperation, by obliging states that ratify the treaty to make certain activities, such as money laundering and corruption, a crime, and by encouraging extraditions and mutual legal assistance. The convention has an additional Protocol Against the Smuggling of Migrants by Land, Sea and Air, though in typical UN fashion, the key achievement of the protocol seems to be the parties' success in agreeing on a definition of human smuggling. And in any event, Thailand and Guatemala have signed the protocol but not yet ratified it, and China has yet even to sign it.

It is spoiler countries like these that are the problem, and in the frustrating game of international crime and crime prevention, the more successful the United Nations is at creating a harmonized system of sovereign law enforcement bodies that agree to cooperate in cracking down on human smuggling, the higher the pecuniary rewards will be for any one particular nation that is induced by some deep-pocketed operator like Sister Ping not to play along. We live in a world in which the flow of ideas and capital and goods and people is largely unimpeded by the quaint restrictions of national boundaries. These global currents are so strong that they sometimes seem inexorable, and the challenge for national governments that want to dam such currents is that the global system is now integrated to a point where a single spoiler jurisdiction can make law enforcement impossible. As long as it is possible to purchase a valid passport in Belize, it will be possible to remain a fugitive and travel the world without tipping off the authorities. Whatever our moral assessment of Sister Ping, what can be said with certainty is that she was a creature of her moment in history—an exponent of free-market capitalism run amok in an ever more borderless world.

Corruption is the common denominator in spoiler countries, and there is little sense in fighting the human smuggling trade without fighting corruption first. The United States should remain alert to the extremely high likelihood of corruption within the ranks of foreign governments. But as the story of Jerry Stuchiner makes clear, it is not merely the underpaid functionaries of developing countries' immigration services who prove susceptible to bribery; occasionally the corruption hits closer to home. "No agency of the government is more vulnerable to corruption than the INS," a *New York Times* investigation found in 1994. "Year after year, dozens of employees are arrested for taking bribes or related crimes." In my conversations with two dozen current and former immigration officials, the persistence of corruption on the front lines of America's immigration service, even after the INS was incorporated into the Department of Homeland Security and rechristened Immigration and Customs Enforcement, was a frequent refrain. On June 26, 2008, Constantine Kallas, the assistant chief counsel of ICE, was arrested at a casino in Highland, California, and charged with accepting thousands of dollars in bribes.

To be fair, in the years since the arrival of the *Golden Venture* some real progress has been made on the problems of human smuggling and abuse of the asylum system. Perhaps the single most conspicuous element of American immigration policy to act as a magnet during the prime years of the snakehead boom was the practice of issuing undocumented asylum applicants with working papers so they could go into the city and find jobs while their claims were processed. In 1995 the government repealed that policy, and the impact of that single, surgical fix was immediately apparent: almost overnight, the number of new asylum applications filed every year dropped from roughly 140,000 to roughly 35,000. In addition, criminal penalties for human smuggling have increased considerably since Sister Ping served her four months in Buffalo, and since 1996 law enforcement has been empowered to pursue snakeheads using the

Racketeer Influenced and Corrupt Organizations (RICO) Act. Together, these changes have succeeded in slowing, if not halting, the snakehead trade and the onslaught of smuggled asylum seekers.

What has not changed, and should, is the essentially arbitrary nature of the determination of whether to grant asylum to an individual who is seeking it or send him back to an uncertain fate. Even taking for granted that the asylum process is bedeviled by fraud, one lesson of the *Golden Venture* incident is that each individual asylum case should be scrutinized with the utmost care, that decisions of such consequence should not be rushed, and that to rush a determination or to paint an entire class of claimants with the same broad brush could result—and often does—in sending individuals home to persecution.

Through a series of "backlog elimination plans," immigration authorities have made some progress on the long delays in processing claims of asylum. But sometimes efficiency is achieved only at the expense of fairness. Recent studies indicate that the asylum process is as arbitrary and unpredictable as ever, and without some effort to oblige asylum officers and immigration judges to harmonize the bases upon which they will grant asylum, it appears that the fate of individuals seeking refuge will continue to be determined not by any coherent policy or sense of justice but ultimately by the luck of the draw.

Moreover, in the years since Sean Chen and his fellow passengers were first bused to York County Prison, immigration detention has gone from the exception to the norm. The sweeping new immigration law that passed in 1996 authorized the "expedited removal" of people who arrive in the United States without proper documents. Genuine asylum-seekers are not supposed to be removed, but those who try to enter the country without documents are subject to mandatory detention while their claims are pending. Like the *Golden Venture* passengers, they are farmed out to various facilities around the country, and there is no limit, in either federal law or agency regulation, on the amount of time an asylum-seeker may be detained. As a result there has been an enormous uptick in immigration detentions. On any given day, some 33,000 people, including children, are jailed on immigration grounds. In 2007 the government held over 300,000 people in total while deciding whether or not to deport them. Immigration detention is now the fastest-growing form of incarceration in the United States.

The immigrants are housed in a network of detention facilities, some of which are owned by private prison companies, and in hundreds of local and county jails. These sites are overcrowded and underregulated. It is possible for immigrants who have committed no crime apart from the civil infraction of entering the country without proper documentation simply to disappear into this system. Health care is substandard, when it exists at all. In 1999 a Chinese woman who had come to America seeking asylum gave birth in a jail cell in Illinois; the guards hadn't noticed she was pregnant. According to a study by the *Washington Post*, in a recent five-year period, eighty-three detainees died in immigration custody. The actions or inactions of medical staff were responsible in a significant number of those cases. But the leading cause of death among those held in immigration detention is suicide.

It is an ironic reflection of American attitudes on immigration that this penal system costs taxpayers an estimated $1.2 billion a year to maintain. That sum is so colossal that if even a fraction of it were redirected to hiring and training asylum officers, immigration judges, and other administrative staff to help process the backlog of immigration cases, and to do so in such a way that people's claims are actually accorded the serious consideration they deserve, it could cut down on the duration of these indefinite prison sentences and the need to jail immigrants in the first place.

After the last of the *Golden Venture* passengers departed from York County Prison in 1997, the facility continued to house immigration detainees. In 1999 the prison underwent an expansion, and that year it became the single largest immigration detention facility in the United States. York might seem, in that respect, to be an expression of America at its most xenophobic and intolerant. But whatever it was that the passengers from the *Golden Venture* had managed to awaken in the people of York somehow persisted long after most of the Chinese men had moved away. The motley coalition that had made up the People of the Golden Vision remains active to this day, arranging legal help and small comforts for the detainees held at the prison and lobbying in Washington for more humane treatment of refugees. The group raised funds to purchase an old property in downtown York, which became International Friendship House, a shelter and halfway house for refugees and other migrants released from immigration detention. They established the Pennsylvania Immigration Resource Center, which offers free legal advice to asylum-seekers, and it comes to the aid not just of the Fujianese but of Bosnians and Iranians, Iraqis, Liberians, and Sudanese. To this day, Bev Church, Craig Trebilcock, Joan Maruskin, and other members of the group continue to work on behalf of the *Golden Venture* passengers, helping them with their efforts to start businesses and purchase property, pay their taxes, and care for their families. And each new congressional term, Bev Church reenters the private bill for consideration by Congress, on the off-chance that more than fifteen years after their arrival on the beach in Queens, the passengers might obtain green cards and become legal residents of the country they call home.

One breezy afternoon in the summer of 2008, I drove from Jacksonville, Florida, to Amelia Island, a pretty, palm-fringed stretch of beach not far from the border with Georgia, where Bill Slattery, the former district director of the INS in New York and the man who first decided to detain the *Golden Venture* passengers, lives today. Following the arrival of the ship in 1993, Slattery's career continued its rapid ascent, and he was nominated to take on the number-three position at the INS. But after a short few years on the job, he was forced to retire from the agency amid a revolt by his subordinates and allegations of corruption. (No formal charges of corruption were ever brought.)

We sat at Slattery's kitchen table and made sandwiches from cold cuts and talked about immigration for hours. Slattery remained angry about the degree to which snakeheads like Sister Ping had exploited the vulnerabilities of the United States, and to this day he is skeptical about the asylum claims of the passengers aboard the *Golden Venture*. He showed no remorse for having thrown the passengers into prison, and mocked as sentimental those who were moved by the thousands of paper sculptures the detainees made during their years behind bars. But when I asked Slattery what he thought should become of the passengers now, I was surprised by his answer. "These people now fall onto the legitimate side," he said. "We're not going to send them back once they've been here this long." Slattery's rationale was pragmatic, he explained. Right now, immigration officials are wasting time monitoring the paroled *Golden Venture* passengers when they could be devoting their energies to stopping new illegal immigrants from entering the country. "So I would support the private legislation," he concluded. "Give them the okay and let them be productive members of society."

The sun was setting by the time I said good-bye to Slattery and drove back along the beach. The waves of the Atlantic were battering the shore. I thought about Sister Ping, who, having failed in her appeal, was now determined to take her case to the Supreme Court. The court would ultimately decline to hear the case. Ah Kay had fared much better, and I marveled at a recent, improbable turn of events: since his release, Ah Kay had been working with his lawyers and his supporters in the government to quietly obtain something that still eluded so many of the passengers from the *Golden Venture:* his citizenship.

I thought about the hundred or so passengers from the ship who had been deported to China over the years and the fact that almost all of them had eventually come back. The resilience of these people was astonishing to me, and it occurred to me that in their sheer determination to make a new life in America, the passengers from the *Golden*

Venture, who were born in China and still speak only broken English, are in some ways more American than I will ever be.

I remembered something that Sean Chen had told me. He was describing the little indignities of being illegal in America, and I asked him whether, knowing what he knows now—knowing about the arduous journey, the years in prison, the perils of an undocumented existence, and, perhaps worst of all, the new prosperity in China, that country he had once risked everything to flee—he felt any regrets. Without hesitation, Sean shook his head. "If you gave me the chance," he said, "I would do it again."

Sister Ping died in prison, from pancreatic cancer, in April 2014. She was sixty-five years old. Her death was front-page news in New York's Chinese-language newspapers, with articles describing her "righteousness," and calling her an "immigration hero." "Her warmth moved everyone," a local man who came from her village back in Fujian told the *New York Times*.

There was a huge funeral procession on the streets of Chinatown, converging at the Grace Gratitude Buddhist Temple, across the street from the building Sister Ping's family still owned at 47 East Broadway. Despite a torrential spring rain, hundreds of Chinatown residents came out to pay their respects. In the vestibule of the temple, dozens of umbrellas were stuffed into a plastic bucket. Incense burned, alongside platters of apples and little bowls of dried fruit, and a framed photograph of Sister Ping. Inside the brightly lit main room, in the presence of the snakehead's coffin, a group of monks in orange robes led mourners from the neighborhood in a rhythmic, funeral chant. Every seat in the room was taken.

Down the Florida coast from where Bill Slattery lives, about a mile off Palm Beach, a rusted freighter lies nestled in the seabed 70 feet beneath the waves. Glittering schools of yellowtail and barracuda thread through the barnacled hatches, and brightly colored coral quilts the deck. On weekends amateur divers descend from power boats above to circle the wreck and rummage through its gaping portals, peering into the dark recesses of the ship's cramped hold. It is as fitting a resting place as any for the *Golden Venture*.

After the ship was auctioned by the marshal's service back in 1993, it was painted red and renamed the *United Caribbean*. For a time it was used to transport cargo up and down the coast, but the aging vessel was not even up to that task, and the new owner abandoned it on the Miami River. Eventually local authorities decided to sink the ship and turn it into an artificial reef for divers. One day in 2000 it was towed out into the Boca Raton Inlet, where holes were cut into the hull and water was pumped into the hold until the ship began a slow descent and sank to the ocean floor.

Every shipwreck tells a story. And if this particular story is in some ways an unhappy one, it is also a story about the awesome power of optimism and bravery and hope, about the many twisting paths that bring strangers from one country to another, and about what it means to be—and to become—American.

Acknowledgments

MY FIRST thanks go to the hundreds of individuals who invited me into their homes and offices and took the time to talk with me over the past three years. Occasionally when I reached someone by telephone for the first time, they would exclaim, "I've been saying someone should write a book about this since 1993," and in that spirit many people became not just sources but co-conspirators, raiding their files and photo albums and Rolodexes and giving me access not just to their recollections but to a rich historical paper trail. It would be impossible for me to thank here everyone I spoke with, or even just those I spoke with on more than one occasion, but I must acknowledge a handful of the most long-suffering sources: Konrad Motyka and Bill McMurry, Bev Church, Joan Maruskin and Craig Trebilcock, Luke Rettler, Jim Goldman, and four other immigration officials, one of them retired, three of them still working in government, who spoke with me off the record and helped connect me with the larger network of veterans of the smuggling wars. A huge thanks also to the unfailingly patient and professional Jim Margolin of the FBI's press office, to Megan Gaffney of the U.S. Attorney's Office for the Southern District of New York, and to Mark Thorn of ICE. Thanks also to Sister Ping's appellate lawyer, Scott Tulman, and to Ah Kay's lawyer, Lisa Scolari.

The book would have been impossible without the cooperation of the passengers who came to America in the hold of the *Golden Venture*. Over the years I had brief interactions with numerous passengers, but

I'd especially like to thank those who spoke with me at greater length: Yang You Yi, Michael Chen, Dong Xu Zhi, Zheng Kai Qu, and most of all Sean Chen. I should also thank Sister Ping, whose note-perfect reply to my early requests for an interview was "What's in it for me?" I appreciate her willingness to indulge me by answering my written questions. Her answers have improved the book beyond measure.

In the early stages of my research I benefited enormously from the scholarship and guidance of several individuals who had been working in this area for years before I showed up. Ko-lin Chin, Peter Kwong, Zai Liang, and the filmmaker Peter Cohn generously shared their work and their time. The academic work of David Kyle, Rey Koslowski, Paul J. Smith, Wenzhen Ye, Peter Andreas, Sheldon X. Zhang, and Dušanka Mišćević was also very instructive, as was the writing on immigration law and policy of Philip Schrag, Peter Schuck, David Card, and George Borjas. James Mills's magnificent opus, *The Underground Empire,* was especially valuable for its portrait of the Fat Man, Dickson Yao. Dating back to the 1980s, a handful of journalists have done work on human smuggling, Fujianese immigration, Sister Ping, and the Fuk Ching gang, and I want to acknowledge my debt to the extraordinary reporting of Seth Faison, Celia Dugger, and Nina Bernstein at the *New York Times*; Thomas Zambito at the *Bergen County Record*; Anthony DeStefano and Mae Cheng at *Newsday*; Ying Chan and James Dao at the *Daily News*; Pamela Burdman at the *San Francisco Chronicle*; Marlowe Hood at the *Los Angeles Times Magazine*; Brook Larmer and Melinda Liu at *Newsweek*; Peter Woolrich at the *South China Morning Post*; and Caryl Clarke at the *York Daily Record.*

Given the truly global scope of this story, I relied on the kindness of numerous sources in foreign countries. I can't name everyone here, but a particular thanks to Matiko Bohoko, Father Michael Sparrow, Reverend Richard Diamond, and Jay New for their help on the Mombasa chapter; to the three colonels in Bangkok, Jaruvat Vasaya ("Col. Dong"), Ponsraser Ganjanarintr ("Col. Jon"), and Apichat Suriboonya ("Col. Phum"); and to the staff at the UN's Office of Drugs and Crime, especially Wang Qianrong, Burkhard Dammann, and Jamnan Panpatama. A hearty thanks to Senior Sergeant Major Pao Pong, now with the Bangkok Immigration Police, and to the tireless Senior Sergeant Major Thana Srinkara of the Pattaya Tourist Police, who helped me find Pao Pong and interpreted our conversation. Thanks also to the American officials who spoke with me in Bangkok but prefer not to be mentioned by name. In Hong Kong, I was especially grateful to Kingman Wong of the FBI for talking to me at such great length; to Yiu-Kong Chu at the University of Hong Kong, for demystifying the triads; and to Wayne Walsh, of the Hong Kong Department of Justice, for agreeing, on my second visit, to meet with me. Thanks also to Bill Benter, who showed me around on both trips to Hong Kong and was my guide on some memorable gustatory excursions.

In Fuzhou and Changle the debts really begin to multiply, and acknowledgment is complicated slightly by the fact that the individual who acted both as mentor and as fixer, and opened doors that I wouldn't have known even to knock on, has asked that he not be thanked by name. But an everlasting thanks to Dr. Tang and to Dr. Li, to Lin Li and her husband, to Jiang Huo Jin in Tingjiang, Fang Meng Rong in Fuqing, Zheng Kai Qu in Changle, and Song Lin, of Yingyu village, who showed me around Ah Kay's hometown with such good cheer that I was reluctant to ask if he was any relation to the Song You Lin from the beeper store on Allen Street. Driving in China is an adventure, and I'm certain I owe my life, along with a newfound taste for sugarcane, to the irrepressible Cheng Wei. A special thanks also to Ben Ross, an American who moved to Fuqing and Fuzhou after college, started an excellent blog, and gave me a terrific rundown on what to look for before I left.

But my greatest debt in both Chinatown and China is to that aforementioned individual who did not want to be named. He did ask that rather than thank him, I honor his grandmother, a woman I never had the privilege of meeting but whose advice—that you should never see the world through the hole in a coin—he relayed to me, and I often have occasion to remember. I honor her here.

As a non-Chinese, and a non-Chinese-speaker, I was reminded on a daily basis of my own limitations, and of the fact that I was ultimately a guest in a culture that was not my own. I would not have been able to write this book without the unflagging assistance of interpreters, who helped me navigate interviews in Cantonese, Mandarin, and Fujianese and provided a crash course in appropriate custom and etiquette. Many thanks to Fei Mei Chan and Lily Lau in New York, and to Sammi Yuan and Jinhua Zhang in China.

At *The New Yorker,* I owe a great debt to Daniel Zalewski, for assigning the original article about Sister Ping, along with David Remnick, Dorothy Wickenden, Emily Eaken, and Raffi Khatchadourian. Thanks also, and especially, to Andrea Thompson. At *Slate,* I'd like to thank Jacob Weisberg and June Thomas for running a three-part series based on my trip to Fuzhou.

I am extraordinarily lucky to have found an editor with the cool, precise mind and affable, unflappable manner of Bill Thomas. From our first conversation, working with Bill has been a pleasure and an education. At Doubleday I'm also grateful to Melissa Danaczko, Nicole Dewey, Emily Mahon, and Rachel Lapal. As ever, I feel profound gratitude to the peerless Tina Bennett, agent, advocate, and friend, who more or less exhausts positive superlatives. Thanks also to Svetlana Katz, Cecile Barendsma, and everyone else at Janklow & Nesbit. A tip of the hat as well to Howie Sanders at UTA, who has been a supporter of this project from our first conversation about it in 2005, and also to Jason Burns.

On the occasion of the Picador edition of this book, I would also like to express my abundant gratitude to my wonderful British editor Ravi Mirchandani, and to Roshani Moorjani, who shepherded this book through publication with her customary passion and care. Thanks also to Kate Green, Siobhan Slattery, and the whole brilliant gang at Picador, and to my dazzling foreign rights team, Karolina Sutton, Helen Manders, and Peppa Mignone.

A good portion of the research for *The Snakehead* was made possible by a fellowship from the John Simon Guggenheim Memorial Foundation, and I am deeply indebted to Edward Hirsh and everyone else at the foundation for affording me that remarkable opportunity.

Michael Auerbach, Michael Hanna, Carl Robichaud, Tim Riemann, Marisa Pearl, Nat Kreamer, Melanie Rehak, Jean Strouse, Craig Winters, Milosz Gudzowski, Danielle Lurie, Daniel Squadron, and Sai Sriskandarajah all helped in ways large and small. Thanks to Linda Barth and her ESL students at Lower East Side Prep, who studied the original Sister Ping article and helped me see the story with fresh eyes. Thanks also to SCSW, albeit in absentia, for supplying an Allen Street anecdote, and for much else besides.

As ever, I'm humbled by the debt I owe to my parents, Jennifer Radden and Frank Keefe, who read through numerous early drafts and offered astute advice. My brother, Tristram, and my sister, Beatrice, are both writers themselves, and on an almost daily basis I turn to one or the other of them for guidance, advice, or inspiration. Thanks also, of course, to Mr. Chopes.

But most of all, this is for Justyna. From the beginning she has supported my decision to waste a perfectly good legal education and devote myself to writing instead—indeed, it was practically her idea. We were married about a year after I started spending time in Chinatown, and she sacrificed an overdue vacation for a research trip to Thailand. (When I brightly suggested that she look up the charming resort of Pattaya in her guidebook, she flipped to the relevant page and read aloud, "A haven for sex tourists, long blighted by overdevelopment . . .") Justyna read the book as it was being written, in thousand-word installments, and has lived with the story for three long years. *The Snakehead* is dedicated to her.

A Note on Sources

THIS BOOK is primarily based on over three hundred interviews conducted between 2005 and 2008 with FBI agents, police officers, immigration investigators, attorneys, White House officials, *Golden Venture* passengers, Chinatown residents and community leaders, and individuals who have worked in the snakehead trade. I also made substantial use of thousands of pages of court transcripts from numerous trials, internal government documents obtained through the Freedom of Information Act, and the records from law enforcement wiretaps and interviews with various criminal suspects.

The vast majority of the people who spoke with me for the book agreed to do so on the record, but in a handful of cases individuals who are still working in government and were speaking without official authorization, or who feared some form of retribution if they spoke with me and then were cited by name, requested that I preserve their anonymity.

No dialogue or scenes are invented, and I have adhered faithfully to the chronology of the events as they actually occurred. If a line is rendered in quotation marks, it is drawn from either a court or a wiretap transcript, or from the recollection of an individual who was present when the words were spoken; in the occasional instances when I attribute thoughts to characters, I do so because they expressed those thoughts either to me or to some other interviewer or during a trial, or because they conveyed the thoughts to someone else with whom I have subsequently spoken.

In many instances the events in the narrative unfolded more than a decade before my conversations with those who went through them, and throughout my reporting I endeavored to correct for the little distortions that our fallible memories can occasionally introduce. Most of the major sources were interviewed multiple times, and wherever possible I tried to corroborate one source's memory of an event with the recollections of another source who experienced it as well. I was also fortunate to uncover vast reams of transcripts and interviews and incident reports in which various people expressed their memories of events on paper mere weeks or even hours after the events unfolded.

Access inevitably drives narrative in any heavily reported piece of writing, and I should note here that if Immigration and Customs Enforcement had been as accommodating in providing me with access as the FBI, the DA's office, and the NYPD were, the book would have balanced the close focus on the investigation of the FBI with an examination of the important work done by the INS and ICE. While ICE did offer some cooperation, that cooperation was both grudging and limited. As a consequence I was obliged to track down former INS officials and current ICE employees who would speak to me only anonymously because they were doing so without authorization. This system worked well enough, and once word got out that I was pursuing the project, people who had worked on Chinese smuggling over the years had a way of emerging from the woodwork and finding me. But I'm keenly aware that for the many law enforcement officials who actually lived and worked these cases, there will be certain glaring lacunae in this book. If the names of some individuals who did their jobs with dedication and valor are not mentioned here, it is largely because ICE, for whatever reasons of its own, did not want this story to be told.

In the summer of 2008, Sister Ping agreed to meet me for an interview, but despite my best efforts and those of her attorney, Scott Tulman, we were unable to persuade the warden at FCI Danbury to allow me to enter the prison for a face-to-face meeting. (The warden's rationale, if you can call it that, was that such a visit might jeopardize the "security situation" at the facility.) As an alternative, Sister Ping agreed to an exchange of written questions and answers, from which I have drawn extensively in the book.

Finally, despite the considerable original reporting that forms the heart of this account, I would not have been able to undertake the project without the groundbreaking work of a number of journalists and academics who have written extensively on the subjects of human smuggling, asylum and immigration law, transnational organized crime, and the history of the Chinese in America. I would like to gratefully acknowledge the work of these individuals, whose particular articles, books, and documentary films are cited fully in the notes that follow.

Notes

CHAPTER 1: PILGRIMS

Apart from interviews with individuals who were on the beach at Rockaway on June 6, 1993, and press accounts of the events in question, this chapter is based primarily on an extensive trove of criminal incident reports filled out by a dozen members of the United States Park Police who took part in the rescue. I obtained these handwritten reports through a Freedom of Information Act request, and in painstaking detail the officers set forth the story of what happened, from the first radio call at 1:46 A.M. until the last of the passengers had left the beach. Because these reports were written within days, and sometimes hours, of the events in question, they have a vivid immediacy and accuracy that are not always possible to achieve through interviews conducted with individuals today, who are recalling events that took place fifteen years ago. Another valuable source in creating the narrative account of events was a large archive of raw footage taken both at the beach and in the triage stations at Floyd Bennett Field by camera crews for *CBS Evening News*.

3 **Dating back to the War of 1812:** The earliest recorded military fortification to be built on the peninsula was known as a "blockhouse" and was constructed during the War of 1812. Fort Tilden was formally established in 1917. On the various installations at Fort Tilden, see Corey Kilgannon, "To the Battlements, and Take Sunscreen: The Joys of Fort Tilden," *New York Times*, July 21, 2006.

3 **"Rockaway" derives from:** Henry Isham Hazelton, *The Boroughs of Brooklyn and Queens, Counties of Nassau and Suffolk, Long Island, New York, 1609–1924*, Vol. 1 (New York: Lewis Historical Publishing, 1925), p. 1011.

3 **At a quarter to two:** Where not otherwise indicated, the account of Divivier's and Somma's involvement in the rescue is drawn from supplemental criminal incident reports filed with the United States Park Police by Steven Divivier and David Somma on June 7, 1993, and June 19, 1993.

4 **At thirty, Divivier:** Kevin McLaughlin and Bill Hoffman, "Chilling Screams Alerted 1st Rescuers," *New York Post*, June 7, 1993; Patrice O'Shaughnessy, "News Honors Cops' Venture," *New York Daily News*, September 27, 1993.

4 **At 98.5 percent white:** David M. Herszenhorn, "Breezy Point, Queens—

Bounded by Gates, Over a Toll Bridge," *New York Times,* June 18, 2001.

4 **The Breezy Point police force:** Elaine Sciolino, "A Cooperative on the Beach Loves Privacy," *New York Times,* September 10, 1984.

4 **To Somma they sounded desperate:** Jim Dwyer, "Desperate Hours," *Newsday,* June 7, 1993; Charles Hirshberg, "Folded Dreams," *Life,* July 1996.

5 **Realizing that they couldn't do the rescue:** McLaughlin and Hoffman, "Chilling Screams Alerted 1st Rescuers."

5 **Charlie Wells, a tall:** Unless otherwise noted, the account of Charles Wells's experience of the rescue is drawn from an interview with Wells on February 22, 2007.

6 **Three off-duty Park Service officers:** Supplemental criminal incident reports filed with the U.S. Park Police by Steven Divivier and David Somma on June 7, 1993, and June 19, 1993.

7 **They flung their arms:** Supplemental criminal incident report, P.O. B. Smith, June 30, 1993.

7 **The men relied on their flashlights:** Supplemental criminal incident report, P. Broderick, June 20, 1993.

7 **But the flashlights began:** Supplemental criminal incident report, Sgt. J. A. Lauro, November 5, 1993.

7 **"We entered the water":** Supplemental criminal incident report, P. Broderick, June 20, 1993.

7 **Those who were too tired:** Details in this paragraph are drawn from supplemental criminal incident report, P.O. M. Lanfranchi, June 19, 1993.

8 **"like a plane crash":** "Freighter Runs Aground with Human Cargo," United Press International, June 6, 1993.

8 **A heavyset Coast Guard pilot:** Unless otherwise noted, all material pertaining to Bill Mundy's role in the rescue is drawn from an interview with Bill Mundy, December 7, 2005.

9 **The chopper's spotlight searched:** Archival news footage, *CBS Sunday Morning,* June 6, 1993.

10 **Before long three Coast Guard boats:** Supplemental criminal incident report, Clay Rice, June 6, 1993.

10 **But just as they approached:** Supplementary case incident report, P.O. G. Arthur, July 28, 1993.

12 **A dozen boats:** Supplemental criminal incident report, Detective William Stray, June 9, 1993.

12 **Most of the survivors:** Archival news footage, *CBS Evening News,* June 7, 1993.

12 **Rescue workers unloaded:** Malcolm Gladwell and Rachel E. Stassen-Berger, "Alien-Smuggling Ship Runs Aground," *Washington Post,* June 7, 1993.

12 **Somma approached the man:** Transcript of an interview with David Somma and Steven Divivier, *Dateline NBC* with Tom Brokaw, August 3, 2001.

13 **Ray Kelly, the short:** *CBS Evening News* footage, June 6, 1993.

13 **Kelly was stunned:** Interview with Ray Kelly, January 6, 2006.

13 **The local and national media:** *CBS Evening News* footage, June 6, 1993.

13 **"These are people who":** Ibid.

13 **It was there that:** Unless otherwise noted, all details relating to Dougie Lee and his experience during the rescue are drawn from an interview with Dougie Lee on February 10, 2006.

14 **There were a few women:** The blankets, the triage tags, and other details of the physical surroundings are drawn from *CBS Evening News* footage, June 6, 1993, and June 7, 1993.

14 **The other officers standing watch:** Richard Pyle, "Ship Carrying Chinese

Aliens Runs Aground Off NYC; at Least Seven Dead," Associated Press, June 6, 1993.

14 **They were desperate:** Diana Jean Schemo, "On the Ship; Survivors Tell of Voyage of Little Daylight, Little Food and Only Hope," *New York Times,* June 7, 2003.

14 **Fearful of tuberculosis:** *CBS Evening News* footage, June 7, 1993.

15 **Many of the survivors:** Ibid.

16 **A team of officers:** These details are drawn from video footage taken by the officers who boarded the ship on the morning of June 6.

16 **"Slippers, purses, money":** Malcolm Gladwell and Rachel E. Stassen-Berger, "Courts Log Tragic Seagoing Saga," *Washington Post,* June 8, 1993.

16 **Working with translators:** Unless otherwise noted, details relating to the interrogation of Amir Tobing are drawn from supplemental criminal incident reports, D. Hecimovic, June 7, 1993, and Edward M. Riepe, June 7, 1993.

17 **In total:** While Kin Sin Lee and Captain Tobing had boarded the *Golden Venture* earlier, the first passengers did not go aboard until February 14, 1993. So for those passengers, the voyage to Rockaway lasted 114 days. The voyage of the Mayflower took 65 days; Nathaniel Philbrick, *Mayflower: A Story of Courage, Community, and War* (New York: Viking, 2006), p. 3.

18 **Before the Chinese boarded:** *CBS Evening News* footage, June 7, 1993.

18 **All that remained on the beach:** Dwyer, "Desperate Hours," *Newsday,* June 7, 1993.

18 **All this jetsam:** *CBS Evening News* footage, June 6, 1993.

18 **The initial count was eight:** Joseph W. Queen, "Drowning Cause of Death for Six Victims," *Newsday,* June 8, 1993.

18 **Along with the bodies of the two cardiac arrest victims:** Ian Fisher, "Waves of Panic Yield to Elation of Refugees," *New York Times,* June 7, 1993.

18 **In the coming weeks:** Detail about the clam dredgers is from an interview with Charles Wells, February 22, 2007.

18 **Little was known about:** supplemental criminal incident report, unsigned, June 16, 1993.

18 **Four of the bodies were:** "Fear and Intimidation Slow Identification of Six Bodies," *New York Times,* September 5, 1993.

19 **Word spread in the neighborhood:** Chris Dobson, "Community Buries Six Unidentified *Golden Venture* Victims," *South China Morning Post,* March 20, 1994. Following the burial, the *New York Times* interviewed a number of the passengers from the *Golden Venture,* who were by then being detained, and learned the identities of the dead—which the passengers knew, but the authorities had not thought to ask. Ashley Dunn, "Nameless Dead in Sea Tragedy Now Identified," *New York Times,* March 31, 1994.

19 **Of the survivors:** Supplemental criminal incident report, Edward M. Riepe, June 7, 1993.

19 **The facility had only:** Vivienne Walt, "Aliens at the Gate," *Newsday,* November 29, 1993.

19 **The *New York Times* alone:** Seth Faison, *South of the Clouds* (New York: St. Martin's, 2004), p. 116.

19 **The man who stepped:** Unless otherwise noted, material on Bill Slattery is drawn from an interview with Bill Slattery on July 7, 2008.

19 **He was extremely ambitious:** Interview with James Goldman, formerly of the INS, May 23, 2007.

19 **"This is the twenty-fourth ship":** *CBS Sunday Evening News,* June 6, 1993.

19 **In the past nine months alone:**

Gladwell and Stassen-Berger, "Courts Log Tragic Seagoing Saga."

20 **The fee to reach America**: During the 1980s the standard fee was $18,000; by 1993 it had risen to $35,000; today it is often as high as $70,000. Interview with Special Agent Bill McMurry and Supervisory Special Agent Konrad Motyka of the FBI, December 15, 2005. (These figures are generally accepted by law enforcement, academics, and members of the Fujianese community I spoke with both in New York City's Chinatown and in Fujian Province, China.)

20 **Strictly speaking, this was**: The distinction between human smuggling and human trafficking is vexing in large part because questions of what constitutes coercion, deception, free will, and exploitation become difficult to resolve in many particular instances. In my conversations with immigration advocates and anti-trafficking experts, I sometimes got the impression that there is an almost willful muddying of the categories, in part because it may seem easier to rouse the indignation of jaded donors and members of the press with suggestions that *all* smuggled and trafficked individuals are being subjected to a contemporary form of slavery. I can see how this might be a useful strategy, but from an analytical point of view it is deeply counterproductive. The fact that individuals are trafficked in great numbers for sex or forced labor is a devastating phenomenon. But human smuggling of labor migrants is also a widespread phenomenon, and a different one: these migrants tend to know what they are getting themselves into, and to suggest that they are exploited in the same manner that teenaged sex workers from Cambodia or Moldova are, or that they are in any meaningful sense "slaves," is to overlook the free will they are exercising in volunteering for the risks of the journey and the debts they will owe upon arrival. On the categorical distinction, see U.S. Department of State, "Fact Sheet: Distinctions Between Human Smuggling and Human Trafficking," January 1, 2005; Brian Iselin and Melanie Adams, "Distinguishing Between Human Trafficking and People Smuggling," United Nations Office of Drugs and Crime, April 10, 2003.

20 **"In effect, slavery here in the U.S."**: *ABC World News Sunday*, Bill Blakemore reporting, June 6, 1993.

20 **Several miles away**: Details from this scene are derived from Weng Yu Hui's testimony in Sister Ping's extradition proceedings in Hong Kong in 2000. See Vicki Kwong and Chow Chung-Yan, "Sister Ping's 'Bad Luck Fears,'" *South China Morning Post*, August 22, 2000.

21 **She had helped arrange**: The fact that one of the dead was a passenger of Sister Ping's is from an interview with Deirdre Gordon and Martin Ficke of Immigration and Customs Enforcement, March 29, 2006.

CHAPTER 2: LEAVING FUJIAN

This chapter is based primarily on Sister Ping's written responses to my interview questions, on her remarks at the sentencing hearing in her trial, and on research and interviews conducted on trips to Hong Kong in March 2007 and February 2008 and to Fujian Province in February 2008. In addition, I relied on the scholarly work of several academics who have written about Chinatowns, the Fujianese, the snakehead trade, and Chinese migration, in particular Peter Kwong and Dušanka Miščević, Ko-lin Chin, Mette Thunø, Zai Liang, and Wenzhen Ye.

22 **No one knows precisely**: On the numbers of overseas Chinese, see

Dudley L. Poston, Jr., Michael Xinxiang Mao, and Mei-Yu Yu, "The Global Distribution of the Overseas Chinese Around 1990," *Population Development Review* 20, no. 3 (September 1994); Cheng Xi, "The 'Distinctiveness' of the Overseas Chinese as Perceived in the People's Republic of China," in Mette Thunø, ed., *Beyond Chinatown: New Chinese Migration and the Global Expansion of China* (Copenhagen: Nordic Institute of Asian Societies, 2007), p. 50. Part of the difficulty in sorting out these numbers is determining who to count—whether sojourners, settlers, the assimilated, the unassimilated. See also Thomas Sowell, *Migrations and Cultures: A World View* (New York: HarperCollins, 1996), p. 180.

22 **America no doubt saw**: The first documented instances of Chinese in North America were in the eighteenth century, though it has also been suggested that some came before that. See Sowell, *Migrations and Cultures,* p. 220. The "beaten into a different shape" quote is from Owen Cochran Coy, *Gold Days* (Los Angeles: Powell, 1919), p. 344.

22 **China was in a state of upheaval**: See Jack Beeching, *The Chinese Opium Wars* (New York: Harcourt, 1975).

23 **At that time America**: Iris Chang, *The Chinese in America: A Narrative History* (New York: Viking, 2003), p. 20.

23 **Young Chinese men began**: Martin Booth, *The Dragon Syndicates: The Global Phenomenon of the Triads* (New York: Basic Books, 2001), pp. 296–97.

23 **But for all their numbers**: Peter Kwong and Dusanka Miščevič, *Chinese America: The Untold Story of America's Oldest New Community* (New York: New Press, 2005), pp. 19–20. (Kwong and Miščević suggest that 3,000 square kilometers is roughly half the size of Rhode Island. It's actually more than that.)

23 **By 1867, nearly 70 percent**: Booth, *The Dragon Syndicates,* p. 296.

23 **Charlie Crocker**: Chang, *The Chinese in America,* pp. 56–57.

23 **Over a thousand**: Ibid., pp. 63–64.

23 **When the Civil War ended**: Kwong and Miščević, *Chinese America,* p. 61.

24 **The demand for Chinese laborers**: Booth, *The Dragon Syndicates,* pp. 296–97. On the origins, history, and current role of the triads and their role in Chinese migration both in the nineteenth century and today, see Yiu Kong Chu, *The Triads as Business* (New York: Routledge, 2000).

24 **Penniless gold rushers**: Kwong and Miščević, *Chinese America,* p. 36.

24 **Once they arrived**: Ibid., pp. 76–77.

25 **"In San Francisco"**: Mark Twain, *Roughing It* (Mineola, NY: Dover, 2003 [1872]), p. 208.

25 **Bloody anti-Chinese purges**: See Jean Pfaelzer, *Driven Out: The Forgotten War Against Chinese Americans* (New York: Random House, 2007).

25 **The law, which strictly**: There had been smaller, state-based limitations on immigration before, often barring paupers, lepers, prostitutes, and the like.

25 **In 1887, one Chinese laborer**: See Chae Chan Ping v. United States, 130 U.S. 581 (1889).

25 **In 1891 the United States**: The position was established in the Act of March 3, 1891 (26 Stat. 1084; U.S.C. 101). See Michael C. LeMay and Elliott Robert Barkan, eds., *U.S. Immigration and Naturalization Laws and Issues: A Documentary History* (Westport, CT: Greenwood, 1999), p. 66. On Ellis Island, see p. 44.

26 **By 1920 fully half**: Sowell, *Migrations and Cultures,* pp. 224–25.

26 **But when Japan attacked**: Kwong and Miščević, *Chinese America,* pp. 202–3.

26 **In the 1950s:** See Tiejun Cheng and Mark Seldon, "The Origins and Social Consequences of China's Houkou System," *China Quarterly,* no. 139 (September 1994).

26 **Sister Ping was born:** Unless otherwise noted, biographical material related to Sister Ping is drawn from written responses from Sister Ping, July 2008. The description of Shengmei is drawn from my visit to the village in February 2008 and from conversations in Fujian Province with people who remember what the village was like in earlier times.

27 **The result was severe food shortages:** Details relating to Mao and the Great Leap Forward are from Jung Chang and Jon Halliday, *Mao: The Unknown Story* (New York: Anchor, 2006), pp. 430–31.

27 **While she was still:** Written response from Sister Ping.

28 **When she was a teenager:** The fact that the Cultural Revolution coincided with Sister Ping's high school years is from a written response from Sister Ping. The fact that schools in the area closed is from the testimony of Weng Yu Hui in United States v. Cheng Chui Ping, aka "Sister Ping," 94 CR 953 (hereafter Weng Yu Hui testimony, Sister Ping trial). Weng came from a village close to Sister Ping's.

28 **Schools and universities:** For a fascinating first-person account of the Cultural Revolution as it played out in Fujian Province for young students like Sister Ping, see Ken Ling, *The Revenge of Heaven* (New York: Ballantine, 1972). These details are drawn from Ling's book.

29 **"That was the trend":** Written response from Sister Ping.

29 **Mao had always been suspicious:** See Chang and Halliday, *Mao,* pp. 94–108.

29 **In the thirteenth century:** Manuel Komroff, ed., *The Travels of Marco Polo* (New York: Norton, 2003), pp. 252–53.

29 **According to legend:** Sterling Seagrave, *Lords of the Rim* (London: Corgi, 1995), pp. 103–7. Accounts of Zheng He's height and the extent of his fleet may be fanciful, but the admiral did indeed exist. He was a Muslim and a eunuch, and a great monument commemorating him stands by the banks of the Min River in Changle today. See Louise Levathes, *When China Ruled the Seas: The Treasure Fleet of the Dragon Throne, 1405–1433* (New York: Simon & Schuster, 1994.) Accounts of just how far Zheng He ventured in the fifteenth century vary, and have been the subject of some recent controversy. See Jack Hitt, "Goodbye, Columbus!" *New York Times Magazine,* January 5, 2003.

29 **By the 1570s:** Thunø, *Beyond Chinatown,* p. 14.

29 **Eighty percent of the Chinese:** Zai Liang and Wenzhen Ye, "From Fujian to New York: Understanding the New Chinese Immigration," in David Kyle and Rey Koslowski, eds., *Global Human Smuggling: Comparative Perspectives* (Baltimore: Johns Hopkins University Press, 2001), p. 193.

30 **Well over a million Chinese:** Kolin Chin, *Smuggled Chinese: Clandestine Immigration to the United States* (Philadelphia: Temple University Press, 1999), p. 13.

30 **It was from Fujian:** Wenzhou, in neighboring Zhejiang Province, was also a source of migrants, more so to Europe in the early years, but increasingly to the United States as well.

30 **In fact, even *Fujian*:** Chin, *Smuggled Chinese,* p. 11.

30 **In New York's Little Italy:** See John S. MacDonald and Leatrice D. MacDonald, "Chain Migration, Ethnic Neighborhood Formation, and Social

Networks," *Milbank Memorial Fund Quarterly* 42 (1964).

31 **Demographers call this:** Ibid.

31 **A more evocative Fujianese expression:** Jason Blatt, "Recent Trends in the Smuggling of Chinese into the United States," unpublished paper, May 2007.

31 **Moreover, everywhere the Fujianese went:** For the role of the overseas Chinese as "market dominant minorities," see Amy Chua, *World on Fire* (New York: Doubleday, 2003), chap. 1.

31 **More than half of Asia's forty billionaires:** Alex Tizon, "The Rush to 'Gold Mountain,' " *Seattle Times,* April 16, 2000.

32 **For generations of Fujianese men:** Confidential interview with the son of a Fujianese ship jumper in Chinatown, New York.

32 **During the 1960s:** Written response from Sister Ping.

32 **Cheng Chai Leung worked:** Ibid.

32 **Eventually he slipped up:** Undated internal INS document, "Progress Reports, 'Operation Hester,' " by Special Agent Edmund Bourke, Anti-Smuggling Unit, New York (hereafter ASU NY).

32 **According to authorities:** Internal INS document, "Alien Smuggling Task Force Proposal," Anti-Smuggling Unit memo, October 31, 1985. That Sister Ping's father was a snakehead himself was confirmed by Konrad Motyka and Bill McMurry of the FBI, at an interview on December 15, 2005.

33 **Historical records indicate:** Zai Liang, "Demography of Illicit Emigration from China: A Sending Country's Perspective," *Sociological Forum* 16, no. 4 (December 2001), citing Yaohua Wang, *An Overview of Fujianese Culture* (Fuzhou: Fujian Education, 1994), p. 15.

33 **The Fujianese were originally known:** Peter Kwong, *Forbidden Workers: Illegal Chinese Immigrants and American Labor* (New York: New Press, 1997), p. 23.

33 **When emigrants slither through:** Testimony of Guo Liang Qi, aka "Ah Kay," in United States v. Cheng Chui Ping, aka "Sister Ping," 94 CR 953 (hereafter Ah Kay testimony, Sister Ping trial).

34 **The poorest provinces:** Thunø, "Beyond Chinatown," p. 6.

34 **So, ironically, economic development:** See Jack A. Goldstone, "A Tsunami on the Horizon? The Potential for International Migration," in Paul J. Smith, ed., *Human Smuggling: Chinese Migrant Trafficking and the Challenge to America's Immigration Tradition* (Washington, D.C.: Center for Strategic and International Studies, 1997).

34 **Some did better:** Liang, "Demography of Illicit Emigration from China."

34 **For this frustrated:** The figure on high school completion is from Susan Sachs, "Fujian, U.S.A.," *New York Times,* July 22, 2001.

34 **Fantastical stories abounded:** Liang, "Demography of Illicit Emigration from China"; Chin, *Smuggled Chinese,* p. 25.

35 **"Here, they're working like slaves":** Interview with Justin Yu, formerly of the *World Journal*, now president of the Chinese Consolidated Benevolent Association, January 4, 2006.

35 **Sister Ping believed:** Testimony of Cheng Chui Ping during the sentencing hearing in United States v. Cheng Chui Ping, aka "Sister Ping," 94 CR 953 (hereafter Sister Ping sentencing remarks).

35 **In high school she had met:** Written response from Sister Ping. The physical description of Cheung Yick Tak is based on my observation of him in numerous encounters at the courthouse

and in the family's restaurant at 47 East Broadway.

35 **Many Fujianese were fleeing:** Kwong, *Forbidden Workers,* p. 29.

35 **Sister Ping and her family:** Written response from Sister Ping. The building was the Kwan Yik Building, Phase 2, Sai Ying Pun, Des Voeux Road West 343. It was built in 1977.

36 **It is not clear how Sister Ping:** The address of the shop comes from an interview with Philip Lam on March 28, 2008. He was a patron when he lived in Hong Kong.

36 **The Cantonese majority:** See Gregory E. Guldin, "Little Fujian (Fukien): Sub-Neighborhood and Community in North Point, Hong Kong," *Journal of the Hong Kong Branch of the Royal Asiatic Society,* no. 17 (1977).

36 **Sister Ping catered to:** Written response from Sister Ping.

36 **Better to be in front of a chicken:** Confidential interview with a Fujianese contemporary of Sister Ping's from Chinatown.

36 **In 1979 she opened:** Written response from Sister Ping.

36 **University students and scholars:** Liang, "Demography of Illicit Emigration from China."

36 **Chinese census bureau figures:** Ibid.

36 **"Every man in the town":** Interview with Steven Gleit, November 11, 2007.

37 **Sister Ping's husband, Yick Tak:** Written response from Sister Ping.

37 **One day in June 1981:** This episode, including quotes, is drawn from Sister Ping sentencing remarks.

CHAPTER 3: EIGHTEEN-THOUSAND-DOLLAR WOMAN

This chapter draws primarily on written responses from Sister Ping in July 2008, the trial testimony of Sister Ping's former customer and associate Weng Yu Hui, and a series of internal INS documents related to Operation Hester, the first investigation of the Cheng family's smuggling activities.

38 **Several months after her meeting:** The details of Sister Ping's initial entry to the United States are from a confidential interview with a current employee of Immigration and Customs Enforcement (ICE), who consulted Sister Ping's file.

38 **"The reason most Fujianese":** Confidential interview with a Fujianese contemporary of Sister Ping's who moved from Hong Kong to New York at roughly the same time.

38 **As soon as she had arrived:** Confidential ICE interview, corroborated by written response from Sister Ping.

39 **The complex was known:** For a terrific account of the history of Knickerbocker Village, see Phillip Lopate, *Waterfront: A Walk Around Manhattan* (New York: Anchor, 2005).

39 **Sister Ping liked New York:** Unless otherwise noted, all of this material is drawn from written responses from Sister Ping.

39 **When they applied:** Ying Chan and James Dao, "Merchants of Misery," *New York Daily News,* September 24, 1990.

39 **The shop next door:** Sister Ping sentencing remarks.

40 **During the slow daytime hours:** See Jane H. Li, "The Chinese Menu Guys," *New York Times,* July 28, 1996. For an empathetic and realistic look at the lives of undocumented restaurant workers and deliverymen, see Sean Baker and Shih-Ching Tsou's film *Take Out* (CAVU Pictures, 2008).

40 **The famous Fujianese entrepreneurialism:** Peter Kwong, *The New Chinatown,* rev. ed. (New York: Hill and Wang, 1996), p. 180.

40 **Employment agencies:** Ibid., p. 178.
41 **In 1960 there were:** Kwong, *The New Chinatown,* p. 4.
41 **Chinatown residents began:** Kwong and Miščevič, *Chinese America,* p. 329.
42 **The criminologist Ko-lin Chin:** Amy Zimmer, "Journey to the Golden Mountain," *City Limits,* January 1, 2004.
42 **The Fujianese called them:** See Elisabeth Rosenthal, "Chinese Town's Main Export: Its Young Men," *New York Times,* June 26, 2000.
42 **Before long this reverse migration:** See Patrick Radden Keefe, "Little America," *Slate,* April 9, 2008; also see Somini Sengupta, "Squeezed by Debt and Time, Mothers Ship Babies to China," *New York Times,* September 14, 1999.
42 **By working long hours:** Chin, *Smuggled Chinese,* p. 119.
42 **After six, or often:** Kwong, *The New Chinatown,* p. 180.
43 **As often as not, they would end up:** Interview with Philip Lam, November 9, 2005. Lam knew Sister Ping during these years, frequented her shop, and rented an apartment from her for a time. She often encouraged him to learn English. On the endlessly complex subject of *guanxi* a great deal has been written, much of it geared to Western businesspeople endeavoring to make sense of corporate culture in China. See, for instance, Frederick Balfour, "You Say *Guanxi,* I Say Schmoozing," *BusinessWeek,* November 10, 2007; and Ying Lun So and Anthony Walker, *Explaining Guanxi: The Chinese Business Network* (New York: Routledge, 2006). For a more sociological approach, see Thomas Gold, Doug Guthrie, and David L. Wank, eds., *Social Connections in China: Institutions, Culture, and the Changing Nature of Guanxi* (Cambridge: Cambridge University Press, 2002). On the role that *guanxi* played in a recent smuggling case in the city of Xiamen in southern Fujian Province, see Simone Menshausen, "Corruption, Smuggling and Guanxi in Xiamen, China," Internet Center for Corruption Research, August 2005.
43 **Local Fujianese began:** Edward Barnes, "Two-Faced Woman," *Time,* July 31, 2000.
44 **In 1984 a young man:** Unless otherwise noted, the account of Sister Ping smuggling Weng Yu Hui to the United States is drawn from Weng Yu Hui testimony, Sister Ping trial.
45 **Snakeheads occasionally refer:** Testimony of "Mr. Lee" (pseudonym), in "Asian Organized Crime," hearing before the Permanent Subcommittee on Investigations of the United States Senate, October 3, November 5–6, 1991 (Washington: Government Printing Office, 1992), p. 385.
47 **The immigrant was thus indentured:** Bill McMurry of the FBI made this observation to me on October 31, 2005.
47 **Western Union charged:** Interview with Steven Wong, of the Lin Zexu Foundation, November 11, 2005; interview with Justin Yu, January 4, 2006; interviews with Konrad Motyka and Bill McMurry, October 31, 2005, and December 15, 2005.
45 **Along the border between Mexico:** INS, "Alien Smuggling Task Force Proposal."
47 **The Fujianese city of Changle:** This figure is drawn from a Chinese-language study by Zhu Meirong of the Fujian Provincial Government's Development Research Center, "Analysis of Fujian Provincial New-Migration Issues and the First Inquiry into Relative Policy," *Population Research* (China) 5, no.

5 (September 2001). The study is cited in Blatt, "Recent Trends in the Smuggling of Chinese."

48 **Drawing on the connections**: Details of Sister Ping's underground banking business are drawn from multiple interviews with Bill McMurry and Konrad Motyka at the FBI and with Chinatown residents who either patronized or were familiar with the service. In addition, both Weng Yu Hui and Ah Kay furnished information about the dynamics of the business at trial. Sister Ping's lawyer Larry Hochheiser would eventually claim that the extent of her crimes was running an unlicensed money transfer service, thereby appearing to concede the truth of that particular allegation against her. But for her part, Sister Ping refused, on the advice of her new lawyer, Scott Tulman, to answer any of my questions about her banking operation.

48 **Various underground banking systems**: See William L. Cassidy, "Fei-Chien, or Flying Money: A Study of Chinese Underground Banking," address at the 12th Annual International Asian Organized Crime Conference, June 26, 1990; Jacques Gernet, *A History of Chinese Civilization* (Cambridge: Cambridge University Press, 1996), p. 325.

48 **"Sister Ping keeps stores"**: Written declaration of FBI Special Agent Peter Lee in a sealed federal criminal complaint against Cheng Chui Ping and Cheng Yick Tak, Southern District of New York, December 1994.

48 **Once Weng Yu Hui**: Weng Yu Hui testimony, Sister Ping trial.

49 **"Her clients are extremely"**: Sheldon X. Zhang, *Chinese Human Smuggling Organizations: Families, Social Networks, and Cultural Imperatives* (Stanford: Stanford University Press, 2008), p. 36.

49 **Soon the Bank of China**: Interviews with Steven Wong, November 11, 2005; interview with Justin Yu, January 4, 2006.

49 **According to the Fujian Statistical Bureau**: Liang, "Demography of Illicit Emigration from China." It should be noted that overseas investment from other countries, like Taiwan, and an array of foreign direct investment that would not be considered remittances are also reflected in those numbers.

49 **But it was rumored**: Interview with Dougie Lee, February 10, 2006.

50 **Weng would go in**: Weng Yu Hui testimony, Sister Ping trial.

50 **They diversified, opening**: Written declaration of Special Agent Peter Lee.

50 **In the waterfront neighborhood**: Konrad Motyka and Bill McMurry first told me about the poultry business, though they did not know precisely where it was. Several people in Chinatown told me that it was in Red Hook. As it happens, there are several poultry slaughterhouses in Red Hook. One of them occupies a small space on Columbia Street and specializes in live chickens, roosters, ducks, and rabbits. Its name is Yeung Sun—the same name as Sister Ping's restaurant at 47 East Broadway.

50 **They continued to operate**: Chan and Dao, "Merchants of Misery."

50 **In the early 1980s**: Prepared testimony of Willard H. Myers III, Center for the Study of Asian Organized Crime, hearing on "The Growing Threat of International Organized Crime," before the House Judiciary Committee, Subcommittee on Crime, January 25, 1996; "Assault on the Dollar," *Asia, Inc.*, February 1995; "Asian Organized Crime," p. 51; interview with James Goldman, May 23, 2007.

51 **The law created**: Weng Yu Hui testimony, Sister Ping trial. (Weng

availed himself of the amnesty, though he had not arrived in the United States until 1984); Willard H. Myers III, "Of Qinqing, Qinshu, Guanxi, and Shetou," in Smith, *Human Smuggling*.

51 **On her visits to Fuzhou**: Chan and Dao, "Merchants of Misery."

51 **The main thoroughfare in the village**: Pamela Burdman, "Back Home in China, Smugglers Are Revered, Feared," *San Francisco Chronicle,* November 19, 1993.

51 **The Chinese state**: Thunø, "Beyond Chinatown," p. 13.

51 **It was an appellation**: Burdman, "Back Home in China."

52 **When Fujianese villagers**: Kwong, *Forbidden Workers,* p. 96.

52 **As the remittance money**: See John Pomfret, "Smuggled Chinese Enrich Homeland, Gangs," *Washington Post,* January 24, 1999. I have visited these houses; they are extraordinarily ostentatious and gaudy, and they tower over even the tiniest villages outside Fuzhou. See Keefe, "Little America."

52 **In the fall of 1983**: Interview with James Goldman, May 23, 2007. Also see Chan and Dao, "Merchants of Misery."

52 **Several years later Frankie Wong**: Interview with James Goldman, May 23, 2007; Dennis Hevesi, "Two Are Slain as a Gang Opens Fire in a Chinatown Gambling Parlor," *New York Times,* November 5, 1987.

53 **One day in February 1985**: Unless otherwise noted, material on the Operation Hester investigation is drawn from an interview with Joe Occhipinti, former chief of the Anti-Smuggling Unit at the INS in New York, who ran the operation, August 3, 2007. Also INS, "Progress Reports, 'Operation Hester.'" The description of the charts is drawn from photographs of the charts shown to me by Joe Occhipinti.

53 **The following month**: INS, "Progress Reports, 'Operation Hester."

54 **The family purchased**: Written response from Sister Ping.

54 **Given his role as second fiddle**: INS, "Progress Reports, 'Operation Hester.'"

54 **In 1986 he was caught**: Internal INS document, "Operation Swiftwater," Report of Investigation, BUF 50/34, October 25, 1989.

54 **This time he was arrested**: Chan and Dao, "Merchants of Misery."

54 **To the investigators**: Interview with Bill McMurry, December 15, 2005.

54 **After customs alerted the INS**: Internal INS document, "Case Management Review: 'Project Hester,'" November 25, 1985.

54 **Occhipinti contacted**: Interview with Joe Occhipinti, August 3, 2007. Also INS, "Alien Smuggling Task Force Proposal."

55 **Sister Ping's father**: Ibid.

55 **It emerged that in January**: INS, "Progress Reports, 'Operation Hester.'"

55 **From the Hong Kong investigators**: Ibid.

55 **Susan, the younger sister**: Ibid.

55 **She was married**: Ibid.

55 **When Susan wasn't in Hong Kong**: INS, "Operation Swiftwater."

55 **The previous spring**: INS, "Progress Reports, 'Operation Hester.'"

56 **During one ten-month period**: Chan and Dao, "Merchants of Misery."

56 **"The smuggling of ethnic Chinese"**: INS, "Alien Smuggling Task Force Proposal."

56 **Occhipinti put together**: Interview with Joe Occhipinti, June 7, 2007.

57 **He had asked for**: Internal INS Memo, "Project Hester Phase II (NYC 50/18.153); Initiation of Grand Jury Investigation," August 3, 1988.

57 **But INS headquarters**: Internal

INS memo, "Project Hester (NYC 50/18.153); Supervisory Conference with Assigned US Attorney," by Joseph Occhipinti, August 16, 1988.

57 **In 1988 he proposed:** Ibid.

57 **As it happened, the INS:** Interview with James Goldman, November 16, 2007. (Goldman was the primary investigator on Operation Hydra.) Also see "Woman Gets a Twelve-Year Term for Promoting Prostitution," *New York Times,* August 6, 1986.

57 **Madame Shih imported:** Hariette Surovell, "Chinatown Cosa Nostra," *Penthouse,* June 1988.

57 **INS investigators believed:** Interview with James Goldman, May 23, 2007.

57 **Madam Shih's son-in-law:** INS, "Progress Reports, 'Operation Hester.' "

57 **Thus, with the inadvertent cooperation:** Interview with James Goldman, May 23, 2007.

57 **Whenever people asked:** The encounter between Occhipinti and Sister Ping was recounted to me by Joe Occhipinti, June 7, 2007.

58 **It became part of her lore:** Before meeting Occhipinti and hearing the story firsthand, I heard several versions of it from other current and former immigration officers.

CHAPTER 4: *DAI LO* OF THE FUK CHING

This chapter draws on interviews with numerous current and former law enforcement officials, from the FBI, the NYPD, and the Manhattan district attorney's office, in addition to the transcript of the Senate Investigations Subcommittee interview with Benny Ong and the transcripts of testimony by Ah Kay at two different trials.

59 **One autumn day in 1991:** Interview with Dan Rinzel, formerly of the Senate Subcommittee on Investigations, November 12, 2007.

59 **"My name Benny Ong":** Quotes from the investigator's interview with Benny Ong are taken from a transcript of the testimony of Benny Ong in "Asian Organized Crime," pp. 145–51.

59 **Born the seventh:** Biographical material on Benny Ong is drawn from Michael Daly, "The War for Chinatown," *New York,* February 14, 1983; Anthony DeStefano, "Federal Investigators Probe Asian Gangs," *Newsday,* November 18, 1993; Anthony DeStefano, " 'Adviser' Holds Court, Lies Low," *Newsday,* February 14, 1993; Peg Tyre, "Final Curtain for 'Godfather' of Chinatown?" *Newsday,* July 28, 1994; Rose Kim, " 'Godfather' of Chinatown Dies," *Newsday,* August 7, 1994; Rick Hampson, "Death Comes to 'The Godfather,' " Associated Press, August 8, 1994; Douglas Martin, "After Benny Ong, Silence in Chinatown," *New York Times,* August 8, 1994; Molly Gordy, "Chinatown Mourning Godfather," *Newsday,* August 17, 1994; Molly Gordy and Mae Cheng, "Paying Last Respects," *Newsday,* August 18, 1994; Eleanor Randolph, "Last Respects for 'The Godfather,' " *Washington Post,* August 19, 1994; Mae Cheng, "Mourning 'Uncle 7,' " *Newsday,* August 20, 1994; John Kifner, "Benny Ong: A Farewell to All That," *New York Times,* August 21, 1994; Molly Gordy, "Hong Kong Connection," *Newsday,* November 3, 1994.

60 **The word *tong*:** Interviews with Ko-lin Chin, November 3, 2005. On tongs, their history, and their role in Chinatown society, see Kwong, *The New Chinatown,* particularly chaps. 5 and 6; Kwong and Miščević, *Chinese America,* pp. 86–87; Ko-lin Chin, *Chinatown Gangs: Extortion, Enterprise & Ethnicity* (New York: Oxford University Press, 1996), introduction; Jane H. Lii, "Tongs and Gangs: Shifting the Links," *New York Times,* August 21, 1994.

61 **In *The Gangs of New York*:** Herbert Asbury, *The Gangs of New York* (New York: Thunder's Mouth, 1998 [1927]), chap. 14. Also see Eng Ying Gong and Bruce Grant, *Tong War!* (New York: N. L. Brown, 1930).

62 **The Flying Dragons did the dirty work:** Booth, *Dragon Syndicates,* pp. 305–6.

62 **But on the occasions:** The Golden Star Tearoom shooting was a famous episode, much written about at the time. See Daly, "The War for Chinatown." (In insisting that he would never have ordered such a massacre, Ong offered a homespun elaboration: "Shoot one guy, easy, nobody knows. Shoot many people, everybody knows. Trouble.")

63 **High above, on a terrace:** Kifner, "Benny Ong: A Farewell to All That."

63 **"The Chinese community is afraid":** Testimony of Kenneth Chu, aka Johnny Wong, former member, Ghost Shadows gang and On Leong tong, in "Asian Organized Crime," p. 35.

63 **Tong leaders of Ong's generation:** T. J. English, *Born to Kill: The Rise and Fall of America's Bloodiest Asian Gang* (New York: Avon, 1995), pp. 55–58.

64 **"There are no norms":** John Kifner, "Asian Gangs in New York—A Special Report," *New York Times,* January 6, 1991.

64 **The 1960 census showed:** Richard Bernstein, "Violent Youth Gangs of Chinatown Reflect Tensions of Complex Society," *New York Times,* December 24, 1982.

65 **"You gotta be strong":** Joseph O'Brien and Andris Kurins, *Boss of Bosses: The FBI and Paul Castellano* (New York: Dell, 1991), p. 215.

65 **A gang of Vietnamese teenagers:** On the BTK gang, see English, *Born to Kill.*

65 **A BTK funeral:** Donatella Lorch, "Mourners Returned Fire, Police Say," *New York Times,* July 30, 1990.

66 **On the Fourth of July:** Jacques Steinberg, "Tourist in Car Killed as She Chances Upon Chinatown Gunfight," *New York Times,* July 6, 1991.

66 **It was a stray bullet:** Metro News Brief, "Queens Man Convicted in Chinatown Killing," *New York Times,* February 14, 1998.

66 **For police and prosecutors:** Interview with Luke Rettler of the Manhattan district attorney's office, December 8, 2005.

67 **"I would have my kids":** Frederic Dannen, "Revenge of the Green Dragons," *The New Yorker,* November 16, 1992.

67 **One day in 1981:** Ah Kay went by several different names. Guo Liang Qi, or Guo Liang Chi, is the Mandarin Chinese transliteration of his name, which he used when he first arrived in the United States. But he also used spellings that more closely approximated the Fujianese pronunciation of his name, Kwok Ling-Kay or Kwok Leung-Kee, both of which were adopted by law enforcement and immigration authorities at various times. For ease, I refer to him the way everyone in Chinatown and law enforcement did: as Ah Kay.

67 **Born to a humble family:** The details of Ah Kay's arrival and early years in the United States are drawn from Ah Kay's testimony in United States v. Zhang Zi Da and Zhang Zi Mei, 96 CR 44 (1996) (hereafter Ah Kay testimony, Zhang Zi trial).

68 **The precise origins:** Dannen, "Revenge of the Green Dragons."

68 **There were a few members:** Unless otherwise noted, details about the behavior and activities of the Fuk Ching gang are drawn from interviews with Bill McMurry and Konrad Motyka on October 31, 2005, and December 15, 2005.

69 **If you wanted to open a restaurant:** "Asian Organized Crime," p. 103.
69 **At the Chinese New Year:** Ibid., p. 51.
70 **It was not unusual:** Interview with Ray Kerr, former head of the FBI's C-6 squad, May 22, 2007.
70 **Nevertheless, the Fuk Ching:** Interview with Dougie Lee, February 10, 2006; interview with Konrad Motyka and Bill McMurry, October 31, 2005; interview with Joseph Pollini, formerly of NYPD, June 7, 2007.
70 **With their connections:** William Kleinknecht, Charles M. Sennott, and Dean Chang, "Empire of Terror," *New York Daily News,* June 20, 1993.
70 **From his early days:** Interview with Luke Rettler, May 30, 2008; Ah Kay testimony, Zhang Zi trial.
70 **In the spring of 1984:** Details of the murder of Steven Lim are drawn from Ah Kay testimony, Sister Ping trial and Zhang Zi trial.
70 **To Ah Kay:** Confidential source.
71 **For their own survival:** Interview with Luke Rettler, December 8, 2005.
71 **Bank accounts were uncommon:** Ibid.
71 **One day in 1985:** The account of Ah Kay's robbery of Sister Ping's house in Brooklyn is drawn from Ah Kay testimony, Sister Ping trial and Zhang Zi trial, from Sister Ping's sentencing remarks, and from written responses from Sister Ping.
72 **Years later a prosecutor:** closing arguments by Leslie Brown in United States v. Cheng Chui Ping, aka "Sister Ping," 94 CR 953 (hereafter closing arguments of Leslie Brown, Sister Ping trial).
72 **When Luke Rettler:** Interview with Luke Rettler, December 8, 2005.
73 **Rettler joined the office:** Interview with Luke Rettler, July 26, 2007.
73 **One problem with the extortion cases:** Interview with Tom Trautman of the FBI, May 3, 2007.
73 **With his languid movements:** Virtually every FBI agent I spoke with who had spent any time with Ah Kay testified to his charisma. Konrad Motyka, Bill McMurry, and Tom Trautman all described what they perceive as his natural leadership abilities.
73 **Once when they patted:** Interview with Joseph Pollini, June 7, 2007.
74 **Still, everyone slips up:** The account of Ah Kay's extortion of Charlie Kwok and his arrest by Dougie Lee is drawn from an interview with Dougie Lee, February 10, 2006, and Ah Kay testimony, Sister Ping trial and Zhang Zi trial.
74 **The massacres at Tiananmen:** Ah Kay testimony, Sister Ping trial and Zhang Zi trial; and Faison, *South of the Clouds,* p. 120.
74 **By the time Ah Kay:** Interview with Bill McMurry and Konrad Motyka, October 21, 2005.
74 **Foochow Paul had left:** Dannen, "Revenge of the Green Dragons."
75 **"Why did Bush step down?":** Confidential source.
75 **Ah Kay had an older brother:** Interview with Bill McMurry and Konrad Motyka, December 15, 2005; hearing transcript in United States of America v. Kwok Ling Kay, et al., 93 Cr. 783, October 12, 1993.
75 **"If Ah Kay said":** Testimony of Tu Wei Chung in State of New Jersey v. Dan Xin Lin, et. al., Bergen County (1995) (hereafter the Teaneck trial).
75 **Ah Kay was attended:** Sentencing hearing in United States v. Kwok Ling Kay, 93 Cr. 783 (JSM), December 4, 1998; report of an interview of Ronald Chao, aka China Man, by members of the FBI and Teaneck Police Department, April 5, 1994.

76 **The most unlikely member**: Unless otherwise noted, details relating to Alan Tam and his role in the gang are drawn from Alan Tam's testimony in State of New Jersey v. Dan Xin Lin, et al., Bergen County (1995) (hereafter, Alan Tam testimony, Teaneck trial); interviews with Luke Rettler on December 8, 2005, and June 26, 2007; interviews with Bill McMurry and Konrad Motyka on October 31, 2005, and December 15, 2005; and a brief telephone conversation with Alan Tam on November 1, 2007.
76 **He was, in the words**: Interview with Bill McMurry, December 15, 2005.
76 **All the money the gang**: The dollar figure is from Alan Tam testimony, the Teaneck trial; the other expenses and the trick with the BMWs come from an interview with Bill McMurry and Konrad Motyka, December 15, 2005.
76 **They hung out, got high**: Alan Tam testimony, the Teaneck trial.
77 **Their turf consisted of**: Ah Kay testimony, Sister Ping trial.
77 **And they policed that turf**: Interview with Chauncey Parker, formerly of the U.S. Attorney's Office for the Southern District of New York, May 29, 2007; sealed complaint, United States v. Ronald Chao, aka "Chinaman," 93 Mag. 1881, August 25, 1993.
77 **The gang had operated**: Ah Kay testimony, Zhang Zi trial.
77 **He elected to open**: Tom Robbins, "The Biz Man and the Thug," *New York Daily News,* June 20, 1993.
77 **The grand opening was**: Details concerning the shootout are drawn from the "Declaration of Thomas Trautman" in the criminal complaint in United States v. Lee Fai Gam, aka "Frankie Lee," 93 Mag. 2224, October 19, 1993.
78 **Governor Mario Cuomo**: Robbins. "The Biz Man and the Thug."
78 **At the same time**: Pamela Burdman, "Inside the Chinese Smuggling Rings," *San Francisco Chronicle,* August 23, 1993. See also testimony of Detective Kenneth Yates, Combined Forces Asian Investigative Unit, Metropolitan Toronto Police Department, "Asian Organized Crime: The New International Criminal," hearing before the Permanent Subcommittee on Investigations of the Committee on Governmental Affairs, United States Senate, June 18 and August 4, 1992 (Washington, DC: Government Printing Office, 1992), p. 28.
78 **"It is unfair to blacken"**: Cited in Ko-lin Chin, "The Social Organization of Chinese Human Smuggling," in Kyle and Koslowski, *Global Human Smuggling,* p. 222.
78 **He raised money**: Chan and Dao, "Merchants of Misery."
78 **But from its opening**: Robbins, "The Biz Man and the Thug."
78 **At the DA's office**: Interview with Luke Rettler, December 8, 2005. Konrad Motyka and Bill McMurry echoed this view that the Fuk Ching and the Fukienese American Association inverted the standard tong-gang dynamic during these years.
79 **A Senate subcommittee found**: "Asian Organized Crime," p. 113.
79 **It outlined the close**: Ibid., p. 68.
79 **On New Year's Eve 1990**: All details of Fang Kin Wah's kidnapping and subsequent experience in court are drawn from an interview with Joseph Pollini, June 7, 2007; an interview with Luke Rettler, July 26, 2007; and the opinion in People v. Hok Ming Chan, 230 A.D.2d 165 (1997).
82 **After the police showed up**: Interview with Joseph Pollini, June 7, 2007.
82 **When it proved too difficult**: Interview with Christine Leung of NYPD, June 8, 2007.
82 **"It was a better business"**: Inter-

view with Steven Wong, November 11, 2005.

CHAPTER 5: SWIFTWATER

This chapter is based primarily on an-interview with Niagara County investgator Ed Garde and on an extraordinary trove of documents that fill several boxes at the Niagara County Sheriff's Office: original investigation reports from Operation Swiftwater, crime scene photos, and transcripts from multiple interviews with Richard Kephart and James Dullan. The material on Sister Ping's role in the Niagara route is drawn from interviews with Patrick Devine of the INS, Peter Lee of the FBI, and Larry Hay of the Royal Canadian Mounted Police, and on Hay's original handwritten investigation notes. Finally, the transcripts and court records documenting the legal cases of Sister Ping and Cheung Yick Tak are now maintained by the National Archives and provided a great deal of valuable material.

83 **On January 3, 1989:** Unless otherwise indicated, details of the Swiftwater investigation and the Cheng family's Niagara operation come from interviews conducted with Sheriff Tom Beilein and investigator Ed Garde at the Niagara County Sheriff's Office on July 11, 2007.

83 **They rolled the body:** The description of the body is based on a series of Niagara County crime scene photographs.

83 **The woman's body:** "Floater (female) Autopsy Report," Niagara County Supplementary Report, ECMC# Mex-1-89, January 4, 1989.

83 **Not far away, the officers found:** Constance L. Hays, "Four Illegal Asian Immigrants Are Believed to Have Drowned in River," *New York Times,* January 6, 1989.

84 **From the woman's luggage:** Niagara County Addendum Report, "Jane Doe, Youngstown," CR 89-CR-5-1, RL 182, January 3, 1989.

84 **Two days earlier:** INS memorandum of investigation, "Malaysian Investigation," File Number BUF 50/34, January 3, 1989; INS, "Operation Swiftwater."

84 **When the woman's body:** INS, "Operation Swiftwater."

84 **Ed Garde called:** INS memorandum of investigation, "Malaysian Investigation," January 5, 1989. These details were confirmed in an interview with Steven Gleit on November 15, 2007.

85 **In 1904 the *Buffalo Times*:** Kwong and Miščević, *Chinese America,* p. 143.

85 **Hong Kong residents:** John F. Bonfatti, "INS Arrests Nine in Alleged Immigrant Smuggling Rings," Associated Press, May 5, 1989.

85 **By the time Haw Wang:** Testimony of Detective Kenneth Yates, Combined Forces Investigative Unit, Metropolitan Toronto Police Department, in "Asian Organized Crime," p. 27.

85 **The previous July:** Gene Warner, " '88 Deaths in River Broke Grip of Smuggling Ring," *Buffalo News,* September 17, 1989.

85 **On January 3:** All details in this paragraph, including the identification of Cheung Yick Tak, are drawn from INS, "Operation Swiftwater."

86 **But when they ran:** INS memorandum of investigation, "Rafters—Lew," File Number BUF 50/34, undated.

86 **A search of *his* toll records:** INS memorandum of investigation, "Malaysian Investigation," March 6, 1989.

86 **Kephart was a cabdriver:** INS, "Operation Swiftwater."

86 **"You know what this":** Testimony of Richard Kephart in US v. Yick Tak

Cheung, Wai Wei Cheng, et al., CR90-113 (1990) (hereafter Kephart testimony).

86 **The investigators took Kephart:** Testimony of Special Agent Peter F. Hoelter in US v. Yick Tak Cheung, Waï Wei Cheng, et al., CR90-113 (1990).

86 **One evening the previous August:** Niagara Regional Police Force supplementary report, May 15, 1989.

86 **There he met three Asian men:** Unless otherwise noted, the details of Kephart's encounter with Paul and first and subsequent smuggling runs are drawn from an INS transcript, interview with Richard Kephart, April 13, 1989.

87 **"He'd come out":** Kephart testimony.

87 **Yick Tak was businesslike:** Testimony of James Dullan in US v. Yick Tak Cheung, Wai Wei Cheng, et al., CR90-113 (1990) (hereafter, Dullan testimony).

87 **He always passed:** Ibid.

87 **He met Yick Tak:** Kephart testimony.

87 **Paul certainly spent:** INS transcript, interview with Richard Kephart by Special Agent Peter Hoelter, April 18, 1989.

87 **He was a risk-taker:** INS transcript, interview with James Dullan, undated.

88 **Paul's favorite expression:** Ibid.

88 **He told Dullan:** Ibid.

88 **After a few trips:** INS transcript, interview with Richard Kephart, April 13, 1989.

88 **He had made "millions":** Ibid.

88 **Through the course of the fall:** Ibid.

88 **Paul said that when:** INS transcript, interview with James Dullan, undated.

89 **Once when they were:** INS transcript, interview with James Dullan, April 13, 1989.

89 **The cabbies were impressed:** INS transcript, interview with Richard Kephart, April 13, 1989.

89 **As fall became winter:** INS transcript, interview with James Dullan, undated.

89 **"The river is rough":** Transcript, INS and Niagara Regional Police Force interview with Richard Kephart, April 18, 1989.

89 **On the night of December 30:** INS memorandum of investigation, "Malaysian Investigation," March 10, 1989.

89 **He could see the light:** Transcript, INS and Niagara Regional Police Force interview with Richard Kephart, April 18, 1989.

89 **Normally it took Paul:** Warner, " '88 Deaths in River."

90 **He had been late before:** INS transcript, interview with James Dullan, undated.

90 **Then they heard something:** Ibid. Kephart initially denied that he thought he heard a scream, but then conceded that indeed he had. INS transcript, interview with Richard Kephart, April 13, 1989.

90 **"That might have come":** INS transcript, interview with James Dullan, April 13, 1989.

90 **Dullan could tell:** Ibid.

90 **They kept waiting:** INS memorandum of investigation, "Malaysian Investigation," March 6, 1989.

90 **Paul had gone down to the river:** Transcript, INS and Niagara Regional Police Force interview with Richard Kephart, April 18, 1989.

90 **"The raft overturned":** Ibid.

90 **There had been four:** Warner, " '88 Deaths in River."

91 **Sometimes Paul used:** Ibid.

91 **They never made it:** Ibid.

91 **In fact, well before the drowning:** Unless otherwise indicated, all material

relating to Patrick Devine's investigation of Sister Ping derives from an interview with Patrick Devine, June 12, 2007.

92 **Devine told the Swiftwater investigators:** INS memorandum of investigation, "Operation Rounder," January 25, 1989.

92 **"The organization appears":** INS, "Operation Swiftwater."

92 **Then suddenly:** Details of Larry Hay's undercover operation at the Toronto airport are drawn from an interview with Larry Hay, December 23, 2005, Larry Hay's testimony in the Sister Ping trial, and the personal notes that Hay took following the incident at the airport on March 28, 1989, a copy of which he gave to me.

92 **Then she and her daughter:** United States v. Tommy Kong, CR 89 46 A (WDNY), Memorandum of Law by AUSA Kathleen Mehltretter, November 3, 1989.

93 **Several months later:** Interview with Larry Hay, December 23, 2005.

93 **After she was transferred:** Interview with Patrick Devine, June 12, 2007.

93 **Sister Ping did not want:** Ibid.

93 **Finally, on June 27:** Defendant's proposed statement of admitted facts, United States v. Chui-Ping Cheng, CR 89 46A (Buffalo, NY), June 27, 1990.

93 **A few weeks later:** Rule 40 affidavit by INS Agent Peter Hoelter, U.S. v. Yick Tak Cheung, aka "Billy," 89 CR 113, July 11, 1989.

93 **Paul and his wife:** INS, "Operation Swiftwater."

93 **He was different:** Interview with Patrick Devine, June 12, 2007.

93 **But many of the investigators:** Ibid. Bill McMurry also expressed the view that because Sister Ping almost always ended up being behind whatever criminal activity her husband engaged in, the likelihood that Yick Tak had somehow independently developed his own smuggling route in partnership with Sister Ping's brother-in-law and that Sister Ping did not play some guiding role in the operation was exceedingly low.

94 **In September a Buffalo federal judge:** "Alien-Smuggler," *Canadian Press,* September 11, 1990.

94 **"I knew what I did":** Ibid.

94 **She volunteered again:** Sentencing hearing, United States v. Chui-Ping Cheng, CR 89 46A, June 20, 1991.

94 **She gave Devine:** Interview with Patrick Devine, June 12, 2007.

94 **Nevertheless, the government:** Sentencing hearing, United States v. Chui-Ping Cheng.

94 **"I'm either the fourth":** Ibid.

95 **Goldenberg pointed to:** Defendant's statement concerning sentence reduction, United States v. Chui-Ping Cheng, CR 89 46A (Buffalo, NY), May 20, 1991.

95 **The prosecutor objected:** Sentencing hearing, United States v. Chui-Ping Cheng.

95 **But the incident wasn't:** Ibid.

95 **When her lawyers:** Ibid.

95 **In March 1991:** "Smuggler of Illegal Aliens Sentenced," Associated Press, March 26, 1991.

96 **Even so, Yick Tak somehow:** Docket in U.S. v. Cheung Yick Tak, a/k/a "Billy," 89 CR 113.

96 **She hated it:** Interview with Special Agent Peter Lee, FBI, January 31, 2006.

96 **She was bitter:** Sister Ping sentencing remarks.

96 **Goldenberg had asked:** Defendant's statement concerning sentence reduction, United States v. Chui-Ping Cheng.

96 **She did have one regular:** Interview with Peter Lee, January 31, 2006.

97 **"Sister Ping had to keep working":**

Interview with Patrick Devine, June 12, 2007.

97 **Upon her release:** Written declaration of Special Agent Peter Lee in a sealed federal criminal complaint against Cheng Chui Ping and Cheng Yick Tak, Southern District of New York, December 1994.

CHAPTER 6: YEAR OF THE SNAKE

This chapter is based on interviews with current and former officials from the FBI, the INS, and Immigration and Customs Enforcement, as well as interviews in Fujian and Chinatown with individuals who came illegally to the United States during the years in question or had other encounters with the snakehead trade. On the growth of the human smuggling business, I relied on the records of several congressional investigations, which are cited in the notes. On the partnership between Sister Ping and the Fuk Ching gang, I drew on the testimony during Sister Ping's trial of Weng Yu Hui and Ah Kay, as well as Ah Kay's deputies Cho Yee Yeung and Li Xing Hua. Ah Kay's testimony in another trial, United States v. Zhang Zi Da and Zhang Zi Mei, 96 CR 44 (1996), was also valuable.

99 **The most widely reproduced:** See Dana Calvo, "Profile in Courage," *Smithsonian Magazine,* January 19, 2004.

99 **On June 5:** Secretary of State's Morning Summary for June 5, 1989, declassified and released by the National Security Archive at George Washington University.

100 **Bush had assumed:** Unless otherwise noted, material on George H. W. Bush's experience in China and his reaction to the events at Tiananmen Square is drawn from George Bush and Brent Scowcroft, *A World Transformed* (New York: Vintage, 1998), pp. 90–99.

101 **Bush's commitment to harboring:** Executive Order 12711, "Policy Implementation with Respect to Nationals of the People's Republic of China," April 11, 1990. The text of the order reads:

> By the authority vested in me as President by the Constitution and laws of the United States of America, the Attorney General and the Secretary of State are hereby ordered to exercise their authority, including that under the Immigration and Nationality Act), as follows:
>
> Section 1. The Attorney General is directed to take any steps necessary to defer until January 1, 1994, the enforced departure of all nationals of the People's Republic of China (PRC) and their dependents who were in the United States on or after June 5, 1989, up to and including the date of this order (hereinafter "such PRC nationals").
>
> Sec. 2. The Secretary of State and the Attorney General are directed to take all steps necessary with respect to such PRC nationals (a) to waive through January 1, 1994, the requirement of a valid passport and (b) to process and provide necessary documents, both within the United States and at U.S. consulates overseas, to facilitate travel across the borders of other nations and reentry into the United States in the same status such PRC nationals had upon departure.
>
> Sec. 3. The Secretary of State and the Attorney General are directed to provide the following protections:
>
> (a) irrevocable waiver of the 2-year home country residence requirement that may be exercised until January 1, 1994, for such PRC nationals;
>
> (b) maintenance of lawful status for purposes of adjustment of status or change of nonimmigrant sta-

tus for such PRC nationals who were in lawful status at any time on or after June 5, 1989, up to and including the date of this order;

(c) authorization for employment of such PRC nationals through January 1, 1994; and

(d) notice of expiration of nonimmigrant status (if applicable) rather than the institution of deportation proceedings, and explanation of options available for such PRC nationals eligible for deferral of enforced departure whose nonimmigrant status has expired.

Sec. 4. The Secretary of State and the Attorney General are directed to provide for enhanced consideration under the immigration laws for individuals from any country who express a fear of persecution upon return to their country related to that country's policy of forced abortion or coerced sterilization, as implemented by the Attorney General's regulation effective January 29, 1990.

Sec. 5. The Attorney General is directed to ensure that the Immigration and Naturalization Service finalizes and makes public its position on the issue of training for individuals in F-1 visa status and on the issue of reinstatement into lawful nonimmigrant status of such PRC nationals who have withdrawn their applications for asylum.

Sec. 6. The Departments of Justice and State are directed to consider other steps to assist such PRC nationals in their efforts to utilize the protections that I have extended pursuant to this order.

Sec. 7. This order shall be effective immediately.

George Bush
The White House,
April 11, 1990

101 **There were roughly:** John Pomfret, "Smuggled Chinese Enrich Homeland, Gangs," *Washington Post,* January 24, 1999.

101 **Reports from inside:** See Matthew Connelly, *Fatal Misconception: The Struggle to Control World Population* (Cambridge, MA: Harvard University Press, 2008), pp. 339–60. For further material on the history of China's one-child policy, see Susan Greenhalgh and Edwin A. Winckler, *Governing China's Population: From Leninist to Neoliberal Biopolitics* (Stanford, CA: Stanford University Press, 2005); and Tyrene White, *China's Longest Campaign: Birth Planning in the People's Republic, 1949–2005* (Ithaca, NY: Cornell University Press, 2006).

102 **The effects of the order:** Malcolm Gladwell and Rachel E. Stassen-Berger, "U.S. Policy Seen Encouraging Wave of Chinese Immigration," *Washington Post,* June 13, 1993.

102 **"The Fujianese thank two people":** Interview with Philip Lam, November 9, 2005.

103 **It was said in New York's Chinatown:** Interview with Dr. Tang Xiao Xiong in Fuzhou, China, February 21, 2008. Dr. Tang lived in New York's Chinatown during the years in question and ran a medical practice that catered to the city's undocumented Fujianese.

103 **The number of Chinese nationals:** "Asian Organized Crime," p. 418.

103 **"Everybody went crazy":** *Sing Tao Daily,* December 2, 1996, as quoted in Chin, *Smuggled Chinese,* p. 9.

103 **Over the past half-century:** United Nations High Commission for Refugees, *UNHCR Resettlement Handbook.* Available at UNHCR.org.

103 **In the past thirty-five years alone:** Ellen R. Sauerbrey, assistant secretary of state for population, refugees, and migration, "Providing Help and Hope

Around the World," *Foreign Policy Agenda* 12, no. 2 (February 2007): 51.

103 **In fact, of the top thirteen countries:** United Nations High Commission for Refugees, "Refugees by Numbers, 2006 Edition" (pamphlet). The United States accepted 53,813 refugees in 2006. The next twelve countries—in order, Australia, Canada, Sweden, Finland, Norway, New Zealand, Denmark, the Netherlands, the UK, Ireland, Brazil, and Chile—accepted a total of 26,889.

104 **The United Nations established:** United Nations Convention Relating to the Status of Refugees, 1951; United Nations Protocol Relating to the Status of Refugees, 1967.

104 **More people were seeking:** Christopher Dickey, "Carter Seeking Major Revision of Refugee Laws," *Washington Post,* March 8, 1979.

104 **With the Refugee Act of 1980:** See 8 U.S.C. §1101(a)(42) and 8 U.S.C. §1157 (a)(1).

104 **They were less concerned:** David M. Riemers, *Still the Golden Door: The Third World Comes to America* (New York: Columbia University Press, 1992), p. 201.

104 **The law envisioned:** The 5,000 figure technically refers not to the anticipated number of people who will be granted asylum each year but to the number of asylees who will be granted permanent citizenship. For a full account of the legislative history of the act, see Edward M. Kennedy, "Refugee Act of 1980," *International Migration Review* (Spring/Summer, 1981): 141–56.

104 **Almost immediately:** Riemers, *Still the Golden Door,* p. 201.

104 **By the time the Bush executive order:** Ira H. Mehlman, "The New Jet Set," *National Review,* March 15, 1993.

105 **If you showed up:** Ibid.

105 **Immigration officials didn't have:** Gladwell and Stassen-Berger, "U.S. Policy Seen Encouraging Wave of Chinese Immigration."

105 **The INS had historically:** Confidential interview with a former INS official.

105 **Gene McNary, who ran:** Joel Brinkley, "At Immigration, Disarray and Defeat," *New York Times,* September 11, 1994.

106 **Bill Slattery, the INS's district director:** Unless otherwise noted, material on Slattery is drawn from an interview with Bill Slattery, July 7, 2008.

106 **When he took the job:** Vivienne Walt, "Aliens at the Gate; New York's INS Director Cracks Down," *Newsday,* November 29, 1993.

106 **"The aliens have taken control":** Tim Weiner, "Pleas for Asylum Inundate Immigration System," *New York Times,* April 25, 1993.

106 **Slattery thought of:** George E. Curry, "Masses Find JFK Airport Is Passageway to Illegal Entry," *Chicago Tribune,* February 23, 1992.

106 **"If I have someone from China":** Mehlman, "The New Jet Set."

106 **Twelve million people:** "Asian Organized Crime," p. 195.

106 **And by 1992:** Mehlman, "The New Jet Set."

107 **"Prove to us that they're Chinese":** Confidential interview with an immigration official.

107 **Each time an arrival:** Mehlman, "The New Jet Set."

107 **The airport had a small:** Ted Conover, "The United States of Asylum," *New York Times Magazine,* September 19, 1993.

107 **"It's not like they're trying":** Bill Slattery, quoted in *CBS News* transcript, "Move to Call for a Moratorium on Immigration in America," July 4, 1993.

107 **Someone could arrive at JFK:** "Asian Organized Crime," p. 195.

107 **The snakeheads knew this:** Mehlman, "The New Jet Set"; Ah Kay testimony, Zhang Zi trial.

108 **One Hong Kong triad:** Greg Torode, "Triads Use HK Agency for Illegals," *South China Morning Post,* March 15, 1993. See also "Asian Organized Crime," p. 190.

108 **One reason for this:** Interview with Neville Cramer, a former INS official, June 1, 2007.

108 **In the midnineties, a federal working group:** Presidential Initiative to Deter Alien Smuggling, "Report of the Interagency Working Group," 1995.

108 **But James Woolsey:** Paul J. Smith, "Illegal Chinese Immigrants Everywhere," *International Herald Tribune,* June 28, 1996. Another article, Jim Mann, Christine Courtney, and Susan Essoyan, "Chinese Refugees Take to High Seas," *Los Angeles Times,* March 16, 1993, cites "INS and State Department officials" who also estimated the number at 100,000 a year.

108 **One senior immigration official:** Gwen Kinkead, *Chinatown: Portrait of a Closed Society* (New York: Perennial, 1993), p. 160.

108 **Sources within China's own Public Security Bureau:** Marlowe Hood, "The Taiwan Connection," *Los Angeles Times Magazine,* October 9, 1994.

108 **The NYPD estimated:** Kwong, *Forbidden Workers,* p. 82.

109 **One expert on the snakehead trade:** Willard Myers, "Transnational Ethnic Chinese Organized Crime: A Global Challenge to the Security of the United States, Analysis and Recommendations," testimony before the Senate Committee on Foreign Affairs, Subcommittee on Terrorism, Narcotics, and International Operations, April 24, 1994.

109 **That would make it roughly comparable:** Pamela Burdman, "How Gangsters Cash In on Human Smuggling," *San Francisco Chronicle,* April 28, 1993.

109 **Other estimates place:** Dele Olojede, "America at Any Cost," *Newsday,* July 19, 1998.

109 **According to Peter Kwong:** Kwong, *Forbidden Workers,* p. 33.

109 **After he was deported:** Ah Kay testimony, Sister Ping trial.

109 **On his journey back to America:** Ah Kay testimony, Zhang Zi trial.

109 **Most people in New York's Chinatown:** Ashley Dunn, "After Crackdown, Smugglers of Chinese Find New Routes," *New York Times,* November 1, 1994. The year 1991 also tended to be the consensus date that emerged in conversations I had with people over three years of research in Chinatown about the advent of boat smuggling.

109 **But an INS Anti-Smuggling Unit memo:** INS, "Alien Smuggling Task Force Proposal."

110 **In some cases:** Weng Yu Hui testimony, Sister Ping trial.

110 **What is clear:** Mann, Courtney, and Essoyan, "Chinese Refugees Take to High Seas"; Pamela Burden, "Human Smuggling Ships Linked to One Huge Ring," *San Francisco Chronicle,* December 30, 1993; Hood, "The Taiwan Connection."

110 **Some have connected:** White House, Office of the Press Secretary, "Background Briefing by Senior Administration Officials" (Rand Beers and Donsia Strong), June 18, 1993; Seth Faison, "Crackdown Fails to Stem Smuggling of Chinese to U.S.," *New York Times,* August 23, 1993.

110 **The snakeheads called the boats:** Blatt, "Recent Trends in the Smuggling of Chinese."

111 **Thailand is extravagantly corrupt:** Interview with Colonel Jaruvat Vasaya of the Royal Thai Police, March 13,

2007; interview with Colonel Ponsraser Ganjanarintr of the Royal Thai Police, March 13, 2007; interview with Mark Riordan, formerly of the INS, June 7, 2007.

111 **By 1992, U.S. authorities:** Interview with Mark Riordan, June 7, 2007.

111 **American document experts:** Confidential interview with a former INS investigator.

111 **Until that point, Bangkok had been:** See James Dao and Ying Chan, "Thai City Hub on Smuggle Route to U.S.," *New York Daily News*, September 24, 1990.

111 **But when authorities:** Weng Yu Hui testimony, Sister Ping trial.

112 **Between August 1991:** Chin, *Smuggled Chinese*, p. 4.

112 **Dating back to 1989:** Interview with Luke Rettler, May 30, 2008.

112 **But Ah Kay had watched:** Ah Kay testimony, Zhang Zi trial.

112 **Ah Kay called the process:** Ah Kay testimony, Sister Ping trial.

113 **Occasionally a passenger would jump:** Testimony of Cho Yee Yeung in United States v. Cheng Chui Ping, aka "Sister Ping," 94 CR 953 (hereafter Cho Yee Yeung testimony, Sister Ping trial).

113 **By the summer of 1992:** Ibid.

113 **Ah Kay was ferociously:** Confidential source.

113 **One day in August 1992:** Testimony of Li Xing Hua in United States v. Cheng Chui Ping, aka "Sister Ping," 94 CR 953 (hereafter Li Xing Hua testimony, Sister Ping trial).

113 **A month after the raft:** Chan and Dao, "Merchants of Misery."

114 **In 1990 a Chinatown journalist:** Ibid.

114 **Sister Ping was angered:** Sister Ping sentencing remarks.

114 **By 1991 a Senate subcommittee:** "Asian Organized Crime," p. 189.

114 **Shortly after Ah Kay:** The account of Sister Ping's meeting with Ah Kay is drawn from the testimony at Sister Ping's trial of Ah Kay, Cho Yee Yeung, and Li Xing Hua.

115 **On the night of September 21:** Cho Yee Yeung testimony, Sister Ping trial.

115 **The night after the pickup:** Unless otherwise noted, the account of John Marcelino's observation of the New Bedford smuggling operation is drawn from testimony of John Q. Marcelino III in United States v. Cheng Chui Ping, aka "Sister Ping," 94 CR 953 (hereafter John Marcelino testimony, Sister Ping trial).

116 **The U-Hauls proceeded:** Li Xing Hua testimony, Sister Ping trial.

116 **She sent Yick Tak:** Cho Yee Yeung testimony, Sister Ping trial.

116 **For Ah Kay she prepared:** Ah Kay testimony, Sister Ping trial.

116 **When the FBI:** Interview with Konrad Motyka and Bill McMurry, October 31, 2005.

117 **She would later claim:** Written response from Sister Ping; Sister Ping sentencing remarks.

117 **Prosecutors would later describe:** Closing arguments of Leslie Brown, Sister Ping trial.

117 **Before long she was offering:** Ah Kay testimony, Zhang Zi trial.

118 **But it has also been suggested:** Interview with Stephen Wong, November 11, 2005. Also see "The Mother of All Snakeheads," Asian Pacific News Service, July 10, 2003.

118 **During the period when Ah Kay:** Interview with Peter Lee, January 31, 2006; written declaration of Special Agent Peter Lee.

CHAPTER 7: MOMBASA

This chapter draws primarily on a dozen hours of interviews with Sean Chen, conducted during several trips to Philadelphia, where he lives today. For additional details in the account of the journey through Burma to Thailand, I relied on the recollections of Michael Chen, one of Sean's fellow passengers aboard the *Golden Venture,* who followed the same busy route from Fujian to Bangkok. During the months that the *Najd II* was stranded in Mombasa, a Kenyan journalist named Matiko Bohoko covered the story for several local papers and boarded the ship. Bohoko still lives and works in Kenya, and in addition to discussing his recollections of the incident with me, he was kind enough to do some additional research and track down some old clippings from the local press. The current and former staff at Mombasa's Missions to Seamen (which is now called the Mission to Seafarers) also supplied valuable memories and documents.

121 **Sean Chen stood:** Unless otherwise noted, all material relating to the experience of Sean Chen in China, Thailand, Kenya, and the United States is based on interviews with Sean Chen, February 6, 2008, and June 5, 2008.

123 **This was Burma's:** Transcript of an interview with Donald Ferrarone, chief, DEA office in Bangkok, 1993–1995, conducted by the PBS television program *Frontline* for an episode called "The Opium Kings" in 1996, available on the *Frontline* Web site (www.pbs.org/frontline).

123 **"When the DEA":** "Khun Sa: Ruthless Burmese Warlord Who Dominated the World's Heroin Trade," obituary, *Times* (London), November 5, 2007.

123 **Sean joined another clandestine:** Some of the details of the general conditions on the crossing into Burma are drawn from an interview with another *Golden Venture* passenger, Michael Chen, December 17, 2005. (Michael Chen's story is told in greater detail in Patrick Radden Keefe, "The Snakehead: The Criminal Odyssey of Chinatown's Sister Ping," *The New Yorker,* April 24, 2006.)

127 **Thai police officers demanded:** Information about raids by the police is drawn from the Michael Chen interview. (Michael Chen's safe house was raided on a number of occasions, and he was thrown into prison.)

128 **The ship's hull was painted:** The physical description of the ship is drawn from the entry on the *Aramoana* (later the *Najd II*) in the New Zealand Maritime Record.

128 **But the chief snakehead:** Weng Yu Hui testimony, Sister Ping trial.

129 **Weng was curious:** Sister Ping sentencing remarks.

129 **Then in 1991:** Weng Yu Hui testimony, Sister Ping trial.

129 **Weng's new business grew:** Ibid.

129 **So unmatched was Sister Ping's:** Interview with Konrad Motyka and Bill McMurry, October 31, 2005. Sister Ping alluded to this situation herself in her sentencing hearing in 2006, when she claimed that those conducting smuggling operations "in her name" had not in fact been employees or associates of hers at all.

130 **Her younger brother:** Weng Yu Hui testimony, Sister Ping trial; interview with Konrad Motyka and Bill McMurry, December 15, 2005.

130 **Weng would put:** Weng Yu Hui testimony, Sister Ping trial. There is some disagreement about the precise number of passengers Weng had. In his testimony in Sister Ping's trial, he said about thirty. But according to government documents, the number was closer to forty. (See, for example, the government's appellate brief in U.S. v. Fei, No. 98-1713, November 4, 1999.)

130 **Mr. Charlie found:** The charter

arrangement was dated July 10, 1992. The registered owner of the ship was Najd Trading and Construction, of Jeddah, Saudi Arabia. See Aung. K. Mynt & 17 Others v. Owners of M/V Najd II, Admiralty Cause No. 21 of 1992 in the High Court of Kenya at Mombasa, ruling, March 23, 1993.

130 **They ran aground**: Internal INS document, "A Chronology of Alien Smuggling by Sea," June 22, 1994; Peter Woolrich, Michael Chugani, and Matiko Bohoko, "Every Day New Details Are Coming to Light of a Mass Exodus," *South China Morning Post*, February 14, 1993; Faison, *South of the Clouds*, p. 122.

131 **In addition to chartering**: Interview with Donald Monica, formerly of the INS, June 9, 2008.

131 **The Indian Ocean**: William Langewiesche, *The Outlaw Sea* (New York: North Point, 2004), p. 62.

131 **Finally, on September 4, 1992**: INS, "A Chronology of Alien Smuggling by Sea."

131 **The *Najd II* hobbled**: Ibid.; confidential interview with an ICE official.

132 **But the port authorities**: "Kenyans Puzzled by Mystery Ship," *Calgary Herald* (Alberta), December 3, 1992.

132 **It would subsequently emerge**: Interview with Donald Monica, June 9, 2008.

132 **One of the ship's officers**: INS, "A Chronology of Alien Smuggling by Sea"; interview with Sean Chen.

132 **After another grueling two weeks**: The *Najd II* arrived in Mombasa on October 6. INS, "A Chronology of Alien Smuggling by Sea."

132 **Kenya was already reeling**: "Kenyans Puzzled by Mystery Ship."

132 **But when the ship entered Mombasa**: "Kenya Detains 240 Chinese Holding Fake Thai Passports," Agence France Presse, November 26, 1992.

132 **To compound matters**: Li Xing Hua testimony, Sister Ping trial.

132 **A delegation from Mombasa's**: Interview with Richard Diamond, who was chaplain at the Missions to Seamen, Mombasa, between 1990 and 2000, February 19, 2007.

133 **As the Kenyan authorities**: Report on the Search of M/V Najd II on 21st Nov 1992, by Jonathan New, assistant chaplain at Missions to Seamen, Mombasa; interview with Jay New, April 5, 2007.

133 **Most of the passengers**: The detail about life preservers is from United States v. Fei, 225 F.3d 167, at 169.

134 **Some constructed small rafts**: Interview with Richard Diamond, February 19, 2007.

134 **In Baghdad or Mogadishu**: For a fascinating account of Fujianese entrepreneurs seeking their fortunes in war-torn Baghdad, see Bay Fang, "Bad Fortune: Big Trouble in Iraq's Little China," *New Republic*, July 10 and 17, 2006.

134 **Dozens of people**: Interview with Richard Diamond, February 19, 2007.

135 **The Kenyans continued**: Erick Omondi, "Mystery Ship Saga Now Deepens," *Kenya Times Shipping Guide*, December 4, 1992.

135 **Eventually, many of them**: Interview with Donald Monica, June 9, 2008.

135 **At one point a delegation**: Ibid.

135 **For a time there was a rumor**: Minutes of the Executive Committee of the Missions to Seamen, Mombasa, January 21, 1993.

135 **According to several people**: Sean Chen, Michael Chen, and Dong Xu Zhi all confirmed this account. The *New York Times*'s Seth Faison reports in his book that all the women on board were raped, but I was unable to corroborate that. Matiko Bohoko reported at the

time and has since repeated in interviews that several of the women were being held as "sex slaves." For what it's worth, Kin Sin Lee, the snakeheads' chief representative aboard the *Golden Venture*, said in testimony that he had heard about rapes on the *Najd II* and that none of the twenty-seven women aboard the *Golden Venture* were raped, in part because he had announced that any man who raped a woman on board would be thrown into the sea. Testimony of Kin Sin Lee in United States v. Kin Sin Lee, et al., 93 CR 694, June 28, 1994.

136 **In November, Weng flew:** Weng Yu Hui testimony, Sister Ping trial.

136 **This was indeed:** Li Xing Hua testimony, Sister Ping trial; Cho Yee Yeung testimony, Sister Ping trial.

CHAPTER 8: THE PHANTOM SHIP

This chapter is based on a research trip I made in the spring of 2007 to Thailand, where I managed to track down Pao Pong, who is now working with the Bangkok Immigration Police, and interview him. I visited the beach in Pattaya where the *Golden Venture* passengers boarded the speedboats, and conducted several interviews with Mark Riordan, the former INS officer who was based in Thailand at the time and worked with Pao Pong to stop the operation. Other major sources include interviews with half a dozen passengers from the *Golden Venture*, most importantly Sean Chen, Michael Chen, and Dong Xu Zhi; notes from law enforcement interviews with Captain Amir Tobing; and court records from subsequent legal proceedings against Kin Sin Lee, Lee Peng Fei, and Sister Ping.

137 **On the evening of:** Unless otherwise indicated, the details of Pao Pong's experience on the night of November 14, 1993, are drawn from an interview with Senior Sergeant Major Pao Pong, Bangkok Immigration Police, and Senior Sergeant Major Thana Srinkara, Pattaya Tourist Police, March 8, 2007.

138 **The Tourist Police had received an alert:** Interview with Mark Riordan, June 7, 2007.

139 **By the time Pao Pong:** Ibid.

139 **But someone had warned the ship:** Kin Sin Lee testimony, transcript of Fatico Hearing Before the Honorable Reena Raggi in United States v. Huag Shao Ming et. al., CR-93-0694, June 27, 1994; also see Anthony DeStefano, "Feds Seeking Ship Suspect," *Newsday*, January 7, 1994.

139 **That night Pao Pong:** Unless otherwise indicated, material relating to Mark Riordan's experience as an INS investigator in Thailand is based on interviews with Mark Riordan on June 7, 2007, and May 20, 2008.

139 **When Riordan questioned:** "Thai Police Bust Human Smuggling Ring, Arrest 68 Chinese," Agence France Presse, February 16, 1993; interviews with Mark Riordan, June 7, 2007, and May 20, 2008.

141 **Mr. Charlie's real name:** Interview with Mark Riordan, June 7, 2007.

141 **A week after meeting:** Weng Yu Hui testimony, Sister Ping trial; Ah Kay testimony, Sister Ping trial.

141 **The ship had been used:** Seth Faison, "Hunt Goes on for Smuggler in Fatal Trip," *New York Times*, July 18, 1993.

142 **In Singapore, Lee met:** Supplemental criminal incident report (based on an interview with Amir Tobing), William Stray, June 7, 1993.

142 **A prosecutor later described:** Interview with Jodi Avergun, former assistant United States attorney in the Eastern District of New York, May 24, 2007.

142 **Lee enlisted a crew:** United States v. Moe, 64 F.3d 245, at 247.

142 **They laid plywood planks:** Undated Coast Guard document, "Post Seizure Analysis—M/V Golden Venture."
142 **Charlie purchased:** Kin Sin Lee testimony, transcript of Fatico hearing.
142 **He gave Kin Sin Lee money:** Supplemental criminal incident report, William Stray, June 7, 1993.
142 **Just before the *Tong Sern* was to leave:** Weng Yu Hui testimony, Sister Ping trial.
142 **It was decided:** Government appellate brief in United States v. Lee, 122 F.3d 1058, Second Circuit Court of Appeals, April 12, 1995.
143 **As the ship headed out:** Complaint in United States v. Moe, 93 CR 00694.
143 **But during Prohibition:** See "Two American Liners Now Fly Panama Flag," *New York Times,* December 6, 1922.
143 **In the years since:** Jim Morris, " 'Flags of Convenience' Give Owners a Paper Refuge," *Houston Chronicle,* August 22, 1996.
144 **Dozens of other countries:** Robert Neff, "Flags That Hide the Dirty Truth," *Asia Times,* April 19, 2007; "Bolivia Waves the Flag," *The Economist,* May 27, 2000; James Brooke, "Landlocked Mongolia's Seafaring Tradition," *New York Times,* July 2, 2004; Langewiesche, *The Outlaw Sea,* p. 5.
144 **But if this system worked:** See Jayant Abhyankar, "Phantom Ships," in Eric Ellen, ed., *Shipping at Risk: The Rising Tide of International Organized Crime* (Essex, United Kingdom: International Maritime Bureau of the International Chamber of Commerce's Commercial Crime Services, 1997).
144 **As the *Tong Sern* sailed:** Jimmy Breslin, "A Familiar Refrain: 'It's Not My Fault,' " *Newsday,* June 8, 1993.
145 **While the *Golden Venture*:** Weng Yu Hui testimony, Sister Ping trial.
145 **Late on the night of April 2:** INS, "A Chronology of Alien Smuggling by Sea"; Aung K. Mynt & 17 Others v. Owners of M/V Najd II, Admiralty Cause No. 21 of 1992 in the High Court of Kenya at Mombasa, ruling, March 23, 1993.
145 **Of the three hundred or so passengers:** Weng Yu Hui testimony, Sister Ping trial.
145 **Nor were they the only ones:** Interview with Donald Monica, June 9, 2008.
145 **He telephoned:** Weng Yu Hui testimony, Sister Ping trial.
145 **Sean Chen was aboard:** Interview with Sean Chen, February 6, 2008.
146 **Kin Sin Lee had selected:** United States v. Moe, 64 F.3d 245, at 247; letter from United States Attorney Zachary W. Carter to United States District Judge Reena Raggi, re: United States v. Kin Sin Lee, et al., 93 CR 694, April 29, 1994.
146 **Sean entered the hatch:** Interviews with Sean Chen, February 6, 2008, and June 5, 2008.
146 **The passengers were divided:** Letter from Carter to Raggi, re: United States v. Kin Sin Lee, et al.
146 **The hold was hot:** Faison, *South of the Clouds,* p. 124.
146 **There was only one bathroom:** Interview with Sean Chen, February 6, 2008.
147 **The air grew thick:** Faison, *South of the Clouds,* p. 124.
147 **Captain Tobing, Kin Sin Lee:** Sam Lwin testimony in United States v. Huang Shao Ming, et. al., 93-0694; transcript of Fatico hearing.
147 **The supply of fresh water:** Mae Cheng, "*Golden Venture* Unfinished Story," *Newsday,* May 31, 1998.
147 **Each passenger was allotted:** Interview with Michael Chen, December 17, 2005.

147 **Their skin broke out:** Melinda Liu, Frank Gibney, Jr., Susan Miller, and Tom Morganthau, "The New Slave Trade," *Newsweek,* June 21, 1993.
147 **When they did:** Letter from Carter to Raggi, re: United States v. Kin Sin Lee, et al.
147 **Kin Sin Lee was clearly fearful:** Interview with Sean Chen, June 5, 2008; Diana Jean Schemo, "Chinese Immigrants Tell of Darwinian Voyage," *New York Times,* June 12, 1993.
147 **He vowed to throw:** Testimony of Sam Lwin in United States v. Kin Sin Lee, et al., 93 CR 694, June 23, 1994.
147 **One man cried:** Interview with Michael Chen, December 17, 2005.
148 **Another man brought:** Schemo, "Chinese Immigrants Tell of Darwinian Voyage."
148 **"I think it changed":** Liu, Gibney, Miller, and Morganthau, "The New Slave Trade."
148 **As the *Golden Venture* neared:** The account of the storm is based on interviews with Sean Chen, Michael Chen, and Dong Xu Zhi.
148 **There were no lifeboats:** United States v. Lee Peng Fei, 225 F.3d 167, Second Circuit Court of Appeals, November 4, 1999.
148 **After two days the storm subsided:** Sam Lwin testimony in United States v. Huang Shao Ming, et. al., 93-0694; transcript of Fatico hearing. INS officials were aware that the ship had stopped at Cape Infanta, a fact that was confirmed for me in a confidential interview with an official at ICE.
148 **Despite the adversity:** The account of the community that emerged is drawn largely from my interview with Michael Chen, but also from interviews with Sean Chen and Dong Xu Zhi.

CHAPTER 9: THE TEANECK MASSACRE

This chapter is based primarily on interviews with law enforcement officials who investigated the Fuk Ching gang, the splinter faction established by Dan Xin Lin, and the murders in Teaneck, New Jersey. In addition to numerous internal FBI investigative files, I drew on a nearly complete case file compiled by the Bergen County Prosecutor's Office during the Teaneck investigation, including crime scene reports, witness interviews, autopsy reports, and so forth. I visited Akiva Fleischmann in Teaneck, and he showed me the house where the massacre took place and walked me through the geography of the neighborhood. I also drew on the testimony of Alan Tam and others at the ensuing trial, and on the terrific coverage of the killings and the trial in the *Bergen County Record.*
150 **On his identity card:** Identity card for Kwok Ling Kay (aka Guo Liang Qi, aka Ah Kay), issued by the Fukienese American Association. The card was shown to me by Luke Rettler, who has held on to it as a memento of the investigation.
150 **One of these newcomers:** Interview/statement of Dan Xin Lin, Bergen County Prosecutor's Office, May 26, 1993.
150 **Dan Xin had been:** Report of an interview with Ronald Chao, aka China Man, by representatives of the FBI and the Teaneck Police Department, April 5, 1994.
151 **Ah Kay was developing:** Interview with Konrad Motyka and Bill McMurry, October 31, 2005.
151 **Dan Xin was ambitious:** Ibid.
151 **Dan Xin had contacts:** FBI confidential informant report, September 23, 1993, File # 281E-NY-196708.
151 **In the summer of 1992:** Report of an interview with Ronald Chao, aka China Man.
152 **"Dan Xin wanted":** Remark by

Prosecutor William J. Murray during Alan Tam testimony, the Teaneck trial.
152 **After the incident in Washington:** Testimony of Tu Wei Chung in State of New Jersey v. Dan Xin Lin, et al., Bergen County (1995) (hereafter, Tu Wei Chung testimony, the Teaneck trial).
152 **Before long, Dan Xin:** Confidential source.
152 **"What are my shortcomings?":** Ibid.
152 **He accused Dan Xin:** Ibid.
152 **Ah Kay thought the move:** Ibid.
152 **He warned Dan Xin:** Ibid.
152 **Ah Kay didn't make:** Ah Kay testimony, Zhang Zi trial.
153 **But on January 8, 1993:** Case report, homicide investigation of Yu Ping Zhang, et. al., Bergen County Prosecutor's Office, February 18, 1994.
153 **"Do it":** The account of this exchange and the shooting at the beeper store is drawn from an interview with Luke Rettler, in which he referred to affidavits filed by the investigating officers, crime scene specialists, and Dan Xin Lin himself, May 30, 2008. (The detail of the singeing of Dan Xin's hair comes from Dan Xin's own account of the incident, delivered to authorities after he escaped unharmed.) Also see Seth Faison, "How a Betrayal Snagged a Chinese Gang Leader," *New York Times,* August 31, 1993.
154 **The police had heard:** Ah Kay testimony, Zhang Zi trial.
154 **Ah Kay was unhappy:** Interview with Konrad Motyka and Bill McMurry, December 15, 2005.
154 **He fell into a depression:** Confidential source.
154 **Because he knew:** Ibid.
154 **Ah Kay hid:** Interview with Luke Rettler, May 30, 2008.
154 **Then one day he left:** Ah Kay testimony, Zhang Zi trial.
155 **When Ah Kay left:** Alan Tam testimony, the Teaneck trial.
155 **Ah Wong, as he was known:** Ibid.; FBI confidential informant report, September 23, 1993, File # 281E-NY-196708.
155 **Ah Kay instructed:** Interview report of Lin, Chang Liang, Bergen County Prosecutor's Office, July 17, 1995.
155 **When Luke Rettler:** Interview with Luke Rettler, July 26, 2007.
155 **Tam found criminal lawyers:** FBI confidential informant report, September 23, 1993, File # 281E-NY-196708.
155 **When Ah Kay had:** Alan Tam testimony, the Teaneck trial.
156 **He also signed leases:** Transcript of an interview with Erica Lugo, sales associate at Century 21 Realty, Bergen County Prosecutor's Office, October 14, 1993.
156 **Alan Tam always specified:** Ibid.
156 **They moved so frequently:** Alan Tam testimony, the Teaneck trial.
156 **The bathroom at a safe house:** Crime scene investigation report, Bergen County Prosecutor's Office, July 12, 1993.
156 **They cooked:** Ibid.
157 **"We watch kung fu movies":** Alan Tam testimony, the Teaneck trial.
157 **They played Nintendo:** Property and evidence receipt, Bergen County Prosecutor's Office, June 14, 1993.
157 **At one of the houses:** Jim Consoli, "Shooters Hunted in Gang Killings," *Bergen County Record,* June 23, 1993.
157 **People assumed:** Witness interview with [name withheld], Bergen County Prosecutor's Office, August 24, 1993.
157 **Then one day Dan Xin Lin:** Interview with Ray Kerr, May 22, 2007.
157 **Dan Xin sat:** Interview with Tom Trautman, May 3, 2007.
157 **But Dan Xin said:** Interview with

Luke Rettler, in which he referred to affidavits filed by the investigating officers, crime scene specialists, and Dan Xin Lin, May 30, 2008.

158 **The FBI coordinated:** Interview with Luke Rettler, July 26, 2007.

158 **He had grown obsessed:** Interview with Konrad Motyka and Bill McMurry, December 15, 2005.

158 **He instructed some of his allies:** FBI confidential informant report, September 14, 1993, File #281E-NY-196708.

158–59 **That March and April:** Case report, homicide investigation of Yu Ping Zhang, et al., Bergen County Prosecutor's Office, February 18, 1994.

159 **He pulled out:** FBI confidential informant report, September 23, 1993, File #281E-NY-196708.

159 **Dan Xin offered:** FBI confidential informant report, September 14, 1993, File #281E-NY-196708.

159 **They visited a gun dealer:** FBI confidential informant report, December 9, 1993, File #281E-NY-196708.

159 **They bought five handguns:** Case report, homicide investigation of Yu Ping Zhang, et al., Bergen County Prosecutor's Office, February 18, 1994.

159 **But they had neglected:** FBI and confidential informant report, September 14, 1993, File #281E-NY-196708.

159 **As the plotters:** FBI confidential informant report, November 12, 1993, File #281E-NY-196708.

159 **Tam said he didn't:** Thomas Zambito, "Gang Insider Turns Accuser," *Bergen County Record,* November 2, 1995.

160 **Tam had always:** Interview with Konrad Motyka and Bill McMurry, December 15, 2005.

160 **On the evening of May 23, 1993:** Interview with Ray Kerr, May 22, 2007.

160 **The next afternoon:** FBI confidential informant report, September 23, 1993, File #281E-NY-196708.

160 **Inside, a man:** Interview report of Lin, Chang Liang, Bergen County Prosecutor's Office, July 17, 1995, and September 20, 1993.

160 **The house was very comfortable:** Thomas Zambito, "Gang Slaying Attempt Detailed," *Bergen County Record,* November 16, 1995.

161 **The doorbell rang:** Interview report of Lin, Chang Liang, Bergen County Prosecutor's Office, July 17, 1995.

161 **Dan Xin looked angry:** Interview report of Lin, Chang Liang, Bergen County Prosecutor's Office, September 20, 1993.

161 **They took him:** interview/statement of Dan Xin Lin, Bergen County Prosecutor's Office, May 26, 1993.

161 **The basement floor was cold:** Interview report of Lin, Chang Liang, Bergen County Prosecutor's Office, July 17, 1993.

161 **One of Dan Xin's underlings:** Charles Young, "Four Deny Role in Teaneck Shooting," *Bergen County Record,* July 7, 1993.

161 **He found a blanket:** Interview report of Lin, Chang Liang, Bergen County Prosecutor's Office, July 17, 1995.

161 **After establishing:** Interview/statement of Dan Xin Lin, Bergen County Prosecutor's Office, May 26, 1993.

161 **Ah Wong had spent:** Thomas Zambito, "Survivor of Teaneck Ambush Tells of Escape," *Bergen County Record,* October 19, 1995.

161 **As afternoon gave way:** Details in this paragraph are drawn from the interview report of Ah Mee Liu (aka "Ming Chen"), Bergen County Prosecutor's Office, February 3, 1994; Zambito, "Survivor of Teaneck Ambush Tells of Escape"; Debra Lynn Vial, " 'These Men Are Real Sweethearts'—Death Scene Painted in Gang Trial Summations,"

Bergen County Record, December 8, 1995; Thomas Zambito, "Six Gang Members Convicted of Murder," *Bergen County Record,* December 16, 1995.

162 **Dan Xin may have**: Interview with Luke Rettler, May 30, 2008.

162 **On the front porch**: Details from this paragraph are drawn from interview of defendant, Chao Lin Feng, Bergen County Prosecutor's Office, May 31, 1993; interview report of Ah Mee Liu (aka "Ming Cheng"), Bergen County Prosecutor's Office, February 3, 1994. Zambito, "Survivor of Teaneck Ambush Tells of Escape"; Robert Hanley, "Teaneck Killings Laid to Chinese Gang's Power Struggle," *New York Times,* May 26, 1993.

162 **Chang heard the shot**: Zambito, "Gang Slaying Attempt Detailed."

162 **But he hardly registered**: Interview report of Lin, Chang Liang, Bergen County Prosecutor's Office, July 17, 1995.

162 **Akiva Fleischmann**: Interview with Akiva Fleischmann, April 19, 2007.

163 **Another neighbor**: Witness interview with [name withheld], Bergen County Prosecutor's Office, August 25, 1993.

163 **Three local kids**: Witness interview with [name withheld], Bergen County Prosecutor's Office, August 26, 1993.

163 **When the officers arrived**: Crime scene investigation report, Bergen County Prosecutor's Office, July 12, 1993.

163 **Akiva Fleischmann still didn't know**: Interview with Akiva Fleischmann, April 19, 2007.

163 **Ah Wong was still alive**: Interview report of Callis Brown, Teaneck Volunteer Ambulance Corps, Bergen County Prosecutor's Office, June 3, 1993.

164 **"Naked oriental male"**: Autopsy Report—ME #0895, Victim Guo Liang Wang, Bergen County Prosecutor's Office, May 27, 1993.

164 **A tenth bullet**: Case report, homicide investigation of Yu Ping Zhang, et. al., Bergen County Prosecutor's Office, February 18, 1994.

164 **Four-Eye was eventually apprehended**: Michael Fechter, "Dishwasher Charged in Gang Killings," *Tampa Tribune,* May 4, 1995.

164 **Shing Chung has never**: Interview with William J. Murray and Tom Goldrick, the lead prosecutor and investigator on the Teaneck case, April 19, 2007.

164 **"Get out of here!"**: Interview of defendant, Chao Lin Feng, Bergen County Prosecutor's Office, May 31, 1993.

165 **In nearby Fort Lee**: Case report, homicide investigation of Yu Ping Zhang, et al., Bergen County Prosecutor's Office, February 18, 1994.

165 **Ray Kerr was asleep**: Interview with Ray Kerr, May 22, 2007.

165 **The killers were held**: Charles Young, "Police Fear Escalation of Gang War," *Bergen County Record,* May 29, 1993.

165 **When a judge set**: Elliot Pinsley and Jim Consoli, "Act of Revenge," *Bergen County Record,* May 26, 1993.

165 **Chang, the Fujianese hostage**: Interview with William J. Murray and Tom Goldrick, April 19, 2007.

166 **In New York, the small band**: This fear was related to me by every law enforcement officer that I spoke with who was involved in the Fuk Ching investigation at the time. See also Ying Chan, "N.J. Ambush Fuels Gang War Fear," *Daily News,* May 27, 1993; Young, "Police Fear Escalation of Gang War."

166 **During the trial of the murderers**: Alan Tam testimony, the Teaneck trial.

166 **Because the Teaneck trial**: Ibid.

166 **"From what I hear"**: Tu Wei Chung testimony, the Teaneck trial.

CHAPTER 10: MUTINY IN THE ATLANTIC

In addition to interviews with law enforcement officials and passengers who were on board the *Golden Venture*, this chapter draws on the accounts of Captain Tobing, Kin Sin Lee, Sam Lwin, and Weng Yu Hui, each of whom gave his version of the mutiny and landing in Queens at one point or another, either in interviews with law enforcement or in testimony related to the various prosecutions that ensued. As indicated in the body of the chapter, the reporting of the *South China Morning Post* put America's intelligence agencies to shame when it came to discerning, in real time, the trajectory of the *Golden Venture*; fifteen years later I found those articles invaluable in puzzling out the voyage of the ship.

168 **The ship's imminent arrival**: Letter from Carter to Raggi, re: United States v. Kin Sin Lee, et al.

168 **When Lee was able**: United States v. Moe, 64 F.3d 245, at 248.

168 **Kin Sin Lee was growing anxious**: Ibid.

169 **Captain Tobing liked this new plan**: Ibid.

169 **But Lee was in no mood**: Supplemental criminal incident report, William Stray, June 7, 1993.

169 **With the matter unresolved**: United States v. Moe, 64 F.3d 245, at 248.

169 **He didn't call it**: Testimony of Kin Sin Lee in United States v. Kin Sin Lee, et al., 93 CR 694, June 28, 1994 (hereafter Lee testimony, Lee trial).

169 **The ship's Burmese first officer**: Government appellate brief in United States v. Lee, 122 F.3d 1058, Second Circuit Court of Appeals, April 12, 1995; Lee testimony, Lee trial.

170 **In Lwin's account**: Testimony of Sam Lwin in United States v. Kin Sin Lee, et al., 93 CR 694, June 23, 1994.

170 **With Tobing locked in his cabin**: Supplemental criminal incident report, Detective William Stray, June 7, 1993.

170 **Lee did not know**: Brief for the defendant appellant, Lee Peng Fei, in United States v. Fei, 225 F.3d 167, before the Second Circuit Court of Appeals, October 1, 1999.

170 **On the morning of June 4**: "Post-Seizure Analysis—M/V Golden Venture," unclassified internal Coast Guard document, August 1993.

171 **As early as October 1992**: Interview with Donald Monica, June 9, 2008.

171 **At least on paper**: Department of Justice limited official use document, "The Immigration Emergency," July 8, 1993.

171 **As it happened, in February 1993**: "Hijacked Merchant Ship Awaits Permission to Land," United Press International, February 10, 1993.

172 **Then the United States turned**: Peter Woolrich and Michael Chugani, "Hong Kong Rejects Chinese Illegals," *South China Morning Post*, February 14, 1993.

172 **The *East Wood* had become**: Interview with Eric Schwartz, former National Security Council official responsible for boat smuggling issues, January 5, 2006.

172 **The UN monitors ultimately concluded**: "More than Five Hundred Chinese Nationals Repatriated from Marshall Islands," Agence France Presse, March 6, 1993.

172 **But no sooner**: Peter Woolrich, "Dreams Crash Land on the Shores of Home," *South China Morning Post*, March 7, 1993.

172 **In a series of stories**: Paul Tyrrell, "Bilateral Deal on Illegals 'Violated,'"

South China Morning Post, March 13, 1993; Peter Woolrich, "China Slammed over *East Wood* Illegals," *South China Morning Post,* March 14, 1993.

173 **Officials in Beijing:** "Peking Denies Detention of *East Wood* Migrants," Central News Agency—Taiwan, March 17, 1993.

173 **What is clear:** E-mail from Ambassador E. Michael Southwick, May 29, 2008.

173 **In 1993 there was:** Interview with Donald Monica, June 9, 2008.

173 **Some at the INS:** Confidential interview, June 6, 2007.

173 **One plan that was briefly:** Interview with Mark Riordan, June 7, 2007; interview with Ben Ferro, former INS official, June 24, 2008.

174 **Don Monica was still trying:** Interview with Donald Monica, June 9, 2008.

174 **On April 15, 1993:** Department of Justice limited official use executive intelligence brief, HQ-EB-93-33, "People's Republic of China: An Update on Current Smuggling Trends," April 15, 1993.

175 **On April 4, 1993:** Peter Woolrich, Matiko Bohoko, and Chris Dobson, "Immigrants Escape in High Seas Drama," *South China Morning Post,* April 4, 1993.

176 **On April 16:** Diplomatic cable from U.S. Consulate in Durban to various recipients in Washington and internationally, April 16, 1993.

177 **The next time Kin Sin Lee:** Lee testimony, Lee trial.

177 **There wouldn't be any:** The details of this conversation are drawn from Weng Yu Hui testimony, Sister Ping trial, and Lee testimony, Lee trial.

177 **But the first officer turned captain:** United States v. Moe, 64 F.3d 245, at 248.

177 **Weng suggested that:** Lee testimony, Lee trial.

178 **If Lwin could:** Letter from Carter to Raggi, re: United States v. Kin Sin Lee, et al.

178 **The following day:** Lee testimony, Lee trial; government brief in United States v. Fei, appellate brief, Second Circuit Court of Appeals, November 4, 1999.

178 **At Charlie's urging:** Lee testimony, Lee trial.

178 **Sean Chen was huddled:** Interview with Sean Chen, February 6, 2008.

178 **Then, around midday:** United States v. Fei, 225 F.3d 167, at 170.

178 **According to some accounts:** Government brief in United States v. Lee, 122 F.3d 1058, appellate brief, Second Circuit Court of Appeals, April 12, 1995.

178 **But according to others:** Letter from Carter to Raggi, re: United States v. Kin Sin Lee, et al.

179 **It is a frequent refrain:** Interview with Mark Riordan, June 7, 2007; see also William Claiborne, "Elusive Ships Frustrate Coast Guard," *Washington Post,* July 21, 1993.

179 **What we do know:** Richard Pyle, "Ship Carrying Chinese Aliens Runs Aground Off NYC; at Least Seven Dead," Associated Press, June 6, 1993.

179 **When the ship reached:** Lee testimony, Lee trial.

179 **Shortly after midnight:** Testimony of Sam Lwin in United States v. Kin Sin Lee, et al., 93 CR 694, June 23, 1994.

179 **As darkness fell:** Lee testimony, Lee trial.

180 **"Let's do it":** Brief for the defendant appellant, Lee Peng Fei, in United States v. Fei, 225 F.3d 167, Second Circuit Court of Appeals, October 1, 1999.

180 **In the last moments at sea:** These details are drawn from interviews with Sean Chen, February 6, 2008, and June 5, 2008.

CHAPTER 11: A WELL-FOUNDED FEAR

This chapter is based primarily on interviews with Bill Slattery, Doris Meissner, Eric Schwartz, and other officials who were involved in handling the difficult policy decisions in the days, months, and ultimately years following the arrival of the *Golden Venture*. Some of the current and former officials in question agreed to speak with me at length about the experience but did not want any facts or assertions attributed to them by name. The chapter also draws on an extensive collection of internal Clinton administration documents and memoranda. These materials were released through discovery in the lawsuit that was eventually filed against the Justice Department on behalf of the *Golden Venture* detainees, and were supplied to me by Craig Trebilcock, of York, Pennsylvania, one of the lead lawyers in that suit.

182 **One historian referred**: Alexander Saxton, *The Indispensable Enemy: Labor and the Anti-Chinese Movement in California* (Berkeley: University of California Press, 1975). Saxton makes a more nuanced point as well, suggesting that the Chinese were indispensable to the development of organized labor in California during the nineteenth century because anti-Chinese animus became a galvanizing rallying force.

183 **In March the *New York Times***: Francis X. Clines, "After Bombing, New Scrutiny for Holes in Immigration Net," *New York Times*, March 12, 1993.

183 **He sounded dire warnings**: Marlowe Hood, "Riding the Snake," *Los Angeles Times Magazine*, June 13, 1993.

184 **Slattery was hard-nosed**: Unless otherwise noted, material relating to Bill Slattery is from an interview with Bill Slattery, July 7, 2008.

185 **Since the inauguration**: Interview with Eric Schwartz, January 5, 2006.

185 **Sean Chen and the other passengers**: Wendy Lin and Jessie Mangaliman, "Woes of Smuggling," *Newsday*, June 10, 1993.

186 **"It's been our tradition"**: Tim Weiner, "Smuggled to New York," *New York Times*, June 8, 1993.

186 **Some snakeheads had been known**: No major cases had been brought against lawyers for cooperating with snakeheads in 1993, but in 2000 one of the most prominent immigration attorneys representing the Chinese community in New York, Robert Porges, was arrested and charged, along with his wife, in a ninety-count racketeering indictment. See United States of America v. Robert Porges, aka "Lawyer Bao," et al., S6 00 Cr. 934 (DLC), United States District Court for the Southern District of New York. Porges and his wife pleaded guilty to racketeering, conspiracy, and tax fraud and were sentenced to serve eight years in prison (though in letters to me from prison, both Robert and Sheery Lu Porges maintained their innocence). See also Elizabeth Amon, "The Snakehead Lawyers," *New York Law Journal*, July 17, 2002.

186 **It wasn't unheard of**: Mark Hamblett, "Government Outlines Case Against Porges," *New York Law Journal*, September 27, 2000.

187 **At Varick Street**: Diane Jean Schemo, "Refugees Blocked from Getting Legal Help," *New York Times*, June 10, 1993.

187 **The attorneys had maintained**: Ibid.

187 **Sean Chen found himself**: Interview with Sean Chen, February 6, 2008.

188 **On that first day**: Melissa Robinson, "Chinese Prisoners Endured Painful Journey for Chance at Freedom," Associated Press, June 9, 1993.

188 **But Sean was beginning**: Seth Faison, "U.S. Tightens Asylum Rules for

Chinese," *New York Times,* September 5, 1993.

188 **On Friday, June 11**: White House meeting agenda prepared by Carol Rasco and Sandy Berger, June 10, 1993.

189 **Before the *Golden Venture***: Pamela Burdman and Ken Hoover, "U.S. Organizing to Repulse Smuggler Ship Invasion," *San Francisco Chronicle,* May 28, 1993.

189 **It emerged that the month before**: Interview with James Puleo, former State Department and INS official, June 10, 2008. Also see Burdman and Hoover, "U.S. Organizing to Repulse Smuggler Ship Invasion."

189 **Before the Oval Office meeting**: Letter from Associate Attorney General Webster Hubbell to National Security Adviser Anthony Lake, June 9, 1993.

189 **"Alien smuggling is a shameful practice"**: President William J. Clinton, remarks on the nomination of Doris Meissner to be INS commissioner, June 18, 1993.

189 **As he concluded**: Gwen Ifill, "President Chooses an Expert to Halt Smuggling of Aliens," *New York Times,* June 19, 1993.

190 **Meissner had been informed**: Interview with Doris Meissner, December 5, 2005.

191 **During the cold war:** Tim Weiner, "Smuggled to New York: Fixing Immigration," *New York Times,* June 8, 1993.

191 **Throughout the 1990s**: Nina Bernstein, "In New York Immigration Court, Asylum Roulette," *New York Times,* October 8, 2006.

191 **If you are a Chinese asylum-seeker**: See Jaya Ramji-Nogales, Andrew Schoenholtz, and Philip Schrag, "Refugee Roulette: Disparities in Asylum Adjudication," *Stanford Law Review* 60 (2008): 15, 25.

191 **One immigration judge in Los Angeles**: Ibid., p. 44.

191 **Interestingly, female judges**: Ibid., p. 47.

191 **"Whether an asylum applicant"**: Ibid., p. 82.

192 **For no other nationality**: Ibid., p. 32.

192 **With one fifth of the world's population**: Nicholas Kristof and Sheryl Wudunn, *China Wakes: The Struggle for the Soul of a Rising Power* (New York: Times Books, 1994), p. 10.

192 **There is a famous story**: This story is true, though the precise wording of Deng's reply varies from one account to the next. See George J. Borjas, *Heaven's Door: Immigration Policy and the American Economy* (Princeton, NJ: Princeton University Press, 1999), p. 3; Kishore Mahbubani, *The New Asian Hemisphere: The Irresistible Shift of Global Power to the East* (New York: PublicAffairs, 2008), p. 314; Adlai E. Stevenson and Alton Frye, "Trading with the Communists," *Foreign Affairs* (Spring 1989).

192 **Shortly after Chang's claim**: Memo from the Office of Attorney General Meese to INS Commissioner Alan Nelson, August 5, 1988.

193 **Instead, the board held**: "Matter of Chang," Interim Decision: 3107, Board of Immigration Appeals, 1989.

193 **Chang's attorney**: Interview with Jules Coven, June 16, 2008.

194 **Tiananmen unfolded**: See 135 Cong. Rec. S. Doc. No. 8241-2 (July 19, 1989).

194 **The bill passed**: Memorandum on Disapproval for the Emergency Chinese Relief Act of 1989, 25 Weekly Compilation of Presidential Documents at 1843-54 (1989).

194 **The executive action**: Executive Order No. 12,711, §4, 55 Fed. Reg. 13,897 (1990). Because of the peculiarity of the regulatory process in Washington, in order for Bush's wishes to take effect, the attorney general needed to

promulgate a "rule" that would be published in the *Federal Register*. But when Attorney General Richard Thornburgh issued his final rule on procedures for determining who would and would not get asylum, he somehow neglected to include anything about family-planning policies in China. No explanation was ever offered for this oversight. Some speculated that it was a drafting error. But the result was that there was no general agreement on how to proceed with asylum applications, and this period of uncertainty happened to coincide with the snakehead boom of the early 1990s and a great proliferation of asylum requests. In practice, immigration inspectors from the INS began following the guidelines established in the executive order, taking an expansive view of who could be granted asylum, while immigration judges and the Board of Immigration Appeals took a much narrower view, following *Matter of Chang* and insisting that simply saying "one-child policy" was not grounds for admission to America. This resulted in great uncertainty for the Chinese, as the result of their cases would vary depending on which of these bodies ended up hearing their claim. In keeping with the legal fiction that people had not entered the country, "exclusion" cases, for those detained at airports or on the beach with wet feet, were heard by the relatively sympathetic INS immigration inspectors, whereas "deportation" cases, for those who were already here, were heard by immigration judges. The frustration for the Chinese who were denied asylum before the BIA, as an opinion in one later case would put it, was that the generous interpretation of American policy had been adopted "in various forms at various times by the President of the United States, both houses of Congress, three Attorneys General and the General Counsel of the INS," but that the BIA had been pretty consistent in its own more restrictive interpretation. Zhang v. Slattery, 55 F.3d 732 (2d Cir. 1995).

194 **In January 1993:** Attorney General Order No. 1659-93, JA 1652, 1664-65.

194 **But in order for a rule:** The chronology that follows is spelled out comprehensively in Zhang v. Slattery, 55 F.3d 732 (2d Cir. 1995).

194 **When Clinton assembled:** White House meeting agenda prepared by Carol Rasco and Sandy Berger, June 10, 1993.

195 **On the campaign trail:** See Howard French, "Haitians See Renewal of Hope with Clinton," *New York Times*, November 23, 1992; Elaine Sciolino, "Clinton Says U.S. Will Continue Ban on Haitian Exodus," *New York Times*, January 15, 1993. On the larger story of the processing of Haitian refugees at Guantánamo Bay, see Brandt Goldstein, *Storming the Court* (New York: Scribner, 2005).

195 **After his nomination:** Jill Smolowe, "How It Happened," *Time*, February 1, 1993.

195 **To Doris Meissner:** Interview with Doris Meissner, December 5, 2005.

195 **Clinton had lost:** See Bill Clinton, *My Life* (New York: Knopf, 2004), pp. 274–78, for a discussion of the Mariel boat lift and Fort Chaffee, and pp. 283–87 for a discussion of the election of 1980. Interestingly, Clinton maintains that he handled the crisis at Fort Chaffee well and that he enjoyed higher support among voters in western Arkansas who had observed firsthand how he managed the situation. But he notes that in postelection polls of those who had voted for him in 1976 but not in 1980, "six percent of my former supporters said it was because of the Cubans."

196 **Even after the *Golden Venture* landed:** Interview with Doris Meissner, December 5, 2005.

196 **The fear among many officials:** Interview with Jonathan Winer, former deputy assistant secretary of state for international law enforcement, March 11, 2008.

196 **Tim Wirth, the undersecretary:** Ibid.

196 **According to the State Department:** Letter to Sandy Berger from Tim Wirth, February 18, 1994.

196 **State prepared a report:** "Asylum Claims Relating to Family Planning in Fujian Province," State Department Office of Asylum Affairs, Bureau of Human Rights and Humanitarian Affairs, August 1993.

197 **Some critics disparaged him:** Hood, "Riding the Snake."

197 **To Bill Slattery:** Interview with Bill Slattery, July 7, 2008.

197 **Following George Bush's executive order:** The Rees memo dates to November 7, 1991, and is titled "Asylum Requests Based upon Coercive Family Planning Policies." It reads, in part, as follows:

> Department of Justice and INS policy with respect to aliens claiming asylum or withholding of deportation based upon coercive family planning policies does constitute persecution on account of political opinion. This policy is embodied in the Attorney General's directives of August 5, 1988 and December 1, 1989; in the President's directive of November 30, 1989; in Executive Order No. 12711, Section 4, published on April 13, 1990 at 55 FR 13897; and in the interim final regulations published on January 29, 1990 at 55 FR 2203 . . . Pursuant to this Department and INS policy, the INS will regard an applicant for asylum (and the applicant's spouse, if also an applicant) to have established presumptive eligibility for asylum on the basis of past persecution on account of political opinion if the applicant establishes that, pursuant to the implementation by the country of the applicant's nationality of a family planning policy that includes forced abortion or coerced sterilization, the applicant has been forced to abort a pregnancy or to undergo involuntary sterilization or has been persecuted for failure to do so. The INS will regard an applicant for asylum (and the applicant's spouse, if also an applicant) to have established presumptive eligibility for asylum on the basis of a well-founded fear of persecution on account of political opinion if the applicant establishes a well-founded fear that, pursuant to the implementation by the country of the applicant's nationality of a family planning policy that includes forced abortion or coerced sterilization, the applicant will be forced to abort a pregnancy or to undergo involuntary sterilization, or will be persecuted for failure or refusal to do so . . . Although the provision of Executive Order No. 12711 for 'enhanced consideration' does not require an INS trial attorney to make an affirmative recommendation based on evidence that he or she sincerely regards as incredible, it is especially important in these cases that the attorney be engaged in a genuine search for truth. The INS attorney should be just as diligent in searching for indications that the applicant or the applicant's evidence may be credible as for indications that it may not be.

197 **In Rees's view:** Isabelle de Pommereau, "Chinese Refugees Turn Waiting into an Art Form," *Christian Science Monitor,* May 30, 1996.

197 **Six weeks before:** Nicholas Kristof, "China's Crackdown on Births: A Stunning and Harsh Success," *New York Times,* April 25, 1993.
198 **Abortion was less common:** Jim Yardley, "Face of Abortion in China: A Young, Single Woman," *New York Times,* May 13, 2007.
198 **But as a tactic:** Kristof, "China's Crackdown on Births."
198 **Rees found it scandalous:** Grover Joseph Rees deposition in Yang You Yi, et al. v. Janet Reno, 852 F.Supp.316 (1994).
199 **"We are making arrangements":** Katy Butler, "Seven Die as Smuggle Ship Runs Aground in New York," *San Francisco Chronicle,* June 7, 1993.
199 **In a memo to Vice President:** Memo for the Vice President, "Immigration Issues," from Donsia Strong, Eric Schwartz, and Rand Beers, July 7, 1993.
199 **A Justice Department document:** Department of Justice limited official use document, "The Immigration Emergency," July 8, 1993.
199 **The solution was to expedite:** Letter from Gerald Hurwitz, counsel to the director, Executive Office for Immigration Review, to Phyllis Coven, assistant to the attorney general, June 15, 1993.
200 **"The Golden Venture is sort of":** White House, Office of the Press Secretary, "Background Briefing by Senior Administration Officials" (Rand Beers and Donsia Strong), June 18, 1993.
200 **After several days:** Unless otherwise indicated, the account of Ann Carr's meeting with Sean Chen is drawn from interviews with Ann Carr, November 21, 2005, and June 10, 2008; a written recollection by Ann Carr of her involvement in the *Golden Venture* cases; Sean Chen's immigration file; and interviews with Sean Chen on February 6, 2008, and June 5, 2008.
200 **There had been many:** See Mary S. Erbaugh and Richard Curt Kraus, "The 1989 Democracy Movement in Fujian and Its Aftermath," *Australian Journal of Chinese Affairs,* no. 23 (January 1990).
201 **The clerk told her:** E-mail from Ann Carr, November 17, 2005. Carr also maintained this account in a sworn affidavit dated August 31, 1993.
204 **The State Department had prepared:** "Asylum Claims Relating to Family Planning in Fujian Province," State Department Office of Asylum Affairs, Bureau of Human Rights and Humanitarian Affairs, August 1993.
204 **The memo conceded:** Ibid.
204 **When the Rutgers criminologist:** Chin, *Smuggled Chinese,* p. 115.
204 **Peter Kwong:** Kwong, *Forbidden Workers,* p. 57.
205 **During the fall of 1993:** "China: Abusive Family Planning Practices and Asylum," memo from Eric Schwartz to Sandy Berger, December 13, 1993; "Processing of Chinese Nationals Who Fear Coercive Family Planning Practices," memorandum by Chris Sale, deputy commissioner, Immigration and Naturalization Service, August 5, 1994.
205 **Eventually the Board of Immigration Appeals:** Matter of G—, 20 I. & N. Dec. 764, Interim Decision (BIA) 3215, 1993.
205 **By September:** Faison, "U.S. Tightens Asylum Rules."
205 **Of those who did succeed:** Kwong, *Forbidden Workers,* p. 50. On the historical presence of large numbers of Christian missionaries in Fujian, see Graham Hutchings, *Modern China: A Guide to a Century of Change* (Cambridge, MA: Harvard University Press, 2001), p. 151.
206 **"It seems we were unlucky":** Faison, "U.S. Tightens Asylum Rules."
206 **One of Sean's fellow inmates:** Nina Bernstein, "Making It Ashore, But

Still Chasing U.S. Dream," *New York Times,* April 9, 2006.

CHAPTER 12: THE FAT MAN

The principal sources for this chapter are interviews with current and former FBI and immigration officials who were involved in the effort to capture Ah Kay and other members of the Fuk Ching gang. For reasons of narrative economy, and because the relevant officials at Immigration and Customs Enforcement made the investigators Karen Pace and Mona Foreman available to speak with me only in a very limited capacity, the story of the capture of Weng Yu Hui is dealt with more briefly than I might have liked. My account of the Fat Man, Dickson Yao, draws on an extensive interview with Richard LaMagna, a former DEA agent who served as Yao's handler and knew him for twenty years. I was eager to interview Yao myself but was told by Jerry Stuchiner that he died several years ago. ("He just kept eating," Stuchiner explained.) James Mills's fantastic 1986 book *The Underground Empire,* which draws on interviews with Yao and input from numerous agents who handled him over the years, paints a picture of this charismatic scallywag. I spoke with Jerry Stuchiner several times and exchanged a handful of e-mails with him, but the portrait of him draws also on the recollections of numerous former FBI, INS, and DEA agents who encountered him over the years. For reasons that become clear in Chapter Sixteen, everyone seems to have a Jerry Stuchiner story. As indicated in the notes, Brook Larmer and Melinda Liu's extraordinary 1997 *Newsweek* article about Stuchiner and Yao was also very useful.

207 **Scores of mourners:** Interview with Konrad Motyka and Bill McMurry, October 31, 2005; Anthony DeStefano, "Gang Leader 'Blew $1 M,'" *Newsday,* August 31, 1993.

207 **He had joined:** Plum Beach was so popular, in fact, that less than two months after that body was discovered, another victim was found on the same beach. See Russell Ben-Ali, "Cops Accused: Family Blames Police in Son's Kidnap Death," *Newsday,* September 29, 1993.

207 **He had been hog-tied:** Interview with Konrad Motyka and Bill McMurry, October 31, 2005.

207 **As the mourners lined up:** Unless otherwise noted, details of the Green-Wood Cemetery raid are drawn from interviews with Konrad Motyka on October 31, 2005, December 15, 2005, and October 19, 2007, and from a photograph of Motyka and Shafer in the cemetery taken following the raid.

208 **Motyka remembered:** Donatella Lorch, "Mourners Returned Fire, Police Say," *New York Times,* July 30, 1990.

208 **Motyka had grown up:** These biographical details are drawn from interviews with Konrad Motyka on October 31, 2005, December 15, 2005, and October 19, 2007.

208 **C-6 was run:** Interview with Ray Kerr, May 22, 2007; interview with Tom Trautman, May 3, 2007.

209 **Nearly three months earlier:** Jimmy Breslin, "A Familiar Refrain: 'It's Not My Fault,'" *Newsday,* June 8, 1993.

206 **Because alien smuggling convictions:** Interview with Jodi Avergun, May 24, 2007.

210 **The judge, Reena Raggi:** Dennis Hevesi, "Judge Rejects a Plea Bargain for Defendants in Ship Death," *New York Times,* April 9, 1994.

210 **When he was asked:** Lee testimony, Lee trial.

210 **And despite his protests:** Pete Bowles, "Smuggler Sentenced," *Newsday,* July 14, 1994.

210 **Several years after he was released:** Jane Hadley and Scott Sunde, "Why Smuggle Pot to NW? Authorities Puzzled; There's Plenty Here," *Seattle Post-Intelligencer,* December 3, 1997.
210 **As investigators questioned:** Interview with Mona Foreman and Karen Pace, of ICE, June 19, 2007.
210 **On the morning the *Golden Venture*:** Weng Yu Hui testimony, Sister Ping trial.
211 **The following month:** Ibid.
211 **Again Sister Ping volunteered:** Ibid.
211 **He never made it to South Africa:** Ibid.
211 **But he kept coming back:** Details of the capture of Weng Yu Hui are from an interview with Karen Pace and Mona Foreman, who led the investigation into Weng and were present at the arrest, June 19, 2007.
211 **He pleaded guilty:** Joseph P. Fried, "An Organizer Admits Guilt in Smuggling," *New York Times,* June 30, 1994.
211 **Within hours of the *Golden Venture*'s arrival:** "Chinese Gang Linked to Grounded Refugee Ship," United Press International, June 8, 1993.
211 **Konrad Motyka was working:** Interview with Luke Rettler, May 30, 2008.
212 **Stories circulated in Chinatown:** Interview with Luke Rettler, July 26, 2007; interview with Tom Trautman, May 3, 2007.
212 **After the killings at Teaneck:** Alan Tam testimony, the Teaneck trial.
212 **When he was asked:** Interview with William J. Murray, April 19, 2007.
212 **Before Tam hung up:** Alan Tam testimony, the Teaneck trial; interview with Tom Trautman, May 3, 2007.
213 **At considerable expense:** Interview with Tom Trautman, May 3, 2007; interview with Luke Rettler, July 26, 2007. The detective who recognized Tam was Margie Yee.
213–14 **Ah Kay was already:** Testimony in United States v. Kwok Ling Kay, et al., 93 CR. 783, October 12, 1993.
214 **When Ah Kay fled:** Interview with Ray Kerr, May 22, 2007.
214 **Of course Ah Kay:** Ibid.
214 **The older man found:** Ibid.
214 **"Are you on the cell phone?":** Ibid.
214 **The members of the Fuk Ching gang:** Interview with Luke Rettler, May 30, 2008.
214 **Like Mock Duck:** Asbury, *Gangs of New York,* p. 282.
215 **Since the *Golden Venture*:** Interview with Konrad Motyka and Bill McMurry, October 31, 2005.
215 **So he started making trips:** Ibid.
215 **He ran up debts:** Ah Kay testimony, Sister Ping trial.
215 **One day in mid-August:** Transcript of a telephone conversation between Ah Kay and "Ah Shu," August 16, 1993.
215 **Under Title III:** Interview with Luke Rettler, July 26, 2007; interview with Chauncey Parker, May 29, 2007.
216 **When Ah Kay's telephone calls:** Interview with Konrad Motyka and Bill McMurry, December 15, 2005.
216 **In New York, Rettler was told:** Interview with Luke Rettler, July 26, 2007.
216 **Standing six feet tall:** Unless otherwise noted, all details relating to the Fat Man, Dickson Yao, are drawn from an interview with Richard LaMagna, July 17, 2008; and from James Mills, *The Underground Empire* (New York: Dell, 1986), pp. 36, 46, 47, 188–201. Yao was still alive when Mills's book came out, and to protect his identity, Mills used a pseudonym, Robert Yang, though he also used Yao's actual code name, the Fat Man. Jerry Stuchiner

confirmed for me that Four Star was Dickson Yao, in an e-mail on July 26, 2007. (Stuchiner had already revealed as much to *Newsweek* in 1997; see Brook Larmer and Melinda Liu, "Smuggling People," *Newsweek*, March 17, 1997.)

217 **The agents knew:** Mills, *The Underground Empire,* p. 799.

218 **Before long the Fat Man:** Interview with Jerry Stuchiner, May 23, 2007.

218 **Short and pugnacious:** This account of Jerry Stuchiner is based on an interview with him on May 23, 2007; Larmer and Liu, "Smuggling People"; and interviews with over a dozen current and former FBI and immigration officials who worked with him over the years.

218 **Still, in 1984:** Larmer and Liu, "Smuggling People."

219 **He developed a habit:** Confidential interviews with two of Stuchiner's former colleagues.

219 **From the Fat Man:** Interview with Jerry Stuchiner, May 23, 2007.

219 **In the days after the *Golden Venture*:** Confidential interviews with three of Stuchiner's former colleagues.

219 **The Fat Man told Stuchiner:** Interview with Jerry Stuchiner, May 23, 2007.

219 **Before long, Stuchiner was paying:** Larmer and Liu, "Smuggling People."

219 **With Hong Kong's changeover:** Interview with Richard LaMagna, July 17, 2008.

220 **Many people who find themselves:** Interview with Richard LaMagna, June 3, 2008.

220 **They even discussed:** Larmer and Liu, "Smuggling People"; William Branigin, "Hong Kong Set to Free Jailed Former INS Agent," *Washington Post,* June 13, 1997.

220 **One day in August 1993:** Interview with Jerry Stuchiner, May 23, 2007.

220 **Stuchiner was excited:** Confidential interview.

220 **Several days later:** Interview with Jerry Stuchiner, May 23, 2007.

220 **Stuchiner wanted to stake out:** Confidential interview.

220 **Instead, the FBI took over:** Interview with Michael di Pretoro, an FBI agent based in Hong Kong at the time, May 8, 2007.

221 **During his time in Hong Kong:** Joseph Treaster, "Arrest Ends Gang Chief's Rich Life on the Run," *New York Times,* September 3, 1993.

221 **On Friday August 27:** Ibid.

221 **Suddenly they were surrounded:** Ibid.; Greg Torode, "Gang Suspect Link Denied," *South China Morning Post,* September 1, 1993.

221 **When the officers searched him:** Treaster, "Arrest Ends Gang Chief's Rich Life"; Torode, "Gang Suspect Link Denied."

221 **Jerry Stuchiner was furious:** Interview with Jerry Stuchiner, May 23, 2007.

221 **For his part, the Fat Man:** Larmer and Liu, "Smuggling People."

221 **As soon as Ah Kay:** Interview with Michael di Pretoro, May 8, 2007.

221 **The following day:** Unless otherwise noted, details of the Green-Wood Cemetery raid are drawn from interviews with Konrad Motyka on October 31, 2005, December 15, 2005, and October 19, 2007, and on a photograph of Motyka and Shafer in the cemetery taken following the raid.

222 **As Motyka rounded up:** Seth Faison, "Gang Leader Is Arrested in Hong Kong," *New York Times,* August 29, 1993.

222 **They wrapped the whole building:** Interview with Tom Trautman, May 3, 2007.

223 **From a high-tech command center:** Interview with Luke Rettler, July 26, 2007.
223 **Several weeks after the roundup:** Interview with Konrad Motyka and Bill McMurry, October 31, 2005.
223 **But in the basement restaurant:** Interview with Konrad Motyka and Bill McMurry, October 31, 2005; closing arguments of Leslie Brown, Sister Ping trial.
224 **In addition to worrying:** Interview with Ying Chan, November 21, 2005.
224 **Chan visited Sister Ping:** Sister Ping sentencing remarks.
224 **Early in 1994:** Interview with Ying Chan, November 21, 2005; Kwong, *Forbidden Workers*, p. 134.
225 **Chan reported the threat:** Interview with Ying Chan, November 21, 2005. These details were corroborated by Dougie Lee in an interview on February 10, 2006.
225 **Dougie Lee, the Cantonese American detective:** Interview with Dougie Lee, February 10, 2006.
225 **Sister Ping denies:** Sister Ping sentencing remarks.
225 **With both Ah Kay and Weng Yu Hui:** Written declaration of Special Agent Peter Lee.
225 **Its agents obtained a warrant:** Ibid.
225 **In March 1994:** Criminal indictment, United States v. Cheng Chui Ping, aka "Sister Ping," aka "Ping Jai," 94 CR 953, December 2, 1994.
226 **The following month:** Transcript of recorded telephone conversation between Guang Yong, Guang Yong's sister, and Ma Ji Son, April 5, 1994.
226 **After months of painstaking investigation:** Criminal indictment, United States v. Cheng Chui Ping, aka "Sister Ping," aka "Ping Jai."
226 **But by then:** Closing arguments by Leslie Brown, Sister Ping trial.

CHAPTER 13: FREEDOM BIRDS

The story of the *Golden Venture* detainees and how they changed the community of York was first related to me by Craig Trebilcock and Bev Church in 2005. They have elaborated on that story in multiple formal and informal interviews, conversations, e-mails, and telephone messages over the intervening years. This chapter is based on their recollections and on extensive archives of letters, photographs, video footage, press clippings, court filings, and paper sculptures that they have each maintained. I made two trips to York, one in October 2005 and one in July 2008. On the second trip, Joan Maruskin arranged a potluck dinner with a dozen members of the People of the Golden Vision, who shared their recollections and are cited in the notes by name. Maruskin also opened up her personal files, including numerous handwritten letters from the *Golden Venture* detainees and scores of back issues of the Golden Vision newsletter produced by Cindy Lobach. The asylum claims of Pin Lin and Sean Chen are based in part on their case files and on multiple interviews with their lawyers, Craig Trebilcock and Ann Carr. The account of the paper-folding is drawn largely from an interview with Yang You Yi, who was one of the most talented folders, and on my own exposure to the sculptures themselves, which seem to ornament every horizontal surface in the homes and offices of the York residents who rallied around the detainees.
227 **To Craig Trebilcock:** Unless otherwise noted, the account of Craig Trebilcock's involvement in the case of the *Golden Venture* detainees is drawn from interviews with Craig Trebilcock, October 28, 2005, and July 23, 2008.
228 **A local joke:** Interview with Joan Maruskin, July 17, 2008.

228 **The town was home:** Interview with Byron Borger, July 22, 2008.
228 **The INS had contacted:** Interviews with Jeff Lobach, July 22, 2008, and July 24, 2008.
229 **It was slow going:** Some of the details of the circumstances under which Pin left China are drawn from Pin Lin, "Request for Asylum in the United States," undated, June 1993, and other items in Pin Lin's case file.
230 **At the foot of the American watchtower:** Serge Schmemann, "On the Central Front in Germany, Quiet Duty and Good Life for GI's," *New York Times,* February 27, 1989.
232 **Craig's secretary Margo:** Interview with Margo Einsig, July 22, 2008.
233 **About a month later:** Unless otherwise indicated, details relating to Joan Maruskin's involvement in supporting the *Golden Venture* detainees are drawn from interviews with Joan Maruskin, July 17, 2008, and July 22, 2008.
234 **Along with Maruskin there was Beverly Church:** Unless otherwise indicated, details about Bev Church's involvement come from interviews with Beverly Church, October 30, 2005, and December 11, 2005.
234 **She drove out to the prison:** Zheng Xin Bin's case is summarized in "*Golden Venture* Chinese Refugees Who Wish Third Country Resettlement," an undated document provided by Craig Trebilcock.
235 **There was Sterling Showers:** Interviews with Sterling Showers, January 22, 2008, and July 22, 2008.
235 **There was Lena Ngo:** Interview with Lena Ngo, July 22, 2008.
235 **There was Rod Merrill:** Interview with Robert "Rod" Merrill, July 22, 2008.
235 **There was Demian Yumi:** Interview with Demian Yumi, July 22, 2008.
236 **There was Cindy Lobach:** Interview with Cindy Lobach, July 22, 2008.
236 **To help them communicate:** Interview with Zehao Zhou, July 22, 2008; Caryl Clarke, "Zehao Zhou: York College Librarian," *York Daily Record,* February 10, 2003.
236 **The members of the group:** Interview with Joan Maruskin, July 17, 2008.
236 **They found passages:** Leviticus 19:33-34. Cited in the mission statement, "Mission of the People of the Golden Venture."
237 **"The Bible is the ultimate":** Mary Corey, "From Refugees to Friends," *Baltimore Sun,* February 21, 1997.
237 **"It's injustice":** Ian Fisher, "A Town's Strange Bedfellows Unite Behind Chinese Refugees," *New York Times,* February 21, 1997.
237 **To Caryl Clarke:** Caryl Clarke, "Plight of Detainees Creates Circle of Friends," *York Daily Record,* June 9, 1996.
238 **Maruskin insisted:** Interview with Joan Maruskin, July 17, 2008.
239 **In the summer of 1995:** "Coercive Population Control in China," hearing before the United States House of Representatives, Committee on International Relations, Subcommittee on International Operations and Human Rights, Washington, D.C., July 19, 1995. At least as of this writing, a portion of the testimony is on YouTube, under the title "Congressional Hearings on China's Forced Abortion Policy." Craig Trebilcock is sitting in the foreground. In the background, you can see some of the paper sculptures on a table.
239 **Chen Yun Fei recounted:** Ibid.
239 **"The crimes that have been committed":** Ibid.
240 **In Bakersfield they caught:** Kenneth Chang, "Freedom Dreams," *Los Angeles Times,* May 15, 1996.
240 **When they learned that the**

women: Julia Duin, "Hopes Frustrated, Refugees from China Languish in Jail," *Washington Times,* September 4, 1996.

240 **On February 29, 1996:** Chang, "Freedom Dreams."

240 **Six months later:** Duin, "Hopes Frustrated."

240 **Word of their predicament had spread:** Interview with Joan Maruskin, July 17, 2008.

240 **In order to secure the deal:** Chang, "Freedom Dreams."

240 **"They have a well-founded fear":** Joan Treadway, "Vatican Intercedes for Chinese Detainees," *New Orleans Times-Picayune,* May 25, 1995.

241 **The church helped the women:** Chang, "Freedom Dreams."

241 **There was one last option:** Interview with Craig Trebilcock, October 28, 2005; the case was Yang You Yi, et al. v. Janet Reno, 852 F.Supp.316 (1994).

242 **"You want a Chinese guy?":** Interview with Joan Maruskin, July 17, 2008.

242 **Several of the passengers went:** "Hunger Strike in York," *Golden Vision Newsletter,* May 18, 1994.

242 **A prison guard caught one:** Melissa Robinson, "Jailed Chinese Aliens Fear Deportation," Associated Press, January 8, 1994.

242 **The inmates were given:** Undated letter from Dong Xu Zhi to Joan Maruskin.

242 **One man developed a tumor:** Julia Duin, "Chinese Waste Away in U.S. Jails After Fleeing Population Control," *Washington Times,* December 17, 1996; Caryl Clarke, "Friends Say Detainee Complained of Stomach Pains for Two Year," *York Daily Record,* February 28, 1996.

243 **As seemed so often:** Interview with Sean Chen, June 5, 2008; Robinson, "Jailed Chinese Aliens Fear Deportation."

243 **One of the passengers:** Caryl Clarke, "Even in Freedom, There Is Fear for Many Chinese Immigrants," *York Daily Record,* December 27, 1996.

240 **One of the York detainees:** The judge was Clarease Rankin, a Philadelphia immigration judge. Dele Olojede, "America—At Any Cost," *Newsday,* July 19, 1998.

244 **While Wang was being held:** Ibid.

244 **Wang was devastated:** Ibid.

244 **Wang had been home:** Ibid.; William Branigin, "Officials Seize 'Mother Ship' Used to Smuggle Chinese Men," *Washington Post,* June 12, 1998.

244 **Some days later:** Celia Dugger, "Sent Back to China, Man Washes Up Again," *New York Times,* June 4, 1998.

245 **The INS immediately moved:** David W. Chen, "INS Moves to Deport Persistent Illegal Immigrant a 2d Time," *New York Times,* June 12, 1998.

245 **But in one final:** David W. Chen, "Chinese Man's Release Ends a Five-Year Tale of Misfortune," *New York Times,* September 10, 1998.

245 **This was nowhere:** Interview with Joan Maruskin, July 17, 2008.

245 **One day in York County Prison:** Unless otherwise indicated, details about Yang You Yi and the paper-folding in York County Prison are drawn from an interview with Yang You Yi, July 23, 2008.

246 **They presented Bev Church:** Interview with Beverly Church, December 11, 2005.

246 **Before long the detainees:** Interview with Cindy Lobach, July 22, 2008.

247 **As word spread:** Interview with Joan Maruskin, July 17, 2008; interview with Cindy Lobach, July 22, 2008.

247 **Soon the proprietor:** It was the Frank J. Miele gallery. Caryl Clarke, "'I Really Wish I Could Have Art for Everybody,'" *York Daily Record,* February 20, 1997.

247 *Life* **ran an article:** Charles Hirshberg, "Folded Dreams," *Life,* July 1996.
247 **"There's some intelligent people here":** Duin, "Hopes Frustrated, Refugees from China Languish in Jail."
247 **The detainees at York:** Interview with Cindy Lobach, July 22, 2008.
247 **Pieces ended up:** Fisher, "A Town's Strange Bedfellows."
247 **A traveling exhibit:** "Fly to Freedom: The Art of the *Golden Venture* Refugees," an exhibit in the Smithsonian Asian Pacific American Program, June 8–September 30, 2001.
247 **Several of the most talented sculptors:** See Isabelle de Pommereau, "For One Refugee, Sculpture Paves the Way to Freedom," *Christian Science Monitor,* October 21, 1996; and Clarke, "'I Really Wish I Could Have Art for Everybody.'" Yang You Yi was given a visa for his artistic ability, but it was later rescinded by the INS on the grounds that after being released from prison he had not continued to enjoy the kind of media acclaim for his artwork that he did while he was in the prison at York. Interview with Yang You Yi, July 23, 2008.
248 **The men clipped the "Made in America" stamps:** Isabelle de Pommereau, "Chinese Refugees Turn Waiting into an Art Form," *Christian Science Monitor,* May 30, 1996.
248 **After one of the men:** June Shih, "Immigration Papers," *Washington City Paper,* May 10, 2001.

CHAPTER 14: THE GOLDFISH AND THE GREAT WALL

The account of Mr. Charlie's capture is based primarily on interviews with Mark Riordan, Karen Pace, and Mona Foreman. The descriptions of Changle, of Sister Ping's village, and of the impunity with which Sister Ping was able to operate in China are based on a research trip to Fujian Province and interviews with acquaintances of Sister Ping's and local Chinese officials. The story of the Goldfish Case draws extensively on Judge Orrick's opinion in the case, as cited in the notes. The Hong Kong meeting between Ah Kay and the prosecutors was described for me by four of the participants: Luke Rettler, Chauncey Parker, Tom Trautman, and Gerry Shargel.
251 **By 1995, only two figures:** Interview with Karen Pace and Mona Foreman, June 19, 2007.
251 **The other was Mr. Charlie:** Interview with Mark Riordan, June 7, 2007.
251 **Mark Riordan, the Bangkok-based:** Unless otherwise noted, details of Mark Riordan's efforts to track down Mr. Charlie are drawn from interviews with Mark Riordan, June 7, 2007, and May 20, 2008.
252 **It was beginning to seem:** Philip Shenon, "Suspect in *Golden Venture* Case Was Leading a Life of Luxury," *New York Times,* November 19, 1995.
253 **On a muggy day:** David Stout, "Suspected Organizer of *Golden Venture* Operation Is Arrested," *New York Times,* November 18, 1995; Shenon, "Suspect in *Golden Venture* Case Was Leading a Life of Luxury."
253 **Mr. Charlie was eventually extradited:** Brief for the defendant appellant, Lee Peng Fei, in United States v. Fei, 225 F.3d 167, before the Second Circuit Court of Appeals, October 1, 1999.
253 **He was sentenced:** Interview with Jodi Avergun, May 24, 2007; Mae Cheng, "Mastermind in Smuggling Plot Gets Twenty-Year Term," *Newsday,* December 2, 1998.
254 **"This case demonstrates":** Stout, "Suspected Organizer of *Golden Venture* Operation Is Arrested."
254 **"He is not a general":** Ibid.
254 **Sister Ping's movements:** Barnes, "Two-Faced Woman"; Ying Chan,

"Smuggler 'Queen' Is Out of Biz," *New York Daily News,* January 19, 1995; interview with Konrad Motyka and Bill McMurry, December 15, 2005.

254 **During the thirteen years:** Burdman, "Back Home in China." Burdman visited Shengmei in the fall of 1993.

255 **Eventually the village saw:** Author visit to Shengmei.

255 **In the wake:** Kwong, *Forbidden Workers,* p. 60.

255 **In Sister Ping's village:** Burdman, "Back Home in China."

255 **At a major intersection:** Author visit to Changle.

256 **Everyone knew where she was:** Confidential interview, Changle, China, March 2008.

256 **At the FBI in New York:** Interview with Konrad Motyka and Bill McMurry, October 31, 2005.

257 **In the spring of 1988:** Unless otherwise indicated, details related to the Goldfish Case and the subsequent fallout are drawn from the comprehensive summary of the facts in Judge William Orrick's opinion in Wang Zong Xiao v. Janet Reno, 837 F.Supp. 1506 (1993).

258 **A mistrial was declared:** Harriet Chiang, "Officials Tied to Drug Case Return to China," *San Francisco Chronicle,* February 13, 1990.

258 **The Justice Department's Office:** Jim McGee, "Perils of International Partnerships," *Washington Post,* May 28, 1996.

259 **In his application for asylum:** Pamela MacLean, "Chinese Drug Smuggling Witness Defects," United Press International, February 6, 1990.

259 **Officials in Beijing were irate:** Harriet Chiang, "China Assails U.S. for Allowing Drug Witness to Seek Asylum," *San Francisco Chronicle,* February 9, 1990.

259 **Wang remained in the United States:** Robert Gearty, "Life and Death in Fishbowl; Chinese Connection to Jan. Slaying Here," *New York Daily News,* July 7, 2003; Robert Gearty, "170 Learn Agony of Ecstasy Bust," *New York Daily News,* April 1, 2004.

259 **But the most damaging legacy:** Constance Hays, "Drug Case Derails U.S.-China Law Tie," *New York Times,* February 20, 1994.

259 **When Judge Orrick declared:** Bob Egelko, "Judge Orders Mistrial After Witness Says He Lied," Associated Press, February 15, 1990.

259 **During a blizzard:** Unless otherwise indicated, details of Rettler's experience on the trip to Hong Kong are drawn from interviews with Luke Rettler, December 5, 2005, July 26, 2007, and May 30, 2008.

260 **There was an expression:** Confidential source.

260 **"I feel like a failure":** Ibid.

260 **For his meeting:** Interview with Gerald Shargel, July 14, 2008. For a terrific profile of Shargel, see Frederic Dannen, "Defending the Mafia," *The New Yorker,* February 21, 1994.

261 **Rettler was impressed:** Interview with Luke Rettler, July 26, 2007.

261 **Shargel had insisted:** Interview with Gerald Shargel, July 14, 2008.

261 **Rettler found it telling:** Shargel confirmed to me that he did indeed visit his tailor during the trip to be fitted for a suit. ("I never go to Hong Kong and come back without a suit," he said.)

262 **Perhaps most significantly:** Letter from Assistant U.S. Attorney Leslie Brown to Judge Michael B. Mukasey, re: United States v. Qui Liang Qi, aka "Ah Kay," S3 93 CR. 783, August 2, 2005.

CHAPTER 15: PAROLE

This chapter is based primarily on interviews with numerous *Golden Venture* passengers who were detained in York, as cited in the notes, and with members of the community in York who were involved in securing and facilitating the release in 1997. Much of the description of the celebration at the church following the passengers' release is drawn from videotaped footage that was taken during the festivities.

263 **On September 30, 1996:** Illegal Immigration Reform and Immigrant Responsibility Act of 1996, Public Law No. 104-208. For a discussion of the legislative maneuvering between 1994 and 1996 that culminated in the act, see Philip G. Schrag, *A Well-Founded Fear: The Congressional Battle to Save Political Asylum in America* (New York: Routledge, 2000). While some critics believe that the law was excessively draconian, others argue that despite some measures designed to curb the snakehead business, the one-child provision in the law would nevertheless continue to serve as an inducement to Chinese to come illegally. See Cleo J. Kung, "Supporting the Snakeheads: Human Smuggling from China and the 1996 Amendment to the U.S. Statutory Definition of 'Refugee,'" *Journal of Criminal Law and Criminology* (Summer 2000).

263 **Bill Clinton had been forced:** Eric Schmitt, "Milestones and Missteps on Immigration," *New York Times,* October 26, 1996.

264 **Before the bill was passed:** Section 601 of the IIRIRA amended the Immigration and Nationality Act by adding the following language: "[A] person who has been forced to abort a pregnancy or to undergo involuntary sterilization, or who has been persecuted for failure or refusal to undergo such a procedure as for other resistance to a coercive population control program, shall be deemed to have been persecuted on account of political opinion, and a person who has a well founded fear that he or she will be forced to undergo such a procedure or subject to persecution for such failure, refusal, or resistance shall be deemed to have a well founded fear of persecution on account of political opinion."

264 **An attorney for the Lawyers:** Celia Dugger, "Dozens of Chinese from 1993 Voyage Still in Jail," *New York Times,* February 3, 1997.

264 **"Dear President Clinton":** Undated letter, *Golden Venture* detainees to President Bill Clinton.

265 **When their lawyers:** Interview with Craig Trebilcock, July 23, 2008; interview with Jeff Lobach, July 24, 2008.

265 **At a certain point:** Interview with Joan Maruskin, July 22, 2008.

266 **After the speech:** Julia Duin, "Goodling's Efforts Led to Freedom for Chinese Refugees," *Washington Times,* March 2, 1997.

266 **"Mr. President":** Celia Dugger, "Chinese Immigrants from Stranded Ship Are to Be Released," *New York Times,* February 15, 1997.

266 **Just over a week later:** Ibid.

266 **"Four years is an awfully long time":** Duin, "Goodling's Efforts Led to Freedom."

266 **The following day:** Ibid.

266 **Beverly Church was at the prison:** Interview with Beverly Church, December 11, 2005.

266 **Joan Maruskin received a call:** Interview with Joan Maruskin, July 17, 2008.

266 **When the news reached Craig:** Interview with Craig Trebilcock, October 5, 2005.

267 **On February 26, 1997:** Unless otherwise noted, these details are drawn from a long videotape of the events in question, filmed by Joan Maruskin on February 26, 1997.

267 **There had been a run:** Interview with Cindy Lobach, July 22, 2008.

267 **Someone had brought:** Ying Chan, "Refugees' Golden Day," *New York Daily News,* February 27, 1997.
268 **The whole community:** Interview with Margo Einsig, July 22, 2008.
269 **A local woman named Ann Wolcott:** Interviews with Ann Wolcott, July 22 and 23, 2008.
269 **For many of the most ambitious:** Interview with *Golden Venture* passenger Chen Guilin, November 22, 2005. For a fascinating look at Guilin's life as a delivery guy in suburban Pennsylvania, see Peter Cohn's 2006 film, *Golden Venture.*
270 **"If I can leave here":** Ted Anthony, "Chinese Detainees Hounded by Government and Gangs," Associated Press, December 11, 1994.
270 **Toward the end of the 1990s:** The precise origins of the Chinatown buses are somewhat murky, inasmuch as there were no companies operating in 1997 and at least three by the end of 1998, but there is general agreement that Fung Wah was the first company. The founder of Fung Wah, Pei Lin Liang, is not Fujianese; he is a former music teacher who came to America from Guangdong Province in 1988.
271 **The Fujianese are great imitators:** For an extraordinary article on the microeconomy that emerged around the intersection in Lower Manhattan where many of the buses take on passengers, see Saki Knafo, "Dreams and Desperation on Forsyth Street," *New York Times,* June 8, 2008.
271 **A price war:** Michael Luo, "In Chinatown, a $10 Trip Means War," *New York Times,* February 21, 2004.
271 **As word spread:** In 1999, during my last year as an undergraduate at Columbia, I was one of those college kids.
271 **Some pointed out:** See, for instance, Fiona Ng, "A Crash in Pennsylvania, and a Cloud over Mott Street," *New York Times,* June 10, 2007; "34 Hurt, Driver Cited for Fung Wah Bus Rollover in Auburn," Associated Press, September 6, 2006; Casey Ross, "Flames Engulf Fung Wah Bus in Connecticut," *Boston Herald,* August 17, 2005; Michael Wilson and Al Baker, "Cheap Buses from Chinatown Get Riders, and Concerns," *New York Times,* February 16, 2003.
271 **There were other reasons:** See, for instance, William Rashbaum, "Man Shot Dead in Chinatown Was Involved in Bus Rivalry," *New York Times,* May 11, 2003; Michael Wilson, "Fatal Stabbing Linked to Chinatown Bus Business," *New York Times,* November 1, 2003.
271 **Eventually mighty Greyhound:** By 2006 Greyhound had cut its prices by more than 50 percent to $15 one way from New York to Boston, which happened to match the Fung Wah price during the same period. Greyhound denied that it was worried about competition from Chinatown buses, though it seems worth noting that in 2003 the bus line also introduced a free round-trip shuttle between Port Authority and Chinatown. See Steve Kurutz, "Urban Tactics: Enter the Dragon Coach," *New York Times,* January 12, 2003.
272 **They ended up:** Bill Cahir, "Congress Leaves Refugees in Limbo," Newhouse News Service, November 29, 2002.
272 **They went to work:** Michael Chen works in Dublin, Ohio. For Normal, Illinois, see Lara Jakes Jordan, "After Horror and Hardship, Chinese Refugees Still Waiting for Permission to Stay," Associated Press, February 1, 2003.
272 **Michael Chen, one of the most:** Interview with Michael Chen, December 17, 2005; Patrick Radden Keefe, "The Snakehead," *The New Yorker,* April 24, 2006.

272 **Less successful was Dong Xu Zhi:** Interview with Dong Xu Zhi, December 18, 2005.

272 **Yang You Yi, the detainee:** Unless otherwise noted, details regarding Yang You Yi are drawn from an interview with Yang You Yi and David Kline, July 23, 2008.

273 **Yang worked sixty hours:** Julia Duin, "Quests for Freedom Yield Only Limbo," *Washington Times,* February 1, 2000.

274 **Clinton had used his power:** Interview with Craig Trebilcock, October 28, 2005.

274 **When Yang You Yi's wife:** Interview with Yang You Yi, July 23, 2008; Caryl Clarke, "Spending Ten Years Apart from Their Family, a Chinese Family Now Adapts to Living in Red Lion," *York Daily Record,* June 30, 2002.

275 **Beverly Church remained close:** Interviews with Beverly Church, December 11, 2005, and June 5, 2007; Caryl Clarke, "No Admittance?" *York Daily Record,* October 3, 1993; Anna Dubrovsky and Barbara Barrett, "The Search for Asylum Endures," *York Daily Record,* February 13, 1998; Allison Klein, "Recovered Gun Believed Used in Killing," *Washington Post,* September 22, 2005; Shepherd Pittman, "Mother Mourning Girl's Slaying May Return to China," *Washington Times,* October 5, 2005; Allison Klein, "A Gruesome Year Leaves Scores of Sad Mysteries," *Washington Post,* January 12, 2006.

277 **Sean Chen had been luckier:** Unless otherwise indicated, details of Sean Chen's release and his experiences after prison are drawn from interviews with Sean Chen on February 6, 2008, and June 5, 2008.

277 **He had walked out:** Order from Judge Sylvia H. Rambo in Sing Chou Chung v. Janet Reno, 1:CV-93-1702, June 6, 1995; order of release on conditional bond for Sing Chow Chung, August 25, 1995; Caryl Clarke, "Detainee Argues for Bail," *York Daily Record,* July 20, 1995.

278 **When he wanted:** This is true not just of the Fujianese but of the Chinese in general. See Sowell, *Migrations and Cultures,* p. 229.

CHAPTER 16: SNAKEHEADS INTERNATIONAL

This chapter draws on interviews with current and former immigration officials who worked with Jerry Stuchiner; the testimony at Sister Ping's trial of Kenny Feng, her Guatemalan associate; an interview with Jerry Stuchiner; and several comprehensive articles about Stuchiner and his investigation of Canales, most notably Larmer and Liu's *Newsweek* piece and Anthony DeStefano's "Destination: Queens."

280 **One summer day in 1995:** Details of Jerry Stuchiner's investigation into Gloria Canales are drawn from Larmer and Liu, "Smuggling People"; and Anthony DeStefano, "Destination: Queens," *Newsday,* June 2, 1996.

281 **He was not happy with the move:** Larmer and Liu, "Smuggling People."

281 **Still, Stuchiner did his best:** Ibid.

281 **Just as Stuchiner was arriving:** For a good summary of the scandal, see Geraldo Reyes and Juan O. Tamayo, "Honduras Gave Passports to China Refugees for Cash," Knight-Ridder, March 17, 1997.

282 **In 1995 alone:** William Branigin, "Immigrant Trafficking Dealt Blow; Arrested Costa Rican Allegedly Smuggled Thousands into U.S.," *Washington Post,* December 26, 1995.

283 **That year a federal working group:** William Branigin, "Report to Clinton Urges Global Attack on Growing Trade in Alien-Smuggling," *Washington Post,* December 28, 1995.

283 **When Stuchiner cracked:** For a useful overview of the Canales case and its significance, see Anthony M. DeStefano, "Immigrant Smuggling Through Central America and the Caribbean," in Smith, *Human Smuggling.*

283 **At that time Honduras:** Branigin, "Immigrant Trafficking Dealt Blow."

283 **When Canales arrived:** Ibid.

284 **"If this isthmus":** DeStefano, "Destination: Queens."

284 **"These new international criminals":** Pamela Burdman, "Inside the Chinese Smuggling Rings," *San Francisco Chronicle,* August 23, 1993.

284 **By the late nineties:** Pomfret, "Smuggled Chinese Enrich Homeland, Gangs."

284 **Many of these people:** Interview with Konrad Motyka and Bill McMurry, December 15, 2005.

284 **It was no longer feasible:** Ashley Dunn, "After Crackdown, Smugglers of Chinese Find New Routes," *New York Times,* November 1, 1994.

285 **Throughout the 1990s:** These routes are included in "Asian Organized Crime," p. 490.

285 **When snakeheads discovered:** Hannah Beech, "Trafficking in Human Dreams," *Time,* April 20, 2007.

285 **After sanctions were imposed:** Misha Glenny, *McMafia: A Journey Through the Global Criminal Underworld* (New York: Knopf, 2008), p. 322.

285 **All the snakeheads needed:** Moisés Naím, *Illicit* (New York: Doubleday, 2005), p. 27.

285 **A handful of snakeheads:** Prepared remarks of Attorney General John Ashcroft, U.S. Border Patrol—Native American Border Security Conference, January 17, 2002; Department of Justice press release, "U.S. Cripples Major International Chinese Alien Smuggling Operation," December 10, 1998.

286 **Snakeheads started sending:** See, for example, Kim Murphy, "Smuggling of Chinese Ends in a Box of Death," *Los Angeles Times,* January 12, 2000; "L.A. Port Officials Find 32 People from China in Containers," Associated Press, January 16, 2005.

286 **Throughout the late 1990s:** Virginia Kice, a Los Angeles–based spokeswoman for ICE, quoted in Lornet Turnbull, Kristi Heim, Sara Jean Green, and Sanjay Bhatt, "Fifteen Days in a Metal Box, to Be Locked Up," *Seattle Times,* April 6, 2006.

286 **A young Fujianese woman:** Tony Thompson, "Snakehead Empress Who Made Millions Trafficking in Misery," *Observer* (UK), July 6, 2003; Kim Sengupta, "On the Trail of the Chinese Snakeheads," *Independent* (UK), May 10, 2004.

286 **In 2000 she was responsible:** J.F.O. McAllister, "Snaking Toward Death," *Time,* July 3, 2000.

286 **Big Sister believed Ping was:** Barnes, "Two-Faced Woman."

280 **But as she continued her boat smuggling:** Interview with Konrad Motyka and Bill McMurry, October 31, 2005.

287 **With stretches of coastline:** Ginger Thompson, "Mexico Worries About Its Own Southern Border," *New York Times,* June 18, 2006; N. C. Aizenman, "Meeting Danger Well South of the Border," *Washington Post,* July 8, 2006.

281 **Sister Ping was hardly:** Jim Rutenberg and Marc Lacey, "In Guatemala, Bush Takes Heat for Raid in U.S.," *International Herald Tribune,* March 14, 2007.

287 **During the period:** Guillermo Vuletin, "Measuring the Informal Economy in Latin American and the Caribbean," IMF Working Paper, International Monetary Fund, 2008, p. 27; Friedrich Schneider, "Size and Measurement of the Informal Economy in

110 Countries Around the World," World Bank, 2002, p. 11.

287 **In some ways Sister Ping's organization:** For more on the emergence of transnational criminal organizations of this sort, see Phil Williams, "Transnational Criminal Organizations and International Security," *Survival* 36, no. 1 (Spring 1994).

287 **Just as the state of Delaware:** On the particular history and role of the Taiwanese community in Guatemala, see Willard Myers III, "Transnational Ethnic Chinese Organized Crime: A Global Challenge to the Security of the United States," testimony before the Senate Foreign Relations Committee, Subcommittee on Terrorism, Narcotics and International Operations, April 24, 1994.

287 **On top of everything else:** Testimony of Kenny Feng in United States v. Cheng Chui Ping, aka "Sister Ping," 94 CR 953 (hereafter Kenny Feng testimony, Sister Ping trial).

287 **She had connections:** INS document, "Progress Reports, 'Operation Hester,'" by Special Agent Edmund Bourke, ASU NY.

288 **Sister Ping's man in Guatemala City:** Closing arguments of Leslie Brown, Sister Ping trial; Kenny Feng testimony, Sister Ping trial; interview with Konrad Motyka and Bill McMurry, December 15, 2006, and October 19, 2007.

288 **Like so many others:** Kenny Feng testimony, Sister Ping trial.

288 **In 1991 Guatemala's consul general:** Pamela Burdman, "Web of Corruption Ensnares Officials Around the World," *San Francisco Chronicle,* April 28, 1993.

288 **Occasionally Sister Ping:** Confidential interview with a former INS agent.

288 **One morning in May 1998:** Testimony of Octavio Urrutia Vidal, of Zacapa, Guatemala, in United States v. Cheng Chui Ping, aka "Sister Ping," 94 CR 953.

288 **Sister Ping was in China:** Kenny Feng testimony, Sister Ping trial; testimony of Special Agent Bill McMurry in United States v. Cheng Chui Ping, aka "Sister Ping," 94 CR 953 (hereafter Bill McMurry testimony, Sister Ping trial).

289 **A woman she had smuggled:** Kenny Feng testimony, Sister Ping trial; testimony of "Sandy" in United States v. Cheng Chui Ping, aka "Sister Ping," 94 CR 953 (hereafter Sandy testimony, Sister Ping trial). Also "Man Pleads Guilty to Conspiracy to Hold Chinese National Hostage," Associated Press, September 19, 2001; John Malcomb, assistant attorney general, Criminal Division, Department of Justice, "Alien Smuggling/Human Trafficking: Sending a Meaningful Message of Deterrence," testimony before the Judiciary Committee of the United States Senate, July 25, 2003.

289 **Jerry Stuchiner knew:** Interview with Jerry Stuchiner, May 23, 2007.

289 **But by the time the ship went down:** Larmer and Liu, "Smuggling People."

290 **Stuchiner and his girlfriend:** Glenn Schloss, "Fake Passport Flight of Fancy Ends in Grief," *South China Morning Post,* August 17, 1996.

290 **He had not realized:** Larmer and Liu, "Smuggling People."

290 **The Fat Man was standing:** Immigration and Naturalization Service Office of the Inspector General, "Inspector General Announces Arrest of INS Official in Alien Smuggling Ring," press release, July 16, 1996.

290 **Herby Weizenblut, the friend:** Glenn Schloss, "Diplomat's Immunity 'Lifted Too Late,'" *South China Morning Post,* August 17, 1996.

290 **As details emerged:** Glenn Schloss, "Investigator from Honduras to Probe Scam," *South China Morning Post,* May 22, 1997.
290 **"I am very sad":** Anthony DeStefano, "Black Eye for the INS," *Newsday,* July 18, 1996.
290 **She was subsequently suspended:** Glenn Schloss, "Envoy Axed After Scam Claim," *South China Morning Post,* July 24, 1996; "Honduran Passport Case Leads to Suspensions," *Orlando Sentinel,* July 23, 1996.
290 **Stuchiner pleaded guilty:** He was sentenced to forty months in prison, but because of a technical error in the prosecution's original charges against him, he was resentenced. See "Ex-Official Resentenced in U.S. Passport Case," *Washington Post,* May 20, 1997; Patricia Young, "Man Jailed for Wrong Crime," *South China Morning Post,* April 18, 1997.
290 **But as the July 1, 1997, deadline:** Larmer and Melinda, "Smuggling People."
291 **The gambit succeeded:** William Branigin, "Hong Kong Set to Free Jailed Former INS Agent," *Washington Post,* June 13, 1997.
291 **For reasons that were never explained:** Confidential interview with a current ICE official.
291 **Some speculated:** Larmer and Liu, "Smuggling People."
291 **Others wondered if the *Golden Venture*:** Confidential interview with a current ICE official.
292 **"The only person":** Confidential interview with a former INS agent.

CHAPTER 17: CATCHING LILLY ZHANG

This chapter is based chiefly on interviews with law enforcement officials who were involved in the handling of Ah Kay during his long cooperation or in the capture of Sister Ping, or both. In describing Ah Kay's cooperation I relied on letters written by federal prosecutors before each of his two sentencing hearings, which spell out in detail the help he offered in over a dozen cases. (I was surprised to find that these letters had been quietly unsealed and were sitting unnoticed in his case file at the courthouse.) The transcripts and other court documents in Ah Kay's case, and in Cheung Yick Tak's, were also helpful, as was the testimony during Sister Ping's trial of Detective Sze-To Yuk Yee, the arresting officer from the Hong Kong police.

293 **Ah Kay gazed directly:** Footage from *CBS Evening News* (New York), April 13, 1994.
293 **By agreeing to cooperate:** Ah Kay testimony, Sister Ping trial.
293 **Because the gang leader:** Interview with Konrad Motyka and Bill McMurry, December 15, 2005.
294 **"I'm benching three hundred":** Interview with Tom Trautman, May 3, 2007.
294 **Like the Fat Man before him:** Interview with Luke Rettler, December 8, 2005.
294 **When Mr. Charlie was captured:** Interview with Jodi Avergun, May 24, 2007.
294 **Ah Kay admitted that he:** Letter from Assistant U.S. Attorney Chauncey Parker to Hon. Judge John S. Martin, Jr., re: United States v. Kwok Ling Kay, July 27, 1998.
294 **When Dan Xin Lin and the other:** Interview with William J. Murray, April 19, 2007.
294 **Nor did Ah Kay merely assist:** Interview with Konrad Motyka and Bill McMurry, December 15, 2005; interview with Luke Rettler, December 8, 2005; interview with Chauncey Parker, May 29, 2007.
295 **So extensive was this proactive:**

Sentencing hearing in United States v. Kwok Ling Kay, 93 Cr. 783 (JSM), December 4, 1998.

295 **"The one thing about Ah Kay"**: Interview with Bill McMurry, December 15, 2005.

295 **Over the years, Ah Kay assisted**: Letter from Parker to Martin, re: United States v. Kwok Ling Kay.

295 **The result was the criminal equivalent**: Interview with Chauncey Parker, May 29, 2007.

295 **Before long, Luke Rettler joked**: Interview with Luke Rettler, July 26, 2007.

295 **Upon his return to the United States**: Judgment in a criminal case, U.S. v. Kwok Ling Kay, 93 CR 783, December 18, 1998. The specific charges to which Ah Kay pleaded guilty were participation in racketeering activity, murder in aid of racketeering, and conspiracy to murder.

296 **Finally one day in 1998**: Sentencing hearing in United States v. Kwok Ling Kay, December 4, 1998.

296 **The federal prosecutor Chauncey Parker**: Letter from Parker to Martin, re: United States v. Kwok Ling Kay.

296 **Neither Ah Kay nor Shargel**: Joseph P. Fried, "Ex-Underboss Given Lenient Term for Help as Witness," *New York Times,* September 27, 1994; Selwyn Raab, "Singing for Your Sentence: How Will It Pay Off?" *New York Times,* September 26, 1994.

296 **"In these five years"**: Sentencing hearing in United States v. Kwok Ling Kay, December 17, 1998.

296 **But the judge, John Martin**: Ibid.

297 **The first thing Ah Kay did**: Interview with Gerald Shargel, July 14, 2008.

297 **But after his sentencing**: Letter from Assistant U.S. Attorney Leslie Brown to Judge Michael B. Mukasey, re: United States v. Qui Liang Qi, aka "Ah Kay," S3 93 CR. 783, August 2, 2005.

297 **Ah Kay had volunteered**: Interview with Konrad Motyka and Bill McMurry, October 19, 2007.

297 **"That's what he was waiting for"**: Confidential interview.

297 **During the years**: Interview with Konrad Motyka and Bill McMurry, October 31, 2005; interview with FBI Special Agent Carlos Koo, who also worked on the Sister Ping case during the 1990s, July 2, 2008.

298 **Eventually Motyka and McMurry**: Ibid.

298 **Occasionally Motyka and McMurry would know**: Interview with Carlos Koo, July 2, 2008.

298 **On one occasion the FBI**: Confidential interview.

299 **The FBI requested**: Interview with Wayne Walsh, Hong Kong Department of Justice, February 19, 2007; confidential interview.

299 **Because she had a range**: INS, "Passenger Activity Report (Official Use Only)," Zhang, L., December 10, 2004.

299 **Indeed, it was rumored**: Interview with Carlos Koo, July 2, 2008.

299 **Yick Tak did not like**: Interview with Konrad Motyka and Bill McMurry, January 10, 2009.

299 **The original criminal complaint**: Sealed complaint, United States of America v. Cheng Chui Ping, aka "Sister Ping," Cheng Yick Tak, Federal District Court for the Southern District of New York, December 16, 1994.

300 **According to the FBI**: Interview with Konrad Motyka and Bill McMurry, October 19, 2007.

300 **Bill McMurry and another agent**: Interview with Carlos Koo, July 2, 2008.

300 **"Since 1993, I have been working"**: United States v. Yick Tak Cheng, 98 CR. 38, sentencing hearing before Judge Deborah Batts, July 14, 2003.

300 **His lawyer said the same**: Ibid.

300 **On January 16, 1998:** All events and dates relating to Yick Tak's subsequent legal history are drawn from the docket in USA v. Cheng, 1:98 CR 38 DAB, before Judge Deborah Betts in the Southern District of New York.
301 **According to one prosecutor:** Confidential interview.
301 **But the biggest mystery:** Confidential interview with a current official at ICE.
301 **Either Yick Tak:** One former INS official who spoke to me on the record and floated the suggestion that bribery could have been involved was James Goldman. Two other officials who would not speak for attribution because they currently work for ICE independently offered the same possible explanation.
301 **When he was finally sentenced:** United States v. Yick Tak Cheng, 98 CR. 38, sentencing hearing before Judge Deborah Batts, July 14, 2003.
301 **But along with both:** I spent several fruitless months appealing to prosecutors, defense attorneys, and judges in both Buffalo and New York City to find some record of the cooperation that Yick Tak provided to law enforcement over the years and some explanation of how he managed to evade any substantial punishment for his crimes. When a sentence is reduced on the basis of cooperation, prosecutors generally write a letter to the judge detailing that cooperation. There is some dispute over whether these letters should be made available to the public, and even if a presumption in favor of making them available is adopted, it still depends on the discretion of the judge in each particular case. Criminal defendants might be less inclined to cooperate with law enforcement if they think that a prosecutor will be describing their every betrayal of their former criminal associates in a letter that will soon be available to anyone who goes to the courthouse to look it up. But it does seem slightly odd that two letters describing Ah Kay's extensive cooperation have been unsealed and now sit in his case file at 500 Pearl Street in downtown Manhattan for the perusal of the general public, but no one familiar with the precise details of Yick Tak's cooperation is willing to release them.
301 **Bill McMurry and Konrad Motyka:** Interview with Konrad Motyka and Bill McMurry, October 19, 2007.
302 **Once McMurry and Motyka:** Interview with Konrad Motyka and Bill McMurry, October 31, 2005.
302 **One day in early 2000:** Confidential interview with a former INS agent.
303 **On April 11, 2000:** Unless otherwise indicated, the account of Sister Ping's arrest at the airport in Hong Kong is drawn from testimony of Detective Sze-To Yuk Yee of the Hong Kong police, in United States v. Cheng Chui Ping, aka "Sister Ping," 94 CR 953 (hereafter Sze-To Yuk Yee testimony, Sister Ping trial).
304 **But it appeared:** Bill McMurry testimony, Sister Ping trial. The passport-stamp description is drawn from my own examination of a photocopy of the pages of the passport, provided to me by the U.S. attorney's office in the Southern District of New York.
304 **In three months:** Closing arguments of Leslie Brown, Sister Ping trial.
304 **Belize has a program:** Anne Sutherland, *The Making of Belize: Globalization in the Margins* (Westport, CT: Bergin & Garvey, 1998), p. 27.
304 **When the agents contacted:** Interview with Konrad Motyka and Bill McMurry, December 15, 2005.
304 **But perhaps the most interesting thing:** Bill McMurry testimony, Sister Ping trial. Also I saw a photocopy of the

book, along with a translated copy, which was used as an exhibit at trial and provided to me by the U.S. attorney's office.

305 **"The arrest of Cheng Chui Ping"**: Press release by U.S. Consul General Michael Klosson, April 21, 2000.

CHAPTER 18: THE MOTHER OF ALL SNAKEHEADS

The trial transcripts from Sister Ping's case form the basis of this chapter, along with my notes from the sentencing hearing and various other court documents. The details regarding Sister Ping's extradition battle are drawn from court documents obtained in Hong Kong and from an interview with Wayne Walsh of the Hong Kong Department of Justice, who represented the government in the proceedings.

307 **For Bill McMurry**: Interview with Bill McMurry, October 31, 2005.

307 **After her arrest in April 2000**: "Hong Kong: Prison Conditions in 1997," Section VII, "Special Categories of Prisoners," Human Rights Watch, 1997; interview with Wayne Walsh, Hong Kong Department of Justice, February 19, 2007.

307 **When a Hong Kong court**: Interview with Wayne Walsh, February 19, 2007; Cheng Chui Ping and Superintendent of Tai Lam Centre for Women & Another, Decision by the Court of First Instance (Hong Kong), Constitutional and Administrative Law List, No. 1985 or 2000, 26–27 September 2000.

308 **She sued the government**: Hong Kong Department of Justice time line, "Cheng Chui Ping aka 'Sister Ping,'" undated document supplied by Wayne Walsh; Mo Pui Yee, "'Big Sister Ping' in Last-Ditch Court Bid," *South China Morning Post,* September 27, 2000.

308 **Amid the flurry**: James Harder, "Mother of All Snakeheads," *Insight on the News,* February 5, 2001.

308 **In December 2002, Sister Ping**: Sara Bradford, "Extradition Blow for Big Sister Ping," *South China Morning Post,* December 13, 2002.

308 **"In the execution of law"**: Ibid.

308 **Sister Ping told the court**: Ibid.

308 **The appeal was unsuccessful**: Peter Michael and Sara Bradford, "'Big Sister' Ping to Be Extradited," *South China Morning Post,* June 12, 2003.

308 **A young FBI agent**: Unless otherwise indicated, details of Special Agent Becky Chan's experience escorting Sister Ping from Hong Kong to the United States are drawn from an interview with Becky Chan, January 3, 2006.

309 **When they arrived at Newark**: Interview with Konrad Motyka and Bill McMurry, December 15, 2005.

309 **Before her capture in 2000**: Ibid.

309 **There were five counts**: See United States v. Cheng Chui Ping, aka "Sister Ping," aka "Ping Jai," 94 Crim. 953, superseding indictment in the Southern District of New York, June 6, 2000. Two additional counts that had been in the indictment were dropped because the Hong Kong Department of Justice deemed them "non-extraditable" offenses.

310 **"Hostage-taking and alien smuggling"**: Closing arguments of Leslie Brown, Sister Ping trial.

310 **"Cheng Chui Ping had nothing"**: Closing arguments of Larry Hochheiser in United States v. Cheng Chui Ping, aka "Sister Ping," 94 CR 953 (hereafter Closing arguments of Larry Hochheiser, Sister Ping trial).

310 **"It wasn't Cheng Chui Ping"**: Opening arguments of Larry Hochheiser in United States v. Cheng Chui Ping, aka "Sister Ping," 94 CR 953 (hereafter Opening arguments of Larry Hochheiser, Sister Ping trial).

311 **Mukasey had heard cases**: See

Dong v. Slattery, 870 F. Supp. 53 (S.D.N.Y. 1994).

311 **"This is a case"**: Opening argument of David Burns in United States v. Cheng Chui Ping, aka "Sister Ping," 94 CR 953 (hereafter Opening argument of David Burns, Sister Ping trial).

311 **"She said that she had bad feelings"**: Weng Yu Hui testimony, Sister Ping trial.

311 **Various former underlings**: Testimony of Cho Yee Yeung and Li Xing Hua, Sister Ping trial.

311 **Larry Hay, the undercover**: Larry Hay testimony, Sister Ping trial.

311 **Kenny Feng, the Taiwanese**: Kenny Feng testimony, Sister Ping trial.

311 **A Fujianese woman**: Testimony of Li Hui Mui in United States v. Cheng Chui Ping, aka "Sister Ping," 94 CR 953.

312 **When he strode**: Interview with Konrad Motyka, December 15, 2005.

312 **For three days he testified**: Ah Kay testimony, Sister Ping trial.

313 **Hochheiser hammered at the credibility**: Opening argument of Larry Hochheiser, Sister Ping trial.

313 **"Make no mistake"**: Opening argument of David Burns, Sister Ping trial.

313 **Prior to Sister Ping's trial**: See Harder, "Mother of All Snakeheads"; and Chuck Bennett, "Sister Ping Ventures Back Home," *New York Daily News,* June 30, 2003.

313 **After pleading guilty**: Sister Ping returned on July 1: United States Attorney, Southern District of New York, "Queen 'Snakehead' Sister Ping Is Extradited from Hong Kong to New York to Face Alien Smuggling and Hostage Taking Charges," press release, July 1, 2003. The events and dates relating to Yick Tak are drawn from the docket in USA v. Cheng, 1:98 CR 38 DAB, before Judge Deborah Batts in the Southern District of New York.

314 **In Bill McMurry's view**: Interview with Bill McMurry, October 31, 2005.

314 **"Sister Ping sat atop"**: Closing arguments of Leslie Brown, Sister Ping trial.

314 **In his closing arguments**: Closing arguments of Larry Hochheiser, Sister Ping trial.

315 **It could not have helped**: Kareem Fahim, "New Jersey Man Shot to Death in a Restaurant in Chinatown," *New York Times,* June 16, 2005.

315 **Hochheiser was especially troubled**: Trial transcript, Sister Ping trial.

315 **Copies of the city's**: Interview with Chan Ching Chuen, president, Fukienese American Association, January 21, 2006.

315 **There was a great upswell**: Zhang Huiyu, "Sister Ping: Living Buddha of Shengmei Village," *World Journal,* May 23, 2005.

315 **Ninety percent of the villagers**: Zhang Huiyu, "Sister Ping on Trial, Villagers Voice Support," *World Journal,* May 22, 2005.

315 **"My sister was just thinking"**: Barnes, "Two-Faced Woman."

315 **Chinatown residents made frequent**: Ibid.

316 **After spending so many years**: Interview with Konrad Motyka, December 15, 2005.

316 **"There are people"**: Interview with Konrad Motyka, October 31, 2005.

316 **For Justin Yu**: Interview with Justin Yu, now president of the Chinese Consolidated Benevolent Association, January 4, 2006.

317 **Throughout the trial**: Interview with Konrad Motyka and Bill McMurry, December 15, 2005.

317 **The press took little notice**: For a discussion of the legal case and the degree to which the atomized, fluid structure of cross-border criminal organizations like Sister Ping's present chal-

lenges for federal prosecutors, see Andrew J. Sein, "The Prosecution of Organized Crime Groups: The Sister Ping Case and Its Lessons," *Trends in Organized Crime* 11, no. 2 (2008).

319 **Yet in 2004 one of the men:** Interview with Beverly Church, December 11, 2005.

319 **"They're picking them off":** Ibid.

319 **So at the beginning:** See for instance H.R. 975, A Bill for the Relief of Certain Aliens Who Were Aboard the *Golden Venture,* 110th Congress, First Session, February 8, 2007.

319 **"They paid the penalty":** Caryl Clarke, "Ten Years Later: The Ship That Altered Lives," *York Daily Record,* February 25, 2007.

320 **"You should see it":** Interview with Craig Trebilcock, October 5, 2005.

320 **In the spring of 2006:** The film is titled *Golden Venture* and features interviews with several of the passengers. Information on the film is available at www.goldenventuremovie.com. I attended the event; quotes and descriptions are from my notes.

320 **"When we saw":** Author's notes from the event, April 26, 2006.

320 **"We almost died":** Ibid.

320 **He had come from Philadelphia:** Interviews with Sean Chen, February 6, 2008, and June 5, 2008.

321 **After perfunctory statements:** All quotes from Judge Mukasey and Sister Ping are drawn from the March 16, 2006, sentencing hearing, Sister Ping trial.

325 **"The potential if she had cooperated":** Interview with Bill McMurry, October 31, 2005.

325 **Prosecutorial calculus:** Closing statement of Leslie Brown, Sister Ping trial.

325 **"I'll be candid with you":** Sentencing hearing in United States v. Guo Liang Qi, 93 CR 78, September 29, 2005.

326 **"He's serving pizzas in Idaho":** Interview with Konrad Motyka, December 15, 2005.

327 **Bill McMurry was thrilled:** Interview with Bill McMurry, October 19, 2007.

EPILOGUE

329 **After President George W. Bush:** For biographical background on Gary Locke, see Gary Locke, "The One Hundred Year Journey," in Don T. Nakanishi and James S. Lai, eds., *Asian American Politics* (Lanham, MD: Rowman and Littlefield, 2003), pp. 359–60. For the 2003 speech, see Carl Hulse and Sheryl Gay Stolberg, "Democrats Say the Nation Heads in 'Wrong Direction,' " *New York Times,* January 29, 2003; Chang, *The Chinese in America,* p. 389.

330 **Migration scholars and refugee advocates:** According to figures maintained by the Department of Homeland Security, an estimated 11.8 million "unauthorized immigrants" were living in the United States in January 2007. See Michal Hoffer, Nancy Rytina, and Bryan C. Baker, "Estimates of the Unauthorized Immigrant Population Residing in the United States: January 2007," Office of Immigration Statistics, Department of Homeland Security, September 2008.

330 **But the business of human smuggling:** Ginger Thompson and Sandra Ochoa, "By a Back Door to the U.S.: A Migrant's Grim Sea Voyage," *New York Times,* June 13, 2004.

333 **The "notable cases" section:** Law Offices of Scott B. Tulman & Associates, PLLC (www.tulmanlaw.com).

333 **Tulman prepared an appeal:** Reply brief for defendant-appellant Cheng Chui Ping, United States v. Cheng Chui Ping, 06-1996-cr.

333 **But the court wasted:** United States v. Ping, No. 06-1996-cr, sum-

mary order, United States Court of Appeals for the Second Circuit, November 19, 2007.

333 **She had her own explanation:** Confidential interview.

334 **When I met with a police officer:** Interview with Colonel Jaruvat Vasaya of the Royal Thai Police, March 13, 2007.

334 **As of 2007, some Chinese estimates:** Blatt, "Recent Trends in the Smuggling of Chinese."

334 **But today the fee:** Interview with Konrad Motyka and Bill McMurry, October 31, 2005.

334 **"The people going away":** Interview with Lin Li, Changle, China, February 20, 2008.

335 **In 2002, for the first time:** Denny Lee, "Years of the Dragon," *New York Times,* May 11, 2003.

335 **"Sister Ping got into":** Zhang, *Chinese Human Smuggling Organization,* p. 223.

335 **I stopped by the church:** Interview with Matthew Ding, November 8, 2005.

335 **There are roughly 200 million:** These figures are taken from the International Organization of Migration's "Global Trends and Estimates," which are in turn drawn from the United Nations' *Trends in Total Migrant Stock.*

336 **And in something of a paradox:** "The smuggler is dependent on the state in a multitude of ways," the scholar Peter Andreas points out. "The most obvious but essential point is that state-created and enforced laws provide the very opening for (and high profitability of) smuggling in the first place." Peter Andreas, "Smuggling Wars: Law Enforcement and Law Evasion in a Changing World," *Transnational Organized Crime* 4, no. 2 (Summer 1998).

336 **Human smuggling is one:** United States Department of Justice, "Distinctions Between Human Smuggling and Human Trafficking," unclassified fact sheet, January 2005.

336 **Afghans are smuggled:** On the Afghans, there are numerous examples; see, for instance, Sarah Smiles, "Boats May Be Work of Syndicate," *Age* (Australia), October 8, 2008. On Ecuadorians, see Thompson and Ochoa, "By a Back Door to the U.S."

337 **The convention has an additional:** Adopted by the General Assembly in 2000, the protocol went into force in 2004.

338 **The United States should remain alert:** Interestingly, there is a positive correlation between countries with major corruption problems and countries with high disparities in income. A fascinating IMF working paper explains the correlation by suggesting that corruption causes income inequality. I wonder if it is not sometimes the other way around. See Sanjiv Gupta, Hamid Davoodi, and Rosa Alonso-Terme, "Does Corruption Affect Income Inequality and Poverty?" IMF Working Paper, May 1998.

338 **"No agency of the government":** Joel Brinkley, "At Immigration, Disarray and Defeat," *New York Times,* September 11, 1994.

338 **On June 26, 2008:** United States Attorney's Office, Central District of California, "Attorney Working for Immigration Agency Arrested for Taking Bribes from Immigrants Seeking Status in the U.S.," press release, June 26, 2008.

338 **In 1995 the government repealed:** David Ngaruri Kenney and Philip G. Schrag, *Asylum Denied: A Refugee's Struggle for Safety in America* (Berkeley: University of California Press, 2008), p. 2.

339 **Through a series:** See, for instance, U.S. Citizenship and Immigration Service, "Backlog Elimination Plan," report to Congress, June 16, 2004.

339 **Like the *Golden Venture* passengers**: Human Rights First, "Background Briefing Note: The Detention of Asylum Seekers in the United States, Arbitrary Under the ICCPR," January 2007.

339 **As a result**: "Detention in America," *60 Minutes* (CBS), May 11, 2008.

339–40 **On any given day**: Dana Priest and Amy Goldstein, "System of Neglect," *Washington Post,* May 11, 2008.

340 **In 2007 the government held**: Nina Bernstein, "Ill and in Pain, Detainees Die in U.S. Hands," *New York Times,* August 13, 2008.

340 **Immigration detention is now**: Nina Bernstein, "New Scrutiny as Immigrants Die in Custody," *New York Times,* June 26, 2007.

340 **In 1999 a Chinese woman**: Ted Gregory, "INS Use of Jails Debated," *Chicago Tribune,* November 15, 1999.

340 **According to a study**: Priest and Goldstein, "System of Neglect."

340 **But the leading cause**: Dana Priest and Amy Goldstein, "Suicides Point to Gaps in Treatment," *Washington Post,* May 13, 2008.

340 **It is an ironic reflection**: Teresa Watanabe, "Report Decries U.S. Treatment of Migrants," *Los Angeles Times,* March 8, 2008.

340 **In 1999 the prison underwent**: Department of Justice, Office of the Inspector General, "The Immigration and Naturalization Service and the United States Marshals Service Intergovernmental Service Agreements for Detention Services with the County of York, Pennsylvania, York County Prison," Report No. GR-70-01-005, June 25, 2001.

341 **The motley coalition**: Interview with Joan Maruskin, July 17, 2008.

341 **Following the arrival of the ship**: Josh Friedman, "NY Head Chosen for Key INS Post: Nomination Brings Praise & Outrage," *Newsday,* May 28, 1994.

341 **But after a few short years**: Molly Gordy, "INS Managers Demand Ax for Boss," *New York Daily News,* December 3, 1996; Molly Gordy, "INS Big Gave Korean Bizmen a Break After a Game of Golf," *New York Daily News,* December 5, 1996; Molly Gordy, "Spying, Fraud, News to Me, Insists Fed," *New York Daily News,* December 5, 1996; Mae Cheng, "Top INS Aide Replaced," *Newsday,* April 15, 1997.

342 **We sat at Slattery's**: Interview with Bill Slattery, July 7, 2008.

342 **I thought about Sister Ping**: Cheng Chui Ping v. United States of America, petition for a writ of certiorari in the United States Supreme Court, October Term 2008.

342 **I thought about the hundred or so passengers**: There is no way to know the precise figure. The *New York Times* puts the number at "at least half," or fifty-five or so; Nina Bernstein, "Making It Ashore, but Still Chasing U.S. Dream, *New York Times,* April 9, 2006. But in interviews with several *Golden Venture* passengers and numerous supporters from York who continue to keep track of the passengers, I have heard that closer to one hundred are now thought to have returned.

344 **On weekends amateur divers**: "United Caribbean Physical Data and Notes," dive notes by Dave Gillings, May 13, 2006, published on the Web site of the Palm Beach County Reef Research Team (www.pbcrrt.org).

344 **After the ship**: Seth Faison, "Part of Immigrant Nightmare Goes on the Block," *New York Times,* August 10, 1993.

344 **Eventually local authorities**: Amy Waldman, "Smuggling Ship to Become a Reef Off Florida," *New York Times,* August 19, 2000.

344 **One day in 2000**: Caryl Clarke, "*Golden Venture* to Sink," *York Daily Record,* August 18, 2000.

Index

Abortion wars of United States, 238–39
Ah Kay (Guo Liang Qi), 166, 218, 225, 318, 322
  arrest in 1993, 221
  asylum request, 74, 109
  beeper-store killings, 153, 154
  charisma of, 151–52
  citizenship application, 342
  cold rationality of, 212
  cooperation with law enforcement, 293–96, 297, 324, 325 (*See also* Sister Ping prosecution *below*)
  deportation and subsequent return to United States, 74
  emigration to United States, 67–68
  ethical concerns regarding his current freedom, 331–32
  FBI's targeting of, 209, 211–16, 220–21
  Fuk Ching gang, joining with, 68, 69, 70–72
  Fuk Ching gang leadership, 74–75, 150, 152, 212
  gambling problem, 214–15
  Golden Venture smuggling operation, 136, 141, 152, 157, 294
  greed and wastefulness of, 151, 152
  human smuggling business, 112–13
  indictment against, 223
  killings by, 70–71
  Lin and, 150–51
  police's targeting of, 72, 73–74
  prison experience in 1980s, 74
  release from prison following Sister Ping's conviction, 325–26
  return to Fujian in 1993, 154, 212
  sentencing of, 296–97
  Sister Ping, robbery of, 71–72
  Sister Ping prosecution and, 260–62, 297, 298, 311–13, 314
  Sister Ping's betrayal of, 118
  Sister Ping's smuggling business, collaboration with, 113, 114–18
  technological savvy, 214
  in witness protection program, 326
Ah Qun (Guo Liang Qun), 75, 160–61, 162
Ah Wong (Guo Liang Wong), 74, 75, 77, 155, 156, 157, 158, 159, 160, 161–62, 163–64
Ai Cheung, 207
Appleton, William, 131, 132
Arcara, Richard, 94
Asbury, Herbert, 61
Asylum system
  Ah Kay's asylum request, 74, 109
  China's political repression and one-child policy, reaction to, 100–3, 192–98, 203–4, 264
  eligibility for asylum, determination of, 192–93
  flood of Chinese asylum-seekers in 1990s, 102–3, 106–9
  Fujianese immigrants and, 196–97, 204
  Golden Venture survivors and, 15, 199–206, 228–32, 232, 241
  Goldfish Case, 257–59
  history of, 103–5
  INS and, 105–7

reforms needed in, 339–40
release of asylum-seekers upon arrival in United States, 105, 107, 109, 184–85, 338
U.S. public reaction against asylum-seekers, 183–84

Baird, Zoë, 195
Balzac, Honoré de, 331
Bangkok, Thailand, 110–11, 126–27
Bank of China, 47, 49
Barr, William, 194
Batts, Deborah, 301
Beeper-store killings, 153–54, 157–58, 294
Belize's role in human smuggling, 304
Berger, Sandy, 196
Boat smuggling, advent of, 109–13
Bonnano crime family, 39
Born To Kill (BTK) gang, 65–66
Breezy Point neighborhood, 4
Brown, Leslie, 314, 326
Buffalo Times, 85
Burke, Gilbert, 10, 11, 12
Burma's role in human smuggling, 123–24
Burns, David, 311, 313
Bush, Barbara, 100
Bush, George H. W., 100, 101, 102, 194
Bush, George W., 329, 334

Calabrian immigrants, 30
Canada's role in human smuggling, 85
Canales, Gloria, 280, 283–84, 289
Canarsie Indians, 3
Carr, Ann, 200–1, 277
Carter, Jimmy, 36, 192
Catholic Church, 102, 240
Center for Immigration Studies, 264
Central America's role in human smuggling, 280–84
Central Pacific Railroad, 23, 24
Chain migration, 30–32
Chan, Becky, 308–9
Chan, Eddie, 62
Chan, Sue, 84
Chan, Ying, 114, 224–25, 323
Chang Liang Lin, 160–61, 162, 165–66
Charlie, Mr. (Lee Peng Fei), 210, 225
arrest and sentencing of, 251–54, 294
background and personal qualities, 141, 252–53
Golden Venture smuggling operation, 130, 131, 136, 140, 141, 142, 168, 170, 176–77, 178
Chau, Ronald, 75
Cheah Fong Yew, 83–84, 90–91
Chen, Michael, 272, 320
Chen, Sean (Chung Sing Chau), 234, 242, 270, 331
American life after prison, 277–79, 320–21
asylum request, 200–1, 234
background of, 121–22
first days in United States, 185, 186
Golden Venture smuggling operation, 121, 122–28, 130, 131, 132, 133, 134, 135, 136, 145–46, 148, 178, 180–81
happiness with decision to come to United States, 343
prison experience, 187–88, 245
Cheng, Monica (Cheng Hui Mui), 35, 50, 71, 93, 97, 302
Cheng, Susan (Cheng Tsui Wah), 44–45, 55–56, 88, 315
Cheng Chai Leung, 27, 31–32, 35, 55, 326–27
Cheng Chui Ping. *See* Sister Ping
Cheng Mei Yeung, 45, 55, 130, 288
Chen Yun Fei, 239
Cheung Yick Tak, 36, 38, 39, 43, 46, 49, 50, 53, 57, 78, 97, 113, 114, 116, 218, 309, 327
arrest in 1997, 299–300
bulk money transport, 54
cooperation with law enforcement, 96, 300–2, 313–14, 324
marriage to Sister Ping, 35
Niagara smuggling route and, 85, 87, 88, 89, 91–92, 93–94, 95–96
U.S. citizenship, 301
U.S. stay in 1970s, 37
Chiang Kai-shek, 216
Chin, Ko-lin, 42, 64, 204
China
Communist restrictions on emigration, 26
Cultural Revolution, 28–29
economic benefits of emigration, 51–52
economic transformation, 33–34, 334
emigration decline in 2000s, 334

emigration reforms of 1970s, 36
Goldfish Case, 257–59
Great Leap Forward, 27
law enforcement cooperation with United States, 257–59
one-child policy, 101–3, 194–200, 205–6, 264
punishment of returned emigrants, 174–75, 245–46
Sister Ping prosecution, refusal to cooperate with, 256–57
Tiananmen Square massacre, 99–101
See also Fujian Province
Chinatown bus system, 270–72
Chinese Exclusion Act of 1882, 25, 26
Chinese immigrants
asylum-seekers, 102–3, 106–9, 192–98, 203–5
Cantonese Chinese, 23, 39–40, 41
Chinese "travel agencies" and, 24
Communist Chinese restrictions on emigration, 26
coolie labor and, 23–24
hostility and discrimination against, 24–25, 182–83
increase in number of immigrants in New York City, 64–65
"Jinshan" name for United States, 22
Locke family's experience, 329–30
nineteenth-century immigration, 22–23, 25
railroad construction and, 23
social isolation of, 25–26
tongs of, 60–64
See also Fujianese immigrants
Chinese restaurants as enduring global feature, 134
Chong, David, 67
Cho Yee Yeung, 115
Church, Beverly, 234–35, 242, 246, 247, 265, 266, 267, 268, 275, 276, 277, 279, 319–20, 341
Citizenship and Immigration Services, 318
Clarke, Caryl, 237
Clinton, Bill, 19, 185, 188, 189, 194, 195–96, 237, 263, 264, 265–66, 274
Cocaine trade, 287
Cohn, Peter, 320
Cold Mountain (film), 273
Communism's toll on human spirit, 230–32
Congress, U.S., 25, 26, 102, 104, 114, 194, 239, 263–64, 319–20
Cosa Nostra, 65
Coven, Jules, 199
Crocker, Charlie, 23
Crucible, The (Miller), 314
Cuban asylum-seekers, 104, 201–2
Cultural Revolution, 28–29
Cuomo, Mario, 78

Dan Xin Lin. *See* Lin, Dan Xin
Deng Xiaoping, 33, 36, 192
Devine, Patrick, 91–92, 93, 94, 97
Ding, Matthew, 335
Dinkins, David, 13
Divivier, Steve, 4–5, 6
Dong, Y. C., 206
Dong Xu Zhi, 272
Drug Enforcement Agency (DEA), 217, 218, 257–58
Dugger, Celia, 265
Dullan, James, 87, 88–90, 92

East Wood smuggling operation, 172–73
Ecstasy trade, 259
Ellis Island, 25
Emergency Chinese Immigration Relief Act of 1989, 194
Extortion racket, 68–69, 71, 73, 76–77

Family Heir Loom Weavers, 273
Fang Kin Wah, 79–82
Fang Lizhi, 100–1
Fat Man (Dickson Yao), 216–18, 219–20, 221, 281, 289, 290, 324
Federal Bureau of Investigation (FBI), 56, 70, 116, 157, 160, 165, 324
Ah Kay and Fuk Ching gang, investigation of, 207–8, 209, 211–16, 220–23
Ah Kay's cooperation with, 293–96, 297
Cheung Yick Tak's arrest, 299–300
Cheung Yick Tak's U.S. citizenship and, 301
C-6 unit, 208–9
Sister Ping, investigation of, 223–24, 225–26, 268, 297–99, 301–2, 304, 309
Sister Ping's cooperation with, 96–97, 118, 324–25
Feich'ien banking systems, 48

Feng, Kenny, 288–89, 311
Flags of convenience, 143–44
Fleischmann, Akiva and Shaya, 162–63
Flying Dragons gang, 61–63, 67, 69
Foochow Paul (Kin Fei Wong), 68, 70, 74
Ford, Gerald, 100
Fort Chaffee incident, 195–96
Freedom Birds sculptures, 250
Fujianese immigrants
accommodations for, 40
America's appeal for, 34–35, 41–42
asylum issue and, 196–97, 204
Cantonese population, separation from, 39–40, 41
chain migration by, 30–31
Cheng Chai Leung's experience, 31–32
Cheung Yick Tak's experience in 1970s, 37
Chinatown, New York, as destination of, 38
Chinatown bus system, 270–72
economic conditions in Fujian and, 33–34
employment for, 40–41
entrepreneurial skills, 31
generational perspective of, 330–31
in Hong Kong, 36
Mexico border crossings, 108
1980s and 1990s immigration to United States, 30, 36
recreational activities, 42–43
remittances to China, 47–49, 50
reverse migration involving U.S.-born children, 42, 43
in Southeast Asia, 29–30
status today, 334, 335
suburbs and small towns, shift to, 269–70, 272
Fujianese organized crime in United States, 116–17
Fujian Province, 29, 30
depopulated condition in 1990s, 254–55
economic boom of 1980s, 33–34
snakehead smuggling business, embrace of, 255
Fuk Ching gang, 225, 309–10, 324
adaptability of, 82
Ah Kay's joining with, 68, 69, 70–72
Ah Kay's leadership role, 74–75, 150, 152, 212
Ah Kay's rivalry with Lin, 150–53
beeper-store killings, 153–54, 157–58, 294
casino operation, 77
extortion racket, 68–69, 71, 76–77
FBI's targeting of, 207–8, 209, 211–13, 221–23
fights with other gangs, 69–70, 77
finances of, 76
Fukienese American Association and, 78–79
gambling by members, 214–15
heroin trade, 70
human smuggling business, 82, 112–13, 156
indictment against, 223
kidnappings for ransom, 79–80, 82
origin and character of, 68
police's targeting of, 72, 73–74, 80–82
safe houses of, 155, 156–57
Sister Ping, robbery of, 71–72
Sister Ping's smuggling business, collaboration with, 113, 114–18
Tam's role in, 76, 155–56
Teaneck killings, 159–67, 294
Fukienese American Association (FAA), 77–79, 222–23
Fukienese Flying Dragons gang, 295

Gambino crime family, 65, 267, 296
Gangs of Chinatown, 335
extortion racket, 73
increase in number of, 64
random killings by, 66
recruits for, 66–67
tongs, relation to, 61–64
warfare among, 64, 65–66
See also Fuk Ching gang
Gangs of New York, The (Asbury), 61
Garde, Ed, 84, 85, 86, 92, 98
Generational model of immigration, 330–31
German Communist experience, 236–38
Ghost Shadows gang, 62, 66
Gleit, Steven, 84
Globalization, 282
Godfather, The, 331
Goldenberg, Stephen, 95, 96, 301
Golden Venture smuggling operation
Ah Kay's account of, 294
Bangkok layover, 126–27
captain and crew for, 142

Mr. Charlie's account of, 253
Coast Guard's failure to prevent landing, 179
deaths of passengers, 11–12, 18–19
destruction of ship documents, 178
documentary about, 320
flag and name changes for ship, 144–45
inadequacy of *Golden Venture* for ocean travel, 141, 145, 146
landing in New York City, 3–13, 177–81
living conditions for passengers, 146–48
loading of passengers in Thailand, 141–45, 146–47
Mombasa layover, 121, 132–36, 145
mutiny against Capt. Tobing, 168–72
Najd II voyage from Thailand to Kenya, 127–28, 130–32
offloading plan, 150, 155, 167, 168, 176–77
overland trek from China to Thailand, 122–26
prosecutions of responsible persons, 209–10, 211, 253–54
provisions for, 142
purchase of *Golden Venture,* 136, 139
sinking of *Golden Venture* in 2000, 344
Sister Ping prosecution and, 310–11, 312, 317
Sister Ping's involvement, 21, 136, 141, 142, 145, 168, 210–11, 310, 312
social bonding by passengers, 148–49
storm at sea, 148
Teaneck killings and, 166–67
Tobing's account of, 16–17
transfer of *Najd II* passengers to *Golden Venture,* 145–46
U.S. government's awareness of, 170–76, 219
U.S. officials' takeover of ship, 16
U.S. waters, approach to, 170
See also Golden Venture survivors' American experience

Golden Venture survivors' American experience
abortion wars of United States and, 238–39
American identity, adoption of, 278–79
asylum requests, 15, 203–4, 228–32, 232, 243
business ventures, 272–73, 277–78
Catholic Church's intervention on behalf of survivors, 240
Clinton administration's policy on survivors' disposition, 196, 197, 197–200, 201, 205
condition of survivors upon arrival in United States, 14
congressional testimony, 239
conversions to Christianity, 238, 240
deportees' fate upon return to China, 243–45
detention of survivors, government's decision on, 185–86, 199
documentary about, 320
Ecuador, female survivors' transfer to, 240–41, 245
family members brought to United States from China, 273–77
female survivors, 188, 239–41, 245
first weeks of freedom, 268–69
foster care for minors, 200
"illegal" designation, 17–18
INS detention facility, 17–18, 19
lawsuit against Clinton administration regarding asylum decision, 241
lawyers' interest in survivors, 186–87
media coverage, 19–20, 247, 265, 268
parolee status after prison, 274, 318–19
permanent resident status, fight for, 319–20, 341, 342
police interviews, 13–17
prison life, 188, 242–41, 245–48, 264–65
prisons in York and New Orleans, transfer to, 187–88
public support for survivors, 233–41
releases from prison, 241–42, 247, 265–68
restaurant work, 272
sculpture-making in prison, 245–48, 266, 267
Sister Ping prosecution, survivors' attitude toward, 317–18
Slattery's views on, 342
struggle ashore and apprehension following ship's landing, 3–13, 178, 180–81
suburbs and small towns, move to, 270, 272

Goldfish Case, 257–58
Gold Future (ship), 174, 175, 176

Goodling, Bill, 266
Gore, Al, 199
Gotti, John, 260, 296
Gravano, Sammy "the Bull," 296
Great Leap Forward, 27
Green Dragons gang, 74–75
Green-Wood Cemetery, 207
Guang Sheng Li, 159–61
Guatemala's role in human smuggling, 287–89
Guo Liang Qi. *See* Ah Kay

Haw Wang, 84, 90–91, 98
Hay, Larry, 92–93, 311
Helms, Jesse, 264
Heroin trade, 64, 70, 123, 124–25, 257
Hezbollah, 219
Hip Sing tong, 60, 61, 62
Hochheiser, Larry, 310, 313, 314, 315, 321
Homeland Security, Department of, 318
Honduras's role in human smuggling, 280–82, 286–87
Honesburger, Terry, 92
Honorable Judge (television series), 308
Hon Tok Lou, 57
Hubbell, Web, 189
Human smuggling
  defining characteristics, 20
  measures needed to combat smuggling, 336–40
  status today, 330, 336
  See also Snakehead smuggling business
Human trafficking, 20

Illegal immigration, origin of concept, 25
Illegal Immigration Reform and Immigrant Responsibility Act of 1996, 263
Immigration and Customs Enforcement (ICE), 318, 338
Immigration and Naturalization Service (INS), 11, 23, 109, 139, 185, 192, 218, 219, 221, 228, 229, 245, 249, 263, 291, 301, 309, 338
  asylum system and, 105–7
  benefits/enforcement dichotomy within, 184, 197
  disaggregation of, 318
  Golden Venture survivors' asylum requests, approach to, 232
  international presence, failure to establish, 173–74
  Meissner's appointment to, 189–90
  Operation Hester, 53–58
  Operation Hydra, 57
  Operation Swiftwater, 85–86, 91–92
  problems of, 105
Immigration patterns today, 335–36
Immigration policies of United States
  amnesty provisions, 50–51
  corruption problem, 338
  crackdown on illegal immigration in 1990s, 263–64
  national security concerns following 9/11 attacks, 318
  progress on problems of alien smuggling, 338–39
  restrictive laws of nineteenth century, 25, 26
  snakehead smuggling business, measures to combat, 188–89
  See also Asylum system
Immigration Reform and Control Act (IRCA) of 1986, 50
International cooperation on immigration, need for, 337–38
International Friendship House, 341

Jennings, Peter, 247
"Jinshan" name for United States, 22
John Paul II, Pope, 242

Kallas, Constantine, 338
Kasi, Mir Aimal, 183
Kelly, Ray, 13
Kephart, Richard, 86–87, 88–90, 91, 92
Kerr, Ray, 157, 160, 165, 166, 208–9
Khun Sa, 123
Kidnappings for ransom, 79–80, 82
King, Martin Luther, Jr., 228, 261
Kin Sin Lee, 16, 17, 141–42, 143, 146, 147, 148, 149, 168, 169–70, 177, 178, 179–80, 209–10, 254
Kline, David, 272–73
Klosson, Michael, 305
Knickerbocker Village, 38–39
Koo, Carlos, 300
Krishan, Vasugee, 90–91
Kristof, Nicholas, 199–200
Ku Klux Klan, 228
Kwok, Charlie, 74
Kwong, Peter, 109, 204

Lake, Anthony, 189
Lantin, Rhona, 66
Lau, Alan Man Sin, 78, 79
Lau, Simon (Four-Eyed Fish), 159, 164
Lau Xing Bau, 130
Lawyers Committee for Human Rights, 264
Lazarus, Emma, 17
Lee, Dougie, 13–16, 73, 74, 80, 81, 225
Lee, Peter, 97, 118, 157, 160, 165, 223, 266, 267, 324
Lian (warlord), 124–25
Life magazine, 247
Life Savers Ministries, 240
Lim, Steven, 70
Lin, Dan Xin, 209, 266, 294
  arrest and conviction of, 165
  beeper-store killings, 153, 154, 157–58
  cooperation with law enforcement, 157–58, 324
  rivalry with Ah Kay, 150–53
  Teaneck killings, 159, 160, 161, 162, 164–65
Little Sister Ping, 286
Li Xing Hua, 75, 215, 221
Lobach, Cindy, 236, 237, 247
Lo Cho, 109
Locke, Gary, 329–30
Lwin, Sam, 169–70, 177, 179–80, 210

Mao Zedong, 27, 28, 29, 32
Marcelino, John, 115–16
Mariel boat life, 104, 195
Martin, John, 296–97
Maruskin, Joan, 233–34, 236, 237, 238, 239, 242, 266, 267, 272, 341
Matter of Chang court case, 192–94, 205
McFerrin, Bobby, 88
McMurry, Bill, 297–98, 299, 300, 301, 302, 304, 307, 309, 314, 316, 325, 327–28, 335
McNary, Gene, 105
Mead, Margaret, 236
Meese, Edwin, 192–93
Meissner, Doris, 189–90, 195, 196
Merrill, Rod, 235
Metropolitan Correctional Center (MCC), 293
Mexico border crossings, 110
Miller, Arthur, 314
Miller, Harriet and Ray, 268
Milošević, Slobodan, 285
Ming Cheng, 162
Ming Wang, 43
Mock Duck, 61, 70, 214
Mohawk Indians, 285–86
Monica, Don, 173, 174, 175, 176
Motyka, Konrad, 207–9, 211, 213, 221–22, 223, 293, 297, 298, 299, 301, 302, 304, 307, 309, 312, 316, 326, 335
Mukasey, Michael, 310–11, 314, 315, 321, 325, 326, 327, 328, 334
Mundy, Bill, 8–10, 11–12

Native American reservations' role in human smuggling, 285–86
New Hong Kong Variety Store, 49
New York Daily News, 114, 165, 224, 225, 315
New York Times, 19, 183, 197–98, 245, 265, 338
Ngo, Lena, 235
Niagara smuggling route, 83–84, 85–96
Nixon, Richard, 100

O'Campo, Calgada Melchoz, 53
Occhipinti, Joe, 54–55, 56–58, 91
Ong, Benny, 59–60, 61–63
On Leong tong, 61, 62
Ooi, Vincent, 90–91
Operation Hester, 53–58
Operation Hydra, 57
Operation Swiftwater, 85–86, 91–92
Oriental Gang Unit of NYPD (Jade Squad), 14, 73
Orrick, William, 258–59

Pai Sheng smuggling operation, 189
Palmquist, Tim and Terri, 240
Panama's ship registration system, 141–44
Parker, Chauncey, 215–16, 260, 261, 296
Pattaya, Thailand, 137
Paul (Minh Hoang), 85, 86–91, 93
Pennsylvania Immigration Resource Center, 341
People of the Golden Vision, 236–37, 241, 246, 247, 267, 319, 341
Peter (Cheng Wai Wei), 55, 88–91, 92, 93, 95–96

Pin Lin, 229–30, 232, 243
Platts, Todd, 319
"Policy Implementation with Respect to Nationals of the People's Republic of China" (Executive Order 12711), 101, 102, 194
Polo, Marco, 29
Pong, Pao, 137–39, 140, 141, 143
Prostitution, 57

Racketeer Influenced and Corrupt Organizations (RICO) Act, 339
Raggi, Reena, 210
Rahman, Omar Abdel, 183
Railroad construction, 23
Rather, Dan, 247
Reagan, Ronald, 101
Red Guards, 28–29
Rees, Grover Joseph, III, 197, 199
Refugee Act of 1980, 106
Refugees. *See* Asylum system
Relative deprivation, 34
Remittance business, 47–50
Reno, Janet, 254
Rettler, Luke, 72–73, 78–79, 80–81, 155, 158, 166, 211, 213, 215–16, 217, 223, 259–60, 261–62, 295
Riordan, Mark, 139–41, 251–53
Rockaway Peninsula, 3
Roosevelt, Franklin D., 26
Rosenberg, Julius and Ethel, 39
Ryan, Nancy, 73

Sandy, 289
Schwartz, Eric, 185
Scolari, Lisa, 325
Serbia's role in human smuggling, 285
Shafer, David, 207, 209, 221–22
Shargel, Gerry, 260–61, 296, 297
Shih, Madame, 57
Shing Chung, 164
Ship registration system, 143–44
Showers, Sterling, 235, 242, 272
Sikh immigrants, 280
Simpson, Alan, 263
Sister Ping (Cheng Chui Ping), 20–21, 129, 218, 286, 337–38
  Ah Kay, betrayal of, 118
  Ah Kay and Fuk Ching's robbery of, 71–72
  arrest and imprisonment in early 1990s, 92–95, 96–97
  building purchase in Chinatown, 49
  the Cantonese, attitude toward, 41
  Chan, contract on, 224–25, 323
  in China in late 1990s to avoid arrest in United States, 254–56
  contempt for authority of government, 28
  conversational style, 308
  cooperation with law enforcement, 94–95, 96–97, 118, 324–25
  diversified business operations, 50
  early years, 26–29, 32
  emigration to United States, 37, 38–39
  flight to Hong Kong in 1994, 226
  Fujian properties, 51
  Hong Kong life and businesses in 1970s, 35–36
  language spoken by, 30
  marriage to Cheung Yick Tak, 35
  media coverage of, 113–14, 224, 225
  Red Guard experience, 29
  relationships (*guanxi*) in Fujian community, 43
  remittance business, 47–50
  restaurant business, 49–50
  retail business, 39, 43, 49–50
  status among Fujianese, 43, 49
  survivalist instinct, 27–28
  sympathetic perspective on, 331
  traveling under assumed identities, 298, 299, 304
  See also Sister Ping prosecution; Sister Ping's smuggling business
Sister Ping prosecution
  Ah Kay's cooperation with, 260–62, 297, 298, 311–13, 314
  appeal process, 333–34, 342
  arrest of Sister Ping in Hong Kong, 302–5
  Cheung Yick Tak's cooperation with, 301–2, 313–14
  China's noncooperation with, 256–57
  defense's strategy, 310
  extradition to United States, 305, 307–9
  FBI investigation, 223–24, 225–26, 268, 297–99, 301–2, 304, 309
  the Fujianese's views on, 315–17
  Golden Venture smuggling operation and, 310–11, 312, 317

Golden Venture survivors' attitude toward, 317–18
government's case, 311–14
indictment, 226, 309–10
jury deliberations, 314, 317
media coverage of, 314–15
sentencing, 327–28
Sister Ping's legal representation of herself, 308
Sister Ping's pre-sentencing statement, 321–24, 326–27
sting operation, plan for, 298–99
trial in New York, 306–7, 310–14, 317, 333
verdict, 317
Sister Ping's smuggling business, 21, 207
Ah Kay and Fuk Ching gang, collaboration with, 113, 114–18
boat-sinking incident, 288–89, 292
documents detailing global operations, 304–5
East Wood smuggling operation, 172–73
exploitative nature of, 332
Fat Man's knowledge about, 219
Golden Venture smuggling operation, 21, 136, 141, 142, 145, 168, 210–11, 310, 312
Guatemala, use of, 287–89
hideouts and way stations throughout world, 211
immigration attorneys, collaboration with, 186–87
media coverage of, 113–14, 224, 225
New Bedford ship, 115–16
Niagara smuggling route, 83–84, 85–96
Operation Hester targeting, 53–58
payment system, 46–47
pipeline nature of, 97
post-*Golden Venture* operations, 225–26, 284, 286–89
reputation among Fujianese, 129, 315–17, 332
Sister Ping's confidence in her immunity from law enforcement, 57–58
Sister Ping's personal involvement in transporting immigrants, 45–46
U.S. authorities' early knowledge of, 52–53, 55
Weng Yu Hui's emigration experience with, 44–47
Skretny, William, 94
Slattery, Bill, 19–20, 105–6, 107, 183–87, 197, 198, 199, 341–42
Smith, Adam, 329
Smith, Chris, 239, 264
Smith, Lamar, 263
Snakehead smuggling business
"acceptable risk" concept and, 317
asylum-seekers and, 101, 102–3, 106, 107, 108, 109
Bangkok arrangements, 126–27
boat smuggling, advent of, 109–13
Canada-to-U.S. route, 85
cargo containers used for transporting clients, 286
Central America's role in, 280–82
Cheng Chai Leung's smuggling business, 32
diversification of routes in 1990s, 285–86
fee to reach United States, 20
Fujian Province's embrace of, 255
Fuk Ching gang's smuggling business, 82, 112–13, 156
Fukienese American Association and, 78
globalization and, 282
international approach in fight against, 283–84
overland route from China to Thailand, 122–26
Pai Sheng operation, 189
revenue of, 109
ship registration system and, 144
"snakehead," origin of term, 33
status today, 335
Stuchiner's passport fraud business, 289–91
"tour guide" aspect of, 45
U.S. measures targeting, 188–89
Wang Wu Dong's experience, 244–45
See also *Golden Venture* smuggling operation; Sister Ping's smuggling business
Somma, David, 4–5, 6, 12
Song You Lin, 75, 153, 154, 157–58
South China Morning Post, 172, 175
Stuchiner, Jerry, 218–20, 221, 280–81, 283, 284, 289–91, 338

Sun Yee On triad, 108
Supreme Court, U.S., 25, 342
Swenson, Eric, 263, 258

Taiwan
  Fujianese immigrants in, 29–30
  human smuggling, role in, 110
Tak Shun Variety Store, 39
Tam, Alan, 76–77, 155–56, 157, 158–60, 166, 212–13
Teaneck killings, 159–67, 294
Terrorist attacks of September 2011, 318
Thailand's role in human smuggling, 111
Tiananmen Square massacre, 99–101
Time magazine, 195
Tobing, Amir, 16–17, 142, 143, 147, 148, 169, 170, 209–10
Tongs, 60–64
Trautman, Tom, 266, 261
Trebilcock, Craig, 227–33, 238–39, 241, 243, 266–67, 319, 320, 341
Triads, 24, 60
Tulman, Scott, 333
Tung On gang, 69, 70, 73, 77
Twain, Mark, 25

Ulloa, Angelina, 283, 290
United Nations, 104, 172
  Convention Against Transnational Organized Crime, 337
  Population Fund, 101
  Protocol Against the Smuggling of Migrants by Land, Sea and Air, 337

Vicksburg Times, 24

Wang Kong Fu, 113, 299
Wang Wu Dong, 244–45
Wang Zong Xiao, 257–59
Washington Post, 340
Wealth of Nations, The (Smith), 329
Weizenblut, Herbie, 281, 290
Wells, Charlie, 5–7, 10–11
Weng Yu Hui, 225, 310, 323
  arrest and sentencing of, 211
  emigration to United States, 44–47
  Golden Venture smuggling operation, 128, 130, 136, 141, 145, 168, 170, 176–78, 210–11
  remittances to China, 48–49, 50
  Sister Ping prosecution and, 311, 313, 333
  snakehead smuggling business, entry into, 128–30
Widener, Jeff, 99
Wirth, Tim, 196
Wolcott, Ann, 269
Wong, Andrew and Chico, 257
Wong, Frankie, 52–53
Woolsey, James, 108
World Journal, 315
World Trade Center bombing of 1993, 183

Yang You Yi, 245–46, 272–73, 274
Yeung Sun restaurant, 49
Yick Tak. *See* Cheung Yick Tak
York, Pennsylvania, 227–28
Yousef, Ramzi, 183
Yu, Justin, 316, 317
Yumi, Demian, 235–36
Yun Lin, 161
Yu Ping Zhang, 161–62

Zehao Zhou (ZZ), 236
Zeng Hua Zheng, 319
Zheng He, Adm., 29
Zheng Xianjuan, 275–77
Zheng Xin Bin, 234–35, 275–77